Redefining *Irishness* in a Globalized World

This ground-breaking book draws on an innovative qualitative audio–visual approach to elicit information from people residing in Ireland what it means to be Irish in the 21st century given the rapidly changing nature of Irish society, in part, due to migration and globalisation. One of the key thought-provoking findings is the centrality of essentialist notions of race in the social construction of Irishness. This book is essential reading for anyone interested in identity formation, socio-psychological theorization of identity and nationhood in Europe and beyond.
—*Daniel Faas*, **Department of Sociology, Trinity College Dublin, Ireland**

This book cuts through the usual fluff about national identities being constructed and fluid, recognizing the gravitational pull of a bureaucratic regression to something less savoury. Remarkably, it does this while retaining a much-needed optimism that is grounded in a deeply felt ethical sensibility. Wonderful!
—*Andrew Finlay*, **Lecturer in Sociology, Trinity College Dublin, Ireland**

Yaqoub BouAynaya wonderfully captures the hard questions of the global challenges experienced as complex national(istic) internal divisions, while providing alternative frameworks of analysis in a rapidly changing Ireland. He very successfully avoids the clichés attached to the cultural wars, offering nuanced insights into the ways in which the dominant group in Ireland are making sense of contemporary Ireland and Irishness. We get a real sense of the processes, the mechanics, by which identity is redefined in Ireland across regions within the continuum of an ever-changing society. Drawing upon multi-disciplinary theoretical perspectives, diverse empirical work and an original qualitative methodology design of audio–visual production, the book will appeal to the widest audience, including those interested in Irish studies and more broadly questions of identity making in national contexts. Yaqoub BouAynaya is a highly skilled writer, who is able to communicate complex ideas in a simple language that is a joy to read.
—*Professor Mairtin Mac an Ghaill*, **Newman University Birmingham, England**

Redefining *Irishness* in a Globalized World: National Identity and European Integration

BY

YAQOUB BOUAYNAYA

United Kingdom – North America – Japan – India – Malaysia – China

Emerald Publishing Limited
Emerald Publishing, Floor 5, Northspring, 21-23 Wellington Street, Leeds LS1 4DL.

First edition 2024

Copyright © 2024 Yaqoub BouAynaya.
Published under exclusive licence by Emerald Publishing Limited.

Reprints and permissions service
Contact: www.copyright.com

No part of this book may be reproduced, stored in a retrieval system, transmitted in any form or by any means electronic, mechanical, photocopying, recording or otherwise without either the prior written permission of the publisher or a licence permitting restricted copying issued in the UK by The Copyright Licensing Agency and in the USA by The Copyright Clearance Center. Any opinions expressed in the chapters are those of the authors. Whilst Emerald makes every effort to ensure the quality and accuracy of its content, Emerald makes no representation implied or otherwise, as to the chapters' suitability and application and disclaims any warranties, express or implied, to their use.

British Library Cataloguing in Publication Data
A catalogue record for this book is available from the British Library

ISBN: 978-1-83797-942-4 (Print)
ISBN: 978-1-83797-941-7 (Online)
ISBN: 978-1-83797-943-1 (Epub)

Printed and bound by CPI Group (UK) Ltd, Croydon, CR0 4YY

INVESTOR IN PEOPLE

For TakiTora, Frances and Mary
peace & love

Contents

List of Figure, Tables, and Appendices   *ix*

About the Author   *xi*

Abstract   *xiii*

Foreword   *xv*
Professor David Theo Goldberg

Introducing *Irishness*   *1*

Chapter 1   Theorizing Identity and *Irishness*   *17*

Chapter 2   'Irish' Identity and the Nation State   *27*

Chapter 3   Legislation, Myth and Progressive Self-constitution   *55*

Chapter 4   Research Methodology and Design   *71*

Chapter 5   Participants' Perceptions of Being 'Irish'   *97*

Chapter 6   Historical *Irishness* and Becoming 'Irish'   *119*

Chapter 7   Recognizing Being 'Irish'   *133*

Chapter 8   Constructing Ethnicity, 'Race' and the Irish Nation   *145*

Chapter 9   *Irishness*, Governance, Migration Controls and **World Views**   *173*

Chapter 10 Epilogue	*213*
References	*245*
Index	*255*

List of Figure, Tables, and Appendices

Figure

Fig. 1.	Stages and Phases of the Research Design.	72

Tables

Table 1.	Details of Preliminary Stage: One-to-One Interviews.	80
Table 2.	Details of the Main Stage: Focus Group Discussants.	84
Table 3.	Key Emergent Themes from the Main Stage Discussions.	87

Appendices

Appendix 1.	Focus Group Discussion Pre- and Post-viewing Questions	94
Appendix 2.	Focus Group Discussion Additional Post-viewing Questions	95

About the Author

Yaqoub BouAynaya is a Lecturer in Sociology at the Institute of Art, Design and Technology (IADT), County Dublin, Ireland. Yaqoub is a Visual Sociologist whose topics of interest intersect identity studies, racial and ethnic studies, eco-sociology, equality and social justice.

Portraits and photographs by Yaqoub Jemil BouAynaya:
www.theconsciouscamera.com
yaqoub@theconsciouscamera.com
instagram: theconsciouscamera

Abstract

This book explores perceived *Irishness* and to what extent identity in Ireland is redefined within the continuum of an ever-changing society. It examines how values associated with identity affect the ways in which individuals participate in their perceived social reality, are perceived by 'others' and are re/presented between the collective local, national, European and global levels. Thus, this study considers the evolution and maintenance of nationalism and relates this to the development of the postcolonial Irish nation state within the context of European governance and globalization.

The methodology takes a multistage approach that seeks to explore individuals' perceived sense of identity, either in stability or flux, by exposure to variations of *Irishness* through the viewing of a multimedia presentation. This novel and innovative qualitative design relies on an audio–visual production made from one-to-one interviews with four individuals of differing backgrounds but who are all Irish citizens. By showing it to eight focus groups, the ambition is to elicit in participants the deconstruction of 'Irish' national identity. Through focus group discussions on identity, ethnicity and citizenship, evidence emerges from the transcribed and thematically analysed conversations.

Consequently, in exploring the processes of socially constructing *Irishness*, this research facilitates insight into the processes which affect an individual's self-understanding and social categorization. Such a reflexive social investigation reveals findings that substantiate an identity theory positing explicit contradictions between individuals' reliance on deep-rooted and inherent notions of *Irishness* in contrast with awareness and a contemporary understanding of identity as being constructed through social experience.

Furthermore, through empirical validation, it postulates the socio-psychological process of *perceived rational pragmatism* as the means by which individuals within *ordo-liberal* liquid modernity perceive of themselves as rational liberated beings. Through reflection, theory synthesis and the embedded agential design, this study informs the reconceptualization of contemporary 'Irish' identity. Its admissions seek to expedite an alternative re-imagination of, 'what it means to be Irish' so as to better complement the aspirations towards an egalitarian-based socio-democracy.

Foreword
Professor David Theo Goldberg

Over the past four decades, globalization has placed pressure on conventional formations and understandings of nation-states and national identities inherited from the past. Capital's global reach sought to soften, if not eradicate, the state's restrictions and controls of capital's movements. This, in turn, troubled states' management of their borders as goods, services, human and financial capital were moved legally and illicitly across borders, in and out of states, in search of resources, opportunities, lower costs, profits and better lives. As Etienne Balibar showed already in the early 1990s, this had the impact of both globalizing national identity and hyper-localizing racial insistence.

'Irish' identity has long been fashioned by pressures within and beyond Ireland itself. In 1850, the then young French surgeon, anatomist and inveterate measurer of skulls, Paul Broca, distinguished between the Irish and English 'races'. At more or less the same time, Thomas Carlyle famously identified Black Jamaicans with Irish 'needlewomen', in ways meant to disparage both. By later that century in both England and the US Irish migrants, in the wake of the potato famine, were being widely characterized as 'a lower race', and, indeed, as 'black'. These characterizations stretched back from both countries to include references to inhabitants of Ireland as well. So, national identities morph as a result of pressures internal and external to the boundaries of state.

Yaqoub BouAynaya's *Redefining* Irishness *in a Globalized World: National Identity and European Integration* addresses the more recent transformations in 'Irishness' within the Irish nation-state as a result of forces and influences both within and outside the state boundaries. As the modern-day Irish economy flourished, it attracted a significant up-tick in labour from near and afar. Ireland's membership in the European Union gave European workers easier access. Like the European birthrate more generally, Ireland's birthrate had declined over the previous three or four decades, and its labour needs likewise opened opportunities to those further afield. The result of push–pull forces led to an influx of migrants from around the world, drawn in by and seeking better opportunities for themselves and their families. These demographic shifts, in turn, have prompted first small and now, as BouAynaya makes clear, more ready pressures on Irish national identity to transform. The result is both a revealing empirical study and a careful sustained analysis of all the possible theoretical accounts for these shifts. The book as a consequence speaks compellingly both to the ways *Irishness* has transformed as a result and how best to think about changes in ethnonational identity more broadly.

BouAynaya is concerned in the book to show how contesting elements in the society are shaped into a frame of interactive and, in an extended sense, shared understanding of *Irishness*. These elements may include conceptions that at present are incomprehensible, considered by consummate 'insiders' even derogatory and unacceptable in current terms of understanding. They transform with time and changing social conditions into features that fashion a new, or newly valued, sense of ethnonational identification. And, in turn, they reorder imperatives of social inclusion and exclusion, refusal and strategic acceptance. BouAynaya is especially concerned to show how to read the fluidities of ethnoracial diversity, their social regulation, remaking and reordering in our current times and conditions.

Ethnonational configuration, in the analysis on offer, is fuelled by the interactive threading of family kinship and lineage, in both the immediate and broader familial senses, and their perceived relation to claimed clan and community connections.

These senses reinforce and are reinforced by a projected understanding of 'nativeness'. This involves the fusing of nativity and the long history of presence, establishing a claim to antique belonging which, in turn, undergirds a hierarchy of 'real' ethnonationals, of those who have ethnonational identity and those who are merely – because new(er) – national citizens. These differentiations quickly come to acquire and be invested with a naturalized – which is also to say a more or less explicit racially asserted – set of meanings and commitments. The force of these formations and their affiliated understandings, in turn, delimit the fluidity of identities as experienced in late modern times. They offer relatedly a contrived and restrictive sense of belonging at a time coming and going and coming again has assumed the lived reality of the world we inhabit. This set of sensibilities in effect evidences a reach for the artifice of conservation, of fixing the supposedly given in place, self-elevating those taking themselves to be 'local', to a greater or lesser degree across the *longue duree*, over the more recently arrived, the coming and – maybe the readily – going.

BouAynaya astutely characterizes those so readily self-elevating as engaging in a process of what he calls a mode of *perceived rational pragmatism*. This can be read as akin to the claim to a local 'common sense' in addressing the shifting terrain of those understanding themselves to be properly belonging and not, the constitutive insiders and perennial outsiders or excluded.

Redefining Irishness, then, critically navigates the driving socio-theoretical literature concerning ethnoracial composition. The book addresses the principal determinants and their contemporary applicability to understanding *Irishness*, and ethnonational identification more broadly. In this, BouAynaya gives us a more generalized critical social vocabulary for comprehending the readily shifting conditions of our times.

Irishness, accordingly, is revealing because, in many ways, exemplary of both the processes and lived impacts of ethnonationalisms more generally. Every ethnonationalism, of course, has unique conditions, prompts, manifestations and elaborations. Yet, they share causes and common grounds of their emergence and growth in given conjunctures. They forge commonalities in their relational interactions, drawing on modes of thinking, adopting and adapting expressions from other places while giving them their own twist. Yaqoub BouAynaya's book, thus, provides a terrifically evocative reading of the applicability of the contemporary literature to the case of *Irishness* while offering us novel insights into how *Irishness* models insights into the workings of ethnonationalisms more generally.

Introducing *Irishness*

Keywords: *Irishness*/'Irish' identity; 'Race'; globalization; nationalism; categorization; modernity; governmentality; democracy; tolerance

Re-imaginations of *Irishness*

What it means to be 'Irish' in the late modern, or even postmodern world,[1] is rooted deeply in the realm of people's consciousness, particularly in the perceived ideas, philosophies and notions of Irish peoplehood. In this book, I explore people's propensity to categorize and give meaning to their social realities. I examine the boundaries of racialized and ethnicized *Irishness*. Such boundaries are considered to be as 'symbolic constructions, forged and reconstituted in a reciprocal process of interaction and reinforced by the *perceptions* of the differences thought to typify' an 'Irish' identity (Tovey et al., 1989, p. ii). In doing so, this book illuminates how people seed, cultivate and nurture through conversation their shared sense of *Irishness*. That is to say, in a primarily qualitative, but also innovative manner, I look to examine and redefine *Irishness* in a globalized world, as well as more broadly inquire into the factors that shape national identity and influence processes of European integration.

By critically evaluating people's responses to discussion on themes relating to individual and collectivized *Irishness*, in this book, I explore re-imaginations of 'Irish' identity in such a way as to produce 'positive' social outcomes. One such 'positive' impact would be the alleviation of intra-societal conflict or conflict that occurs within society. According to Tovey et al. (1989, p. i), problems in civic Ireland are deemed traceable to the inability of the Irish 'as a people to express a coherent and authentic sense of Irish identity, or a broadly acceptable philosophy of what it means to be Irish in today's world'. By mitigating social conflict among an increasingly diverse population residing in Ireland, an overarching consideration is to advocate more inclusive understandings of *Irishness*. Thus, a central purpose detailed herein is to recognize harmoniously and assess particularities of

---

[1]For further debate on *Modernity versus Postmodernity*, please refer to Habermas and Ben-Habib's (1981) aforementioned italicized title.

Redefining *Irishness* in a Globalized World:
National Identity and European Integration, 1–16
Copyright © 2024 by Yaqoub BouAynaya
Published under exclusive licence by Emerald Publishing Limited
doi:10.1108/978-1-83797-941-720241001

Irishness, while, at the same time, exploring and pushing the boundaries, towards answering the question: 'who are the "we" who seek a shared future on the island of Ireland?'

The Social Construction of Identities and Knowledge-Based Society

This book sets out to acknowledge and investigate the theoretical 'de-centrings of modern thought' (Hall, 2000a, p. 145). I explore the frailty or ambiguity of identities and relate these to what Hall (2000a) defines as 'the relative decline, or erosion, the instability of the nation-state, of the self-sufficiency of national economies and consequently, of national identities as a point of reference, there has simultaneously been a fragmentation and erosion of collective social identity' (p. 146).

As such, it is an exploration of the sense of anxiety and fear within the ambivalence of identity, due to a loss of both the fixity of the individual and social identity, intertwined with the directionality of capitalist globalization and what Bauman (2001, pp. 121–122) elaborates as *liquid modernity*. As implied, *liquid modernity* describes a sense of continual change or condition where 'change is the only permanence …' (Bauman, 2012, p. viii). In this sense, identity is understood as inherently ambiguous because in its current condition, it is both linked territorially to nationality yet undermined by post-/late-modernist theory.

The focus is on Irish 'life politics' (Bauman, 2001), which are described as 'identity construction, negotiation and assertion' (p. 121). *Irishness*, nation state identity and pan-European notions of identity are investigated from the perspective of individuals living in Ireland. However, from the outset, the presupposition is that these identity formations are seen as existing to provide a sense of perceived fixity, yet are destabilized at their core when understood simply as social constructs. The frailty of such constructs becomes visible when exposed to the rapidity of change associated with globalization and ensuing apparent post-/late-modernity. Thus, I explore a newly emergent territory, which, in many ways, might be termed 'a terra incognita' (Bauman, 2000, p. 48) whereby new processes of identification emerge.

By exploring the constructed nature of 'Irish' identity, I compose a proposition of an 'imaginary political re-identification, reterritorialization' and to struggle for, as Hall (2000a) emphasizes, 'a change of consciousness, a change of self-recognition, a new process of identification …' whereby 'the emergence into visibility of a new subject' (p. 149), or subjects may be conceived, the reason being the conceptualization and envisaging of a new sense of belonging that is complementary to post-/late-modern constructivist theory. In other words, not taking the absoluteness of past truths but also emphasizing the importance of understanding how we make meaning of our lives and construct our knowledge. In a similar vein, by understanding and unravelling the construction of identity formations, this book provides the possibility to represent alternative identities of *Irishness* and allow for the postulation of the existence of that which may be, at present, un-representable, excessive and abject (Coates, 1997, p. 78*f*.; De Lauretis, 1987). As Coates (1997) summarizes from Judith Butler's, *Bodies that Matter: On the Discursive Limits of "Sex"*, 'The abject ... is always contained in that which is excluding or expelling it. The "return of the abject" radically destabilizes that from which it was expelled, opening the site to reconfiguration and resignification' (p. 79). Similarly, 'otherness' can be seen as the abject of currently conceived notions of 'Irish' identity; while 'the other' may exist in Irish society, or attempt to enter it, instead of becoming part of and redefining 'Irish' identity, its unrepresented status is simultaneously preserved and it may even be exiled figuratively, through the maintenance of predefined closed notions of *Irishness* and physically through state intervention, such as in its extreme through repatriation, deportation or fencing off, walling and closure of borders. Although a somewhat paradoxical nexus, the stance I take is the assertion that, while allowing for collective solidarities that are inclusive of that which is abject, the re-identification of the Irish collectivity is conversely required to accommodate specific traditional cultural values, attitudes, behaviours, norms and historic repertoires.

Importantly also, I relate such concerns of contemporary identity formation with macro-processes in the construction of *knowledge societies, globalization* and their potential effects towards *mono-culturalization*. Accommodating both processes of *globalization* and, at the same time, maintaining cultural identity, thus, unfolds complexities. From the macro perspective, juggling processes of *globalization* with the preservation of culturally specific repertoires relates to the construction of contemporary *knowledge societies*. Knowledge-driven societies purportedly allow for re/conciliation between the notion of identity in ambiguity. This is because knowledge-driven societies submit that there is nothing that can truthfully bind subjects together other than a singular collective 'humanity', but juxtapose this against the notion of fixed yet multifarious individual identities that are layered over an imaginary true self.

As the report by UNESCO (2005) entitled *Towards Knowledge Societies* elucidates, 'the concept of knowledge societies encompasses much broader social, ethical and political dimensions' (p. 17). It continues by advancing that

> there is a multitude of such dimensions which rules out the idea of any single, ready made model, for such a model would not take sufficient account of cultural and linguistic diversity, vital if individuals are to feel at home in a changing world. (UNESCO, 2005, p. 17)

The report proceeds to detail how knowledge and culture, in their various forms, lend to the development of any society through scientific progress and the adoption of modern technologies. In recognition of the importance of diverse knowledge/s and cultural understandings, the UNESCO (2005) report continues by claiming that 'it would be inadmissible to envisage the information and communication revolution leading – through a narrow, fatalistic technological determinism – to a single possible form of society' (p. 17).[2]

Yet, the directionality of at least developed nations seems to be on course for a confined *nihilistic determinism*, an unavoidable condition where society is void of values. In parallel, in an Irish and broader context, Inglis (2008) sought to explore and describe 'to what extent local everyday life is becoming global' but, in particular, how 'Western culture is seeping into the everyday lives of more and more people' (p. 2). This is viewed as a 'mono-culturization' and erosion of discrete traditional practices which have evolved and developed over millennia and are passed down through processes of socialization (Inglis, 2008, p. 2). Such cultural practices derived from an unquestioned, pre-disposed way of being in the world, or a particular *habitus*,[3] that produces a sense of belonging and collective identity (Inglis, 2008, p. 2).

With the eradication of identities constructed through notions of fixity and territorial association, be it nation state or beyond, comes the threatening extinction of local or indigenous forms of knowledge. This leads to the contestation that, according to Clifford (2000, p. 105), 'Westernization' may not necessarily have been a linear progress. Yet almost simultaneously, Clifford (2000) compounds this previously stated view by reinforcing the notion of some sort of distinction, based on advancement between pre-modern and modern, by claiming that, 'Most histories of global development have had few second thoughts about people on the margins: "pre-modern" societies are destined either to assimilate or to vanish in a relentless homogenizing process' (p. 105). Though it reads quite definitively, by ascribing such terms, that explicitly suggest temporal positioning along a notion of progress that is linear, such statements subtly reinforce a *fatalism* leading towards an assimilated oneness that is concomitant with current trends in *globalization*. What Clifford is attempting to acknowledge, however, is, in fact, highlighting the flaw in such ascriptions and shedding light on what becomes obscured by some, yet constant, rhetoric of *globalization* and *acculturation*. Such *cultural assimilation* occurs when each generation of a minority group becomes incrementally similar to the majority or dominant group. Often said people, fully or partially, assimilate the *status quo* norms, values, attitudes, behaviours and beliefs. Clifford (2000) describes that '… visions of globalization tend to smooth over the constant (re)articulation of cultural identities and differences …' (p. 105). In contrast, Holton (2005) attempts to provide a critique of the *fatalism*

---

[2]Such technological determinism may eventually correspond to the posit made by Marx whereby science and general progress are seen as interrelated and integral to the dominance of machinery through objectified labour over 'The worker' so that, 'The worker appears as superfluous to the extent that his action is not determined by [capital's] requirements' (Marx, 1857/1973, p. 695). For more on this, please refer to *The Grundrisse* (Marx, 1857/1973).

[3]For more on the concept of *habitus*, please refer to *Outline of a Theory and Practice* by Pierre Bourdieu (1977a, 1977b). *Habitus* refers to 'a subjective but not individual system of internalized structures, schemes of perception, conception, and action common to all members of the same group or class' (Bourdieu, 1977a, 1977b, p. 86).

Introducing Irishness   5

many associate with *globalization*, by rejecting 'the view that globalisation happens, driven by various markets or technology, leaving human actors to adjust as best as they can' (p. 2). Instead for Holton (2005, p. 2), globalization is both a consequence of human activity and also a situational environment intended for human activity.

The UNESCO (2005) report is seen to attach discreetly, yet very purposely, the conditionality of the necessity to respect and follow scientific reasoning by avowing not only is

> [...] the fate of languages threatened with extinction. What is also at stake is the space we should make for local or indigenous forms of knowledge within knowledge societies whose development models highly value the codification forms specific to scientific knowledge. (p. 18)

As such, promoting diversity also requires the nurturing of creativities and new knowledge as it emerges from the mélanges of contemporary society. As conveyed by UNESCO (2005),

> Such a prospect fulfils not only an abstract ethical imperative, it above all aims to raise in each society an awareness of the wealth of the forms of knowledge and capacities it possesses, in order to increase their value and take advantage of what they have to offer. (p. 18)

I would retain several reservations towards a rationale that places as superior scientific logicality; however, instead of getting distracted by critiquing the nuances in what is stated in the UNESCO report, with regard to the development of *knowledge societies*, within this book, I strive to go beyond the limiting aspect of fostering diversity for the benefit of scientific gain, by placing the processes of redefining identity and re-identification as central, not only to the emergence of new forms of identities, but as paramount to the preservation of collective consciousnesses as a multitude of forms that may also evade or transcend what may be considered *ethnocentric* scientific thought.

The Ethical Imperative of Knowledge, Categorization and Classification

In introducing the overarching approach of this study, it must be acknowledged that, from the onset, I disregard categorizations by the state, or otherwise, and instead provide access and voice to all those who are interested. Such an approach is considered to mitigate cross-cultural misconceptions and promote solidarity among differences. Thus, within this book, I account for the unavoidable politics of research and places centrally within it, as a component of the institution of academia, *The Ethical Imperative of Knowledge* (Larson, 2001). The content herein is centred on the acknowledgement and supposition that truth is not a singular absolute, but rather established by perspectives that are produced and give order to experience (Larson, 2001).

Integral to knowledge construction is the paradoxical question, namely that 'unless one knows definitively what truth is how does or will anyone ever know when they have attained that knowledge which is truth?' Correspondingly, Larson (2001) argues that 'there is no definable objective position by which one can say what forms of organization are universally and absolutely valid' (p. 2). What becomes apparent is that in attaining knowledge the issues of perception and of who gets to be the judge of a truth claim become more the determinant. This relates to questions of power, societal influence and identification, where '... some discourses of truth are means of entrenching social hierarchies or practices of exclusion via class, race, sex, etc.' (Larson, 2001, p. 3). Accordingly, the methodological approach documented within this book is not merely about the attainment of knowledge as an end goal but to acknowledge the subjectivity of our understanding of what is deemed *significant knowledge*, as opposed to *substantive knowledge* (Crevoisier, 2015, p. 194), and to structurally embed within the methodological process means by which individual subjectivities are actively accounted for; where hierarchical distributions of knowledge/power are diminished to give greater equalized weight to contributing voices, actors or subjects.

Of particular concern is the influence exerted by those who wield power over processes that produce knowledge. As a consequence, in recognizing and justifying firstly, the *subjectivity* of knowledge acquisition and secondly, the inherent relationship between knowledge and power, only then can this study be deemed pertinent in mitigating imbalanced power relations, through its integrated methodology and incorporated reflexivity. The specific methodological approach taken is central to fulfilling both the objective of, and obligation in accounting for, *the ethical imperative of knowledge*. In this respect, key to the overall strategy and inbuilt methodology is the acknowledgement that for the populous to acquire knowledge, and intellectuals are no longer essential. As Foucault (1977) states, 'the masses know perfectly well, without illusion; they know far better than the intellectual and they are certainly capable of expressing themselves' (p. 207). For Foucault (1977), there exists a system of power which subtly, yet to a profound level, penetrates an entire societal network, whereby 'Intellectuals are themselves agents of this system of power: the idea of their responsibility for "consciousness" and discourse forms part of the system' (p. 207). Such an implication can lead us in divergent ways, either towards discrediting knowledge itself and slipping into a regressive stance or discerning new understandings that better complement our globalized reality. This book fits in neatly by investigating where alternative thinking may arise in contrast to power found in *manifest authority*.

From the position of Ireland as a contemporary Western, industrialized and information technologically driven society, which aspires to evolve into a *knowledge society* basing its economy on research and development, the fact that knowledge and power can be viewed as 'essentially contested concepts' (Gallie, 1955; Heaney, 2000, p. 102) would seem as pertinent a consideration as ever. What is implied here is to consciously scaffold politics with the incorporation of ethics. To achieve such would be to purposefully deliberate on new and emergent principles that might inform how we are to live together in this globalized 21st century. As James (2006) argues, 'unless this is given priority, the current debates over *post-nationalism* and cosmopolitanism, globalism and localism, are bound to end up repeating, in late-modern or postmodern terms, the dead-end modernist arguments over the relative merits of nationalism and internationalism' (p. 294). Dilemmas relating to each are further expanded upon in Chapter 2.

If academia is a strand of civil society and inevitably plays a role in shaping politics as an integral component of *polity-public*, this would substantiate the argument that from within such institutional structures there is, and should be, recognition of *the ethical imperative of knowledge* production.[4]

From here, as a means of introducing the theoretical, conceptual and legal positioning discussed in the subsequent chapters, it is necessary to advance issues relating to categorization and classification, as situated in knowledge formation. The foundation of the structured society is the human ability to make binary distinctions (Lévi-Strauss, 1978, p. 22f.; MacCormack & Strathern, 1980, p. 2). The mind builds up its perceptions of the world by perceiving opposites or contrasts. MacCormack and Strathern (1980) add that 'the human mind seeks analogies with other contrastive phenomena and upon finding them encompasses the analogies into its system of classification' (p. 2).

On a conscious level, people are aware of concrete manifestations rather than the relations themselves, but for *structuralists*, the unconscious tendency to perceive relations is fundamental to the mind. Inglis (2008) informs us, 'our knowledge of the world begins with classification systems ...' and later considers that 'classifying people as similar and different is embedded in social life, both in the micro-events and practices of everyday life and in the macro-strategies of organizations, institutions and nation-states' (p. 5). Such informs our understanding of culture and society within which myth arises so that individuals' minds 'structure myth, and in a feedback loop myth instruct our perceptions of the phenomenological universe' (MacCormack & Strathern, 1980, p. 6).

Beyond this is to consider reinterpreting how we see our phenomenal universe and create orders through the classifications we are socialized to understand and construct. The justification for this being the acknowledgment that, '... the unity of knowledge is nothing else than the very unity of the social collectivity extended to the universe' (Durkheim & Mauss, 1963, p. x). The fact that there are multifarious classifications and structures of society implies that, with such simultaneous variations across *space-time*, conceptualizing social collectivity in an alternative form may produce new forms of knowledge and new ways of existence that mitigate certain redundant social dilemmas of our time, thus reducing social conflict. Though not frivolous is the consideration as to whether society creates minds that categorize, or whether conversely, the individual mind has the intrinsic capacity to learn to classify and re-classify anew. It may well be that it is an interplay between both. Nonetheless, the focus is also the task of interrogating

---

[4]This quite suitably complements Gallie (1955) fitting description of democracy as being built on 'essentially contested concepts' (p. 184*f.*).

the order produced by classificatory schemes and to see if such order creates preventable and illogical bias.

Like all concepts underpinning the construction of the self, there is no essentialist perception of 'race' or ethnicity as formations of an absolute identity. The human mind has to be educated to think and visualize 'race' and/or ethnicity (Gilroy, 1998, p. 838), to perceive it and to re/imagine its existence. It is not an absolute descriptive term; it is a *floating signifier* that refers to concepts of classification and the making meaning of practices within culture (Hall, 1997). For Goldberg (2009), 'race' is argued as

> not simply a set of ideas or understandings. The category represents, more broadly, a way (or a set of ways) of being in the world, of living, of meaning-making. Those ways of being, living, and representation differ across space and time, between the regions .... (p. 152)

Furthermore although 'race' has its antecedents in pre-modern times, Goldberg (2009) argues that, 'race is an irreducibly modern notion defining and refining modern state formation' (p. 329) particularly within the contemporary era of world-transforming globalization. 'Race is a foundational pillar of modernizing globalization, both in shaping and coloring the structures of modern being and belonging, development and dislocation, state dynamism and social stasis' (Goldberg, 2009, p. 329f.). For Lentin (2008), 'race' acts 'as a more abstract signifier for separating human groups socially, politically and economically. As such, culture, ethnicity, religion, nationality and (but not always) skin colour can all stand for race at different times' (p. 490). Thus, 'race' can be viewed as a structuring feature of modern Irish society, as well as other societies such as Britain (Gilroy, 1990, p. 114).

Gilroy (1998) makes the ethical plea in *Race Ends Here* to counter racism and injustices by making 'a more consistent effort to de-nature and de-ontologize "race" and thereby to disaggregate raciologies' (p. 839). Linking to the ethical imperative proposed, the approach from the outset is to incorporate into the conceptual framework a research strategy that undermines and disturbs 'the persistent normative claims of raciology' (Gilroy, 1998, p. 840) and ethnicity that are based on a false biological or pseudo-scientific theory. That is not to attempt to make 'race' or ethnicity obsolete but rather to interrogate their foundations and confront the reification of 'race' and ethnicity, within the process of analysis and through re-definition and re-construction, rather than *deracination*.[5]

Thus, a core precept is the subversion of *racio-ethnic* constructions while simultaneously recognizing and acknowledging cultural ways of life as inherent to

---

[5]For more on such debates, please refer to works such as Between Camps: Nations, Cultures and the Allure of Race (Gilroy, 2000), 'Ethnicity Denial' and Racism: The Case of the Government of Ireland Against Irish Travellers (McVeigh, 2007), Alana Lentin's (2015) article, What does 'race' do? and Kapoor's (2013) work, The advancement of racial neoliberalism in Britain.

ethnicity. Racism exists where 'race as ordering, as management, sedimentation, sifting, as correction and disciplining, as empowering some while causing "others" to buckle under that power has always relied on a plurality of processes' (Lentin, 2015, p. 1403). 'Race' and forms of racist *governmentality* are also observable in more contemporary times as *racial neoliberalism* (Goldberg, 2009; Kapoor, 2013; Lentin, 2015, p. 1403), are existent and require study and exposure as having groundless foundations requiring undermining. The difficulty, then, is the technique with which to simultaneously expose the falseness of *political racelessness* which attempts to render 'race' invisible, thus disguising *racio-ethnic* injustices, while concurrently discrediting 'race' as an identifier of differentiation. Further to this, endeavour is to frame what is detailed within this book in an open manner that underscores the liquidity of identity and culture and mitigates what Gilroy (1990) describes as 'ethnic absolutism', which is understood as, '… a reproductive, essentialist understanding of ethnic and national difference which operates through an absolute sense of culture so powerful' (p. 115). Gilroy (1990) considers *ethnic absolutism* as having the capacity to place people into groupings that are distinguished differentially according to their social and historical situations in a manner that fixes them, 'understood to be mutually impermeable and incommensurable' (p. 115).

> Nonetheless, it is not to reject *nationalism* outright but to uncover modes of national development that have occurred and are still emergent, most importantly, to analyse if such have a tendency towards *ethnic absolutism* or, in contrast, perturbs national *insiderism*. A supposed ethnically 'Irish' identity 'is a group identity that encapsulates all other identities and roles (gender, class occupational, local or regional etc.); and it defines and delimits the acceptable range of relationships one may claim with both insiders and outsiders to the group' (Tovey et al., 1989, p. 5). The purpose is not only to test the range of what is acceptable, but to investigate the effects of the decentring of modern thought on the formation of identity, whereby ethnicity is understood predominantly as a self-consciously produced social construct. Furthermore, an undertaking is to make less ambiguous what it means to be 'Irish' by denying archaic or even fabricated notions of group affiliation. Instead, it is to make contemporary *Irishness* less arcane by embracing the existential reality of 'fluid' or 'liquid' modernity and allowing for the formation of a perceived authentic identity that better complements such current theory.

However, a prior difficulty to this relates to the reproduction of ethnic distinctions. Divulging two main arguments, Barth (1969) presents the perspective that instead of social isolation, exposure and social interaction between assumed ethnicities can reinforce ethnic distinctions:

> First, it is clear that boundaries persist despite a flow of personnel across them. In other words, categorical ethnic distinctions do not

depend on an absence of mobility, contact and information, but do entail social process of exclusion and incorporation whereby discrete categories are maintained despite changing participation and membership in the course of individual life histories. Secondly, one finds that stable, persisting, and often vitally important social relations are maintained across such boundaries, and are frequently based precisely on the dichotomized ethnic statuses. In other words, ethnic distinctions do not depend on an absence of social interaction and acceptance, but are quite to the contrary often the very foundations on which embracing social systems are built. Interaction in such a social system does not lead to its liquidation through change and acculturation; cultural differences can persist despite inter-ethnic contact and interdependence. (p. 9f.)

From an Irish perspective of self-interest, what becomes clear relates to the balance between the perceived degeneration of values gained from ethnic distinction and the merits gained by accepting contemporary modernity to its fullness. However, from a more independent position, in this book, I comprehend and explain the power dynamics of social processes of exclusion and incorporation, as well as patterns of stratification, dominance and subordination. As Tovey et al. (1989) state, for the reconstitution of identities, ethnic or otherwise, '... power relations are of immense significance in understanding how specific ethnic identities or systems of meanings have emerged and have taken the forms they have' (p. 7). If Irish society is becoming more diverse and certain once assumed group identifications are not made superfluous and/or categorizations of ethnic distinctions do not alter accordingly, more inequitable power relations have and will continue to emerge. With such an emergence, it is probable that increased internal social conflict will arise. In particular, by examining how categorizations affect certain groups on the margins of what is deemed to be 'Irish', proposals towards mitigating conflict may be postulated. Furthermore, if the motivation is towards a transformation of social relations and alleviation of hegemonic social conditions, then it is not only to look at the mundane ways in which individual acts seed prejudiced conditions but to extrapolate and theorize beyond the individual acts as they are manifested.

Exploring 'Irish' Identity

Espoused herein is my explicit aim of capturing the consciousness of participants' ways of perceiving 'Irish' identity as it is imagined at this early period of the 21st century. This book addresses such voids in debate within the Irish context. As Monahan (2009, p. 216) states, 'the frailty of concepts such as identity, nationality and history in the light of the problematic and flexible notion of perspective'. Thus, I reveal misconceptions of *Irishness* which may then motivate ethical self-transformations and positive modes of resistance to an inequitable social order that relies on mythological perceptions of 'Irish' identity. This is because such fallacies or false notions perpetuate power inequalities within Irish society and, thus, are undemocratic. Fundamentally, they do not prescribe to democratic principles, such as autonomy, *constitutionality*, *egalitarianism*, freedom and justice. What then emerges is a proposition that challenges undemocratic views by questioning a broader audience, people's perceptions of identity and evoking response. As a consequence, the results and findings, detailed within this book, contribute to the derivation of thoughts and contestations pertinent to matters relating to identity, citizenship and constitutionality.

By exploring 'Irish' identity as expressed by inhabitants within the contemporary 21st century nation state of Ireland, it could lead to the re-conceptualization of 'Irish' identity within an era of fluid, or even *liquid modernity*.[6] Consequently, the central question being posed explicitly is,

> To what extent is identity in Ireland being redefined within a globalised world?

Additionally within this book, I query, reveal and evaluate people's collective rationale for perceiving 'Irish' identity and citizenship and contrast this with constitutional legislation introduced in 2004 following the Irish Citizenship Referendum. In accordance with the outcome of the 2004 Irish Citizenship Referendum,[7] changes in the Irish constitutional legislation indisputably created augmented restriction of citizenship for children of 'foreigners' while contradictorily maintained the granting of rights to citizenship to children and grandchildren of Irish living abroad from within the broader Irish diaspora.[8]

Furthermore, the book explores and assesses theoretically the criteria for membership of the Irish national collective, which are seen to rely on concepts of the nation in racialized terms. Specifically conjectured is whether or not the shift towards *jus sanguinis* citizenship is contrary to the aspirations of a social democratic state but representative of developments of supranational governance and European integration. I query whether or not the change in emphasis towards *jus sanguinis* citizenship relies on subject constitution through *governmentality* or a form of governance that is founded on anachronistic colonial rationale. That is to say, to some extent, this book investigates theoretically if an emphasis towards bloodline descent citizenship acquisition is dependent on the top-down governance of individuals and if such government control is an outmoded remnant of *colonialism*.

---

[6] Bauman (2000) defines *'Fluid' modernity* as 'the epoch of disengagement, elusive, facile escape and hopeless chase. In "liquid" modernity, it is the most elusive, those free to move without notice, who rule' (p. 120).

[7] Henceforth, the 2004 Irish Citizenship Referendum is referred to interchangeably as the 2004 ICR.

[8] For a more detailed Sociological account of the Irish diaspora in the context of globalization, please refer to Gray (2002) and, for a more Gender Studies orientation, MacPherson and Hickman's (2014) edited book on, *Women and Irish Diaspora Identities: Theories, Concepts and New Perspectives*.

In the contemporary context, colonialism should not be understood in its simplest form, as the territorial extension of a nation's sovereignty but should be understood as the multifaceted control or governing influence of people. New forms of *colonialism* are better comprehended as dominance and control of individuals, and of social governed collectives or groups, across a multitude of facets of people's lives. As such, *supranational governance* and certain configurations of European integration can also be quite easily understood as *colonialism*, under the pretence of *regionalization*, without the blatant territorial conquests of previous historical epochs (further elaborated within Chapter 3).

> Fitting at this point is to advance that I express the normative position of opposing the retreat of that which is progressive. One practical and reflexive way of analysing the regressive/progressive paradigm is through the expansion of the analysis of individuals' conceptions of nationality, identity and belonging. This requires probing into formations of self-identifications so as to make enquiries into concepts of people's own experience, of individuals' comprehension of the psychological process and ultimately the nature of the self in relation to society (Heald, 1989, p. 59). An appropriate way to achieve this is through facilitated focus group discussions, which may lead to self-realizations and contribute to an understanding of perceived *Irishness* in contemporary 21st-century Ireland. To this end, the study provides insight into perceived *Irishness* and compares such findings with the foundational rationale behind the enactment of *jus sanguinis* legislation through the 2004 Irish Citizenship Referendum. This is explored through the facilitation of group discussions on processes of (re)identifications (the methodology of which is detailed in Chapter 4). By exploring an in-depth understanding of contemporary 'Irish' identity, along with redefinitions of self-identification, the objective is to disclose potential alternative understandings of citizenship and belonging that are more inclusive (Brandi, 2007, p. 43; Crowley et al., 2006, p. 22). Details below provide further justification for the argument that such legislative changes can, and should, be interpreted as regressive rather than progressive.

From here, I highlight disparities that exist between individuals' concepts of identity and socio-theoretical hypotheses. Central to this is my desire to facilitate deliberation which may provide creative insight into envisaging more apt, contemporary notions of *Irishness* and identity. It is for this reason that the study incorporates participatory, reflexive and grass-root phases using contemporary technological means of communication.

The methodological approach adds depth through phases that incorporate discussion, after a period of reflection, on the drafting of more inclusive citizenship policies. One such phase involves relevant stakeholder participation allowing for open debate and negotiation so as to redistribute power more evenly in the decision-making process.[9] Thus, this study reflexively seeks to recognize and positively influence the emergent nature of society through the promotion and facilitation of inclusive civic engagement, community involvement and intercultural communication. It is not simply an interpretation of experience, but it actively acts as a catalyst of social enrichment. To an extent, this study could be, 'understood as the transformative capacity of human agency' (Moriarty, 2006, p. 20) through its methodological processes, dissemination capabilities and objectives.[10]

Within this book, specific theorization is postulated and is seen as adding to the body of knowledge. The question is,

> does or could this study spur on a transformative self and collective redefining that could advance greater societal enhancement and a novel state of intercultural enrichment?

To give an outline of how this question might be addressed, the subsequent section provides a brief overview of the structure, chapter content and findings of this book. It includes a concise outline of the topics covered, as well as the concluding motif of contemporary *Irishness*.

Overview

As the overall approach of this study is grounded in an exploratory style, it is pertinent to clearly detail the trajectory of thought, discussion and analysis. The aim within the context of contemporary Ireland has been detailed heretofore. As it is deemed vitally relevant, detailed above is consideration of the ethical imperative in knowledge acquisition in addition to processes of categorizations. The introduction and initial chapters together encapsulate this book within more focussed and confined limits pertaining to perceived *Irishness* but also set the scene in both a purposefully expansive and exploratory form which is in keeping with the overall aims and objectives of the study.

In order to justify and complement the central aims presented, the introductory section has created a more enclosed setting of Identity Studies within the more narrowed scope and discipline of Sociology. Specifically, it orientated towards looking at 'Irish' identity through the prism of ethnic and racial studies. Rather than placing 'Irish' identity into a discrete definable locality, it highlighted the unfixed arrangement and fragility of such concepts through a historical

---

[9]For more on power and participation, please refer to work by Gaventa (1980), entitled, *Power and Powelessness*.
[10]Such a methodological approach is akin to the concept of Public Sociology, which was re-introduced by Michael Burawoy during his presidential address at the annual American Sociological Association meeting in 2004 (Fatsis, 2014). For further detail on the 2004 presidential address, please refer to *For Public Sociology* (Burawoy, 2005).

account of the evolution of the concept of identity and its interrelated discursive vocabularies.[11]

Then spilling over into Chapter 1, the book develops by focussing on theoretical issues and detailing the theoretical framework employed. Initially delved into are questions around identity formation and *subjectification* in a more general sense. The construction of 'Irish' national identity is examined from the theoretical perspective of *essentialism* within a *social constructivist* framework.

Chapter 2 describes how *Irishness*, which is centred on national identity formation, then evolved into a critique of the assumed fixed nature of the nation state itself. The evolution of the supposed homogenous nation into what may be termed the racial state is shown to provide justifications for authoritative population migration control. Theoretical rationale is related to hegemonic neo-colonial knowledge/power relations, which are illustrated as having been manifested in the passing of the 2004 ICR. What is interpreted and theorized as a regressive shift in Irish constitutional legislature is depicted as copper-fastening the racialization of the Irish nation state. It is through the deconstruction of notions of identity that resistance to excessive state power and its anti-heterogeneous predilections can be asserted; the overarching supposition being that commonalities prevail over difference among a diverse population.

Following this, Chapter 3 describes and details *jus sanguinis/jus soli* legislation in the historical context. This is detailed in relation to the manifestation of social policy in legislative terms as it is fixed within the constitutional amendments following the 2004 Irish Citizenship Referendum.

> Chapter 4 explains the methodological approaches, as well as the underlying principles guiding each approach. The foci are a description of the phases of the design, the sampling style and methods, the process of analysis and the methodological conclusions, including limitations. A description of the methodology is detailed within this chapter. The methodology takes a multiphase approach that seeks to explore individuals' perceived sense of identity, either in stability or flux, by exposure to variations of *Irishness* through the viewing of a multimedia presentation. This novel and innovative qualitative design relies on an audio–visual

---

[11] In order to provide a more decentred approach to describing the socially construction of *Irishness*, in addition to mitigating assumptive claims on *Irishness* and the potential reification of 'Irish' identity specifically, this introduction expressively avoids chronicling a literature review of broader studies into *Irishness* as the explanatory foundation of this research. Instead, discursively interwoven throughout, references are made to literature where appropriate. For additional sociologically orientated research into *Irishness*, please refer to works by Daniel Faas, Richard Layte, Ronit Lentin, Elaine Moriarty, Brian Fanning, Máirtín Mac an Ghaill, Sean Ó Riain, Mary Corcoran, Declan Kiberd, Kieran Keohane, Pat O'Connor, Gavan Titley, Brian Conway, Michel Peillon, Tom Inglis, Stephen Loyal, Andreas Hess, Robbie McVeigh, among others.

production made from one-to-one interviews with four individuals of differing backgrounds but who are all Irish citizens. By showing it to eight focus groups, it elicits in participants the deconstruction of 'Irish' national identity. Through focus group discussions on identity, ethnicity and citizenship, evidence emerges from the transcribed and thematically analysed conversations.

The central concepts that come to the fore in the results from the cross-analysed data are discussed in Chapters 5–9. Chapter 5 presents participants' perceptions of being 'Irish'; Chapter 6 details historical *Irishness*, Chapter 7 compares 'being' with 'becoming' Irish; Chapter 8 documents the construction of Ethnicity, Race and the Irish nation; Chapter 9 describes *Irishness* in the context of economics, state governance and world views. The sections interlink and instead of visualizing the directionality of the discussions in a linear progression, it is easier to imagine the topic as iterative, which paints an overall picture of individuals' perceptions of 'Irish' identity. Consequently, in exploring the processes of socially constructing *Irishness*, this documented monograph facilitates insight into the processes which affect an individual's self-understanding and social categorization. Such a reflexive social investigation reveals findings that substantiate an identity theory positing explicit contradictions between individuals' reliance on deep-rooted and inherent notions of *Irishness* in contrast with awareness and a contemporary understanding of identity as being constructed through social experience.

The concluding 10th chapter reviews themes of *Irishness* sequentially and discusses section by section the considerations deemed pertinent to the overall exploratory purposes of the study. In keeping with the grounded methodological approach advocated, a central postulation is proposed based on empirical information reviewed. Thus, the development of the thesis postulated in Chapter 10 is presented as contributing to knowledge within the discipline of Sociology and field of ethnic and racial studies. Theorization is expounded based on the data analysis, and well-informed inferences are posited, analysed and justified. Through empirical validation, it postulates the socio-psychological process of *perceived rational pragmatism* as the means by which individuals within *ordo-liberal liquid modernity* perceive of themselves as rational liberated beings. Through reflection, theory synthesis and the embedded agential design, this book details a thesis which informs the re-conceptualization of contemporary 'Irish' identity. Its admissions seek to expedite an alternative re-imagination of, 'what it means to be Irish' so as to better complement the aspirations towards an egalitarian-based socio-democracy.

Overall, this book documents a qualitative approach to sociological research that gives voice to everyday lay people residing in Ireland. It evidences conversation

16   Redefining Irishness *in a Globalized World*

and interaction between such individuals focussing on prominent topics relevant to the current times we live in, such as national identity, citizenship, inclusiveness, *regionalism*, *globalization/localization*, migration regimes and *governmentality*.

Chapter 1

Theorizing Identity and *Irishness*

Keywords: Essentialism; social constructivism; performativity; subjectification; migration; racism; hybridity; exclusion; post-colonialism

Homogeneity/Heterogeneity

Within this chapter, I primarily explore theoretical concepts relating to identity and *Irishness*. This chapter further expands on and develops sociological and philosophical theorization from those familiarized in the introduction and together provides the underpinning justifications of the study.

Initially, the general problematic aspect of identity is highlighted and deliberated drawing primarily from renowned contemporary theorists and scholars. From the examination of theory, an initial proposition conveyed is that instead of being seen as a rationale which is inherently contradictory, *essentialism* can be seen to exist, residing within *social constructivism*.

Problematizing Identity

The theoretical foundations of this study are based on constructivist identity theory. Thus, it would seem fitting to examine the processes which contingently produce and reproduce collective identities and to consider the propensities of individuals to identify with particular collectivities.

Individuals and groups are viewed as preserving repertoires of possible identities or identities that are multi-layered (Hall, 1996, p. 4). Hall's (1996) suggestion is that,

> If we translate this essentializing conception to the stage of cultural identity – is it that collective or true self hiding inside the many other, more superficial or artificially imposed 'selves' which a people with a shared history and ancestry hold in common and which can stabilize, fix or guarantee an unchanging 'oneness' or

> cultural belongingness underlying all the other superficial differences. It accepts that identities are never unified and, in late modern times, increasingly fragmented and fractured; never singular but multiply constructed across different, often intersecting and antagonistic, discourses, practices and positions. (p. 3f.)

For Hall (2000a), the logic of identity is that it has,

> a kind of existential reality ... the logic of the language of identity is extremely important to our own self-conceptions. It contains the notion of the true self, some real self, inside there, hiding inside the husks of all the false selves that we present to the rest of the world. (p. 146)

The suggestion is also that subjects maintain ways of presenting themselves to the world that are dependent on the credibility and usefulness of such identity in differing circumstances. Post-structuralists[1] view increasing globalization and migration-related diversity as creating fragmented societies within which people's identities are 'hybrid and shifting' (Faas, 2010, p. 11).

Contemporary identities are seen as multiple, performative, liquefied and multidimensional. In 'The Presentation of Self in Everyday Life', Goffman (1959) considers perceptions and performance at the level of the individual and the interpretation of individuals' physiognomies, or facial features indicative of an ethnic origin, by not only looking at the perspective of the other but at

> [...] the point of view of the individual who presents himself before them. He may wish to think highly of him, or to think that he thinks highly of them, or to obtain no clear-cut impression; he may wish to ensure sufficient harmony so that the interaction can be sustained, or to defraud, get rid of, confuse, mislead, antagonize, or insult them. (p. 3)

As Butler (1993, p. 12) discusses, albeit in the context of sexuality, but which could also be interpreted across many inscribed characteristics of *subjectification*, this poststructuralist perspective is a 'rewriting of discursive performativity' where production through the performative is recognized as 'the reiterated practice of *racializing* interpellations' (Butler, 1993, p. 18). Importantly, Butler (1988, p. 528) sees the ascription of interiority as itself a publicly regulated and sanctioned form of essence fabrication (further discussed in the next section). Hence, subjects are influenced by their surrounding environment, social incentive structures, demands for local conformity, broader cultural changes and the

---

[1] Although some may not self-subscribe as post-structuralists, examples of such thinkers include Judith Butler, Michel Foucault, Gilles Deleuze, Jacques Derrida, Jacques Lacan, among others.

influence of manipulative techniques used by cultural or political entrepreneurs. Bauman (2000) places the human condition within the concept of *fluid modernity* where the individual is '... now malleable to an extent un-experienced by, and unimaginable for, past generations' (p. 8).

This is reliant on the notion that observable heterogeneity among individuals is translated into collective perceptions, goals and behaviours. From this, identities are malleable, tradable and deployable at different points. Contemporary theory suggests that individuals have repertoires of identities that are activated differently in response to changing incentive structures, and it is recognized that some actors have a disproportionate influence on modes in the commencement or consolidation of specific identities at the group level, such that power relations differ within the societal milieu.

With reference to Foucault's (1977) work, for example, *Discipline and Punish*, I explore the interrelationship between 'power-knowledge' and discourse in the creation of modes of self-policing among the populace, namely, self-identification and the identity formation of 'the other'. However, rather than decentralizing 'the subject' by placing emphasis on 'a theory of discursive practice' (Foucault, 1970), I seek to reconceptualize 'the subject' in an attempt to, 'rearticulate the relationship between subjects and discursive practices' (p. xiv). According to Hall (1996), this is considered where '... the question of identity reoccurs, or rather, if one prefers to stress the process of subjectification to discursive practices, and the politics of exclusion which all such subjectification appears to entail, the question of *identification*' (p. 2). These dimensions are further elaborated on in Chapter 3 under the concept of 'the colonisation of the self'.

However, from this Foucauldian perspective, what is then highlighted is the manner in which, through societal constructs, the cyclical nature of the nation state is not only initiated but also perpetuated via the reproduction of collective identifications. The cyclical nature of this paradigm creates a tendency for the nation state to gravitate towards emphasizing homogeneity over accommodating differences. In order to define the nation as described by members within society, through discourse and negotiation, participants in this study contribute their perceived views of *Irishness*.[2] From here, an exploration to compare such definitions against identity theory, as well as the state's role in constructing national identity is conducted. The rationale of identification is related to justify/falsify the legislative boundaries that are drawn to fashion difference between the 'them' and 'us' of contemporary Irish society.

In drawing on the interconnectedness in understanding 'us' and 'them', Bridget Anderson (2013) opens the fittingly titled book *Us and Them? The Dangerous Politics of Immigration Control* by stating that,

> The politics of immigration reveal the volatility of categories that are imagined as stable, including citizenship itself. Judgements

---

[2]For supplemental contemporary views on *Irishness* as expressed by members of the public, please refer to the pilot study by the author (BouAynaya, 2011).

about who is needed for the economy, who counts as skilled, what is and isn't work, what is a good marriage, who is suitable for citizenship, and what sort of state-backed enforcement is acceptable against 'illegals', affect citizens as well as migrants. The exclusion of migrants helps define the privileges and the limitations of citizenship, and close attention to the border (physical and metaphorical) reveals much about how we make sense of ourselves ... citizens and migrants define each other, and that they do so through sets of relations that shift and are not in straightforward binary opposition. (p. 2)

The politics of immigration is the key aspect of Anderson's (2013, p. 2) understanding of the modern state which depicts itself as a *community of value*. Similar to active everyday life, members who exhibit shared values, such as common ideals and behaviour, undertake certain rituals of social relations within the community and it is these commonplace activities, underpinnings of identity, that are explored within this book. In a sense, this study empirically investigates, through analysing subjective opinions on issues of identity, ethnicity and citizenship, not only the composition of the *community of value* but also its durability and perpetuation. This is placed within a national specificity with a focus on Ireland. However, to avoid what Fossum (2012) terms 'nationalism's "reification fallacy"' or in other words, 'the propensity to accept as an already fact that which one wants to have come into existence' (p. 341), what are also considered are identities and conceptions of the self and other that may not be nationalist but based on perhaps a novel or somewhat different form of identification. Although *cosmopolitanism* (refer to Chapter 2) does not necessarily need to be interpreted in juxtaposition with nationalism, it would provide one such concept as a point of reference.

Furthermore, this study seeks to relate dominant normative understandings that comprise the *community of value* and investigate the interrelation of such with legislation specific to citizenship and migration. This is achieved by considering legal constructs as normative, as well as both the citizen and migrant. Finally, the intention is to investigate if new concepts of forms of identification can be attained through purposively constructing scenarios for deliberation specifically on the topic of new processes of re-identification or redefining *Irishness* (as described in Chapter 4 on research methodology).

Essentialism within *Social Constructivism*

Previous models of identity that rely on 'primordial' or 'essential' characteristics of individuals or groups suggest the descriptive nature of identity. *Primordialism* bases its assumptions on the notion that the true political or social nature of an individual or group, and their identity, is fixed or static. It places people within 'zoological' groups, where their essential characteristics are divined with the assumption that accurate predictions can be made about the preferences, perceptions and behaviour of their members without relying on sound empirical information to make such judgements. The approach relies on theory that contrasts with such notions of identities as being 'rigid, long-standing and primordial; that resist assimilation and erosion from education, secularization and modernization' (Oberschall, 2010, p. 180).

Instead, this thesis develops on socio-psychological theorists, such as Tajfel (1981, p. 150) who posit that social identity creates in-group preference or *ethnocentrism*, which is a derivative of social categorization. Intrinsic to this is the rejection of 'the other'. Such theories lead to active social separation by which minorities create space in which they can better shape and control their shared political environment within a representative democratic landscape of inevitable subordination (Butler & Ruane, 2009, p. 84). Accordingly, 'Self esteem, social identity, and ethnocentrism are validated in social interactions with like-minded persons' (Oberschall, 2010, p. 180). Similarly, the politics of identity (Huntington, 1996, p. 125) considers concepts of primordial ethnic identities unconvincing and favours the construction of group identities through social psychology of intergroup relations such that power holders may create identities using semiotics and myths to emotionally affect populations and contrive nationalistic solidarities. As Oberschall (2010) states,

> Manipulative elites assume fragility in ethnic group relations and social construction of identities, as Identity politics does, but highlights top-down more than bottom-up mobilization. Elites contend for power by manipulating social divisions and blowing them out of proportion with threat, fear and hate discourse and propaganda, and with no-compromise, aggressive, crisis politics. (p. 181)

When conceptualized from the sociological perspective and related to what is edifying, association by identity can be similarly compared with culture, which is seen as a unique approach to life of a group with, 'meanings, values and ideas embodied in institutions, in social relations, in systems of belief, in mores and customs, in the uses of objects and material life' (Clark et al., 1976, p. 10). Furthermore, Clark et al. (1976) propose that culture, '… embodies the trajectory of group life through history: always under conditions and with raw materials which cannot wholly be of its own making' (p. 11). Similarly, McRobbie (1977) describes resolutely that,

> […] culture is about the pre-structured but still essentially expressive and creative capacities of the group in question. The forms which this expressivity takes are 'maps of meaning' which summarize and encapsulate their social and material life experiences. But these cultural artefacts or configurations are not created out of nothing. Individuals are born into what are already constructed sets of social meanings which can then be worked on, developed and even transformed. (p. 45)

Taking this *social constructivist* approach, 'Irish' identity can be interpreted as 'the accumulated legacy of previous generations and how they are interpreted today' (White, 2008, p. 84).

This defining process of self-identification by the inhabitants of the island of Ireland requires exploration and scrutinization, so as to oppose a political schema that, relying on mythological concepts and falsities, implements immigration policies and legislation that could be interpreted as exclusionary. As Billig (1995) highlights,

> This nationalist way of thinking, even when it is ingrained as habitual, is not straightforward. Just as a dialectic of remembering and forgetting might be said to sustain 'national identity', so this 'identity' involves a dialectic of inwardness and outwardness. The nation is always a nation in a world of nations. 'internationalism' is not the polar opposite of 'nationalism', as if it constitutes a rival ideological consciousness. Nationalism, like other ideologies, contains its contrary themes, or dilemmatic aspects. An outward-looking element of internationalism is part of nationalism and has accompanied the rise of nationalism historically. (p. 61)

Although Billig (1995, p. 69) argues that not only should national identity be seen as 'an inner psychological state' but that it ought to be conceptualized as a '... form of life which is daily lived in a world of nation states' (Billig, 1995, p. 68). Skey (2011, p. 332) stresses that 'moreover, it is a form of life so entrenched and taken-for-granted in many parts of the world that it is rarely commented upon', thus emphasizing the banality of *nationalism*. These considerations are further elaborated on in Chapter 2, under the heading of 'The Nation State and Identity'. Subsequent to this, I consider how such perturbance, of the perceived fixity of the nation state, may relate to identity itself as fluid, dynamic and adaptable within *late-modernity*.

Post-modernists contend today that 'identities are social constructs, not defined or limited by language, race, ethnicity or any other concrete criteria' (White, 2008, p. 87). The late-/post-modern world has fragmented all of that which provided people with fixed and firm locations as individuals (Ní Chonaill, 2009, p. 49). Although Brah (1996, p. 123) suggests, 'identity is neither fixed nor singular; rather it is a constantly changing relational multiplicity', 'Irish' identity seems to be persistently reconstructed, reinvented and redefined from an essentialist perspective. This provides the rationale for mechanisms of power and control whereby the construction of identities is visibly interrelated with difference and exclusion (Hall, 2000b, p. 234). The emphasis on

> The notion that identity has to do with people that look the same, feel the same, call themselves the same, is nonsense. As a process, as a narrative, as a discourse, it is always told from the position of the Other ... written in and through ambivalence and desire. (Hall, 2000a, p. 148*f*.)

What is fascinating is that identity is still defined effectively with the portrayal of 'the other', through an understanding that is essentialist, which is maintained by government and media, ultimately shaping the direction of policy-makers in dealing with contemporary societal issues and profoundly influencing public opinion. In fact, it has even been contended that, 'racism in Ireland was organised not by extreme right groups, but by ordinary journalists, politicians and writers' (Lentin & McVeigh, 2006, p. 4). Moreover, the suggestion is that although it is recognized that social identity theory proposes that conformity stems from psychological processes, being a member of a group is defined as the subjective perception of the self as a member of a specific category (Nass et al., 1995), suggesting a more constructivist understanding of personal, in-group identity.

Yet in the Irish context overall, there may be an alternative or third space of in-betweenness that intertwines the dialectical arguments of *essentialist* notions of identity within a framework that is reflective of *social constructivism*. Such blurring of identity politics is dissimilar to Bhabha's (1994, p. 162*ff.*) concept of *hybridity*, which is seen to create spaces that are inclusionary, and, in fact, is more insidious in its apparatus of regulation, control and ultimate continual exclusion of the Irish antonym. Like the contestation of gender essentialism, being truly Irish or the false 'other' is only what is socially compelled and is in no sense ontologically necessitated (Butler, 1988, p. 528).

Furthermore, the binary relationship between 'insider' and 'outsider', with its reliance on primordial theorization based on false assumptions, plausibly has a tendency to facilitate ethno-political conflict. Thus, unless contested through notions of inclusiveness, there is a grain of truth in Campbell's (1998) argument to suggest that the territorial state is the source of not only the marginalization of 'the other' but also the exclusion and rejection of the 'outsider'. Similarly, Hardt and Negri (2000) historicize that, 'wherever modern sovereignty took root, it constructed a Leviathan that overarched its social domain and imposed hierarchical territorial boundaries, both to police the purity of its own identity and to exclude all that was other' (p. xii). According to Campbell (1998),

> This is because inscribing the boundaries that make the installation of the nationalist imaginary possible requires expulsion from the resultant 'domestic' space of all that comes to be regarded as alien, foreign and dangerous. The nationalist imaginary, thus, demands a violent relationship with the other. (p. 13)

Ultimately, if the criteria for membership within the Irish national collectivity rely on concepts of the nation in racialized terms, then this dependency on essentialist principles is not only regressive, but it is contrary to the aspirations of a social democratic *body politic*. It may even be seen as representative of developments in supranational governance that relies on subject constitution through *governmentality* and anachronistic colonial rationale (further elaborated in Chapter 2).

If the dynamics of collective identity formation and change were instead seen as fluid, rather than from an *essentialist* stand point, it would more likely build on more accurate perceptions that could mitigate ethno-political conflict within and between societies. By focussing on the constructed nature of identity not only is it possible to, as White (2008) suggests, 'gain a better understanding of the way in which the Irish have defined their identity based on a national conceptualization of their archaeological, historical, and cultural past' (p. 82), according to *postcolonial* scholarship it should also elucidate a more accurate understanding of 'Irish' identity that is inclusive. Consequently, from this perspective, there are three main aspects that are focussed on throughout this book and the discussions

24 Redefining Irishness in a Globalized World

within in order to explore the methodologies of national, community and individual representation, thus questioning the maintenance of the mythopoeic aspects of 'Irish' national and local identity (Monahan, 2009, p. 217). These are:

1. questioning interpretations of the historical;
2. exploring national homogeneity/heterogeneity; and
3. investigating essentialisms of identity.

This chapter has provided an overview of the central considerations in relation problems associated with perceived notions of identity, specifically *Irishness*, as well as in relation to identity, conceptions of *subjectifiction* and *performativity*. Importantly what is introduced is that neither concepts of identity nor the nation state are portrayed as static but rather deduced as social constructs, which leads into the next chapter on, 'Irish' identity and the nation state.

Furthermore, following notions based on contemporary identity theory, I tacitly assume that through specific forms of *social construction*, ideas that are reliant on *essentialist* notions become ingrained in the collective conscience of people claiming *Irishness*. At this point, my proposition is that such dispositions of self-identification be the basis of this exploratory piece of writing.

Chapter 2 follows on by focussing on Imagining *Irishness*, the nation state and identity and how historical constructions of 'Irish' identity more precisely contributed to the development of a distinctive national identity associated with the establishment of contemporary Ireland. I question the very notion of the nation state and then disentangle notions around *nationalism* to show how, in its current form, it imbues subject constitution based on *racialized* notions. This leads to discussion on nation building, contemporary *neoliberal governmentality*, towards querying plausible dilemmas of the post-national nation state.

Chapter 2

'Irish' Identity and the Nation State

Keywords: Nation state; racialization; biopower; community; marginalization; interculturalism; ethno-national; borders; historicity; cosmopolitanism

In order to place theory within the spatio-temporal context of Irish society, this chapter leads on by delving into how *Irishness* has been imagined and also to describes the historical construction of 'Irish' national identity. Such continuous re-constructions, from historical times to present-day circumstances, highlight the interplay between the nation state and identity formation. This is provided as a backdrop or prequel to contextualize temporal changes in Irish citizenship acquisition. Such contextualization is measured in a theoretical manner.

Thus, within this chapter, it is theorized that more static definitions of identity, as have been challenged in the previous chapter, are also in conflict with the natural progression of any labile contemporary society. Consequently, the ability to freely self-identify is dependent on mechanisms that counter the subjugation of a given minority. If such arrangements are not in place, inequitable power relations occur. Such mechanisms are seen as crucial to the ideological framework of any egalitarian social democracy.

Imagining *Irishness* and the Nation State

> We have an image of ourselves as a modern, liberal democracy with a commitment to the rule of law and the protection of human rights. To some extent, this image may be justified. But there may also be significant blind spots in our self-appraisal as a society. (O'Reilly, 2013, p. 131)[1]

---

[1] O'Reilly's (2013) remarks are made specifically with regard to a critical piece on the Irish state's asylum process, suggestively entitled, 'Asylum seekers in out republic: Why have we gone wrong?'

Developments in print media and capitalism through the industrial revolution assisted the documentation, preservation and dissemination of what would have been more capricious and transient aspects of pre-industrial oral cultures. New, more encoded modes of communication helped the development of the modern nation state. Anderson (1983) refers to such organizational developments of the state as 'imagined communities' (p. 46), which were made imaginable by 'the convergence of capitalism and print technology on the fatal diversity of human language'. Synchronously,

> the rise of the nation state brought about a transformation in the ways that people thought about themselves and about community. It could be said to have brought about a transformation of identity, even bringing into popular vocabulary the notion of 'identity' itself. (Billig, 1995, p. 61)[2]

National identity is, thus, imagined and invented by a group seeking to forge a collective fortitude through commonalities of identification (White, 2008, p. 87). Continuing along similar lines of thought, Gellner (1983) makes the suggestion that 'nations as a natural, God-given way of classifying men, as an inherent though long-delayed political destiny [were/are] a myth' (p. 48*f.*). Anthias and Yuval-Davis (1992, p. 17) emphasize, however, that Gellner roots nationalism and cultural homogeneity as a necessary functional requirement of modern societies. Nationality as a means of classification fastens the contemporary nation within an illusion that is not only based on an eternal reality but also is seen as transhistorical (Wodak et al., 1999, p. 1). This fixity, based on a teleological understanding of the nation as an organization of individuals and communities that are homogeneous, is as Monahan (2009) states, 'established in ritual, cultural performance and historiography which can be usefully seized upon and manipulated by benign, but also corrupt, power systems' (p. 110). When looked at both historically and from the regional, pan-European level, according to Gaine (2008):

> It is clear that countries within Europe have had very different histories with regard to racial and ethnic differences. The colonial past of several countries has, it is argued, infected the rest with assumptions about visible non-European 'others', but many have also struggled to construct an imagined homogeneity despite significant internal diversity ... this sublimating of internal diversity was always problematic and temporary, and that it took the arrival of noticeable numbers of 'foreigners' within the European project to highlight the need to protect people – citizens or not – against the threat of being treated differently and worse because of their physical appearance or aspects of their culture. (p. 35)

---

[2]According to Billig (1995), this quote is in reference to Gidden's (1990) work.

The basis for an assessment of the criteria for membership of the Irish nation collectivity is seen to rely on concepts of the nation in racialized terms. Similar to most modern nation states, Ireland is defined as a 'racial state' (Goldberg, 2002; Lentin, 2007; Lentin & McVeigh, 2006, p. 11), where 'race' and state are inseparable and are defined through the racialization of *Irishness* (Lentin & McVeigh, 2006, p. 11). The state utilizes *biopolitical* measures that are blatantly racialized to manage, regulate and mainstream immigration with the unquestioning support of broader society and practically all social policy analysts. Thus, 'the politics of immigration control, which only a decade ago appeared to be the preserve of the "loony right", becomes a core principle of the developing racist state' (Lentin, 2007, p. 435; Lentin & McVeigh, 2006). Similarly, Billig (1995) in discussion on national identity in the world of nations perceives the evolution of modernity with notions of the sovereign nation state, and its associated vocabulary on identification, as not only being acceptingly adopted but also imposed by colonial powers. 'The new imposed identities (such as belonging to the United Tribes of New Zealand) were part of a more general outlook on the world. In this sense, nationalism involves a theoretical consciousness' (p. 63). Billig (1995, p. 63) continues to describe how Etienne Balibar (1991),

> [...] has written that there is 'no racism without theory (or theories)'. The racist may hate unthinkingly, yet as Balibar implies, racism distinguishes between 'our race' and 'other races', 'our racial community' and 'theirs'. At the very minimum, the racist shares some common-sense theory of what a 'race' is; why it appears important; how 'races' differ; and why 'ours' should remain unmixed. By the same token, there is no nationalism without theory. Nationalism involves assumptions about what a nation is: as such, it is a theory of community, as well as a theory about the world being 'naturally' divided into such communities. The theory does not need to be experienced theoretically. Intellectuals have written theoretical tomes about 'nation'. With the triumph of nationalism, and the establishment of nations across the globe, the theories of nationalism have been transformed into familiar common sense. (p. 18)

Specifically embedded in this study, I also reflect on the concept of subject constitution, which is further elaborated in the following sections. Suffice to say at this point, in summary, I query if subject formation, via methods of *governmentality* and anachronistic rationale, allows the state and its constituents to conceptualize and reinforce an overly superficial depiction of 'Irish' identity. That is to say, I question if from the top down, the Irish state perpetuates shallow depictions of *Irishness* so as to maintain a form of governance based on reasoning that is inconsistent with the existential circumstance of contemporary Irish society.

Community can imply a stable local environment of people, not simply merely existing but also functioning effectively for mutual benefit. In studies on *Community* by Thornton (1997), the recognition is that 'community tends to suggest a more permanent population, often aligned to a neighbourhood, of which family is the key constituent part. Kinship would seem to be one of the main building blocks of community' (p. 2). In contrast, Halberstam (2003, p. 315), in reference to Jean Luc Nancy's work, maintains that *community* is now as moribund and redundant as many view the Christian ritual of communion. Halberstam (2003) adds, further '... quests for community are always nostalgic attempts to return to some fantasized moment of union and unity reveals the conservative stakes in community for all kinds of political projects' (p. 315). Though Halberstam (2003, p. 315) emphasizes the urgency for the reconsideration of subcultures, one could also interpret it as pointing towards the necessity to reconsider notions of the singular homogeneous identity and also to the consideration of the existence of multifarious identities that contend with the community and its inevitable pursuit for homogenization. Similarly, the desire for unity and stability of identity among a particular community is seen as manipulating both internally, but less explicitly, and externally so as to obliterate heterogeneity, thus notably silencing and subordinating already marginalized people within the status quo (Nichols, 2010, p. 116). According to Goldberg (2002), the homogeneous nation 'is to be viewed as heterogeneity in denial, or more deeply yet as the recognition of heterogeneity at once repressed' (p. 16). Thus, its construction creates exclusions, which are masked by the modern racial state's blatant, yet mediocre, attempts to portray images of accommodation of difference through celebrations of multiculturalism or interculturalism (Lentin & McVeigh, 2006, p. 11). Nonetheless, both rely on acknowledgement of differences in ethnicities and are expectant of 'the exotica of difference' (Hall, 2000a, p. 152).

A second critique of multiculturalism relates to the notion of *dominant universality* whereby an attempt to create an identity as 'human beings' might only be an attempt by the dominant to be universal. *Dominant universality* leads to the assumption that, if identity is ambiguous, there is essentially nothing to bind humans together other than a singular collective humanity. Such a proposition provides justification for the re-conceptualization of contemporary Irish collectiveness. Without such, paradoxically what is suggested is that *universalism*, which facilitates *multiculturalism* through postmodernist identity theory, may promote ethnocentric norms, values and interests that are associated with hegemonic power and *globalization* (Bhabha, 1990a, p. 208). At the level of the individual, such Universalist rationale '... takes all perspectives into account, the impartial subject need acknowledge no subjects other than itself to whose interests, opinions and desires it should attend' (Young, 1990, p. 101). In other words, our globalized reality, together with certain universalist thoughts, may nourish the self-interested individual, rather than promote collective cross-cultural solidarities. Further critical engagement in relation to the contradictions associated with universalist thinking and multiculturalism is detailed below (under the heading of 'The Dilemmas of the Post-national Nation State').

For all intents and purposes, a more critical view would see the state using notions of diversity, equality and integration to persuade racial and religious minorities to conform, requiring compromise and compliance to gain entry and acceptance into the mythical homogeneous state. This over-obligation towards acquiescence and conformity could be understood as the development of a stratified racist society (Gilroy & Ouseley, 2005). Supplementing this, Moriarty (2006) describes how a dialectical constitutive matrix of migration controls and politics of care, '... shape belonging in Ireland, where systems of racialized governance become routinised through euphemisms, myths and stories' (p. 126).

This study examines the modes and mechanisms of the group and individual in the representation of 'otherness'. It elucidates the problematic, trans-historical aspects of identity and difference, which are presumed to account for the dominant configuration of knowledge/power but similarly create space for resistance and counter-hegemonic knowledge acquisition (Nichols, 2010, p. 130). Furthermore, an intrinsic component is a reflexive core that, upon circumspection, dictates the directionality of the study towards being itself a space for resistance.

Power is seen as integral to state control, which, in turn, is seen as a mechanism to manage those who are given membership of the state, as well as to exclude 'others' that are viewed as un-associated with the state. The modern racial state manipulates an array of apparatuses to wield power over recognition and as Lentin and McVeigh (2006) propose:

> The state is a central player in racial matters; the modern state carries out racial classification, surveillance and punishment of the population; it distributes resources along racial lines; it simultaneously facilitates and obstructs racial discrimination. (p. 11)

The state defines and reinforces criteria for membership through categorization and the creation of notions of homogeneity under one nation. Similarly, Goldberg (2002) proposes,

> The state has the power by definition to assert itself or to control those within the state ... [and] the power to exclude from state protection. In these senses, the modern state has readily lent itself conceptually to, as it has readily been defined by, racial formation. For central to the sorts of racial constitution that have centrally defined modernity is the power to exclude and by extension include in racially ordered terms, to dominate through the power to categorize differentially and hierarchically, to set aside by setting apart ... [These are] processes aided integrally by ... the law and policy-making, by bureaucratic apparatuses and governmental technologies like census categories, by inventing histories and traditions, ceremonies and cultural imaginings. (p. 9)

To a degree this book questions in an Irish context, 'the racist criteria for membership in the national collectivity itself' (Anthias & Yuval-Davis, 1992, p. 22). It counters the defining of nationhood under homogeneous, essentialist notions and dispel notions that heterogeneous populations are necessarily divisive. It reveals and contributes greater understanding of racism by recognizing that particular state configurations that racialize, maintain inequalities by placing prominence on difference rather than commonality, thus creating, 'a system of subordination' (Lentin & McVeigh, 2006, p. 10).

The Nation State and Identity

As set forth in the introduction, this book focusses on processes of identification, as well as the relation of knowledge/power to identity formation, rather than fixing on the assumption that identities are immutable notions of belonging or possessions with permanency (Skey, 2011, p. 342). By studying the extent to which identities are made meaningful through everyday expression by 'ordinary' people, I assess the making of meanings or concepts relating to identity. In particular, I explore how nation state identity has become 'sedimented' in the Irish context (Laclau, 1990).[3] More generally, it is commonly presumed that for most of the world, 'national identity' has supplanted or assimilated ethnic identity as the most important form of identification (Tovey et al., 1989, p. 9), yet oddly enough ethno-national identifications still persist even against the tides of regionalization and globalization.

Nevertheless, by placing emphasis on the essence of identity formation as a social construct, I do not neglect consideration of debate on nationalism or globalization. Instead, by approaching identity as socially constructed, it simply permits the perspective that the permanency of the nation cannot be assumed. Tovey et al. (1989) elaborate, in the past

> nationalist ideology portrayed 'the nation' as an already existent fact – as a natural consequence of differences in culture. However much of the activity of national movements was devoted to constructing and constituting the nation which was to control its own affairs and command its citizens. (p. 14)

In contrast to perceiving the nation as naturally essential and enduring, this study is potentially more accurate in conceiving of political communities as defined by members themselves, in nationalist terms or not. Such a tack is 'therefore also a way of avoiding nationalism's "reification fallacy", the propensity to accept as an already established fact that which one wants to have come into existence' (Fossum, 2012, p. 342). A further dilemma of such false reification, whereby an abstract notion is assumed to be a concrete objective truth, is that it may also progress to an understanding of political organization as being integral and inseparable from conceptions of nation states. This creates a tautology about the nation that is normative (Levy, 2004, p. 160). By not following the presumption that the nation is a predetermined fact of social enquiry, I attempt to overcome what Beck (2003) concedes, 'to some extent, much of social science is a prisoner of the nation state' (p. 454).

---

[3] Butler (1988) also describes 'a sedimentation of gender norms that produces the peculiar phenomenon of a natural sex, or a real woman, or any number of prevalent and compelling social fictions, and that this is a sedimentation that over time has produced a set of corporeal styles which, in reified form, appear as the natural configuration of bodies into sexes which exist in a binary relation to one another' (p. 524).

Conversely, however, the existential reality is that a majority of people are prisoners of nation state formation, even with globalized migratory flows and technological advancements in transportation. Within this era of flux, people privileged enough to be in a position to migrate, and traverse the globe, still may find themselves disadvantaged. As Anderson (2013) suggests, 'immigration is not just about "them" but is fundamentally about "us"' (p. 9). Similarly, the transposition of this would be to point out what Billig (1995, p. 61) indicates as nationalist thinking that involves conceiving the 'us' and 'them' and the assumed naturalness of the world divided into nation states. This occurs whereby the psycho-social cognizance or perceived notions of the world become implicated in the othering of particular individuals and peoples based on fixed demarcations of national identities, borders and boundaries. The nation state, similar to national identity, as seen through the lens of *social constructivism*, simply becomes naturalized for a particular dominant group. That is, the nation state defines itself based on what it characterizes as essential traits of the ruling or majority population. As Laclau (1990) elucidates, with such naturalization 'the system of possible alternatives tends to vanish and the traces of the original contingency fade' (p. 35).

Thus, it is not necessary to make the presumption of the nation state as naturalized; instead, such notions are recognized as integral to the shaping and informing of individuals' national identities. The approach taken within this project is towards 'reactivation' through disruptive work of the socio-political by developing a thesis that articulates a more accurate comprehension of self and collective identity, not only within the current collectively conceived nation state of Ireland but also within global humanity. By disrupting 'the sedimented forms of "objectivity" [that] make up the field of what we call the social' (Laclau, 1990, p. 34), this study facilitates the recognition of potential alternatives and modification of past and present understandings. Laclau (1990) conjectures a retracing of the historical so as to demystify and bring about a restoration of more accurate understandings:

> The moment of original institution of the social is the point at which its contingency is revealed, since that institution, as we have seen, is only possible through the repression of options that were equally open. To reveal the original meaning of an act, then, is to reveal the moment of its radical contingency – in other words, to reinsert it in the system of real historic options that were discarded ... by showing the terrain of original violence, of the power relations through which that instituting act took place. (p. 34)

Importantly, in what could be accurately related to the socially constructed notion of Irish homogeneity, *revivalism* and the birth of the Irish nation state, Laclau (1990) points out, 'insofar as an act of institution has been successful, a "forgetting of the origins" tends to occur ...' (p. 34). Such recognition of the amnesia surrounding a more truthful understanding of the historical development of the nation state of Ireland provides impetus for this study's progression.

In keeping with this trend of thought, Skey (2011) states there have been a '... growing number of empirical studies that are now shifting attention to focus on forms of nationalism and identification at the level of the everyday' (p. 342). Similarly, Chaney (2002) asserts, 'The everyday is generally the bedrock of social reality, what can be taken for granted' (p. 4). In summarizing the argument for the justification of his piece of work entitled, *Banal Nationalism*, Billig (2009) concludes

> By looking upwards towards the global or downwards towards secessionist moments, analysts have avoided looking directly at one of the most important social phenomena of the age. They have left an enormous hole right at the centre of the study of contemporary nationalism. (p. 351)

Billig (2009) continues, in reference to the United States, 'If the most powerful nationalism passes unrecognized and unstudied as "nationalism", then there is what ... [one] might call an elephant in the sociological room. The academic avoidance of this metaphorical elephant certainly merits critical engagement'.

From the positions of Laclau (1990), Skey (2011) and Billig (2009), it becomes evident that there are fundamental knowledge gaps that can be recognized which require further in-depth exploration. One such lacuna relates to the study of the historical context, development and progression of *nationalism*, taken from a critical position that views the very concept, of the globe comprising the collective of nation states, as a socially fabricated phenomenon. This also raises the problem of 'adopting the tenets of methodological nationalism, whether in the academic sphere or elsewhere, part of a wider – and largely entrenched – set of processes that legitimizes and naturalizes discourse of the nation' (Skey, 2011, p. 334). A void in research specific to 'Irish' identity and its conceived socially constructed actuality, relates to researching at a more localized level, or as Skey (2011) implores, it is at the level of the everyday 'that we must try and understand how and why identities are lived and made meaningful' (p. 334). Similarly, in remedying the bias relating to contemporary analysis that places over-emphasis on principles and ideals, '... and to arrive at a more complete picture of the social realities of toleration ...' Dobbernack and Modood (2011) maintain that, 'we need to be concerned with local practices of accommodation and conviviality that are often supported by pragmatic reasons, as well as with local and contextualized moral reasons for granting toleration' (p. 16).

These vacuums in study are to an extent accommodated for within the methodological approach employed.

At a deeper level, I also explore issues relating to *neo-liberal governmentality*. In consideration of the ideology of *neoliberalism*, Goldberg (2009) provides a laconic description:

> Neoliberalism is the undertaking, then, to maximise corporate profits and efficiencies by reducing costs – most notably as a consequence of taxes, tariffs, and regulations. It has touted itself as the defender of freedom. But it is a peculiar sort of freedom to which neoliberalism is committed. It seeks above all to protect and

expand the freedom of *flows* of capital, goods, and services, and more recently information. It is expressly for letting the market regulate itself so far as the artificial constraints of politics allow. It thus places faith in the market's capacity to optimize resource allocation and expand employment capacity as a result of sustained profitability, subsequent economic growth, and 'trickle-down' charitability. It follows that neoliberalism is committed to denationalizing industry and deunionizing labour power in the name of limiting state regulation, reducing public costs, and freeing capital and its interests from constraint. The perceived result is dramatically if not completely to roll back the need for public funding, institutions, and resources. (p. 332)

Complementing this understanding, the notion of *governmentality* is seen as focussing on integral connections between the micro- and macro-political strata but also defines developments of new structures of socio-political order. *Neoliberal governmentality* then is less to dispense with the state than profoundly shift state priorities; to redirect the nation state to epitomize private interests and relentless economization. Fittingly, as Lemke (2001) explains, 'by means of the notion of governmentality the neo-liberal agenda for the "withdrawal of the state" can be deciphered as a technique for government ... shifting the regulatory competence of the state onto "responsible" and "rational" individuals' (p. 12). In ways, the government could be seen as another strand of aristocracies wanting to emulate 'the owners franchisees, and top managers [who] want to control subordinates, but they want their own positions to be as free of rational constraints – as inefficient – as possible' (Ritzer, 2011, p. 145). Yet this would seem to complement the more classical notion of the nature and power of authority in *bureaucracy*, one where 'the office hierarchy is monocratically organised' (Weber, 1948, p. 197) and where emphasis is placed on structure. In this way, *bureaucracy* is identified with supposed reason 'and the process of rationalization with mechanism, depersonalisation, and oppressive routine' (Gerth & Mills, 1946, p. 50).

In contrast to this, according to Lemke (2001, p. 13*ff.*) is the Foucaultian view that 'the neo-liberal strategy does indeed consist of replacing (or at least supplanting) out-dated rigid regulatory mechanisms by developing techniques of self-regulation ...' (p. 13*ff.*). Lemke (2001) continues by insisting that 'political analysis must start to study the "autonomous" individual's capacity for self-control and how this is linked to forms of political rule and economic exploitation' (p. 13*ff.*). In keeping with Foucault's orientation towards the analysis of two distinct directives of research that are described as intersecting at many points but refer back to a common axis, this study directly includes, 'the examination of the *technologies of the self* by which processes of subjectivization bring the individual to bind himself on his own identity and consciousness and at the same time, to an external power' (Agamben, 1998), while indirectly incorporating, 'the study of the political techniques ... with which the State assumes and integrates the care of the natural life of individuals into its very center' (p. 11) through structures of modern power.

Such *subjectification* is related to the concept and study of *biopolitics*, which can be précised as the politicization of 'bare life' (*zoë*) in contrast to 'qualified life' (*bios*). Throughout civilization sovereign power has been and is acquired by whomever has the authority to regulate the *state of exception* (Agamben, 2005). The *state of exception* affords the state self-authorization to possess extraordinary power, and even extrajudicial power to restrict, restrain and even disappear, disobedient subjects or unruly populations in the name of securitization (Goldberg, 2009, p. 334).

This circumstance occurs when the sovereign, through self-legitimation, frees itself from legal restraints to its power that might have ordinarily applied. The appropriately termed concepts of *biopolitics* or *biopower*, as described by Agamben (1998, 2005), may be understood as the continuous contestation of political control over 'bare life'. Explicitly, it is the supremacy of the sovereign to transcend or alter at a whim the rule of law of the land in the name of the public 'good' and to empower it so as to determine who can be included into the political body and who is to be excluded. As Agamben (1998) points out,

> after all, human politics is distinguished from that of other living beings in that it is founded, through a supplement of politicity [*policita*] tied to language, on a community not simply of the pleasant and the painful but of the good and the evil and of the just and the unjust. (p. 9*ff.*)

At a philosophical level, this book questions the link between politics of exclusion, sovereign power and 'bare life', through the recognition of the concept of *biopolitics*, as developed by Michel Foucault, Hannah Arendt and Giorgio Agamben, among others. From the onset, it adopts a methodological approach that reveals insight into such a concept as *bio-power* by acknowledging and advocating that, as Agamben (1998) states,

> Only within a biopolitical horizon will it be possible to decide whether the categories whose opposition founded modern politics (right/left, private/public, absolutism/democracy, etc.) – and which have been steadily dissolving, to the point of entering today into a real zone of indistinction – will have to be abandoned or will, instead, eventually regain the meaning they lost in that very horizon. And only a reflection that, taking up Foucault's and Benjamin's suggestion, thematically interrogates the link between bare life and politics, a link that secretly governs the modern ideologies seemingly most distant from one another, will be able to bring the political out of its concealment and, at the same time, return thought to its practical calling. (p. 10)[4]

---

[4]Lentin (2009) provides further argument specifically with regard to the state of the Republic of Ireland and how it has created a 'state of exception', in which state racism combines with the Foucauldian notion of *biopolitics*.

In concluding this section and tying these concepts together, I investigate perceived *Irishness* via the intersectionality of subjective descriptions of self-identity and everyday life, *banal nationalism* and the supposed sedimented nature of the nation state within the psyche of subjects. As well as this, reflection on the relationship between the nation state, *governmentality* and *biopolitics* is made in relation to how such processes affecting the self, or selves, might be interpreted within participants' responses. When considering the analysis of the subject in Western civilization towards developing the concepts of the discipline and docility of bodies Foucault (1993) stresses that one needs to

> [...] take into account not only techniques of domination but also techniques of the self. Let's say: he has to take into account the interaction between those two types of techniques – techniques of domination and techniques of the self. He has to take into account the points where the technologies of domination of individuals over one another have recourse to processes by which the individual acts upon himself. And conversely, he has to take into account the points where the techniques of the self are integrated into structures of coercion and domination. The contact point, where the individuals are driven by others is tied to the way they conduct themselves, is what we can call, I think government. Governing people, in the broad meaning of the word, governing people is not a way to force people to do what the governor wants; it is always a versatile equilibrium, with complementarity and conflicts between techniques which assure coercion and processes through which the self is constructed or modified by himself. (pp. 203–204)

It is for the precise reasons clarified above that this piece of socio-political research is being conducted. Such also provides justification for the more qualitative methodology taken which focusses on, if not oxymoronic, the (post-)modern sovereign Irish subject, so as to more fully comprehend its antonym or opposite, the abject made that is at once excluded. To inquire into such, it is first necessary to deconstruct and relate the historical context of the emergence of 'Irish' identity and nationhood.

The Historical Construction of 'Irish' National Identity

The rapid transformation of Ireland, along with the pace and scale of fluctuating migration shifts, Ní Chonaill (2009) would argue, have 'engendered notable dislocations of collective and personal identity. Home and belonging have become increasingly salient issues, a struggle to cultivate a place within a world/nation that is rapidly metamorphosing' (p. 48). In part, this book places prominence on the defining of a contemporary 'Irish' identity within a rapidly altering society.

'Irish' national identity relates to what are viewed to be identifiable traits of *Irishness*, which are intricately linked to perceptions of what is traditional (Marshall, 2000, p. 15). With regard to critiquing contemporary claims of a past

Celtic civilization in Ireland, White (2008) is supportive of the view 'that perceptions of ethnicity and identity are influenced by the context in which they are formed' (p. 86). The notion of a common heritage is continually shifting with the recreation, restatement and reinterpretation of the nation so as to provide credibility for present-day claims of nationhood (White, 2008, p. 85). Yet this simplistic notion of *Irishness* rooted in homogeneity and upon which the national ideal of 'Irish' identity is founded conflicts with historical accounts of a society that has come out of a melange of people through settlements, invasions, movement and migration. The Irish have, though not undisputed, an ancestry that has been traced back to the end of the last Ice Age, approximately 8,000–6,000 BCE. Such lineage is associated with the origins of the Celtic civilization of Western Europe rather than central Europe. Since, the Neolithic period waves of immigrants from various geographical locations settled and contributed to the genetic variability of the Irish (White, 2008, p. 83).

Thus, it would seem that there is a contradiction between the cultural location of 'Irish' identity and its relationship to the historical epoch. Even more puzzling is that the construction of a 'prototypical' cultural identity in Ireland (Marshall, 2000, p. 16), which has led to the imagined notion of a homogeneous society, still persists against a backdrop of genetic and archaeological challenges to the origins of 'Irish' Celtic identity (White, 2008, p. 83*f.*). Such identification with a national ideal, in which the criteria of *Irishness* are restricted to somewhat mythological notions of *homogeneity*, has detrimental effects on the liberal nature of a society through the creation of cultural distinctions or boundaries of difference that are exclusionary.

O'Toole (2000) refers to 'the governing Irish consensus' that persisted for most of the last century as 'a monolithic and static culture' (p. 22) with a degree of apparent *homogeneity*. The homogeneous nation was made of an 'old Irish identity based on Catholicism, nationalism and rural values' (O'Toole, 2000, p. 22). However within this, there have always been 'elusive ambiguities in Irish identity' which allow space to manoeuvre how the Irish define these terms and 'to re-imagine who "we" are' (O'Toole, 2000, p. 22). Marshall (2000, p. 16) refers to the construction of a stereotypical 'Irish' identity being founded on the entirety of main defining traits, those being: 'white', heterosexual, Irish speaking, Irish born, settled and Catholic.

This racialization of *Irishness* as a distinct identity seems to have stemmed from the historical experiences of both people from Ireland living abroad and those within Ireland who saw opportunity to advance through competing modes of social identification. Two distinguishable groups emerged, the Irish as emigrants who attempted to incorporate themselves as equals into a dominant 'white' Anglo culture, and the Irish as nationalists who attempted to detach themselves from a dominant Anglo culture. For both, the unifying characteristic, which had the potential to elevate the status of being 'Irish', was through the advancement of an 'Irish' identity filled with ambiguity (O'Toole, 2000, p. 26). The transition to a post-colonial Ireland saw those advocating an independent free-state utilize contrived notions of the nation to cultivate public defiance towards the imperial power at the time (White, 2008, p. 87). As O'Toole (2000) states, 'Irishness couldn't simply be transformed from black to white. It had to remain ambiguous' (p. 26).

Although contemporary *Irishness* may be considered ambiguous (O'Toole, 2000, p. 27), pre-contemporary 'Irish' identity was also reliant on ambiguity or distancing from reality, particularly in time. As De Paor (1979) elaborates,

> when we ask if there has been a continuous and literally *identifiable* Irish identity, we confront this ambiguity – this evasiveness, this insistence by many Irish writers and nationalistic leaders that we in Ireland are not what we seem on the surface to be, but something else, older, wiser, truer; to be found not here and now but only in the past and in the future. (p. 22)

Modern 'Irish' identity is undeniably dependent on the recognition of a distinct identity formed from distinctive cultural traditions and religious affiliations but also dependent on racial similarities. In fact, historically, the ambiguity of *Irishness* lies within the ambiguity of a racial theory, developed on notions of racial superiority/inferiority. The main instance of this lies in the contradictory conception that the Irish, while being 'white', could also be cast as inferior. In truth, racial theory has always relied on ambiguous assumptions, and as O'Toole (2000) comments, 'being white had nothing necessarily to do with skin colour' (p. 27).

With the expansion of the British monarchical empire, that can be seen to have been irredeemably *assimilationist*, within the early modern period, the conquest of Ireland was envisioned to make sure that the people of Ireland would completely integrate into English civilization (De Paor, 1979, p. 27*f.*; Tovey et al., 1989, p. 14). Nonetheless, rather than a process of incorporation, Gaelic life and its institutions would be subjugated and condemned to inferiority to the British monarchic system of rule.

The preoccupation of English colonialism in Ireland was to thwart the decay of *Englishness* in Ireland, a concept that had been first articulated in 1297 (Crowley, 2005, p. 23). This raises another aspect of ambiguity whereby

> accompanying centralization there is also marginalisation; together with the idea of the legitimate language there is also the question of that which is excluded; for our purposes, along with an emergent sense of Englishness as a form of cultural identity, there is also the problem of Irishness in its various forms. It is this which lies at the heart of debates around 'degeneration'; the cultural and political identity and loyalty of the Old English, the New English and the Gaelic Irish ... the triumph of the English language and the new forms of cultural identity that accompanied it were at one and the same time brash and insecure. (Crowley, 2005, p. 29*f.*)

Furthermore, Crowley (2005) reveals

> [...] another aspect of the great fear, which haunts colonial rule at the time: *cultural hybridity*. He has an Irish name but we know many of the Old English took Gaelic names; he speaks English yet he does so with clearly Irish pronunciation. (p. 32)

With the turning of the 20th-century emphasis on Celtic racial distinctiveness through the revival of Irish language, the development of a national literary movement and the codification of national sports created the foundation of the modern 'Irish' identity. The artificial construction of this Celtic identity was achieved through political myth making by Irish nationalists 'whose political aspirations could only be satiated by achieving complete independence from the British crown' (White, 2004, p. 325). Similarly, Tovey et al. (1989) corroborate, 'the nativism of the Gaelic League was rooted in origin myths which elevated the cultural and social residues surviving in the western islands and the Gaeltacht into the fountainhead for a new society' (p. 18*f.*).

With *Celtic revivalism* came what is termed *national parallelism* which, in the Irish context, sought to de-anglicize Ireland while elevating Irish status from one of inferiority in comparison to the English (De Frëine, 1978, p. 51*f.*; Kiberd, 1995, p. 265; Tovey et al., 1989, p. 16). Tovey et al. (1989) make apparent that 'the clearest and strongest expression of this strategy of "national parallelism", it could be said, was the attempt of the Gaelic League to revive the Irish language as the counter of the language of the English nation' (p. 16). Thus, throughout *Celtic revivalism*, particularly in relation to language, ambivalence again becomes apparent in Irish society. It is suggested that in the wake of the Famine, the English language was necessary for effective emigration accordingly, from a utilitarian perspective, the Gaelic language could be discarded by those who emigrated while reproduced through cultural *revivalism* (Fanning, 2010, p. 400). Irish language was continued to symbolize identity formation and national cohesion, while English language remained for utilitarian functions (Tovey et al., 1989, p. 23). According to Lee (1989), following *cultural revivalism*, it became evident that

> a certain paradox was involved here. English was allegedly embraced as the reputed language of economic growth. When adequate growth failed to materialise, emigration became the alternative. Once again English was embraced as the reputed language of effective emigration. Thus both economic growth, and lack of economic growth, apparently encouraged the drift to English. (p. 665)

Nation Building and Essential *Irishness*

Nation-building inevitably shifted the emphasis of social reproduction from a cultural nationalist perspective towards a *utilitarian liberalist* perspective that focussed on development and modernization (Fanning, 2010, p. 400). Aspects of *nationalism* that were seen to impede Irish economic development were eroded, and 'arguably developmentalism undermined the political salience of essentialist representations of Irish identity' (Fanning, 2010, p. 402). Nevertheless, essentialist claims about 'Irish' identity generated by Irish nationalism managed to persist.

With Ireland's rapid socio-economic changes, the inherited basis of Celtic identity has had to be continually redefined and adapted (White, 2008, p. 89). The construction of a modern 'Irish' identity, defined by a narrow set of criteria, seems to have carved out a niche of self-recognition and self-assurance that masks its ambiguous foundation. Furthermore, such identity construction attempts to position itself, poised between the conflicting ideals of nation state and globalization, with the resultant effect being that 'the boundaries that structure Irish society are being remodelled. Some have dissolved, some have proved resilient to change, and some have crossed over each other melding or producing uneasy interfaces' (Peillon & Corcoran, 2004, p. 3).

What seems to be the case in contemporary Ireland is the emergence of a post/late-modern *Irishness* where 'Irish' identity has been renegotiated between the diametrically opposed ideals of the traditional and the global. In *Global Ireland: Same Difference*, Inglis (2008, p. 38) relies on the notion that Ireland has transformed quite suddenly 'from a homogenous type of white, English-speaking, Catholic society to one with a mix of race, ethnicities and religions' (p. 38). Although the generalized view of a homogenous nation seems to reproduce, as has been contested, fixed and false notions of 'race' and ethnicity, Inglis's view that *Irishness*, as it is perceived, has become more varied with global flows and globalization may be accurate. Additionally, as Inglis (2008) elaborates, '... the concept of glocalization helps us understand how these flows became integrated and adopted to Irish conditions' (p. 38*f.*). As substantiated by O'Donovan (2009, p. 98), post/late-modern *Irishness* manifests itself as two processes of identity formation, which are referred to as 'regressive nationalism' and 'glocalization'. *Glocalization* is the process whereby societies negotiate the relationship and interchange between the local and the global (Inglis, 2008; O'Donovan, 2009; Ritzer, 2011; Robertson, 2001). With *glocalization*, as Inglis and Donnelly (2011) suggest 'it may well be, then that local attachment and identity not only become adapted to globalization, but complement and sustain each other' (p. 129). Yet, O'Donovan (2009, p. 100) also points out evidence that contemporary Ireland has adopted a *regressive nationalist* approach which 'can result in closed constructions of identity, often leading to xenophobic expressions of identity' (p. 100).

Within the context of recent Irish history, spanning a timeframe from the early 1990s onwards, what becomes evident is a subtle shift towards reshaping the existent state through the establishment and prominence of what are deemed to be sufficient market freedoms under *neoliberalism*, while deemphasizing the historical. Again what seems to be a blatant utilitarian approach is taken mirroring what Foucault refers to in his Lecture on 14 February 1979 (La naissance de la biopolitique) as *Ordo-liberalism* (Lemke, 2001, p. 5*ff.*), as described below. In parallel with post-war Germany, Ireland has more recently shifted social policy to possess the primary function of inhibiting any anti-competitive mechanisms that capitalist society could produce. Such promotion of *neoliberal* competitiveness is being achieved through 'the universalization of the entrepreneurial form, and the re-definition of law' (Lemke, 2001, p. 5). This is whereby, according to Grewal and Purdy (2014, p. 5), the affirmative use of political power has seen the restructuring of law and social life along market lines, from labour relations to educational institutions to the professions generally. Similarly for Ireland, as historicized with Germany, 'a new notion of time asserts itself, organized no longer in historical but in economic categories. Hence it no longer entails notions of historical progress but instead economic growth ...' (Lemke, 2001, p. 5). If a by-product for Germany was the ability to forget and annul German history, for Ireland, the by-product could easily be assumed to be the capacity to overcome obsessions of historical colonial oppression and potentially help defuse more recent sectarian conflict, nonetheless, with such a shift of the nation state's focus and trajectory, the categorical question to ask would be: 'what may have been neglected?'

Legitimating the Irish state with reference to economic growth rather than by defining it in terms of an historical mission may have resulted in neglect of adequately interrogating identity constructions. With such neglect, along with the globalized economic predicament Ireland struggled through, having not fully attained 'a form of sovereignty limited to guaranteeing economic activity' (Lemke, 2001, p. 6), arguments may well revert to a mythological narrative that is partial and closed-minded, leading to anti-immigrant sentiment. It is for this reason that further investigating identity constructions within such an era of *liquid modernity* may well prove an important avenue for examination in relation to the amelioration of the social dilemmas of our time.

According to White (2008, p. 90), there is evidence of an association between nationalism and anti-immigrant sentiment. As O'Brien (1971) writes, in 'Nationalism and the Reconquest of Ireland',

> even under the most benign definitions of nationalism, much more is subsumed than simple affection for one's fellow citizens, and one's native place. Collective selfishness is there, aggression, and the legitimation of persecution, with at the back of it all, the old doctrine of the superiority of one's own nation, the Herrenvolf, on whatever scale of values, whether of triumph or of suffering, the Volk may rest its assumed superiority. (p. 8)

The materialization of this regressive reformulation of 'Irish' identity was evident when the Irish electorate, voting in the 2004 ICR, opted to repeal the constitutional provision that automatically granted birthright citizenship to all children born within the state (O'Donovan, 2009, p. 101). This was seen as 'a fundamental philosophical shift in Irish law from the principle of citizenship based on birth within the territory to citizenship based on blood descent from the citizenry' (Mancini & Finlay, 2008, p. 577). Over a similar timeframe populist politics also sought to marginalize refugees and asylum seekers with the implementation of oppressive provisions that further segregated people through dispersion to Direct Provision centres and forbidding opportunity for employment.[5]

---

[5] As documented by the state's Reception and Integration Agency (RIA, 2011) officially 'Direct provision is a means of meeting the basic needs of food and shelter for asylum seekers directly while their claims for refugee status are being processed rather than through full cash payments. Direct provision commenced on 10 April 2000 from which time asylum seekers have received full board accommodation and personal allowances of €19.10 per adult and €9.60 per child per week'. The RIA (2011) continues by stating that no RIA staff are present at the centres, 'However, from time to time, RIA staff visit the centres to ensure that asylum seekers needs are being met and to ensure that they have access to all the relevant services'.

Alongside this is the process of *glocalization* which makes the assumption that communities have agency in selectively controlling the interaction between the global and the local whereby the homogenization/heterogenization of culture is geographically specific (O'Donovan, 2009, p. 103*f.*). Irish society attempts to be inclusive of foreign investment and foreign labour where necessitated, while creating boundaries that are exclusive or limiting on access and integration of 'other' peoples and cultures that might perturb the imagined homogeneity of contemporary 'Irish' identity.

When unveiled, *regressive nationalism* and the notion of *glocalization* become implements by which an unprincipled *utilitarian* approach to Irish developmental (post/late-)modernity is achieved. It juxtaposes a modern 'Irish' identity that endorses 'developmental modernity' where, in the opinion of Fanning (2010), 'competitive corporatist national interest' (p. 410) towards immigration has prevailed against an *ethno-nationalist protectionist* approach. Either way, when both are framed exclusively from an *Ordo-liberal* perspective (as above), society overly focusses on the economics of material gain irrespective of the means by which this is achieved.[6]

Conversely however, within both, beneficial aspects can be derived which allow for progress that more adequately supports the aspirations of the development of an egalitarian and democratic society and the supposed ideals of the Irish nation. 'Good' governance could prioritize equitable wealth distribution and more inclusive rules of belonging, as well as allowing for a melange of both developmental and cultural attributes that seek the progressive development of a modernizing society.

Against the backdrop of supranational governance and globalization the state can be seen in constant confrontation, scrambling to define the national 'Irish' identity as a means of population control, to manage ethnic diversity and preserve the imagined homogeneity of the Irish nation (Fanning, 2002; Ní Chonaill, 2009, p. 51; O'Donovan, 2009). However, for the state preoccupied with order, 'heterogeneity is marked as a problem or a pathology' and homogeneity is seen as 'a kind of idée fixe; it is a driving force in the construction of a cohesive social identity and moral community, in modern state formation, in the racialized postmodern city' (Giroux, 2006, p. 40). Globalization is embraced for its economic benefits as it simultaneously vies with the nation state's hold on identity formation. Through migration, it brings with it heterogeneity which David Theo Goldberg describes in an interview with Giroux (2006) as a 'natural drive':

> Trying to de-anchor the question of belonging ... it's not just that condition of stasis, of being with; it has to do also with a romantic imaginary that is not bound by 'being'. This then drives the

---

[6]An example of the application of an *Ordo-liberal* perspective can be seen with the increased privatization of property. Under such a doctrine, this can be seen to function to both exacerbate inequality by elevating cost and, thus, access through the purchasing for leasing by consortiums and vulture capitalists, as well as re-homogenizing and re-securing the status quo hierarchy whereby property privatization is equated with nationalist identification. As Goldberg (2009) comments, 'Where the welfare state, with all its contradictions and failings, produced a modicum of social egalitarianism, the neoliberal state exacerbates inequality, further privileging the already privileged' (p. 332).

curious to the unknown, to engage with those you're not expected to engage with, and so on. (p. 42)

In contrast, modernity and the development of the nation state into a modern *governmentality* by seeking 'the project of ordered governance' became dependent on the propagation of racial self-definitions as the classification and ordering method by which to define and differentiate each nation state as distinct. Thus, for David Theo Goldberg, the construction of a national identity that relies on homogeneity is fundamentally and 'deeply unnatural' (Giroux, 2006, p. 43).

The Dilemmas of the Post-national Nation State

Indispensable for any society that purports to be democratic are structures and mechanisms that allow for broad definitions of identity that are inclusive and labile. As White (2008) states, 'Irish identity is not transferred genetically. It has been created in the past and is constantly being modified and changed by those who identify themselves as Irish today' (p. 89). Therefore, unless identity is constructed with complete homogeneity, interpreted as unanimously identical among the members of a society and maintained within complete isolation geographically, then temporally society could be perceived as somewhat predetermined. However, notwithstanding the effects of generational changes and the accepted fact that all humans are unique individuals, this is an inconceivable possibility, even within contemporary 21st-century Ireland or among humanity globally. As Parekh (2000) points out, cultures are 'unique human creations that reconstitute and give different meaning and orientation to those properties that all human beings share ... and give rise to different kinds of human beings' (p. 122).

Thus, definitions of identity that are static will conflict with the natural progression of any labile society. If mechanisms are not in place that counter the subjugation of a given minority and the inability to freely self-identify, inequitable power relations occur. Furthermore, restricting the freedom to self-constitute creates and perpetuates inequalities, which is diametrically opposed to the supposed ambitions and aspirations of an egalitarian social democratic state. As such, it is plausible to view such a restrictive and narrow mode of identification, which exerts tension on society, as a flaw of democracy and as such, a society that preserves an exclusionary approach to identification as a *flawed democracy*.

Leading on from this, equally the problem with *liberal multiculturalism* is not only that it is based on an essentialist concept of identity, but that it fails to deal with issues of unequal power and resources (Finlay, 2004, p. 140). *Liberal multiculturalism* relies on the notion of *tolerance* but is somewhat blind to the interplay between tolerance and power, particularly the tolerating agent's superior position of power. From the perspective of the tolerant proxy, Goldberg (2009) provides an explanatory description as,

> I have the power and position to tolerate you. I am active; you are passive, powerless to affect me in my tolerating save to get under my skin, make me even less accepting of your distinction. My social power to tolerate turns on all those like me likewise disposed towards you. (p. 157)

Both through the reliance on *essentialisms* and through the process of tolerance, power becomes inequitably shared, which conflicts with the ideals of a supposed multicultural and *liberal democracy*. *Liberal democracy* itself becomes self-contradictory.

As detailed by Joppke (2007, p. 39), globalization brings with it a deficiency of national identity, which leads to a lack of sense of citizenship, or membership of the state. The apparently tolerant state responds by creating levels of citizenship statuses and re-tightening of access. However, it becomes paradoxical or in Orwellian terms, 'doublethink' as, 'the space for the re-nationalization of citizenship is limited by norms of equality and non-discrimination, which allow only universalistic answers to the question of identity' (Joppke, 2007, p. 39). According to Joppke (2007), 'states can no longer impose substantive identity as a pre-condition for acquiring citizenship' (p. 44). In parallel with this, the contemporary liberal state becomes bound by maintaining an ostensibly neutral stance towards the multitude of different peoples. Again, the unity of such a society is only possible if the society remains universalistic. Thus, paradoxically, unity under such a social order can only be exclusionary unless global or planetary (Joppke, 2007, p. 45). To counterbalance this and justify nation state-based liberal ideals, 'deep contradictions within liberalism emerge when confronted by migration, which mean that, in practice, liberalism often stops at the border ...' (Anderson, 2013, p. 11; Cole, 2000).

When unravelling issues relating to border formations such as taking into account security and migrant subjectivities, Latham (2010) proposes that,

> What is unique about border agents and the border itself – the external as well as the internal borders – is the salience and scope of what is being secured: access to a social space in its entirety rather than admission to any discrete, limited institutional space or right to use specific resources. This matters especially because what can be denied to migrants at the border is the potential for a broad range of agency and mobility once inside a national space – however restricted this agency may be because of internal policing and social and political exclusions. (p. 190)

This relates to the contradiction within liberalist ideology and highlights that ultimately, at the official point of access, it is exactly here that discretion rules over reason and it is at this point where control is wielded whereas, once having being granted access into the jurisdiction, supposed liberal logic and reason are implemented through laws and systems of justice. As Latham (2010) argues perhaps in order to overcome such a liberalist predicament 'a multiversal understanding of societies' (p. 185) is required as well as a leaning towards creating policies that encompass concepts such as *flexible citizenship* (Ong, 1993, 1998).[7]

---

[7]Ong (1993, 1998) denote flexible citizenship to be a form of citizenship chosen by individuals based on primarily on their own perceived economic needs rather than more social-based citizenship such as association with community or the sharing of political rights. It relies on flexible strategies that the individual deploys so as to maximize

Latham (2010) reveals that the framing of the state/society/territory complex, which we associate with the Westphalian polity, is organized in accordance with assumptions of a perhaps dated 'single citizenship state-society' (p. 187). Under such conditions, *incorporation* occurs whereby migrants are expected to become subsumed either temporarily or with permanency into 'a part of the constellation of social and political spaces we more conveniently but problematically call a national society' (Latham, 2010, p. 186). However, the compounded problem that arises relates to individual's subjectivities which may not neatly fit decisively into designation or sorting, such as, 'race', religion, class and disposition (Latham, 2010, p. 188). This brings us back again to the issue of national identity or perhaps, from a more sociological perspective, it relates to 'identity systems that read deeply into your body and life, which …' according to Latham (2010), '… is consistent with the official hermeneutic of the social fabric' (p. 189).[8]

Cosmopolitanism as the panacea?

One way to resolve such a dated system of single or dual citizenship state-society might be based on *cosmopolitan* standards. Nonetheless, contradictions associated with universalistic orientations may also be present in relation to the concept of *cosmopolitanism* and may be relational to Martha Nussbaum's understanding of the implications of such a conception. For Nussbaum and Cohen (1996), *cosmopolitanism* is simply an allegiance to 'the worldwide community of human beings' (p. 4). This *cosmopolitan* view towards a worldwide community, rather than national identity, is 'more adequate to our situation in the contemporary world' (Nussbaum & Cohen, 1996, p. 74).[9] Scheffler (2002, p. 114) expands on this by detailing that at the core, *cosmopolitanism* centres on the notion of reciprocity between each individual, as a citizen of the world, and their relationship with the global community of which they are a part and to which they thus owe allegiance. The natural progression of such a conceptual understanding is that it represents the 'acknowledgement of some notion of common humanity that translates ethically into an idea of shared or common moral duties towards others by virtue of this humanity' (Brown, 2011; Lu, 2000, p. 245). Further to this, Brown (2011, p. 53) explains that, 'explicit within cosmopolitanism's ethical orientation is a concern for global justice with the expansion of corresponding moral duties which can broaden the scope and responsibilities of justice to include those beyond state

---

their position in an era of global capitalism. Ong (1993) coins the term to describe Overseas Chinese who opportunistically 'search for citizenship abroad that will facilitate their strategies of flexible (financial) accumulation and their attempts to evade political costs and debits of minority entrepreneurs in Western countries' (p. 770).
[8]Hermeneutics is the branch of knowledge dealing with interpretation, especially literary texts and religious scripts, such as the bible.
[9]Within Brown and Held's (2010, p. 155) book, *The Cosmopolitan Reader*, they note that Nussbaum's views on the topic of *cosmopolitanism* and specifically *patriotism* have since changed in significant ways. They refer to Nussbaum's (2008) work entitled 'Toward a Globally Sensitive Patriotism'.

'Irish' Identity and the Nation State   47

borders' (p. 53). Scheffler (2002) dichotomizes *cosmopolitanism* into being relevant to justice and culture:

> For the cosmopolitan about justice, the idea of world citizenship means that the norms of justice must ultimately be seen as governing the relations of all human beings to each other, and not merely as applying within individual societies or bounded groups of other kinds. For the cosmopolitan about culture, meanwhile, the idea of world citizenship means that individuals have the capacity to flourish by forging idiosyncratic identities from heterogeneous cultural sources, and are not to be thought of as constituted or defined by ascriptive ties to a particular culture, community, or tradition. (p. 114)

However, a dilemma which unfolds, though this should not be seen to detract from the overarching tenets associated with *cosmopolitanism*, relates to the commitment to devoting attention to people at a familial level, community level and national level, in contrast to the commitment to equality, above and beyond all, including prevalence over the nation. As Scheffler (2002) points out, with an accentuation of *cosmopolitanism*, it may be interpreted as 'simply the inevitable consequence of a serious commitment to equality' (p. 118) and as such taking a staunch *cosmopolitan* perspective means the rejection of the nationalist proposition 'that the members of an individual society owe each other some things, as a matter of justice, that they do not owe to non-members' (Scheffler, 2002, p. 118). This relies on a binary understanding of *cosmopolitanism* that is in direct conflict with, and juxtaposed against, *nationalism*. As Brown (2011) explains, *cosmopolitans* such as Nussbaum, Tan and Waldron, 'often contend that traditional conceptualizations of the state are inappropriately insular and that statist defences regarding the protection of culture, nationality and national patriotism ignore pressing issues of common humanity and planetary coexistence' (p. 54).

With such an association, what then becomes inherent in the concept of *cosmopolitanism* is that it denies 'adherence to the values and traditions of a particular community ... and accordingly, is not inclined to treat an individual's relationship to a particular cultural community as a potential source of special responsibilities' (Scheffler, 2002, p. 116). Thus, *cosmopolitanism* is supposedly more representative of a viable way of contemporary life that prioritizes *egalitarian* values superseding the national and that this can only be achieved effectively through the rejection of specific community or national values. Similarly, for MacIntyre (1994), partiality towards one's nation in the form of *patriotism* creates the same predicament. However, having historical bonds and connections to a community justifies the virtue of *patriotism*, whereby MacIntyre (1994) deduces,

> *If* first of all it is the case that I can only apprehend the rules of morality in the version in which they are incarnated in some specific community; and *if* second it is the case that the justification of morality must be in terms of particular goods enjoyed within the life

of particular communities; and *if* third it is the case that I am characteristically brought into being and maintained as a moral agent only through the particular kind of moral sustenance afforded by my community, *then* it is clear that deprived of this community, I am unlikely to flourish as a moral agent. Hence, my allegiance to the community and what it requires of me – even to the point of requiring me to die to sustain its life – could not meaningfully be counterpoised to what morality required of me. (p. 312)

This *morality of patriotism* which recognizes that there are 'underived special responsibilities to the members of one's own community' is considered by Scheffler (2002, p. 119) as utterly incompatible with the devotion to *cosmopolitan* notions of the equal worth of persons.

Conflicting with this perspective is the Kantian view that the national is a delusion whereby people view their own nation as inherently superior to 'others' (Kleingeld, 2003, p. 299). An interpretation of Kant's work by Kleingeld (2003) is used to elevate and propound the compatibility of *cosmopolitanism* and *patriotism*. If, as according to Kant in his work on *Toward Perpetual Peace*, one can be a 'citizen of a supersensible world' (Kant, 1795/1996, p. 323), then this would imply that all rational beings belong to a single moral community regardless of their nationality, religion, customs and so on (Kleingeld, 2003, p. 301).[10] Further to this, Kant refers to *cosmopolitan law* (*Weltbürgerrecht*) based on the maxim of benevolence, resulting in beneficence that transcends any boundaries. Kleingeld (2003) describes the Kantian logic as being, 'according to cosmopolitan law, states and individuals have the right to attempt to establish relations with other states and their citizens, but not a right to enter foreign territory' (p. 302). Continuing in reference to *Toward Perpetual Peace*, written in 1795, Kant is shown to describe that 'strangers have the right to "hospitality", which is the right "not to be treated with hostility because of [their] arrival on someone else's soil"' (Kleingeld, 2003, p. 302). Equally too, *cosmopolitan law* would strongly criticize *(neo-)colonialist* practices. The basis for this is because Kant sees the essence of *republicanism* – freedom, equality and independence – as being a source, rather than a hindrance, towards realizing cosmopolitan ideals. According to Kleingeld's (2003) interpretation of Kant, true *patriotism* or at least,

> Civic patriotism does not imply the notion of a nation in an ethnic sense. Thus, it is not in principle (conceptually) impossible to give up one's citizenship in one state in favor of that in another, although it depends on immigration and emigration laws whether it is a real option. (p. 304)

This reasoning would seem to at least partially overcome the paradoxical juxtaposition between *egalitarianism* and *ownership*. *Civic patriotism* within the virtues

---

[10]Presumably, in this context, 'beings' refer to humans; however, if one were to consider rational beings beyond humans, this would also be compatible with *posthumanism*.

'Irish' Identity and the Nation State 49

of *cosmopolitanism* hints towards more favourable conditions being entrusted to all in relation to mobility, hybridity and citizenship transference according to affiliation.

Although recognizing that the socially constructed elements of an individuals' values, attitudes and behaviours may contradict notions of *liberal universalism* that are considered transhistorical, MacIntyre's (1994, p. 312) argument (as quoted above), rests on the assumption that the community described is fixed, it inhibits any logical deduction of the development of community at a global level or the transformation of a community over time or even the transformation of a person's loyalty temporally. If *community* was to be conceived as singular, at the global level, then that could provide reason and justification for universal ideals even from a subjective perspective. In a way, the advancement towards a global comprehension of specific moralities would lead to a level of what could be termed *pseudo-objectivity*. This could be interpreted as a state of *universalism*, through the amalgamation of subjectivities along the same alignment. The conundrum would be if such were to require a homogenization of an array of cultural relativities, would this go against the very ideals of liberalist thinking? Obviously, to affirm universalist assumptions would let the liberalist off the hook, whereas *cultural relativism* forces the liberalist to think beyond *multiculturalism*.

The reconciliation then is not the complete rejection of either but a fusion of both liberalism and multiculturalism in the form of *interculturalism*. *Interculturalism* means that *cultural relativism* is not only recognized as constituent to what is universal, but it is in essence universal for the liberalist. Similarly, pitching *cosmopolitanism* against nationalism omits a notion of complementarity that may exist, whereby the community or nation may endorse and place weight on egalitarian principles that are practically analogous to the hypothetical universal ideals of *cosmopolitanism*. In fact, Scheffler (2002, p. 118) acknowledges that one may have a sense of responsibility to family and community and that this can occur concurrently with concern for the greater good of humanity. Accordingly, Scheffler (2002) admits 'it is, therefore, not at all apparent why a commitment to equality should be thought incompatible with a recognition of underived special responsibilities' (p. 118).

As Fossum (2012) suggests, supplementing Kantian *cosmopolitan patriotism*, a progressive nation does not necessarily require functioning which is in conflict with cosmopolitanism ideology and importantly harmony can be achieved through inclusive modes of governance. Fossum (2012, p. 337) substantiates the argument that potentially not only might the supranational provide for *cosmopolitanism*, but potentially, although it 'appears as the least likely candidate for cosmopolitan vanguard' (p. 337), the nation state may well be compatible with *cosmopolitanism* as 'State-based democratic constitutionalism is, after all, founded on a set of universal principles' (Fossum, 2012; Habermas, 2018). In contrast, Brown (2011) contends that 'many cosmopolitans have seen the state more as an inconvenience to work around than an empirical background condition that needs to be thoroughly worked in' (p. 54). Brown (2011, p. 54) not only finds that cosmopolitan theory renders the state morally and empirically ineffectual but also makes ambiguous the normative role states could play in developing a cosmopolitan order.

50 *Redefining* Irishness *in a Globalized World*

Leading on from this is the consideration of the mergence of nation and state in becoming a singular nation-state. Appiah (1998) deduces from a *social constructivist* perspective that the state is perhaps a more predetermined notion than that of the nation, which helps distinguish the nation from state. Appiah's (1998) contention is that *liberalism's* emphasis on the state could be justifiable and maintains,

> Because human beings live in political orders narrower than the species, and because it is within those political orders that questions of public right and wrong are largely argued out and decided, the fact of my being a fellow citizen of yours – someone who is a member of the same order – is not morally arbitrary at all … it is exactly because the cultural variability that cosmopolitanism celebrates [and] has come to depend on the existence of a plurality of states that we need to take states seriously …. Nations matter morally, when they do, in other words, for the same reason that football and opera matter: as things desired by autonomous agents, whose autonomous desires we ought to acknowledge and take account of, even if we cannot always accede to them. (p. 96)

In contrast, Appiah (1998) contends,

> States, on the other hand, matter morally intrinsically; they matter not because people care about them, but because they regulate our lives through forms of coercion that will always require moral justification. State institutions matter both because they are necessary to so many modern human purposes and because they have such great potential for abuse. (p. 96)

Quite simply put by Brown (2011),

> […] whether we like it or not, we currently live in a world largely dominated by states and if cosmopolitan theory is to have greater pertinence, then it is prudent to engage better with the state and to offer reasonable ideas about bringing the state back into cosmopolitanism. (p. 55)

These arguments indicate that the obstacle for either the *cosmopolitan* or *liberal nationalist* is the exclusivist propensity of the nation state. Such a propensity towards being restrictive is consistently seen as based on the need for preserving national distinctness and homogeneity, rather than, a nation state that is postnational and promotes communities of inclusion (Fossum, 2012, p. 337). The current order of such nation states, thus, seems bound in a type of circular logic whereby preserving homogeneity requires an exclusivist propensity which gives the nation-state predisposition towards notions of a homogeneous collectivity. Such a tautological argument provides not only for the exclusion of the potential for change but it confines any understanding of the assumed homogeneous nation state as innately un-falsifiable. Yet the composition of the nation state is never static and, in fact, such supposed notions of homogeneity may well be fallible. Not only does this tautological justification for the overbearing nation-state which is reliant on exclusive modes of citizenship regimes precisely link back to the notion of a 'flawed' democracy (as stated above), but it sheds light on the significance of identity formations.

Appiah (1998) claims that, by viewing cosmopolitanism as liberalism, cosmopolitanism can be reduced to the fundamental belief that 'the freedom to create oneself – the freedom that liberalism celebrates – requires a range of socially transmitted options from which to invent what we have come to call our identities' (p. 97). For Appiah (1998, p. 98), identities are both ascribed and are open to manipulation and reshaping both from within the self and externally. It is through language that the subject contemplates their identity and it is language that acts as catalyst in the shaping of new individualities.

In a way, the notion of a *post-national nation state* unfolds a predicament not only in terminology but also in its very production, which may relate to the inability of the nation state to recognize and fully uphold the universality of human rights when concerned with the individual as an autonomous being, or, as Fossum (2012) emphasizes, 'the ultimate unit of concern' (p. 337) for the nation state. This is because such concern would suggest universality in the association of *biopower* attained by the nation state from any given individual equally. Predominantly, the quandary would be, how can the nation state provide for all the individuals of the world equally and conversely, how can all the individuals of the world provide reciprocation to one nation state that is not global? Furthermore, the very *biopower* acquired by one nation state that is not global cannot be universal because if it were, such a scenario would equate to a diminishing of its very own authority. This could not be the case, unless of course, it were operating extrajudicial power which would go against the very ideological foundations of *cosmopolitanism*, as such power would manifest disproportionately. Equally, the dilemma created relates to the paradox of maintaining democratically legitimate states, with liberal policies committed to the idea of an inclusive community, while simultaneously placing central the autonomy of the individual. This progresses towards the *post-national civic-state* that is reliant on inclusivity,[11] and, in turn, implies an onus away from *jus sanguinis* citizenship acquisition, to the contrary of the outcomes of the 2004 ICR.

The introduction and opening two chapters provide an overview of the central considerations in relation to both perceived notions of identity, specifically *Irishness*, and in relation to national identity, conceptions of political organization, such as the nation state, cosmopolitism, regionalism and so forth. Importantly, neither concepts of identity nor the nation state are portrayed as static but rather deduced as social constructs.

---

[11] For more on the liberal state or civic state, please refer to works by Will Kymlicka and Yael Tamir, such as Tamir's (1993) book entitled, *Liberal Nationalism*.

52 *Redefining* Irishness *in a Globalized World*

From here the attention is then drawn towards how social constructs such as identity and *Irishness*, which in actuality are abstract, become entrenched and embedded in reality. Thus, specifically, the subsequent chapter exposes the formation of identity and *Irishness* in both the more tangible and concrete sense, through legislation and governance, as well as through socio-psychological processes, such as manipulation via media misrepresentation and publicized elite, yet falsified discourse. By interrelating the theory presented heretofore with specific legislative and policy changes, in addition to proven fabrications that influence the conscience of the populous, Chapter 3 closes with the argument for progressive self-constitution.

Subsequent to this, the introduction and initial three chapters, which present the theoretical foundations, governance and legislative frameworks, are specifically interrelated to the findings chapters (Chapters 5–9). Although the theoretical review argued heretofore informs the general construction and directionality of analysis, it is not imposed onto the findings. Instead, consistencies and incongruities along general themes are shown to emerge from the data obtained. Somewhat iteratively, such findings are then related back to the theory contended hitherto, which together is combined to provide the basis for deliberation and the construction of inferences in the concluding section, Chapter 10.

'Irish' Identity and the Nation State 53

54 Redefining Irishness *in a Globalized World*

Chapter 3

Legislation, Myth and Progressive Self-constitution

Keywords: Republicanism; liberal; citizenship; subsumption; integration; mythology; colonization of the self; empire; neoliberalism; institutionalization

This chapter places the 2004 Irish Citizenship Referendum and its outcomes within the context of the Irish nation state, as it has evolved into its contemporary condition. In it, I make theoretical considerations drawing from the discrepancy between the outcomes of the 2004 ICR and the foundational ideology of the purported democratic republic of Ireland.

The racialization of state and institutional policy is further evidenced. Following this, considerations of self-understanding are made comprehensible not only as a benign feature of modernity but also as a characteristic that is susceptible to manipulation from unequal power relations within society. An example of such that I provide is in relation to the public and media discourse leading up to the 2004 ICR. The Irish Citizenship Referendum in 2004 and its outcomes are theorized as an illogical political shift in constricting the definition of *what it is to be 'Irish'*, which contradictorily is juxtaposed with the embracing of supranational European Union governance by the Irish state (Constitution of Ireland [1937] 2004).

From here, I consider the dilemma relating to perceptions of identity as inherent within Universalist thought is discussed to form the critique of a democracy based on *liberal multiculturalism*. Drawing from assumptions in relation to the antithetical stance taken by the government provides the basis for the current change in perception of citizenship acquisition. From this, I then posit that *jus sanguinis* citizenship could, in fact, be interpreted as a relic of colonial subordination/'otherness'.

In conclusion, I propose that the logicality and rational foundation of contemporary society be debated and contested to illustrate the underlying requirement to resist knowledge/power formulations that prioritize the *subjectification* of identity. Foucault's notion of *self-constitutionality* is seen as a prerequisite force in overcoming power that attempts to influence the 'reflexive conscience' of members of a community as a counterbalance to power that thrives on the propagation of notions of the collective in essentialist and exclusionary terms.

Jus Sanguinis Legislation and the 2004 Irish Citizenship Referendum

From an historical perspective, it is unambiguous that *jus sanguinis* citizenship is a conception of the monarchical system of acquisition, which granted sovereignty over all conceived in the territory based on bloodline descent. According to Honohan (2010), 'origins in many countries [of *jus sanguinis* citizenship] lie in a legacy of British law …' (p. 2) or common law. In contrast, the origin of *jus soli* citizenship, irrespective of ethnicity, is quintessentially republican, centring round civic participation. Similarly, Lentin (2009) asserts that,

> The term 'nation' derives from nascere (to be born), thus the passage from divinely authorized royal sovereignty to national sovereignty means that in the transformation of 'subject' into 'citizen', birth – or bare natural life as such – becomes the immediate bearer of sovereignty. (p. 6)

This change in citizenship criteria can be viewed as a progression from more traditional notions of feudal allegiance towards socialization, and links with Foucaultian theory of the development of the modern nation state. In the case of Ireland what has continued, to some degree since the late 19th century, is the notion that 'Irish no less than European nationalism all distinguished, to some extent, the "true" Germans, French, English or Irish from lesser peoples and races, through sectarianism, anti-Semitism or colonial ideologies of racial superiority …' (Fanning & Mutwarasibo, 2007, p. 449). Supplementing this, contemporary racializations of *Irishness* have their historical antecedents in references to belonging, ideological descriptions of a monocultural and homogeneous Ireland, and other such nationalist ethnocentrisms (Fanning & Mutwarasibo, 2007, p. 450).

The 27th Amendment of the Constitution Act 2004 entitled, *Irish Citizenship of Children of Non-national Parents*, was passed on the 24 June 2004 (Constitution of Ireland ([1937] 2004). It fundamentally affects Article two of the Irish Constitution under the heading of 'The Nation'. Article two declares,

> It is the entitlement and birthright of every person born in the Island of Ireland, which includes its islands and seas, to be part of the Irish Nation. That is also the entitlement of all persons otherwise qualified in accordance with law to be citizens of Ireland. Furthermore, the Irish nation cherishes its special affinity with people of Irish ancestry living abroad who share its cultural identity and heritage.

Legislation, Myth and Progressive Self-constitution   57

The 2004 Irish Citizenship Referendum, with the signing of the 27th Amendment (as quoted above), revised the last example of unrestricted birthright citizenship, *jus soli*, among the members of European Union nations (Mancini & Finlay, 2008, p. 575). During its introduction by the Irish government at that time it 'was accompanied by a populist politics that emphasized distinctions between "nationals" and "non-nationals"' (Fanning, 2010, p. 395). Viewed from a manifest perspective of exclusion, this can be seen as the creation of obstacles to citizenship for those without a hereditary connection to the nation. Delving into it deeper it can be revealed as 'the changing of the rules of belonging in Ireland' (Moriarty, 2006, p. 132) with the establishment of identity and notions of *Irishness* being based on bloodline descent.

The passing of the Irish Citizenship Referendum in 2004 meant the amendment of Article nine of the Irish Constitution, under the heading of 'The State', with the insertion of a new section stating (Constitution of Ireland ([1937] 2004),

1. Notwithstanding any other provision of this Constitution, a person born in the island of Ireland, which includes its islands and seas, who does not have, at the time of the birth of that person, at least one parent who is an Irish citizen or entitled to be an Irish citizen is not entitled to Irish citizenship or nationality, unless provided for by law.
2. This section shall not apply to persons born before the date of the enactment of this section.

Essentially such an amendment meant the removal of the provision for protection of guaranteed citizenship to all Irish-born children, including those born to economic immigrants and asylum seekers, and instead placed citizenship within the national legislative realm. The implications are that birthright citizenship is now determined at the discretion of the Justice Minister operating under a government mandate and is no longer a constitutional right. The creation of such a barrier to citizenship for persons without any blood descent in Ireland contradicts universalistic notions of a national republic and creates a new hierarchical order within the state. From a broader perspective, differentiated access to citizenship maintains economic inequality both within and between countries. Furthermore, for Ireland, this restrictive access works 'to limit temporal and ethnic change in the composition of "the Irish Nation"' (Mancini & Finlay, 2008, p. 576).

Within the timeframe of the constitutional vote, when Ireland's economy was proliferating and the country had become a net in-migration nation, the assumption might have been that with the expansion of the EU eastwards, Ireland wished to create restrictions to citizenship as a control mechanism to curb the provision of state welfare to new arrivals. However, the constitutional change was inconsequential to children born of European parents or the parents themselves as labour migrants who, under EU law, would have been and are lawfully entitled to such provisions. Furthermore, it cannot be seen as a state mechanism to curtail immigration as with retrospection, the European Migration Network report reiterates that, '… it was after the 2004 EU enlargement that immigration reached unprecedented levels, peaking at 109,500 in the year to April 2007' (Quinn, 2010, p. IX). Instead, it would seem to have been blatantly introduced to target the restriction of access to citizenship to those beyond the European zone, such as asylum seekers, undocumented workers and non-EU immigrants. Even during the so-called unprecedented peak levels in 2007, according to the figures provided by the OECD (2010, p. 212), people from developing regions beyond the EU constituted less than 10 percent of all immigrants or less than 1 percent of the total population of the Irish republic.

The onus on the attainment of citizenship biasing *jus sanguinis*-based criteria rather than both *jus soli* and *jus sanguinis* criteria can then be seen as an increased restriction on accessing EU citizenship, vis-á-vis Irish citizenship, to people beyond Europe while conversely acting as a discursive expansion on 'the notion of "the Irish nation" in bloodline terms' (Lentin, 2007, p. 434). Thus, the 2004 ICR, which was hastily proposed and passed, can be viewed on a supranational level as an apparent requirement to harmonize or converge with legislation of other EU states (Garner, 2007, p. 439; Moriarty, 2006, p. 168). At the very least, the 2004 ICR, occurring within a similar timeframe to changes in employment legislation and EU expansion and mobility,[1] is suggestive of a more managed approach to immigration nationally, complementary to EU-driven policies. Nonetheless, in all conceivable instances, there seems to be, on the one hand, the fabrication and perpetuation of a national identity that is based on nationhood, while contradictorily, there is the development of the post-colonial Irish nation state within the context of supranational European Union governance.

> In general, when citizenship acquisition is analysed within a comparative European framework, it could be argued that Ireland is at the more liberal end of the spectrum of a nominally diverse range of nation-state policies. For instance, although it has not been empirically proven in the context of Ireland, a cursory comparison would suggest that with the passing of the 2004 ICR, Ireland has followed suit in the reversal trend towards more restrictive, differential citizenship in conjunction with the Netherlands, Britain and France (Bauböck et al., 2006, p. 23; Joppke, 2007, p. 41; Koopmans et al., 2005, p. 73). Nevertheless, Irish policies still emphasize a more *culturally pluralist/multiculturalist* conception of citizenship in contrast to countries, such as Germany

---

[1] The Equality Act 2004 was enacted in July 2004 under the auspices of implementing the principle of equal treatment for men and women, irrespective of racial or ethnic origin, as regards access to employment, vocational training and promotion and working conditions. In relation to mobility, on 29 April 2004, Directive 2004/38/EC of the European Parliament and of the Council was drafted with an overarching focus on the right of citizens of the Union and their family members to move and reside freely within the territory of the Member States. Within the same period, on 1 May 2004, 10 new countries joined the EU: the Czech Republic, Cyprus, Estonia, Hungary, Latvia, Lithuania, Malta, Poland, Slovenia and Slovakia.

and Switzerland. However, such comparative analysis becomes a somewhat frivolous argument when debating the complementariness of *jus sanguinis/jus soli*-based citizenship legislation with egalitarian socio-democratic ideologies. Although Ireland's legislation on citizenship acquisition is comparably liberal, at the level of the nation state the constitutional change is a regressive step and highlights an inconsistency between Irish nation state governance ideologies and transnational governance practices.

Mythological Representations of *Irishness*

Brandi (2007) and Garner (2007) independently allude to the role political and public discourse played in shaping perceptions prior to the 2004 ICR and to the creation of such misconceptions. In a critical analysis of discourse, Brandi (2007, p. 40) holds that the Irish government, in a strategic manoeuvre, successfully constructed a process of ideological *naturalization*. In the analysis of primary texts and speeches, Brandi's (2007) thesis propounds

> A strategic ideological manipulation and reframing of events taking place throughout the texts, by resorting to the recurrent use of specific discursive strategies. The demonisation of 'non-national' pregnant mothers and the polarisation of immigrants into two distinct categories of good deserving and bad undeserving ones emerge with clear evidence from the analysed texts. Hence, the impact of [then Minister for Justice, Equality and Law Reform] McDowell's pronouncements in the reproduction and reinforcement of popular racism is stressed. (p. 26)

For example, within the months leading to the election debate concerning the 'loophole', both state ministers, in particular Minister McDowell, and hospital Masters/managers presented the argument for constitutional change. The argument's justification based on alleged claims of numbers of foreign women placing strain on the Irish maternity system are now seen as baseless as they are, 'clearly unsubstantiated by any statistics ... [although] repeatedly referred to by supporters of the "Yes" vote throughout the 90-day campaign' (Garner, 2007, p. 440).

An obvious conclusion is an appeal for the reassessment of the outcomes of the 2004 Irish Citizenship Referendum within the public sphere but also to devise a contemporary form of citizenship that complements the aspirations of an egalitarian socio-democratic nation such as Ireland. The difficulty, as Kiberd (2000) alludes to, is the question 'where is the lawyer who can offer a constitutional definition of identity as open rather than fixed, as a process rather than a conclusion?' (p. 630). It is this conundrum, and its associated constituents that inform, inspire and feed into the development of this study.

Returning to what was discussed earlier in the section entitled, 'The Historical Construction of "Irish" National Identity' in Chapter 2, not only is the ICR

2004 evidence of regressive nationalist tendencies within public, political and legislative realms it is, inadvertently or not, a form of constitutional techno-legal tool that complies with Lemke's thesis of *Ordo-Liberalism*. O'Reilly (2013) makes reference to the current Irish President Michael D. Higgins who reflected on the divide between the economy and society and how the interests of the economy have taken precedence over the interests of society. President Higgins remarked at the launch of Up the Republic on 13 November 2012 by pronouncing that 'Economy and society need to be reconnected through a shared sense of ethics and values that both operate in the same moral universe' (O'Reilly, 2013, p. 139).

It would seem Higgins is critiquing in contemporary Irish society what has become a blatant and perplexing encounter between liberal economic ideals and regressive sentiments that combine to produce *Ordo-Liberalist* tendencies.

A Relic of Colonial Subordination/'Otherness'

Further to above, with the benefit of retrospection, in 2004, the referendum on Irish citizenship is seen as having been hurriedly pushed through. At a supranational level, it may be indicative of an apparent requirement to converge with the laws of other EU states laws (Garner, 2007, p. 439; Moriarty, 2006, p. 168). In addition, suggestive of the racialization of state policy, the introduction of nationality laws can be seen to directly affect only parents that are asylum-seekers and economic migrants from developing world nations who attempt to claim residence rights through having an Irish-born child, a supposed 'loophole' in Irish legislation (Garner, 2007, p. 439). As Finlay (2004, p. 340) states, 'leaving the "Irish Granny rule" intact gives substance to the allegation of racism'. Consequently, a component of this study, thus, assesses whether the legislative changes coincided with perceptions from the general public, or, whether it was more indicative of institutionalized administrative racism. Such administrative racism would manifest through the required process of immigration and the expansion of the racial state. At the very least, the 2004 ICR is not only symptomatic of unbalanced power relations, but it is indicative of a regressive self-understanding.

Further to this, what becomes evident is that, theoretically, the shift to *jus sanguinis* citizenship from 2004 in Ireland is less representative of supposed liberal rationale; as Honohan (2010) points out the term 'liberal' ought to denote policies that are non-discriminatory and inclusive and specifically stresses the importance of the consideration that '*Jus soli* broadly constitutes a "liberal" mode of access to citizenship' (p. 1). Thus, in contradiction to what Honohan (2010) refers to as a 'liberalizing trend' (p. 1) among other nations over more recent times, Ireland, through the constitutional amendment on citizenship, would seem to be taking regressive steps towards defining nationhood, where perceptions of *Irishness* within members of the group are based on theoretically inaccurate and superficial notions of intrinsic inheritance. False perceptions are conceived from *essentialist* notions of 'the other' and illusions of difference rather than the recognition of commonality. Anxiety is driven by fabricated perceptions, and this promotes submission to the *racialization* of the Irish nation state.

This theorization is more indicative of *neo-colonialism*, which, under the guise of *neoliberalism*, is a continuation of intentional, unidirectional colonial power.

In an attempt to ground theory to some sort of authenticity, specifically with regard to the case of Ireland, this colonial power does not necessarily manifest itself within traditional notions of territorial acquisition; rather it manifests itself primarily in two intertwining ways.

Firstly, it is manifested through the legislature and policies of Ireland, as a sovereign nation state, with regard to its citizenship harmonization and its compliance within *neo-liberalist* policies of the European Union, which operates mechanisms of equality and inclusion internally, while stringently controlling access through exclusionary mechanisms for those beyond its borders (Anthias & Yuval-Davis, 1992, p. 41; Fanning & Mutwarasibo, 2007, p. 446). Although the expected result of *neoliberal* ideology would suggest a unidirectional shift in governance away from the state and onto the level of society, thus resulting in a reduction or limitation of governance, according to Lemke (2001), the prevalence and importance of the state have not diminished and that,

> On the contrary, the state in the neo-liberal model not only retains its traditional functions, but also takes on new tasks and functions. The neo-liberal forms of government feature not only direct intervention by means of empowered and specialized state apparatuses, but also characteristically develop indirect techniques for leading and controlling individuals without at the same time being responsible for them. (p. 11*ff*.)

Similarly, Goldberg (2009, p. 333) argues that the state is not dismantled under *neoliberalism* but instead is remade to become the centre of control and management of demographics with the shifting modalities of movement. *Neoliberalism* demands the reduction of taxation on the wealthiest and corporations, together with, tightening social welfare commitments such as subsidized education, healthcare and pensions. In conjunction with this, the institutions of the neoliberalizing state invest in repressive apparatuses of control and policing of the public and beyond. Such repressive state functionalities are seen to include the police, military, prisons, homeland security, border control and so on (Goldberg, 2009, p. 333).

As Benhabib (2004) states, though more suggestive of a benign directionality of governance,

> the EU is caught in contradictory currents which move it towards norms of cosmopolitan justice in the treatment of those who are within its boundaries, while leading it to act in accordance with outmoded Westphalian conceptions of unbridled sovereignty toward those who are on the outside. (p. 13)

That 'the negotiation between insider and outsider status has become tense and almost warlike' (Benhabib, 2004, p. 13), for Benhabib seems to be an inadvertent phenomenon. However, it could be viewed more insidiously as a mechanism of the neo-colonizer in the representation of 'Otherness', which subsequently plays a major role in elucidating transhistorical problems of identity or difference and accounts for a dominant configuration of knowledge/power. The state administration, by selectively according rights and entitlements to subjects defined through their racialized categorizations, is intentionally contriving mechanisms that are antiquated in a supposed post/late-modern technocratic age that is based on the universality of logic and reason. In creating this discretionary power, the state is restricting equal access to the territorially circumscribed nation state.

Historically, as Hardt and Negri (2000) describe, when making the distinction between 'imperialism' and what they attempt to coin in their thesis, 'Empire',

> The sovereignty of the nation-state was the cornerstone of the imperialisms that European powers constructed throughout the modern era .... The boundaries defined by the modern system of nation-states were fundamental to European colonialism and economic expansion: the territorial boundaries of the nation delimited the center of power from which rule was exerted over external foreign territories through a system of channels and barriers that alternately facilitated and obstructed the flows of production and circulation. (p. xii)

However, what this thesis would like to consider is that within more contemporary configurations of power, *colonialism* is still present in its reconstructed form and it is not so alien, or not as 'altogether different from "imperialism"' as Hardt and Negri (2000) would have us to believe. Hardt and Negri (2000) initially base their overall argument of *Empire* on a decentralized location of power at the level of the global, which would seem overly ideological and represent a transition towards effective *multipolarity*. What is postulated is that 'The passage to Empire emerges from the twilight of modern sovereignty. In contrast to imperialism, Empire establishes no territorial center of power and does not rely on fixed boundaries or barriers' (p. xii).

Hardt and Negri (2000) make the assertion that, 'It is a decentered and deterritorializing apparatus of rule that progressively incorporates the entire global realm within its open, expanding frontiers' (p. xii) and with clouded idealism that somehow defines *Empire* as an all-encompassing, authoritative yet benevolent force '... Empire manages hybrid identities, flexible hierarchies, and plural exchanges through modulating networks of command. The distinct national colors of the imperialist map of the world have emerged and blended in the imperial global rainbow.'[2] If such a nonthreatening interpretation of the current

---

[2] This study finds it more fitting to describe current trends within the European context as simply, 'the maturation of the new imperial design' (Hardt & Negri, 2000, p. 246) that is reliant on a globalized disciplinary regime. Rather than a complete paradigm shift leading to 'Empire', though perhaps 'Empire' may well be apt in describing the end game scenario as envisaged by an elitist few, what is now visible on the global stage is *neo-imperialism*.

directionality of *globalization* were the case it might be heartening from a Lockean humanist perspective. However, I would like to advance the claim that what can be observed is merely a transition towards *neo-colonialism* primarily benefiting core countries or cosmopolitan cities of power and influence globally while maintaining structures of usurpation.

Thus what this book would suggest as the second manifestation of power, intrinsically interdependent on the first, and in which Ireland is also complicit, is the continuation of intentional, unidirectional *neo-colonial* power operating at a supranational level of governance (such as in the EU), particularly its reliance on global financial hegemony, including disproportionate access to resources, labour and property.[3]

From the macro perspective, it is this power of *neo-colonial capitalism* interconnected with *neoliberal* nation state governance which is a core deliberation within this book. An example of such macro processes interplaying with more micro-level organization is evidenced in Ireland's acceptance of *Eurocentric* institutional racism. Such institutional racism relies on transhistorical processes of ontological obsession and falsity within discourse, and these may have been the main drivers behind the regressive changes in Irish citizenship. In other words, if racist categorization can be conceived, it may not necessarily exist, and if narratives are told, they may not necessarily be fact. With the European Union, new categorizations of inclusion/exclusion have been created. Without being overly simplistic and 'pretending that immigration is simply the result of poverty and the acts of individual immigrants' (Sassen, 2005, p. 36), when it clearly is more complex which Sassen attests, it is still important to recognize, as Mancini and Finlay (2008) conclude, that often immigrants,

> are the ones whose livelihoods in their home countries are compromised by inequitable trade relations, among other factors, and who come to *our* wealthy countries only to be exploited under *our* inequitable civic relations.[4] (p. 11)

Although as Sassen (2005) suggests migration 'flows are bounded in time and space and are conditional on other processes; they are not mass invasions or indiscriminate flows from poverty to wealth' (p. 37), it is exactly the fact that they are bounded in economic and power-driven conditionalities which is at the heart of mobility. These inequitable power relations remain persistent between and among nation states.

---

[3]This aspect of property relates to both physical ownership of property, and also the notion of 'Citizenship as Inherited Property' as theorized by Shachar and Hirschl (2007). Shachar and Hirschl (2007) point out 'that the analogy between inherited property and birthright citizenship permits us to see the latter in the light of the former: as a carefully regulated system for limiting access to scarce resources to those that "naturally" belong within its bounds as the heirs – not of "one's body" – but of the *body politick* itself' (p. 275).
[4]Emphasis in italics added.

To be more specific, in relation to the association between affluence and mobility, Latham (2010) points out that migrants 'face a precarious positionality in a racialized and gendered global political economy, exacerbated through securitized citizenship regimes regulating access to prosperous zones through mechanisms of subsumption' (p. 191). If *subsumption* is understood as, at the disposition of the state, the granting to a person the choice to either *assimilate* or *integrate* into the said state then an individual's access to capital, financial, intellectual (training) and social (family) become vital resources and bargaining chips in the negotiation process (Latham, 2010, p. 21).

Positing such a theorization on the second manifestation, namely that of unidirectional transnational power, would also seem to complement Ahmad's (1992) reference to the potential of elites acting within a 'global offensive of the Right, global retreat of the Left, and retreat also of that which was progressive even in our canonical nationalism' (p. 192). This may apply to Ireland and its placement within, 'the unprecedented imperialist consolidations of the present decade' (Ahmad, 1992, p. 192). Ireland, be it explicit or not, has taken an *assimilationist* approach to *supranational governance* by adopting *jus sanguinis*-based citizenship. This would seem to facilitate a condition that is more nuanced than the notion of a flawed democracy (as detailed in Chapter 2), what Chandler (2010) refers to as a 'façade democracy' (p. 150) in reference to the promotion of external policies, in the name of 'good governance', but with the resultant effects of excluding liberal rights. Although Chandler's reference is with regard to external intervention, it could also be applicable to an array of incremental processes towards harmonization, including exclusionary controls on people from beyond the European zone. To this effect, Ireland would seem all too keen to pursue a conceptualization of *Eurocentric neoliberalism*, relying on frameworks that may not in reality be inherently liberal. The removal of birthright citizenship would seem contradictory to the notion of *liberal democracy* that is dependent on the civic-republican 'ideal of self-governance which defines freedom as the rule of law among a community of equals who are "citizens" of the polis, and who have the right to rule and be ruled' (Benhabib, 2004, p. 2).

With a slight twist of interpretation, a parallel can be made of the *subsumption pathway*, which is discussed by Latham, in reference to the granting of access to the state to migrants. Accession to the nation state is designated not only if judged as a non-threat to the EU fabric but also with the assuredness towards a kind of 'subsumption pathway' (Latham, 2010, p. 191). If a play on Latham's words can be made, the poorer nation is to become part of the sea of European unity either anonymously as any other weak nation, or assertively as a cultural entity or perhaps as a welcome but temporary guest. For the individual who is not subsumed then it will be the migrant's children who will be 'subsumed' (Brubaker, 2001; Latham, 2010). In this instance, Latham (2010) is implying that eventually integration through *assimilation* into the larger collective, rather than *intercultural* sharing, will inevitably occur, but it may not happen for several generations. Likewise, if the nation is not soon to be subsumed, then it will be the nation's children collectively who will become assimilated. If such a process could be projected, this would beg the question, where does this leave the liberalist notion of egalitarian-based democratic self-governance? A further consideration reverts back to issues of the development and promotion of a *knowledge society* through the recognition of different forms of knowledge (as advanced in the Introduction), as well as *cultural relativism, subjectivity* and subject formation.

Governmentality and the Colonization of the Self

Consequently, in relation to mythological representations of *Irishness* and processes affecting individuals' self-constitution, what can be seen in contemporary Ireland is not only a regression with *jus sanguinis* citizenship being a relic of colonial exclusion, subordination and 'otherness', but what Foucault refers to as a sophisticated system of governance that causes the *colonization of the self*. According to Nichols (2010, p. 140), the formation of *colonialism* and *imperialism* is not merely seen by Foucault as a physical invasion and territorial occupation, nor as a formal system of governance, but as the colonization of the imagination, of forms of possible knowledge and of the representation of historical events and localities (as proposed in the Introduction). Through projects of social construction, it is a colonization of the privileged self, by the naturalization of mythological notions of identity, ethnicity and 'race' that perpetuate exclusionary practices. Although this is in reference to a wide set of disciplines such as literature, philosophy, social science and art, it could also be applicable to 'the mechanics of disciplinarization and institutionalization, the constitution, as it were of the colonizer' (Spivak, 1988, p. 294). Accordingly, Foucault does not tie down the mechanics of the constitution of 'otherness' to any version of imperialism (early or late, pre- or post-). Thus, in the context of Ireland, perhaps what becomes evident is an occupation of the Irish imagination conceived round mythical 'reformulations of Irishness' (Fanning & Mutwarasibo, 2007, p. 440); notions that have become more institutionally racialized through the passing of the 2004 ICR.

The centrality of the mode of representation of 'otherness' prior to the 2004 Irish Citizenship Referendum election and post-election is indicative of a form of *governmentality* that is constituted by knowledge and the exercise of power, which provides the method by which *neo-colonialism/neo-imperialism* creates exclusion. Foucault (1977) and Said (1978, 1994), among other theorists, would view the colonial discursive field through text and language as being central to the mis/representation of 'otherness' and, therefore, the method by which exclusions are created. Contrary to this, Ahmad (1992) would argue that actions speak louder than words and that more emphasis is warranted on political coercion, techniques of governance, along with studies of the cultural, which play major constitutive roles in elucidating transhistorical problems of identity or difference and account for dominant formations of knowledge/power (Nichols, 2010, p. 123*ff*.). The apparatus that substantiates Ahmad's position is well described by Joppke (2003), who argues that citizenship legislation comprises 'legal-technical mechanisms' that are controlled by dominant political forces where 'states modify these rules if they saw a concrete need or interest for it' (p. 436). It is possible to render both stances applicable when scrutinizing the issues surrounding the 2004 ICR. Thus, the 'process of exclusionary nation building' (Fanning & Mutwarasibo, 2007, p. 440) is achieved by the inscribing or scripting of subjects together with more formal mechanisms of *governmentality*.

Autonomous and Progressive Self-constitution

This thesis would like to posit that if Ireland is to seek progress under liberalist ideals, it is critical that *liberalism* is also recognized as being a potentially repressive tool of exclusion, which is inherently self-contradictory (Joppke, 2007, p. 46). What arises with the conflation of *tolerant universalist post-nationalism*, as discussed earlier, with an *intolerant autonomous liberalism/regressive nationalism* is a *universalist post-nationalism* that is simultaneously tolerant and intolerant. This could be interpreted as a form of *neoliberalism* that is repressive and disciplining and as Joppke (2007, p. 47) states, 'allows illiberals of many stripes ... to pursue their altogether different agendas', which often clash with the consensus ideals of *liberalism*. However, this does not provide an adequate solution to overcoming the paradoxical issues involved in identity formation, *liberalism* and 'good' governance. The rationale behind the 2004 Irish Citizenship Referendum based on *liberal multiculturalism* raises two major dilemmas. The first problematic issue is the 'top-down and managerial' approach, while the latter problem is that the rationale remains based on sediment and concrete relativism, which embeds the defining boundaries of a group such that the differentiation between identities remains fixed and unalterable (Finlay, 2007, p. 340).

To account for this and to counter the potential of the enlargement of an authoritative trans/national *neoliberalism*, it would be more fitting to theorize the notion of identity and citizenship within contemporary society in more accessible terms that can constantly be negotiated from a micro level, bottom-up, autonomous perspective. To remove the overbearing aspects of *neoliberal governance* would require an alternative approach to self-identification. The collective imagination of people co-existing on the island of Ireland could potentially desire the construction of a society that is inclusive by its own self-defining conventions. For this, the Irish would need to re-imagine their identity from an experiential perspective that incorporates a more holistic understanding of the self, the society, civic rights and responsibilities. This would entail the recognition of identities as constructed and an acceptance of multiple/hybrid identities that can be moulded into building blocks to complement each other (Grillo, 2003, p. 161). Thus, a reasonable objective would be the creation of a contemporary sense of belonging and *Irishness* that promoted autonomy within a broader range of defined contributions. Such characteristics of belonging could stem from the enduring ideals of what may be referred to as 'love' and 'pride', or through the re-identification with our humanity, or even new identification with our post-humanity. Thus, the only difficulty, and slight illogicality, would be in making the material immaterial and, reciprocally, the intangible matter.

Only then is it possible to envisage Ireland consenting to citizenship criteria that are more inclusive, facilitate *interculturalism* and build on unity of citizenry through tangible aspects of belonging such as rights and responsibilities, symbiotic interrelations and communal solidarities through the recognition of difference grounded in non-essentialist understandings. Perhaps, this can only be imagined through the development of a system of governance that seeks to ground solidarities through commutual exchange between the individual and public, public and state. Quintessential would be recognition of the justifiable argument that, as described by Thoreau (1849) in the essay 'Civil Disobedience', the authority of government ought to have the approval and consent of those it governs. Thoreau's (1849) stance is that 'The progress from an absolute to a limited democracy, from a limited monarchy to a democracy, is a progress toward a true respect for the individual'. Thoreau (1849) then implores in his closing, 'Is a democracy, such as we know it, the last improvement possible in government? Is it not possible to take a step further towards recognising and organizing the rights of man?' (p. 39) It may be that human rights have afforded us such advancement. However, the question posed, based on *liberal individualism*, obliges the individual to be free from, or at least be aware of, the mechanisms of power inherent to Western social organization that can shape and manipulate the individual's perspective. 'There will never be a really free and enlightened State until the State comes to recognize the individual as a higher and independent power, from which all its own power and authority are derived, and treats him accordingly' (Thoreau, 1849, p. 39); similarly, there will never be a really free and enlightened individual until the individual comes to recognize the mechanisms of *governmentality* that shape and impinge on the life of individuals.

The elimination of essentialist thinking is not detrimental to perceived self-expression; it is more an opportunity for a greater understanding of the intersubjectivity of identity. If, as *social constructivism* suggests, 'people belong to groups because they believe they do so' (White, 2008, p. 87), the only fixation constraining the Irish from a progressive understanding of the Irish collectivity is allowing for the broader recognition of what may constitute being 'Irish'. *Social constructivism* is merely the method by which identification within a culture occurs, such that, according to Charles Taylor, 'one is not born a man, as if humanity were an attribute given at birth: one becomes human through their anchoring in a cultural tradition. In short, particularities make one human' (Benoist, 2004, p. 14*f.*). As Benoist (2004) states, 'the human condition requires that the individual be always embedded in a value system, in a cultural, socio-historical field, which will allow him to understand himself. Men are *situated* beings' (p. 25).

The fact that *essentialist* notions attempt to entrap individuals' identity in a sense of fixity and subject formation is taken for granted as being socially determined. Consequently, 'resistance to power requires a subject who is capable of actively and self-consciously fashioning its own identity' (Armstrong, 2008, p. 22). The imperative and driving motivation hereafter is to resist the highly cultural forms of modern power,

> which categorizes the individual, marks him by his own individuality, attaches him to his identity, imposes a law of truth on him which he must recognise and which others have to recognise in him. It is a form of power which makes individuals subjects. (Foucault, 1982, p. 212)

That is to say, to increase the ability to practice freedom without discrimination of 'insider' and 'outsider' requires the acknowledgement that,

> Freedom lies in our capacity to discover the historical links between certain modes of self-understanding and modes of domination, and to resist the ways in which we have been classified and identified by the dominant discourses. This means discovering new ways of understanding ourselves and one another, refusing to accept the dominant culture's characterization of our practices and desires. (Sawicki, 1991, p. 44)

Seeking Knowledge of the Discursive Practice

As discussed above, this postulated theory makes the supposition that the reinforcement of *essentialist* notions is achieved by the *colonization of the self* through mechanisms that influence and shape formations of knowledge/power. Thus, to approach the root cause of knowledge/power formations that influence 'the negotiation between insider and outsider' (Benhabib, 2004, p. 13), it is deemed fitting that this study queries individuals' perceptions of *Irishness* so as to assess any inconsistencies between individuals' perceived realities and legislation as it definitively exists at present.

Following from Foucault's (1970, p. xiv) view emphasizing greater requirement to seek knowledge of the discursive practice and less of the 'knowing subject' though both are intrinsically interrelated, Hall (1996) states,

> It seems to be in the attempt to rearticulate the relationship between subjects and discourse practices that the question of identity recurs – or rather, if one prefers to stress the process of subjectification to discursive practices, and the politics of exclusion which all such subjectification appears to entail, the question of *identification*. (p. 2)

Accordingly, this study places the discursive and narrative as paramount in better understanding perceived *Irishness* among individuals within contemporary Irish society. Thus, intrinsic to the design is the assumption of the conception of identity from a non-essentialist perspective but as a historically constituted social construct that is processual and infinitely mutable in character.

This chapter questioned the legislative constitutional changes that occurred in 2004 and the logicality and rational foundation of contemporary society. Having narrowed the focus of the study from both broader theoretical contemplations and specific genuine accounts to arrive at the point of querying *subjectification*, and the *processes of identification*, the following chapter progresses by detailing the methodological style employed. Moving from the more ontological, albeit perturbed account of identity and *Irishness* as presented thus far, Chapter 4 overlaps

Legislation, Myth and Progressive Self-constitution 69

by presenting and describing the epistemological way in which the empirical information is attained to explore relevant themes on 'Irish' identity. Following this chapter, Chapter 4 presents the innovative methodology, the underpinning methodological theory, design and ethical considerations in the context of the overall aims and objectives of this study.

Chapter 4

Research Methodology and Design

Keywords: Grounded theory; participatory; reflexivity; multistage; dominant group; neopragmatism; social identity; self-constitutionality; cultural hegemony; discourse analysis

Initially, this chapter discusses the design of this study, highlighting the two interconnected stages involved, as well as the sequential phases within each. The overall design is described as centred on a constructivist Grounded Theoretical framework. Such a methodological approach acknowledges the social construction of meaning achieved through the participant/s and researcher,[1] along with the assumption that processes of identification and their associated characteristics, such as meaning and belonging, are subjective and independent of the particularisms of individuals. From this vantage point, the circumspective benefits of such a methodological stance are advanced. In particular, emphasis is placed on reflecting the opinions of the contributors and building reciprocity between the individual and collectivity that, from the normative positioning theorized in the previous chapters, would stress *egalitarianism*, participatory development and social amelioration.

The overall design is illustrated graphically showing the two stages and the respective phases within each (please refer to Fig. 1).[2] Within the section describing the overall design, an account of the Research Framework provides explanation of the novel design features and includes an account of the rationale for

---

[1] Henceforth, the researcher is referred to interchangeably as the researcher, facilitator or author.

[2] The study herein proceeds from a preliminary study entitled *Perceived Irishness: An Exploration of the Superficiality of Identity Using a Reflexive Social Experimental Approach* (BouAynaya, 2011). The preliminary/pilot study was completed in 2011, and the dissertation was submitted in partial fulfilment for a Master of Philosophy in Race, Ethnicity and Conflict at Trinity College Dublin.

Redefining *Irishness* in a Globalized World:
National Identity and European Integration, 71–96
Copyright © 2024 by Yaqoub BouAynaya
Published under exclusive licence by Emerald Publishing Limited
doi:10.1108/978-1-83797-941-720241005

72 Redefining Irishness in a Globalized World

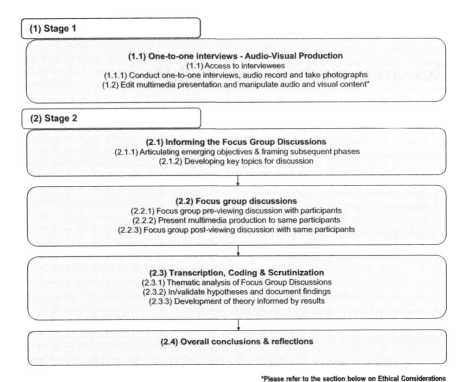

*Please refer to the section below on Ethical Considerations

Fig. 1. Stages and Phases of the Research Design.

expansion through the incorporation of additional components. Subsequent to description of the overall design, details on ethical considerations and limitations are provided.

What is intrinsically incorporated into this research methodology is a multistage approach. This multistage methodological design comprises both one-to-one interviews and focus group discussions which aimed to analyse the performative constitution of identity (Butler, 1988). This is analogous to what Butler (1990, p. 139*ff.*; 1993, p. 95*ff.*) refers to as 'performativity', whereby power asserting itself in identity formation can be observed in participants through societal regulation of moral judgement, values and beliefs which is constructed, continued or contrarily destabilized through performance. Additionally, the methodology is centred on a reflexive design that seeks to evoke a specific response from participants. Incorporation of a reflexive element throughout its approach means that the process by which the data are collected will consistently be questioned and justified (McRobbie, 1977, p. 46). Reflexivity also seeks substantiation and confirming refutation of theory in a more iterative, but holistic manner. To an extent, such an approach addresses aspects relating to the knowledge/power paradigm theorized by Foucault (1977) (as detailed in the previous chapters) and the questions posed by Gunaratnam (2003), explicitly '... how we produce knowledge about difference, and how what we know (or what we claim to know) is caught up with specific histories and relations of power' (p. 3). The reflexive approach taken in this study is seen as integral to the overall project design and essential to the fulfilment of several key objectives, particularly in relation to knowledge production and mythological notions of *Irishness*.

The focus of the study is on a qualitative participatory, reflexive and grassroots democratic stage using current technological means of communication. This stage expands and delves deeper into the scrutiny of perceptions of 'Irish' identity and extends to a larger number of individuals across more diverse geospatial settings. Similar to the aspirations and outcomes of work by Byrne and O'Mahony's (2012, p. 72),[3] the research demonstrates through collaborative interaction how researchers and members of society can produce meaningful social interventions that may be somewhat emancipatory and transformative for the individual, the wider community and broader society.

Both the methodology and sequential stages facilitate discussions that are examined through the process of discourse analysis, deriving from Derrida's (1967) notion of deconstructing discourse as documented in, *Of Grammatology*.[4] Similar to the consideration that '... the "subject" of knowledge then becomes the text' (Spivak, 1997, p. 320), this study is based on an interwoven analysis of participant's opinions prior to and responses after viewing a multimedia presentation through thematic discourse analysis. This is applied so as to deconstruct not only the 'subject's' understanding but also negotiation of identity and to document its formation within interactive conversation. In addition, focussing on conversation discourse means that important characteristics of 'the *linguistic production relations* within which it is produced' (Bourdieu, 1977b, p. 647) allow for the recognition of language as a symbolic power relation. This takes into account the authoritative use of language, of which Bourdieu (1977b) writes,

> Language is not only an instrument of communication or even of knowledge, but also an instrument of power. A person speaks not only to be understood but also to be believed, obeyed, respected, distinguished. Hence the full definition of competence as the right to speech, i.e. to the legitimate language, the authorized language

---

[3]Byrne and O'Mahony (2012) researched *Family and Community: (Re)Telling Our Own Story*. In it Byrne and O'Mahony (2012) describe, 'The collaborative interaction and the transdisciplinary meeting of the three knowledges of sociologist, artist, and the local combined to collectively tell a narrative of a people and place, rooted in history but connected to contemporary familial and community relationships. Recognizing that local knowledge of place, kinship, and custom could be framed and presented from the perspective of local knowers and made visible within an academic and cultural context has been both emancipatory and transformatory for those involved' (p. 72).
[4]Written by Jaques Derrida in 1967 and translated by Gayatri Chakravorty Spivak in 1997.

which is also the language of authority. Competence implies the power to impose reception. (p. 648)

As the aim in creating such a novel research model is to focus on thematic discourse and discussion analysis, the study relies on several main methods of sampling that, in turn, depend heavily on access and recruitment in their own specific ways. Similar to Willis's (1977, p. 3) view, such a focussed interest on 'the cultural' dictates the qualitative methods and the approach employed in the research, as well as the reflexive format of the presentation.

In acknowledging that a priori assumptions are made when considering the subjectivity of identity formations, it is a '... necessity to identify life experience as partial within which contradictions are to be expected' (Gunaratnam, 2003, p. 6). This necessitates taking into account ethical considerations and corollaries when conducting such research on perceived identities with a variety of subjects. Thus, as far as is possible ethical issues are dealt with thoroughly and effectively to fully comprise aspects, such as, insuring all participants at the various stages and phases are properly informed, have given consensual agreement to take part and for the usage and storage of data in its different forms. Also assuring all participants are provided the possibility to opt-out at any stage of their participation. Finally, outcomes and limitations of the design are addressed at the end of this chapter.

An Iterative Approach to *Constructivist Grounded Theory*

Methodological theory primarily takes into consideration the usefulness and benefit of the conjectural perspective in meeting the objectives of the study in addition to its complementarity to the overall reflexive design. Therefore, it adopts a 'neopragmatic perspective' (Hansen, 2006, p. 294). Rather than defining 'truth' as objective, transcendent and based on indisputable realities, it redefines 'truth' in a pragmatic way, as local and utilitarian (Hansen, 2006, p. 294). As such, it negates from being over saturated by the array of theoretical propositions *post/late-modernist relativism* entails and instead opens space for the synthesis of novel observational accounts and theoretical propositions. By implementing a *neopragmatic utilitarian* approach to the selection of methodology, in conjunction with the foundational notion of identities being primarily socially constructed, I advocated a Grounded Theoretical approach throughout. This is because central to this thesis is the objective to provide an intercultural and multi-individual process in which the voices, perspectives and opinions of the participants are given the greatest priority while acknowledging 'the importance of a multiplicity of perspectives and "truths"' (Mills et al., 2006; Strauss, 1987; Strauss and Corbin, 1990, 1994, 1998).

Furthermore, this study relies on interpretive work and coding. Thus, as Strauss and Corbin (1994) stipulate, '... interpretations must include the perspectives and voice of the people who we study' (p. 274). A similar justification for such a theoretical approach is that, as Thomas and James (2006) suggest, it is impossible to detach oneself from one's own preconceptions in the collection and analysis of particular data.

However, instead of taking a more purist Grounded Theoretical approach that begins with inductive logic, uses emergent strategies, relies on comparative inquiry and is explicitly analytic, the *constructivist* Grounded Theory approach,

> [...] assumes that people construct both the studied phenomenon and the research process through their actions. This approach recognizes the constraints that historical, social, and situational conditions exert on these actions and acknowledges the researcher's active role in shaping the data and analysis. (Charmaz, 2011, p. 359*f*.)

Adopting such a methodological approach is appropriate when taking the stance in arguing for the subjective nature of the attainment of knowledge and endorsing *post/late-modernist* thought which is seen as *anti-essentialist*. It is complementary to the research framework and the fundamental underpinning theory relating to the ethical imperative of knowledge acquisition (as discussed in the initial chapters). Correspondingly, the ethical imperative of knowledge acquisition is reflected in the research paradigm chosen, which emphasizes the 'constructedness' of reality and the denial of the existence of any objective truth (Mills et al., 2006, p. 26). The *constructivist approach* takes a relativist ontological position which is considered 'asserting instead that realities are social constructions of the mind, and that there exist as many such constructions as there are individuals (although clearly many constructions will be shared)' (Guba & Lincoln, 1989, p. 43). Additionally, the *constructivist approach* allows for the recognition of the co-construction of meaning through an interrelationship between the researcher and participants which provides a more post/late-modernist *epistemological* justification for adopting such an approach (Hayes & Oppenheim, 1997; Mills et al., 2006; Pidgeon & Henwood, 1997).

It would seem an impossibility to approach this research void of preconceived ideas that would require corroboration or falsification. Nonetheless, formulated through an iterative analytic process there are a set of common characteristics that resemble Grounded Theory but have also evolved into what is termed *constructivist Grounded Theory*. The methodological approach implements sensitivity towards a variety of theories, critical literature review, comparative analysis of gleaned data, verification of meanings, identification of key categories, translation of interpretations into coding, the drafting of diagrams and memos, along with examination through testing (McCann & Clark, 2003; Mills et al., 2006).

Methodological Justification: Focusing on the Dominant Group

The topic of this research is, but not limited to, the dominant national group *id est*, people who would self-subscribe to being entirely Irish and having an 'Irish' identity. It is a combination of both theoretical and empirical investigations exploring identity and belonging in everyday speech related to daily experience. Similar to Skey's (2011) work entitled, *National Belonging and Everyday Life: The*

Significance of Nationhood in an Uncertain World, the methodological approach places at the centre of attention what is considered a rather under-explored area or lacuna in academic research (Skey, 2011, p. 28). Specifically, it studies the role played by ordinary people in processes of identification and practices of belonging. To an extent, it is alternative as the methodology does not confine itself to a qualitative study of viewpoints from a supposed ethnic majority; it remains open and actively encourages contribution from individuals beyond the mythological boundaries constructed within the imaginary homogeneous nation. By focussing on the micro-sociological and scrutinizing even the notion of dominant ethnicity/group/population, while mitigating reification of essentialist notions, this methodological approach does not trap itself in its own bind of contradictions in relation to the book's overall framework.

As detailed previously, I focus on perceptions of *Irishness* through discourse analysis. Discourse primarily from individuals who may, or may not, ordinarily associate themselves within the dominant group of Irish society is analysed. The justification for such a discursive analytical approach relies on the desire to conduct empirical research that focusses on what Widdicome and Wooffit (1994) describe as '... discourses – systems of meanings and concepts which provide a coherent way of representing the world – through which persons are ascribed identities' (p. 4). Discourse analysis shifts the focus of analysis towards language, interaction through dialogue, the ways in which identities are narrated through language and so on. Furthermore, when taking into account the issues and complexities of dominant and minority group dynamics, it can be related to Gramsci's writings which, according to Lears (1985, p. 589), 'stressed the centrality of language in cementing a given group's prestige and cultural leadership' (p. 589). Not only is language central to the process of identity formation, language usage is a component in shaping society. This is because Gramsci views society as a labile system where ruling-class domination may persist or it may shift through changing discourses. As purported by Lears (1985), this Gramscian view means that society is in a constant process where counter-hegemonies operate. Lears (1985) summarizes, 'Gramsci's vision of society involves not a mechanical model of base and superstructure but a complex interaction of relatively autonomous spheres (public and private; political, cultural, and economic) within a totality of attitudes and practices' (p. 571). By focussing on discourse, it allows the researcher to consider language expressions as indicative of various processes of acculturation. As such, it assists in transcending an understanding of subjects' viewpoints that might otherwise be seen as trapped within the duality of compliance and resistance. Likewise, using conversation analysis recognizes that

> Language is not a neutral medium that passes freely and easily into the private property of the speaker's intentions; it is populated – overpopulated – with the intentions of others .... The word in language is half someone else's. It becomes one's 'own' only when the speaker populates it with his own intentions, his own accent, when he appropriates the word, adapting it to his own semantic and expressive intention. Prior to this moment of appropriation, the

word does not exist in a neutral and impersonal language ... but rather it exists in other people's mouths, in other people's contexts, serving other people's intention; it is from there that one must take the word, and make it one's own. (Bakhtin, 1981, p. 294)

Widdicome and Wooffit (1994, p. 4) claim that discourse analysis may not adequately challenge traditional socio-psychological assumptions, nor might it do enough to address aspects relating to power, gender, class and racism. Nonetheless, Widdicome and Wooffit (1994, p. 4) suggest, it can mitigate such shortcomings by incorporating work by social philosophers such as Foucault, Derrida and Lacan. In order to account for this, the analytical approach to researching discourse is consistently scrutinized within a constructivist Grounded Theoretical framework that iteratively draws from social philosophical theory. Furthermore, an approach that validates the use of focus group discussions rather than one-to-one interviews becomes justifiable because respondents' identities are seen as an interactional resource in the production of discursive action (Widdicome & Wooffit, 1994, p. 5). Discourse analysis places emphasis upon three interrelated key points of interest. It allows the researcher to gain an understanding of, firstly, the constructive properties of language use; secondly, the ways individuals constitute society through their membership or lack of and thirdly, it underscores the link between individuals and society by analysing social identity as a derivation of group membership or social category ascription, thus group affiliation (Widdicome & Wooffit, 1994, p. 5).

Building Reciprocity Between the Individual and the Collective

This study addresses not merely challenges in relation to identity but brings to the fore the interconnected challenges related to sovereignty, state or collectivity. With globalization and trans-Europeanization and the consequences of such affecting the saliency of belonging, a feature that requires consideration is the reciprocity between the individual and state/collectivity with regard to individuals' rights and responsibilities, respectively. An additional consideration is the depreciating power of the nation state in managing its affairs, particularly its diminishing authority over the national economy because of its bind to *neoliberal* free-market ideologies and current trajectories in globalization.[5]

---

[5]In 'Regulating Immigration in a Global Age: A New Policy Landscape', Sassen (2005, p. 38) discusses how the state's regulatory role and autonomy have been affected by internationalization and the proliferation of bi- and multi-lateral agreements. Rosenau (1992) describes how, 'governments have undergone a narrowing of the range in which their authority and legitimacy are operative' (p. 256) which is substantiated by Hardt and Negri (2000) who claim, 'in step with the processes of globalisation, the sovereignty of nation-states, while still effective, has progressively declined' (p. xi).

From understanding transformations at both a spatial and temporal level, this study, in an innovative manner, conceptualizes alternatives to counter the negative effects of mis/conceptions propagated within society through its reliance on both synthesis (bottom-up) and decomposition (top-down) systems of knowledge ordering. Inherent to the design is a space created that allows for the re-evaluation of *Irishness* by participants, evoked at a personal level, as well as the production of information that can add to the body of knowledge relating to socio-political and socio-psychological theory.

Some of the main benefits of this design are that it reflects the opinions of the contributors and participants at any given time; it is replicable and easily reproduced with further potential for its expansion and practical value. Although having a component that is centred on an interactive design, another fundamental benefit is that it is not simply empirical sociological research nor is it social technology/praxis (sociological theory applied to social practice). This study consciously carves out a third space by attempting to advance socio-psychological knowledge while being an agent of social amelioration, through initiated reflection on self-identification and self-differentiation. Thus, an important benefit of such a study is that its success not only rests in the possibility of contributing to knowledge theory but also to advocating change in social reality (Agassi, 1990, p. 2). It allows for an evaluation, albeit minor, and potential formulation of theory and raises awareness of concealed mechanisms that influence individuals' perceptions of identity and reality. What is advantageous in the overall design is that it does not purport to challenge the philosophical objection that 'rests on the claim that truth is inaccessible, so that there is no possibility of objectivity in the social sciences, so that there is no need to try to be objective' (Agassi, 1990, p. 3). It not only recognizes the subjectivity of participants' realities, which is appropriate for the social sciences, it also attempts to develop *reflexive self-constitutionality* at the individual level interwoven with empowerment at the level of the collective.

Added to this, theory such as *cultural hegemony* implies that capitalists and institutions defend the *status quo* so as to maintain and legitimize hegemonic power. Gramsci (1971) provides a loose definition of *hegemony of culture* somewhat ambiguously as,

> the 'spontaneous' consent given by the great masses of the population to the general direction imposed on social life by the dominant fundamental group: this consent is 'historically' caused by the prestige (and consequent confidence) which the dominant group enjoys because of its position and function in the world of production. (p. 12)

Such maintenance cannot be seen as absent from within the field of social science as though the social sciences have somehow remained unadulterated from the long extending reach of *capitalism*. In particular, preservation of the hierarchal order occurs when institutions are encouraged to support specifically chosen empirical sociological research and as such this can be understood as inherently subjective, serving the general interests of both the sociologist and the benefactor, as it were. As mentioned, contrary to this argument is acknowledgement of the subjective nature of the study and the circumstance that it cannot expect to be interpreted as an extensively representative empirical study.

With such an approach that relies on the inherent subjectivity of its processes, the participants and the researcher relate to each other in a participatory fashion so that the researcher can consider aspects of attitudes and behaviour relative to the thematic discourse and discussion analysis. The participatory process during discussions allows for improvization by the researcher, along with self-representation by the participants and reflection, so that amendments or adjustments can be made to their own self-portrayal and understanding.

Conversely, as I was working within the constraints of an independent powerbase, that being the Department of Sociology at Trinity College Dublin, it also provided a benefit because it legitimated the project by requiring standards of ethics, methodological approach and production. It also allowed the project freedom to be conducted without necessarily being exposed to other external influences, thus, with a degree of impartiality, which was conveyed to the participants.

Design Innovation

As introduced earlier, the design can be seen as split into two main constituent stages (illustrated in Fig. 1). The first stage was the production of an audio–visual presentation in the form of one-to-one interviews. This was then integrated into the second stage, whereby discussants were shown the audio–visual presentation midway through their focus group discussion. This overall process was seen as the catalyst for the construction of interrogations that would allow unravelling of core issues relating to perceptions of *Irishness*. It also tested the validity of the incorporated stages. The methodology overall emphasized the necessity to re-evaluate perceptions of *Irishness* that are more inclusive of 'the other'.

In exploring perceived *Irishness*, within contemporary Irish society, and its formation through social construction as a means of reinforcing belonging, the focus group discussions assessed the means of subordinating self-identification under the nation/'Irish' antonym. The process sought to examine perceptions of *Irishness* within members of the collective and to illuminate the superficiality of such perceptions. Thus, the initial investigation focussed on questioning perceptions of *Irishness*. It also examined if 'Irish' identity could be influenced through a reflexive social experimental approach. In doing so, it aimed to observe perceptions conceived from essentialist notions of 'the other' and illusions of difference. The study expanded on the de-centred aspect of identity formation and attempts to create space for discussion on governance and the proactive re-conceptualization of alternative identities, through deliberation and self-reflection on processes of identification.

Conducting focus group discussions with members of the public in Irish society connects with academic arguments on identity and nationalist ideology which are related to the perceived positioning of the self and assumed practicalities of the lived experience of ordinary individuals (Tovey et al., 1989, p. 25f.). It also takes into account the conceivably 'racial state' (Goldberg, 2002; Lentin, 2007;

Lentin and McVeigh, 2006) and how, as Tovey et al. (1989) further expound, individuals might perceive themselves as

> subjects of this, and not some other, state (the subjects of this state's laws, the audience for this state's public service broadcasting, the participants in this state's education or welfare institutions and so on). It can be argued that such experiences are what, in the contemporary world, define and create the 'people' which the state claims to represent. (p. 26)

Or, as De Paor (1979, p. 25) advised several decades ago,

> romantic nationalism and impatient anti-nationalism, in their various forms, have made it difficult for us to see Ireland as a whole, and we need to get down more and more to local detail in order to understand the present direction of our society.

By adopting a design that centres on focus group discussions and questionnaires, it advocated a bottom-up approach and engendered thought on the process of identification with members of the public realm who are the fabric of a given society. Conducting such work aided in the provision of more precise understandings of identity, in particular, identity formations in the Irish context, and how identity functions, both through its formation as an individual project and its role of interacting in social and cultural contexts (Schwartz, 2001, p. 9).

The study relied on visual and auditory stimuli in the form of narration within a multi-media presentation that I produced specifically for the study. The method used for the creation of a multi-media presentation was dependent on one-to-one semi-structured interviews (please refer to Table 1). Following this, focus group discussions were conducted, which provided a body of transcribed raw information that was then analysed as the focal point for the development of the book's thesis. Data analysis techniques involved a thematic approach to group discussions, pre- and post-viewing, which were then analysed and compared through coding. From this coded information, not only did the informative data reveal key themes, it informed the directionality of the study both theoretically and methodologically. As such, it can be seen as in keeping with theoretical aspects of participatory research by maintaining an inductive approach.

Table 1. Details of Preliminary Stage: One-to-One Interviews.

Date of Interview	Alias	Gender	Interview	Age
05 July	Laura	Female	Interviewee 1	25–35
11 July	Dijwar	Male	Interviewee 2	18–25
01 August	Niamh	Female	Interviewee 3	18–25
11 July	Kevin	Male	Interviewee 4	34–45

The overall design is in contestation with the assumptions made by those advocating the achievements of liberal democracy specifically in relation to the public sphere whereby it is recognized as open to all equally (Coates, 1997, p. 89). Instead, it is purposely designed to recognize and mitigate what Fraser (1990) describes: 'where societal inequality persists, deliberative processes in public spheres will tend to operate to the advantage of dominant groups and to the disadvantage of subordinates' (p. 65*f.*). By disregarding such social structuring, the methodology allows for 'parallel discursive arenas where members of subordinated groups invent and circulate counterdiscourses, so as to formulate oppositional interpretations of their identities, interests and needs' (Fraser, 1990, p. 67). In this way, the methodological approach could be viewed as having a participatory democratic form that promotes deliberation between the public sphere within Irish society and the *subaltern counterpublic* that is present and, from an egalitarian perspective, deserves acknowledgement and repositioning. The aim of the design is not to focus on conflict or hierarchical positions, but rather to be both affective and effective through engagement and reflection on processes of re-identification so as to potentially resolve certain challenges in relation to 'Irish' identity and its socially constructed formation.

The Preliminary Stage: Production of the Multimedia Presentation

Stage 1 involved the production of a multimedia presentation. The multimedia presentation was created from information gathered from one-to-one semi-structured interviews with four individual contributors. These individual contributors were selected on the basis of their status relative to the conditionality of *jus sanguinis* and *jus soli* Irish citizenship and nationality. As detailed in Chapter 3, the Irish constitutional referendum on citizenship in 2004 removed emphasis from *jus soli* nationality (nationality right based on territorial place of birth) and placed greater emphasis on *jus sanguinis* rationale (nationality right based on bloodline descend). The primary reason for selecting such participants was to assess if current citizenship legislation fails to account for the heterogeneous make up of Irish society. In becoming a less inclusive mode of governance, it may be incongruent with contemporary societal perceptions of *Irishness*. If this were plausible, the criteria for membership of the Irish collective as defined by law may be misrepresentative and require re-evaluation.

The only requirement for the first stage was that the contributors are physically present and conform to the ethical requirements, such as consensually agree to contribute. The individual interviewees were selected by purposive sampling, which required utilizing gatekeepers within organizations and beyond.

The data for the preliminary stage were collected through a one-to-one interview process and discussion involving the utilization of audio and visual equipment. Notes were also taken during the course of the conversations. Thus, the multi-media presentation was created using excerpts of audio recordings from the interviews, incorporated with visual material from the interviewees. Individuals' portraits were documented through the medium of photography and interlaced with still images of other visual material, such as objects of personal value, personal lifestyle, old photographs and memorabilia.[6]

As detailed above, individual interviewees were selected according to their appropriateness for the study. This prejudice was not seen to be excessively problematic within the remit of the overall investigation, as the criteria and categorizations were already normative and legally bound within Irish society. One concern was that relying on such categorizations may have been seen to reinforce stereotypical notions that then become integrated into the research itself. However, this was mitigated for by virtue of the open and inclusive selection process conducted for the focus group discussions, which is at liberty from the current legal criteria that define entitlement to being/becoming an Irish citizen.

The Main Stage: Focus Group Discussions and Analysis

The Second or Main Stage expanded on an exploration of participants' perceived views of *Irishness* and made comparisons with the state's role in constructing national identity. The rationale of identification was related to justify/falsify the legislative boundaries that are drawn to fashion difference between the 'them' and 'us' of contemporary Irish society. This Second Stage was constructed with the explicit intension of creating the foundations to support deliberation on Irish identification and potentially alternate conceptualizations of 'what it means to be Irish'. It relied primarily on opinions from participants from urban, semi-urban and rural backgrounds.

At a spatial level, Stage 2 concentrated on opinions obtained through multiple focus group discussions within Dublin city, suburban and commuter environments, other more rural towns and villages, as well as an extrajudicial extension to incorporate opinions from Belfast, Northern Ireland. The locations of the eight focus group discussions were Belfast, Limerick, Drumondra, Naas, Leixlip, Clondalkin Drogheda and Coolock. Although this was by no means seen to represent and cover the geographical expanse of Ireland at a shallow level, instead such a sampling approach provided rich and deep data looking more at socio-psychological determinants that may play a role in influencing individuals' perceptions of, and sensitivities to, their own realities. As Inglis and Donnelly (2011) suggest 'one of the advantages of an open-ended, qualitative approach to social research is that it can bring to the surface issues and processes that were not identified at the outset as being significant' (p. 136). It must be noted that although initially this was conducted in a relatively targeted manner, which aimed at revealing information from specific cohorts, participants may or may not have

---

[6]These were requested to be brought prior to the interview and the interviewees were given as much freedom as possible to bring objects that were personally felt to be relevant to each of them. To create a good rapport with the contributors, the author took a reflexive approach and was as open as possible about the research and the researcher's personal position. This was done within an environment that was congenial to the contributors, where they could be most comfortable and relaxed.

had strong associations with the specific geographic localities where the discussions were held. It was assumed, however, that focus group discussions did include city urban, suburban, town lands and rural residents, as well as individuals who were students, unemployed or working professionals in age ranges between young teenagers up to retirees (please refer to Table 2).[7]

In adopting a multistage approach that was methodologically iterative and reflexive, the findings, results and conclusions were to some extent interrelated to allow for reflexive re-theorization.[8] Through a process of theory and methodology synthesis that has an element of reflexivity, modifications and adaptations enhanced both the subsequent Stage 2 process and the overall findings. Referring to theory of the nation state and identity formation, it was not expected that criteria, other than association with Irish nationality or exposure to Irish society, would have had any major influencing effect on the outcomes of the research. The reason for this was that association with Irish nationality and exposure to Irish society are the two major factors believed to influence perceived *Irishness* in individuals. Thus, the study, using an exploratory approach to identity, primarily focussed on these criteria.

The main focus involved thematic focus group discussions and required completely independent groups of participants. Focus group discussions were recruited via canvassing networks, associations, institutions, youth and community groups, educational organizations and so on primarily through online emailing, follow-up calls and communications. A letter for further circulation outlining the request for participation was also attached to each email sent to potential correspondent gatekeepers/participants.

The participants of each focus group were assembled to take part in a discussion whose thematic focal point is primarily on 'Irish' identity and included questions on themes relating to ethnicity and citizenship. Within each thematic focus group discussion, the participants initially had a pre-viewing conversation on issues pertaining to identity, ethnicity and citizenship and then viewed the multimedia presentation prepared (lasting 20 minutes), and this was followed up with the same participants taking part in a focussed group discussion post-viewing.[9]

---

[7] For an overview of an historical account of more *in situ* methodological approaches and development within the Chicago School and the Birmingham School, please refer to Colosi's (2010) work.

[8] This more constructivist approach to Grounded Theory is quite similar to Thornberg's (2012) proposal of an informed Grounded Theoretical approach. Both compensate for the impossible position of pure induction. As Thornberg (2012) claims, in an informed Grounded Theory approach, 'the researcher takes the advantage of pre-existing theories and research findings in the substantive field in a sensitive, creative, and flexible way' (p. 255).

[9] The methodological approach is quite similar to O'Connor's (1997) work on audience studies; however, the object of the analysis in this case is to investigate both the extent and ways in which representations of *Irishness* are perceived and discussed among groups of individuals both prior to and after viewing a multimedia production created by the researcher. Additionally, the participants own representations of 'Irish' identity were simultaneously incorporated into the study, rather than separated.

Table 2. Details of the Main Stage: Focus Group Discussants.

Date and Location of Discussion	Alias	Gender	Age	Nationality	Profession
11 March Belfast (E)	Tony	Male	36–45	Irish	Trade unionist
	Molly	Female	36–45	Irish	Migrant support worker
	Reagan	Female	46–55	Irish	Finance/office manager
24 March Limerick (F)	Adrian	Male	>65	Irish	–
	Charlie	Male	56–65	Irish	Retired
	Maebh	Female	56–65	Irish	Retired
	Dale	Male	46–55	Irish	Teacher
	Juliana	Female	26–35	Irish (UK born)	Homemaker
07 April Drumcondra (G)	Carroll	Female	46–55	Scottish/Irish	Community development worker
	Alana	Female	56–65	Irish	Operator
	Eddie	Male	>65	Irish	Retired marketing manager
	Ryan	Male	46–55	Irish	Self-employed
	Ciara	Female	46–55	Irish	Adult literacy tutor
20 May Naas (H)	Colin	Male	15–17	Irish	Student
	Liam	Male	15–17	Irish	Student
	Alan	Male	13–14	Irish	Student
	Glenn	Male	13–14	Irish	Student
	Eithne	Female	25–35	Irish	Youth worker
28 May Leixlip (I)	Michael	Male	13–14	Irish	Student
	Kim	Female	13–14	Irish	Student
	Blathnaid	Female	13–14	Irish	Student
	Noel	Male	15–17	Irish	Student

(*Continued*)

Table 2. (Continued)

Date and Location of Discussion	Alias	Gender	Age	Nationality	Profession
29 July Clondalkin (J)	Kelsey	Female	18–25	Irish	Student
	Dana	Female	18–25	Irish	Student and restaurant staff
	Kathleen	Female	18–25	Irish	Unemployed
	Brady	Male	18–25	Irish	Fitter
	Cillian	Male	18–25	Irish	Student
	Christine	Female	36–45	Irish	Youth information officer
15 August Drogheda (K)	Amy	Female	36–45	(Congo) French	Unemployed
	Irena	Female	36–45	Polish	Nurse
	Gerek	Male	36–45	Polish	Driver
	Emmanuel	Male	36–45	Togolese	Actor
	Luis	Male	56–65	Spanish	Pilot
	Toben	Male	–	Nigerian	Business
	Hubert	Male	46–55	French	Journalist
	Dillon	Male	–	South Africa	Retired journalist
	Diarmuid	Male	56–65	Irish	Retired defence forces
	Izabela	Female	36–45	Romanian	Teacher
	Rachel	Female	46–55	Nicoraguan	Assistant
	Busayo	Male	46–55	Nigerian	Missionary
	Ezinwa	Female	46–55	Nigerian	–
	Machie	Male	36–45	Nigerian	Event management and business analyst
	Kasper	Male	46–55	Poland	–
	Karina	Female	26–35	Poland	Care worker

(*Continued*)

86 Redefining Irishness in a Globalized World

Table 2. (Continued)

Date and Location of Discussion	Alias	Gender	Age	Nationality	Profession
26 November and 02 December Coolock (L)	Tierney	Male	56–65	Irish	Tour guide/author/radio presenter
	Peadar	Male	66–75	Irish	Retired (industrial chemist)
	Aileen	Female	46–55	Irish	Radio producer
	Keela	Female	36–45	Irish	DJ/radio
	Grainne	Female	26–35	Irish	Sports officer/media publicity
	Emmet	Male	46–55	Irish	Radio presenter/researcher/producer
	Conlaoch	Male	66–75	Éirenach	Retired teacher

The data collection tools that were used in the second stage are pre- and post-group discussions with observation referring to open-ended interrogations for qualitative analysis and the completion of a factsheet to record contributors' information such as age bracket, profession, gender and so on. Adhering to conventions of researching both interviews and focus group discussions, the questions were asked sequentially in a standardized format. During each focus group discussion, identical pre- and post-viewing questions were asked (please refer to Appendix 1). This was conducted in order to maintain consistency and the potential for accurate cross-comparative analysis. Lacking congruity would otherwise have made any comparison unreliable.

During the discussions, an audio recorder was used discreetly. The advantage of this was that an exact documentation of the conversation during the discussion was recorded. Data were also collected from recording the participants' discussion after viewing the presentation. During later focus group discussions, additional questions were also deliberated towards the latter part of the discussions (please refer to Appendix 2).

A thematic approach to data analysis of the group discussions was conducted. The transcribed information contained in both the one-to-one interviews and focus group discussions (pre-/post-viewing) were compared, using an interpretive technique of coding. Segments were labelled with a 'code' so as to associate data segments together and inform the research objectives. The coded themes were drawn up in a table (please refer to Table 3), their associations were cross-referenced and their interconnected relationships were graphically illustrated. From the coded information, the occurrence of significant changes in opinions,

Table 3. Key Emergent Themes from the Main Stage Discussions.

Perceived Characteristics of *Irishness*	Perceptions of Being 'Irish' and Becoming 'Irish'	History, Law and Privilege	*Irishness*, Economy and the State	Conversation Analysis and Changing Views
Family	Calling oneself Irish/feeling Irish	History	Welfare state (benefits)	Perception
Home	Feelings/emotions (as Irish)	Change (and history)	Education	Perspective
Clan	Affinity (want, feel, desire)	Colonialism/non-colonial	External cultural influence	Blurring historical reference points
Feud/Feudal	Pride	Law (abiding)	Migration (em-/im-)	Language use (1st, 2nd, 3rd person)
Grudge/Begrudge/belittlement	Becoming a citizen /v/ being 'Irish'	Passport	Cultural relativism	Dominating conversation
Conflict/compromise	Insider/outsider/self-subscription	Privilege	Economy	Changing topic
Parochialism (parish)/tribal	Temporal/Spatial (experience/exposure)	Anti-establishment	Work	Altering topic (slight)
Sport	Ethnicity	Anti-activist	Transnational governance	Hidden information
Ritual	Getting the nuances	Travelling community (minority groups)	Globalization/financial capitalism	Absence of empathy
Community	Outsider view	Natural justice	Corporations	Ambivalent
Waning religion	'Race'	Borders	Americanization	Recognizing ambiguity
Anti-puritan	Racism	Egalitarian/fair	Consumerism/materialism	Egocentrism

(*Continued*)

Table 3. (Continued)

Perceived Characteristics of *Irishness*	Perceptions of Being 'Irish' and Becoming 'Irish'	History, Law and Privilege	*Irishness*, Economy and the State	Conversation Analysis and Changing Views
Paganism	'Race' and ethnicity – inherent amd extrinsic	Hierarchy	Competitive (sport, etc.)	Collective-centrism***(ethnocentrism)
Spirituality	Colour	'Good' citizen/'bad' citizen	Future	Adopting views of interviewees
Mythology	Subtle prejudice	Rights and responsibilities (r&r)	Technology	Defensive reactions to interviewees
Travel abroad	Being open-minded	Entitlement	National interest	Self/family/friends as reference
Generosity	Tolerance	Ownership*	Patriotism	Gender dynamics
Friendliness (outgoing, not too serious)	Adaptation	Belonging	*Perceived rational pragmatism*	Persistent interjections
Inquisitive/intrusive	New Irish/new Ireland	Acceptance	Liberal dilemma	Media influence
Cultural superiority/ dominant position	Change (and diversity)	Assimilation	Neo-liberalism	History as reference
Hidden culture (–)	Advancement/progress	Integrate/participation	EU governance	Multimedia influence
Satire	Evolution	Effort	Agency	Anti-American sentiment
Social problems (suicide, etc.)	Fear (perceived danger)	Jus soli	Social amelioration	Changing views
Roots		*Jus sanguinis*	Rediscovery	Use of anecdotes

Heritage (old/new)
Tradition
Nostalgia
Internal cultural influence
Conformity – performance to fit in
Authentic/unique *Irishness*
Misconceptions
Drinking
Feeling rules/etiquette
Physical affection
Accents
Language
Physiological traits
Nationalism
North/South context (N-S context)
Hard working
Rural/Urban divide
Generational
The famous 'other'

Citizenship
Hybrid identity
American Irish/diaspora
Cultural capital/social entrepreneurs
EU identity

Beyond EU identity

Critique of system/law
Direct provision
Reimagining *Irishness*

Freedom
Force (enforcement/)

Process of self-'othering'

variations in phraseology and alterations in terminology by participants were examined. Such scrutiny looked at both individual and collective contributions in a comparative manner that focussed on similarities and differences and, through cross-referencing, also examined different individual and collective contributions over the different stages.

Ethical Considerations

The fundamental ethical issue related to its structural design and, in particular, the stages which encountered aspects from the manipulative approach to the multi-media production. However to overcome this, within both stages, the participants were never considered passive recipients of stimuli nor were their responses viewed in a negative or hostile way. The participants were informed that they were not being given the full information, and a pre-requisite to the discussions was that participants provide consensual agreement to partake in the research and dialogue. Participants younger than consensual age were required to have parental consent in advance of the focus group discussions and were themselves agreeable to contribute as research participants. Parental consent was acquired via the signing of a parental consent form which was provided to parents several days in advance of each respective focus group discussion organized.

Other ethical issues to arise related to the selection of the original interviewees who were willing to provide the researcher with the information for the multimedia presentation. Both the interviewees and all the participants involved were expected to participate voluntarily. No recompense for partaking in the research was awarded.[10] It was ensured that the interviews take place in a quiet and discreet setting. For the one-to-one interviews, all interviewees were pre-disposed and willing to answer personal questions and to be visually recorded. This was ensured through verbal agreement of informed consent.

Participants for Stage 1 that required privacy, anonymity or their information kept confidential were not sought. However, pseudonyms were used with information provided by participants in the one-to-one interviews, the focus group discussions and questionnaires. It was requested that all participants of Stage 2, the focus group discussions, to complete a short questionnaire and provide informed consent to the author/facilitator using data from the questionnaire and data from the group discussions, directly associated with the speaker or not. Participants were also asked for informed consent for the raw audio and visually recorded data to be used. Once consensual agreement had been made, it was agreed that all data be stored indefinitely by the researcher. Participants were informed that the data from the interviews were to be used for the research and research dissemination purposes only unless further consensual agreement was made to allow the data to be used for other purposes. A clause of this being that a request was made that

---

[10]Refreshments, such as water and snacks, during the interview and discussion stages were provided.

data could be documented and published as part of the research indefinitely and that the data and photographs become the proprietary rights of the researcher.

The possibility was provided for interviewees and participants to opt out during the interview stage for any particular question/s that the participants were unwilling to have recorded and/or used in the study.[11]

Overall, by having all the appropriate safeguards in place, to the best of my ability and knowledge, this study did not have any psychologically or emotionally harmful effects on anyone involved. Although the multi-media presentation was purposely altered, because the actual information was truthfully revealed during the same time-period, it was not found to have any negative effects on the participants. The participants were informed of the theme of the research beforehand; consequently, all ethical issues of concern were mitigated for to the best of my ability. Though unlikely, it is considered that if any negative effects were to have occurred, they would have been be greatly outweighed by positive effects.

A further concluding ethical consideration was the personal positioning of the researcher. It is plausible that because of my personal situation participants might have been reluctant to provide wholly honest answers to the questions for fear that it might offend the researcher. Conversely, it is also plausible that participants perceived themselves in a more neutral setting that facilitated them to be able to more outwardly express and self-reflect on their personal views on a topic that might otherwise be unspoken. As facilitator, I endeavoured to answer any questions pertinent and relevant to the research topic. Where necessary and where related to the theme of the research my personal circumstance was explained to participants. When queries relating to the origins or ethnicity of me were made, I, as facilitator, attempted to accommodate them from my subjective perspective. Where necessary, I openly provided personal opinions in relation to the research topic but kept it at a minimal level so as not to unduly influence the discussions.

A final consideration was that I as author continually sought to incorporate the raw data into the thesis with the clear endeavour to keep a required constituent of a Grounded Theoretical approach, 'the participant's voice and meaning present in the theoretical outcome' (Charmaz, 1995, 2001; Mills et al., 2006). Thus, by emphasizing both facilitator and participants as contributors to the reconstruction of the finalized

> Grounded Theory model, my ethical obligation, to 'describe the experiences of others in the most faithful way possible' (Munhall, 2001, p. 540) could be seen as fulfilled to the best of my ability. Furthermore, even within such an interpretive framework, the study was conducted without compromising on the capacity of the researcher to analyse the data with as much of a degree of impartiality as is possible.

---

[11] Although one participant from one of the focus group discussions was unable to attend the discussion to completion, all participants were agreeable and amenable to answering all the questions posed and allowing me to use all the information as requested.

Limitations and Reflections

As the study detailed in this book was conducted taking into account a strategy that incorporated a reflexive element and several stages involving numerous contributions, it was pertinent that a flexible approach be taken so as not to discredit the overall design expectations. Thus, the main hurdle encountered initially related to both the recruitment of interviewees and participants for the discussions and questionnaires. It was found that in recruiting individuals for the multi-media presentation, all of the interviewees had more complex backgrounds and histories than were initially expected and categorized. Instead of subtracting from the research, this provided additional depth and was deemed a beneficial influence to the end product, as well as the study overall. Scrutinized further, it is indicative of the true complexities of individuals' circumstances, which are not coherently or adequately reflected in legislation, social policy or even people's perceived notions of *Irishness*, including my own. It became a reaffirmation of the underlying uniqueness of each and every human being. As Parekh (2000) contends, though perhaps overly simplistic, it is not a totally mistaken assumption to concede that 'human beings are naturally unique and that human uniqueness somehow underwrites moral and cultural diversity' (p. 43). In relation to the four interviewees for instance, none had resided exclusively in Ireland for the duration of their lives, yet all had differing circumstances relating to the legislative criteria for Irish citizenship, either prior or post the 2004 ICR.

It was anticipated that there would be significant interest in public debate on 'Irish' identity, yet turnout was poorer than expected. The limitation of this also was that those that participated showed an active interest in civic involvement and generally expressed a personal interest in the wider issues relating to identity. In the consideration of the recruitment of participants for the main stage, numerous agencies and organizations were canvassed as well as gatekeepers, such as the Dublin City Council. Nonetheless, canvassing campaigns and meetings with organization representatives proved to be unfruitful for the most part.

I describe a component of the research methodology, as well as the thesis synthesis as proactively attempting to mitigate gender bias. Nonetheless, a further limitation was that it did not take into account the diverse gendered orientations that exist and as such, limited the analysis of gender as an influencing factor that might shape differences in notions of *Irishness* as perceived by individuals. Furthermore, participants' sexual orientation, or potentially more importantly participants' perceptions on sexuality, was not explored. The inclusion of such probing may have unembellished either complementary views concerning the more labile socially constructed nature of identity, as perceived by participants in Ireland, and/or it may have simply exposed certain paradoxical conditions. A further concern relates to the dominance of contributions from male participants which inevitably had a greater influence in determining not only projected perceived notions of *Irishness* but also the overall outlook of

'Irish' identity that may have become somewhat male-centrically constructed.[12] Generally however, in gender binary terms, there was relatively adequate balance both within and between all of the one-to-one interviews and the focus group discussions.

Moving on from this chapter on methodology, and the previous chapters that discursively provide an overview on literature and research pertaining to *Irishness*, directly and less explicitly, the succeeding chapters present empirical data obtained in thematic sequence. Chapter 5 focusses attention on perceptions of being 'Irish'. It descriptively details being 'Irish'. In keeping with the sequence of discussion on identity formation, as presented in the initial chapters, and so as to maintain a level of procedural integrity as described above, the themes are described in a direct and relatively unprejudiced manner. The themes in the first findings and results chapter commence with family and in an interrelated succession develop to describe home, genealogical lineage, clan, feudalism and community, as perceived by participants of the study.

---

[12]Where possible the researcher attempted to moderate such effects and take into account concerned raised by Oakley (1981, 2016) about 'the complex political and social relationship between researcher and researched' (p. 195).

Appendix 1. Focus Group Discussion Pre- and Post-viewing Questions

Focus Group Discussion Questions
Pre-viewing Questions for Participants:
Ethnicity:
1. What are the characteristics of *Irishness*?
2. How would you describe a distinctive Irish ethnicity (way of life, society)?

Identity:
3. What does it mean to be 'Irish'? (Elicit if being born in Ireland is essential.)
4. How do you personally identify with *Irishness*?

Citizenship:
5. What are the criteria for being 'Irish'? (Elicit if Irish decent is essential.)
6. Who is entitled to be an 'Irish' citizen?

Post-viewing Questions for Participants:
A. Having viewed the presentation, have you any comments you would like to make?
B. Do you have any additional outlook from what you said prior to viewing the presentation?
C. What makes someone 'Irish'?
D. What is the difference between being 'Irish' and being an Irish citizen, do you think?
E. Of those interviewed, two people were born in Ireland and two were not, do you think being born in Ireland is an essential criterion for being 'Irish', why/ why not?
F. Of those interviewed, one person has no link by descent to Ireland and one person has mixed descent. Do you think having Irish decent is an essential criterion for being 'Irish', Why/why not?
G. How can someone become Irish?

Reveal that the information I provided has been switched
(Elicit what that reveals about participant's presumptions about identity)

Appendix 2. Focus Group Discussion Additional Post-viewing Questions

Additional questions (AQ) developed that were informed by the Preliminary Phase/pilot study

1. *Universal and democracy based on liberal multiculturalism*
   (a) How would you describe 'liberal democracy' (or liberal and democracy)?
   (b) What are your opinions of *multiculturalism*?
   (c) *How do you see European governance in relation to Irish governance?*
2. *The criteria for Irish citizenship*
   (a) What helps ground you or what might disturb your sense of identity?
   (b) Please describe if and how you feel influenced by things around you, media, etc.
   (c) How would you allocate citizenship (taking into consideration the multimedia presentation viewed)?
3. *Mythical representations of* Irishness
   (a) *Do you know about the outcomes of the 2004 Irish Citizenship Referendum?*
   (b) *If so, what is your opinion of them?*
   (c) *Are you aware of other legislation that affects access to the provisions of the state, if so, please tell me about them?*
4. *Autonomous and progressive self-constitution*
   (a) *How might we re-imagine identity in the 21st century?*
   (b) How would you describe your sense of belonging?
   (c) *Would you consider alternative understandings of citizenship and, if so, what might they be (i.e. what would be the criteria)?*

96 *Redefining* Irishness *in a Globalized World*

Chapter 5

Participants' Perceptions of Being 'Irish'

Keywords: Home; family; cultural transmission; genealogy; clan; belonging; parochialism; community; begrudgery; feudalism

The purpose of this, and the following findings chapters, is to explore information pertaining to perceived *Irishness* that emerges from the transcribed material documented from the recordings taken of the eight focus group discussions. When describing the characteristics of *Irishness*, both the behavioural and the physical were discussed, the primary focus, however, being the behavioural and attitudinal. 'Irish' identity is viewed from the micro- to macro-level of social interaction and behaviour. The aim of this introductory results and findings chapter focusses primarily, though not exclusively, on participants' perceptions of being 'Irish'. It details emergent themes that arose during the discussions in a fluid and coherent manner. The chapter progresses by describing in sequence notions associated with the central themes of family, clan, parochialism and community.

The importance of the role of the direct family in identity formation is prevalent throughout. Leading from this, discussion of the perceived role of the mother emerges. Hereditary links and the wider family links with 'Irish' identity are discussed. Home is presented as a central theme connected to family. This chapter then continues by linking conceptions of family, wider family and genealogical lineage, with notions of clan. Clan lineage is seen to extend back to pre-medieval times which connects with perceived views on social life, in the past. The notions of grudge and *begrudgery* are associated with feudalistic social life and feudal conflict. Evolving from the collective sense of clan and feudalistic allegiances, though perhaps not through expansion, is localized *parochialism*. The closing main theme discussed is community, within the subtext of traditional and rural Irish life.

Immediate Family, Cultural Transmission and Sacrifice

According to Inglis (2008),

> the question of sameness and difference lies at the heart of social life ... the most fundamental of these begins with seeing and understanding ourselves and other members of our family, clan, group, community or nation as similar, and others as different (p. 5).

It is, thus, fitting to commence the findings from such a position. Consistent among most discussions was the topic of family (as recognized among the interviewees). The importance of family cannot be understated in relation to what people deem as important to them and also with regard to identity formation. This is evidenced in the responses both by the interviewees from the one-to-one interviews and by participants from the focus group discussions. Carroll sums up this in the post-viewing comment, 'I think what was interesting though was the, eh, similarities, like of the four, kind of quite diverse people, like all more or less said that their family or somebody in their family was most important to them.'

One aspect of family exhibited is in reference to the immediate family of participants and the internal behaviours, everyday habits and relationships expressed. Family is seen as a mechanism whereby more nuanced cultural aspects of everyday life are taught and learnt naturally. Similarly, for Byrne and O'Mahony (2012, p. *60f.*), family was historically and is associated with stability and connectedness. In the Drumcondra focus group discussion, Eddie quite insightfully acknowledges that, '... culture tends not to be a taught subject as it were, [it's] like something you absorb from your family, your friends, your relations, the people around you.'

Tony describes what it means to be 'Irish' and expresses how *Irishness* within the family is reproduced and the forms it takes through socialization and familial choices.

Tony: It's funny you know, 'cos choosing language, I know Molly and me have probably a similar decision making process, choosing the language option and the kind of music option and the, the learning option in my family, I found was – and not choosing Catholicism was extremely important, I had no relationship with the church neither do my children

This control over specific forms of re/production of 'Irish' identity within the immediate family, even relative to wider family circles, is also evidenced at later stages within the discussions. Noteworthy is the importance of religious choice or non-choice (see below).

Dale describes how she personally identifies with *Irishness*: she has ascribed an association with *Irishness* to her sons and later how she, habitually through her lifestyle, creates a sense of everyday normality to being 'Irish'.

Dale:	I gave my two boys Irish names ...
YB:	Are they Irish, like Gaelic Irish names, or?
Dale:	Well like Donal and Aodhan,[1] but Aodhan is spelt the Irish way, (pause) em, (pause), I cook traditional Irish dinners, like bacon, cabbage and stew and stuff like that, they're my favourite dinners, and I like Irish music, rebel songs now not the country songs

This seems suggestive of an order of importance in relation to identifying with *Irishness*; the continuation of family, maintaining traditional cultural habits, as well as proscriptive and prescriptive norms (Coleman, 1990, p. 247), such as those that underline the traditional family role of the mother, and those for preserving personal association with nationalistic sentiments and sentimentalities.

This aspect of personally identifying with *Irishness* through family and habitual behaviours is also referred to by Dana in the Clondalkin focus group. Dana feels she is very family orientated and considers that she and her family 'would be very family-ish'. For instance, Dana refers to her family life complementing media programmes which portray the family congregating on special occasions such as Christmas.

In the Drumcondra focus group discussion, Carroll provides a slightly different account; however, Carroll has similar thoughts on the perceived importance of immediate family on cultural transmission. Although Carroll describes how having parents of different nationalities can complicate what might be deemed as essential criteria for being 'Irish', she feels an obligation to appreciate her mother's Scottish identity.

Carroll:	So I feel like I have to be part of that, to, recognise her ordinary life or whatever, and that part of my family
Eddie:	Well that's a different, it's a different if you like, culture too
Carroll:	There's a lot of similarities but it's different you know
Eddie:	Similar, but it's a different culture, and ...
Carroll:	Yeah, and you have to acknowledge that's part of you
Eddie:	Well, you can only, you can only acknowledge it but ... it, it is part of you ... it's part of who you are
Carroll:	I feel, if you weren't saying it, or you weren't part of it and my kids weren't born in Scotland but I take them back once a year, you know my family there, you know, where capable ... because I think it's part of ... my mother coming through, kind of thing, you know

Not only does this extract of conversation suggest an element of innateness in cultural diffusion through direct family lines, but also it indicates an obligation towards a sense of continuity and longevity that is trans-generational. It seems similar to White's (2008) suggestion that 'Irish identity exists based on the accumulated legacy of previous generations and how they are interpreted today by the

---

[1]The names Donal and Aodhan are pseudonyms for Dale's son's names.

inhabitants of the island' (p. 84). The comments also imply a level of assumed factuality of a familial or bloodline innateness associated with national identity, although such perceived notions do not overtly consider White's (2008) summation who continues, 'thus, the search for blood origins is as fruitless in the Irish context as it is in other historical analyses of the origins of nations' (p. 84).

Within the Drogheda focus group discussion, according to what is documented on the factsheet handed out, Izabela self-subscribes as Romanian (see Table 2). Having lost Izabela's own job in Romania and migrated to Ireland to start a new life, Izabela considers that 'of course' Izabela and Izabela's children are Romanian. This is challenged by several of the other participants who question whether the temporal longevity of exposure to Irish culture and being brought up in Ireland will affect Izabela's children's sense of identity.

Toben: That's fine, but you are assuming your children will be Romanian ...
Izabela: Yeah I speak in Romanian in the house, I, I spoke with my children about Romanian history, I
Toben: No, I understand that, when your children grow up ... to a certain age ... and they want to identify with a country ... will you be surprised if the kids (choose to be Irish)?
Izabela: I'm not sure, I'm not sure, if you eh, if you, speak with your children, about your country, not every day, but constantly and you, if you visit your country, your family there, because my mother will be Romanian, my brothers, my, my mother-in-law, all my family is in Romania, and I don't forget
Toben: No yeah, I understand that

What is emphasized is how Izabela self actively transmits cultural information and exposure to members of Izabela's own immediate family so as to intentionally shape the development of Izabela's children's identity in a way that may differ from being 'Irish'. The fact that Izabela recognizes the self-requirement to proactively do this suggests that either the children themselves, though more likely their surrounding exposure to Irish society, will impinge on Izabela's wishes by influencing Izabela's children's sense of identity. Although Izabela is adamant to remain Romanian, like Toben, Irena feels that longevity and exposure might change how Izabela self-identifies by later stating following from the conversation above, 'it's impossible you know, because you grow old with this country ...' Izabela's desires to maintain strong connections with Romania seem to complement what Inglis and Donnelly (2011) recognize: 'people may move around the world, they may be open to change and other people, but they also identify strongly with and remain attached to the place in which they grew up' (p. 128*f.*).

What also seems worthy of attention is the manner in which the role of women in the family is described and stressed within several of the focus group discussions and also by the last interviewee, Kevin. Continuing from Kelsey's historical account of pre-colonial Ireland as a more matriarchal kind of society, in the Clondalkin focus group, Dana compounds family and home with a description of the mother.

Dana: But the woman like the, everyone like actually, there's, like talks about the typical Irish mother like ... where the Irish mother does everything for, in the family home and all ... yeah like it's actually like the, even do you ever see like the Royle family, like the tv series like and it's all, like they (slight pause) ... it's an English programme like, but it's based on like the writer was, she was like, had Irish parents or whatever like, so it was eh, it was, like the woman in it is based on an Irish mother, like she does absolutely everything like ... like the man does nothing like and she doesn't complain or anything like, the woman, like she raises the kids and what not but like your man from Iraq never, just said his da like, the, his mother never came into it at all like, and I bet yea she raised him and all like

There are intersecting aspects being discussed in this excerpt of conversation relating to reinforcing gender roles, media influence and perceived cultural specificities that may be influenced by the class perspective of the contributing participants of this focus group discussion. In this instance, evidenced is the interplay between culture and family. As Gilroy (1990) describes 'culture is reductively conceived and is always primarily and "naturally" reproduced in families' (p. 114). Further to this, Dana seems to be almost idealizing her notion of the Irish mother as possessing natural care giving characteristics to manage and maintain the proper functioning of family life. By pointing out that the interviewee, Dijwar, with an Iraqi background didn't refer to the maternal side of Dijwar's own family in the multi-media production, Dana seems to assume that his mother must have been his primary carer. Interestingly, such a *universalized* assumption could be understood in contradiction with the supposed uniqueness of the strong, hard-working yet caring Irish mother.

The role of the mother in the family is also discussed in the Limerick focus group discussion. Initially, in response to the contribution made by the interviewee Kevin in relation to a general desire by most, irrespective of nationality, creed, 'race' and religion, wanting to live peaceful and content lives, the response by the discussant Charlie is to say, 'I think that most people's lives are caught up with, with eating, working and rearing families.' The conversation then slightly shifts towards Irish society, indicative of the participant's desire to promote the prominence of motherhood in Irish society more specifically.

Charlie: And getting on, I think, you know about the Irish, going back centuries, emigrated, one thing is they did work and I think that comes from, it's like mothers go[ing] back centuries here, they always wanted their children to get on, it was nearly, they would starve ... and save money to educate their children, and that is, I don't know whether it is in other cultures, but it is definitely in the Irish culture
Juliana: That it's well worth not spending money on the parents, we'll say, they wouldn't spend it on themselves but they would use it
Adrian: They would yes
Charlie: To put their children to have a better standard of living

This historical recognition of sacrifice and hard work for the benefit of the succeeding generation, particularly by the mother and parents, is quite revealing. On the one hand, it provides the sense that in Irish society, although under colonial rule, such behaviour would have challenged the hierarchical order of governance. When compared with the more stratified society of Britain, perhaps what is assumed is that the Irish needed to think more strategically about labour and climbing the social ladder, whereas within the aristocratic or bourgeois strata of British society, social positions were assumed fixed.

An alternative way in which the comments made above might be interpreted, in relation to parental sacrifice, might be that it complements the ethos of *Roman-Catholicism*. Furthermore, within the context of the preceding conversation, such an elevated valuing of parental sacrifice is seen as contrasting with other cultures which are perceived to have less of an ethos of hard work, familial care and education. If the latter were the case, by presenting what may be a partial view of Irish society, it could be interpreted as quite *ethnocentric*. In ways, what emerges is that, through differentiation and emphasis on 'insider' cultural values and norms, the member constructs their perspective that is *ethnocentric* and lacks an empathic view of the differentiated other either within or beyond Irish society. This notion is developed later in Chapter 7.

Wider Family as a Lineage to *Irishness* and Notions of Home

Another way in which family is described is how, more broadly, family provides the bridge between the individual and Irish collective. Being born into the family innately fixes the individual to Irish society. Family, or more specifically having family lineage in Ireland, is considered to be a primary differentiating factor between being 'Irish' and being an Irish citizen. (This aspect is developed further below in the description of becoming Irish, *jus sanguinus* citizenship.) Ryan describes the difference between being 'Irish' and being an Irish citizen by stating: 'I think being Irish maybe suggests you have em, maybe a lineage way, there could be time, so you'd have lines say family, family before that, family before that in various ... different parts of Ireland.'

Similarly, although Kelsey states that she was born in Great Britain, in describing if being born in Ireland is an essential criterion for being 'Irish', or not, Kelsey justifies her own position in relation to her wider family circumstance.

Kelsey: I was born in Birmingham and I would consider myself Irish, like I, lived over here and then I came back a few weeks later, or a couple of months later and I would, I'm, like my whole family's Irish, my aunties and me uncles, me grannie and me granddad, I wasn't born in Ireland and I can get that dual passport scenario as well, but, I am Irish so I'm gonna stick with my Irish passport, so yeah I'm no, I wasn't born in the Coombe or the Rotunda like you guys but, (slight pause) I think I'm Irish, do you consider me Irish?... Brady is shaking his head, like, 'I can't, she's not Irish' (laughter) ...

Dana: I never [hear] him say it again
Kelsey: [what] would you think Dana?
Dana: I don't know, it's like your whole family's Irish but you weren't born there and you live here, that's, that's Irish like ... but like if you, if your ma and da are Irish but you grew up in England the whole time then you'd probably consider yourself English like

Both Kelsey and Dana recognize longevity or the temporal dimension of exposure to a specific society as trumping connections that one might have through family (this is later contradicted below in the Limerick group conversation). Kelsey asserts her right to be considered 'Irish' by virtue of lineage. However, more nuanced aspects also emerge in relation to the micro-social interaction that occurs.

Although, as stated, Kelsey self-subscribes as being 'Irish', she seeks the approval of this from the other participants in the focus group discussion and even jokes at the idea that one of her peers might not be so forthcoming because of stances taken previously in the conversation. By being ambivalent and initially stating as a response to Kelsey's inquiry 'I don't know ...' Dana quite subtly elevates her status as superior to her peer but then affords and ascribes to Kelsey the right to self-claim to be 'Irish'. With the knowledge of Kelsey's life history differing from what might be perceived as the norm, this provides others the slightest of opportunities to differentiate, thus shifting power dynamics, which ultimately create subtle inequitable relations. This exemplifies the link between 'power-knowledge' and discourse in the creation of manners of self-policing among the population, as alluded to by Foucault (1977).

As an aspect of how someone can become Irish, Tony briefly mentions, 'having a family here'. However, after viewing the presentation, it was acknowledged in the Belfast focus group discussion that family was barely mentioned in relation to *Irishness*.

Molly: but they touched on things we didn't even touch on, we didn't even [talk] about community, about family, em, you know grandparents and that thing, they touched on that which is very close to us, not just
Tony: well, it goes without saying doesn't it?
Reagan: [...] you look at the start where, you know, where they were ... talking about community, family you know, (pause) that's everybody's different perspective on what Irishness is and what their citizenship is

Molly appears to highlight the importance of the intergenerational aspect of family in relation to *Irishness* and its integral link with locality and community (developed further below), to which Reagan responds in a way that could infer that family is so integrally bound with *Irishness* that it does not need to be stated. Reagan's subsequent comment seems to acknowledge the multivariate ways in which *Irishness*, as well as Irish citizenship can be perceived subjectively.

The assumption which may be held generally is that family is a core transmitter of particular value systems in terms of specific ethical and moral positions (as introduced above). In one instance, the impression is that the excuse of family connection trumping lived experience is rejected, as Reagan describes, '... I think of my cousin, he was born in London, grew up and moved to Canada but his mother's Irish ... but he still says that he's, he has Irish family, yet, he'd never lived in Ireland in all his life (pause).' At a later point, when describing how someone can self-subscribe to being 'Irish', Tony seems to emphasize family as a factor justifying any claim to being 'Irish' by stating, '... most progressive people wouldn't have a problem with you saying I'm (an) Irish person, I can live here, I have family here ...'. However, in relation to this, what is particularly revealing within the Belfast focus group discussion is the participants' recognition of their own position within their immediate family. With regards to changing views, with perhaps the rejection of parental standpoints and the suggestion of how this might reflect broader social change, here, the participant Tony is discussing the rejection of traditional religious belief and choice of language.

Tony: Oh yeah, I'm in the minority in my family
Molly: So am I
Tony: There's no, I mean, I've got sixty-one cousins, sixty-two cousins and em, I would be the only one, one of them that is raising their kids as atheists ... last count one girl who's eighteen and one who is eight, so there is no atheists in my family
Molly: There's no atheists, no socialists, no feminists in mine so
Tony: And I'm the only Irish speaking family out of all of those, so we are atheists and Irish speaking ... and the rest are catholic and English speaking

This exchange and disclosure suggests a broader desire to actively differentiate from 'others' not only outside one's kin but importantly to differentiate away from the dominant position of their respective family group members, at least in relation to religion, political view, language affiliation or considerations of gender norms. What also emerges is that language, in the view of the participants, is a key attribute of a distinctive *Irishness*. Adopting Irish language seems to be a means of differentiation and a process of 'self-othering' away from his family group. One could infer too that Irish language is viewed in Bourdieusian terms as a form of *cultural* or *linguistic capital* that provides greater authenticity to claims of *Irishness* than merely the ability to speak English (as discussed below and in Chapter 9).[2]

Such a leaning towards Irish language does not seem to be purely about communicating, understanding and deciphering, but expressly language, as overtly described above, is an instrument of action or power (Bourdieu, 1977b, p. 645). In its contemporary form, it goes beyond *national parallelism* associated with Celtic revivalism (De Frëine, 1978, pp. 51–52; Kiberd, 1995, p. 265; Tovey et al., 1989, p. 16), as it is not simply the countering of one language over another but

---

[2] For more on language, Irish (American) ethnicity and Bourdieusian concepts of *Capital*, please refer to Sullivan (2016).

rather capitalizing off both English and Irish proficiency. The acquisition of Irish language expands beyond linguistic competence to become a form of *linguistic capital* for the individual. As discussed in Chapter 2, Lee (1989, p. 665) refers to a certain paradox which existed within Irish *cultural revivalism* and the utilitarian retention of English language. What is evidenced in contemporary times is a shift from justifications based on the ideology of cultural revival and preservation that has slipped towards the more economic and *neoliberal* based rationale on *cultural capital*. Nonetheless, speaking Irish language is a matter of choice and exposure, unlike more supposedly innate constructed identifiers, such as physiological traits, which means one of the qualities of the Irish language is its potential as a more inclusive, rather than exclusive or divisive, form of identifier.

One of the driving forces that influenced Dale's desire to have her family repatriate to Ireland from Britain is seen as the desire to be closer to all of Dale's wider family in Ireland. Although having been raised in England, an association with Ireland as home is made through both experience of visiting Ireland on holidays and cultural exposure to people from within the Irish emigrant community in England. Unlike the assumption that is mentioned earlier in the Clondalkin focus group discussion (see above), longevity of stay in Britain does not seem to have had an impact on Dale's sense of self-identification; family and the idea of home seem to influence more powerfully Dale's choice of affiliation.

Dale: [...] so all my mother's friends were Irish, all my friends over there, they, their parents were Irish, every holiday we've ever had as a child was in Ireland, we would holiday twice a year, then we moved over here and I was like, I was actually the one who made my mother come home, I begged her, 'please I wanna go home, back home, cos over there'

Maebh: You call it home even though you were always in England ...

Dale: Do-yea-know so, em, because I, but my father was very over protective of me over in England and we'd been mugged a few times and stuff like that, and I don't blame him like, but when I came here I had so much freedom and all our family were over here and I love them dearly like, you know, my cousins, and even my friends then that I was friends with back then in nineteen ninety six when we were on holidays, they're my best friends still here now in Ireland, like, do-yeah – no so ... I just love it here

There seems to be a real sense of association of the notion of home with family and friendship even though Dale spent most of her younger formative years in England, which she might have referred to equally as home, yet didn't. Home, family and friendships seem to combine to provide the emotional justification to love being 'Irish' in Ireland.

Parentage, family and home, as well as the importance of language, are also interrelated in an anecdotal account provided by Machie in the Drogheda focus group discussion. In this instance, the anecdotal account provided is somewhat inverted because they are being looked at within the African context.

Machie: I know an Irish guy, I met him eh, in a night spot, an Irish guy, he's white, he's an Irish guy... and he turns to me and says 'are you from Nigeria?' 'Yes, I'm from Nigeria' and he starts to speak my language to me, like one of the languages ... and I looked at him like, 'hang on a sec., where does this guy come from?' and he told me that yeah, he told me that he was actually born in Nigeria, he was born in the Northern part of Nigeria, his whole family was there

YB: Ok

Machie: [For example] the American guy, and he was born in Nigeria but he's an Irish person so he's not relating to the fact that even though his parents are Irish, he's now living here, but we were, he thinks Africa is, 'oh yeah Africa is home, you know that's where I'm from' but he's still Irish, I would see him and say he's an Irish person straight away, but he says, on his passport he is from Nigeria and since when a situation like that, even up to today, there are a lot of people that now that ah, from a certain (long pause) diaspora ...

Family, sense of home, the acquisition and proficiency of a specific language, place of birth and the possession of Nigerian citizenship are described. What appears evident as a key determining factor to allow the subject to be considered Nigerian relates to a person's outward appearance. Although when the question is posed to Machie, as to whether such a person can ever be considered Nigerian, Machie responds with an admission that shifts towards the notion of hybrid identities, by stating, 'in my eyes, yes, he can be Nigerian, there are many Chinese-Nigerians right now, yep'.

Thus identity, as seen from the negotiation of self-subscription by an 'insider' and from the ascription onto the individual by an 'outsider', is seen to be contestable. In fact, the notion of hybridity is challenged within the conversation when Emmanuel interjects to ask, 'did you, did you say, Chinese-Nigerian?' to which Machie responds, 'yeah' and Emmanuel concludes quite categorically, 'that means they're not Nigerian'. This rejection, of even the ascription of a hybrid identity, reinforces what might be implied from Machie's comment; that a hybrid identity does not equate equally to what is perceived as a purer form of singular national identity (further discussed in Chapter 7). It seems to be a definitive rejection and closing off of what Bhabha (1990a, p. 211; 1990b, p. 189) describes as a 'third space which enables other positions to emerge'. Emmanuel adamantly rejects the notion of this third space where new negotiations of the meaning of representation might create unique identities by displacing the histories that constitute them (Bhabha, 1990a, p. 211; 1990b, p. 189).

Friendliness, one of the attributed characteristics of *Irishness*, emerged during the discussion on family and home in the Drogheda focus group discussion. As most of the participants have migrated to Ireland, it gives them a unique perspective on such topics. Although the conversation is initiated by a person who perceives himself and would likely be perceived as Irish, Diarmuid is quite cautious in his opening remarks and distances himself from the viewpoint of the Irish being particularly friendly.

Diarmuid: From the tourists I've spoken to they say the Irish are particularly friendly ...

Irena: But for example for me, I think that home for them is like just like a case, my home is my castle, and it's very difficult to go inside the home when you are a stranger, for them, when you are a closer friend, it's ok, but yet now when you are a stranger, and you are not very close, home is closed you know ... you're friendly on the street

Izabela: Yes on the street, in the park ... but home is, is closed for strangers

Dillon: This is probably why the pub is a hub ... because people don't tend to use their homes to entertain as much as, in South Africa you had more at home you know ... your friends would visit you -

Izabela: I think ... not just with stranger, between Irish

The conversation soon shifts to discussing Christmas and the dynamics of family and home in the Irish context.

Izabela: How it was in Ireland and here in Ireland, nothing happens in Christmas on the street ... it does in the house between the family, but in our country I think the, maybe in France, I'm not sure maybe in France but in Romania, Spain and Nigeria, in Togo, everybody visiting and sing songs and you know

There is a clear distinction made here between Irish cultural activities at the season of Christmas, in comparison with other countries of which the participants have firsthand experience and knowledge. Home seems to be more clearly demarcated into the private sphere and is not shared beyond family. The public space, particularly the public house, is designated as an alternative location for socializing with friends and acquaintances beyond family.

Overall, identity is closely bound with that of parental influence on cultural transmission and the transference of specific value systems which occurs during a child's development within the family. Although the notion of family may be perceived as the basic unit of social organization, it may not be the primary influencing factor on identity formation. The social construction of how one self-identifies and is identified by others would seem to rely on how one frames one's own perceived position in relation to a combination of family, home, locality and community. Certainly with changing and more diverse family structures, one would expect that a child's development of core aspects of their identity will occur through socialization beyond the family. That is to say, institutions, such as education and friendship, are likely also to play an increased influence on an individual's self-identification.

Genealogical Lineage and Clan

Relevant to the topic of family and genealogical lineage is the notion of clan. In the Clondalkin focus group discussion, a distinctive Irish ethnicity is somewhat ironically joked about in association with family names. Names identify an individual

108 Redefining Irishness *in a Globalized World*

as belonging to an identifiably Irish family. Linking in with the notion of family, names and cultural transmission (discussed above), family names are described as symbolizing descent from an Irish clan. Being 'a Murphy, O'Connor, O'Brien' (Kelsey) appears to connect the individual to a sense of 'traditional' *Irishness*.

Kelsey: It's like, you just like saying, 'well you're obviously like em, a brand of Irish' like there's no sort of (slight pause) international in there like, I'm [Kelsey's own surname], that's kind a German so like I'm obviously like some sort of in, like outbred

Cillian: An outbred (laughter)

Kelsey: Like your Scottish name, you're like outbred (referring to Dana's name), Kathleen you're screwed (laughter) ...

Dana: Yeah, it's like em, yeah if you were like a Murphy or something it's like you've been Irish like for like hundreds and thousands of years or something... that's what people would probably say ... whereas if you had a name that was outside Ireland, you'd be like, 'ah well maybe your grandparents came over ... on a boat or something' (slight laughter) (pause)

YB: So how would you describe that distinctive Irish ethnicity then?

Kelsey: Well you can kind a say like, 'oh he's Murphy', or whatever (slight laughter) ... so you can say like, well obviously he's a descendant from like an Irish clan ... where like I might've (slight pause), like I mean I'm kind of more of a Norwegian brand, kind of brought over, so like I'm kind of, I was probably more, I was probably a Viking, like my ancestors (laughter) ... and it is that I, I actually have more of a Viking ancestral, where Murphy would be more of an Irish clan'

Christine: A true Celt kind a, isn't it?

Brady: Celt yeah

Kelsey: Yeah, don't know (slight laughter) ... and if you're like, say your name was like Conor, like you dropped the 'O' like, so you took the 'C' (slight laughter) ... do-yea-know what I mean? (slight laughter) ... I don't know what I do, trying to judge people by names, do you know like

In this instance, clan is not only seen as a grouping of people within the current timeframe; it has connotations of longevity over an historical epoch, is seen as trans-generational and seems quite situated within a fixed time and the geographical space of Ireland. Synonymous with notions of being a member of an Irish clan is the idea that, one is affiliated with Ireland over multiple generations going back to pre-Christian times. Apparently, family name becomes a label or an identifier of a person's association with the perceived notion of a consanguineous relation, kinsman or clan. In this context, notions of family and clan match certain interpreted definitions of kinship as being reliant on 'irreducible genealogical connections' (Fortes, 1969, p. 52; Strathern, 1973, p. 21). By self-referencing as 'an outbred' because Kelsey doesn't necessarily possess such a family name, and instead possesses a name that may have come from abroad, Kelsey is self-conceived as somewhat of an 'outsider' and differentiates from 'others' that might be members of an Irish clan, legitimated through their surname.

In the Coolock focus group discussion, the connection between family and clan is reiterated in direct relation to the participants' own lives. Although taking place in response to conversation on the Traveller community, it is implied more generally to include the settled community.

Aileen: But I think that that sense of clan goes through families, you know, whether traveller or not in Ireland, we in our family, this year, now not my family but my cousins, they had five new babies this year, everyone's delighted because it makes our clan stronger
Tierney: Yeah, you're right
Aileen: You know, it reinforces our clan ... makes us stronger like you know

In this extract of conversation, family and clan seem to be compounded into one, almost making them synonymous. The slight distinction rests between what might be the immediate family and the extended family. The sense that a numerical increase of offspring within the clan group strengthens and reinforces the clan would seem to emphasize the importance of bloodline connections and imply a greater loyalty based on wider familial interconnections.

Clan, Feudalism and Grudges

A positive characteristic that emerges is the notion of loyalty and also the sense of *kinship paternalism*. Clan is seen as a very important characteristic of *Irishness* and according to Emmet, 'family is at the root of everything that we are really'. In contrast to this, a further aspect of family is initially introduced in the Coolock focus group discussion within a thread of conversation that commences with 'grudge' (or *begrudgery*). Similarly, Inglis (2006) flags such a condition within the context of self-indulgence by describing it in Irish culture as the 'habit of putting people down, belittling those who are ambitious and begrudging their success' (p. 34). Although Inglis (2006) attributes it to Catholic culture, self-deprecation and self-denial, in this instance, the sense of the Irish having a propensity towards begrudging 'others' is related to the association with family feuds, *feudalism* historically and reference to the Travelling community in contemporary society (as introduced immediately above). Seemingly, inter-family grudges are seen as a primary motive for the formation of the clan, *parochialism* and the aspect of wider community life. This would also seem to manifest itself in the participation and spectatorship of sports today.

Tierney: Grudge is a huge part
Grainne: But even the GAA and the parish
Tierney: Go to any wedding in Ireland -
Emmet: So loyalty then
Tierney: There's grudge being played out
Emmet: Loyalty (slight pause)

Grainne: To your community
Peadar: That's the opposite ... the other side of it
Emmet: Well even down to, as you said, communities or, whether the travelling community or even families
Aileen: Or your sporting club or
Emmet: Your loyalty can be split in a family and that can split families for years
Tierney: You're with us or against us
Emmet: Yeah, so loyalty would be yeah something that
Aileen: It's demanded
Conlaoch: But yet there is the 'geish', I mean the, here you have an absolute responsibility for the incidence, if you give birth to a child, you have an absolute responsibility for rearing that child for the rest of their lives and this works to the whole society, the, this is imbedded in our society and there's responsibility for caring for your clan or your people and this is where your grudge comes in

This extract highlights how the participants unanimously consider that the notion of family expands into clan and community. Several participants seem to suggest that this creates conflict because of what they perceive as a primal sense of grudge that ensues with such social formations.

Continuing from this clannish, feuding and grudging perspective of Irish life is the closely related sentiment of *begrudgery* or belittlement. What could be perceived as a negative notion of *Irishness* was barely touched upon in all of the focus group discussions and when discussed by two groups, it was either briefly stated or implied. The notion was directly stated but not given space to be developed or actively continued by the contributor in the Coolock focus group discussion. In partial answer to describing characteristics of *Irishness*, Emmet exclaims, 'we've a great propensity for *begrudgery*' yet it was not followed up nor did other participants refer to it.

In the Drumcondra focus group discussion, a subtle comment is made during the conversation which focuses on becoming Irish. Although when asked about the criteria for being 'Irish', the participants immediately began reflecting on the imaginary 'outsider' wishing to become Irish, and selecting the criteria according to what they perceived would be required for that stranger to enter into being 'Irish'. It is within this context that a subtle reference might be inferred to relate to the specific notion of *begrudgery*.

Ciara: I think if you are Irish, if you adopt the kind of (cough), the kind of traditions of Ireland and the behaviour, like we saw, participation, being willing to talk and share with other people and, kind a fully participate in Irish society, I think that, that makes you Irish, irrespective of where you originally come from, I mean you can have a dual, you can be Irish and Nigerian at the, at the same time I think
Ryan: Yeah ... yes, just not be, too confident

This somewhat flippant remark at the end of the snippet from Ryan is quite significant. It is suggestive of a level of social control. It demands of an individual, in this case the example provided being an Irish-Nigerian which in itself is also quite revealing, that a person must not be too confident as it might evoke in members of society a feeling of *begrudgery* towards the said individual.

The Community that Unifies or a Community of Distinction

Within the Belfast focus group discussion, when 'Irish' identity is stripped back from its more generalized associations such as language, music, family, religion and so on, community is seen as a foundational characteristic. What also becomes evident within this focus group discussion is the particular condition of the Northern Irish context, mainly made relevant to the period prior to the peace agreements.[3] One participant describes how there was a community divide.

Reagan: [There was a] massive divide within rural community where you couldn't go, it's changed now for my children, my children are old teens so they have a different perception of community, they're very em (pause), there wouldn't be a racist bone in their body, they wouldn't be sectarian, they don't even understand the history sometimes, where the people distrust ... each other so much because of differences

It would seem that the historical legacy of the recent conflict in Northern Ireland has imbued the term 'community' with overly negative connotations; yet also as a concept, it seems copper-fastened to identity formation. As is revealed below, the conflicting use of the term 'community', not only within the Belfast focus group discussion but by several other participants, seems to highlight how it reifies difference rather than transcending perceived and constructed notions of difference.

The notion of a singular collective community is more frequently used when statements emphasizing positive collective action are linked to collective functioning.

Positive collective action relates both to the sense of benefits and to reciprocal responsibilities such as support, civic participation and community group action. Positive collective action is, thus, also linked to the more generalized use of community or 'the community'.

For instance, within the Belfast focus group discussion, for 'the community to function', Tony concurs with what is self-perceived as the necessity and importance of a common good by most of the interviewees. From the general conversation, there is an onus of responsibility, not just for an individual's self-development but also for the community. In answer to how someone can become Irish, along

---

[3] According to the Irish Department of Foreign Affairs and Trade (DFA, 2016), 'the Good Friday Agreement is the cornerstone of our commitment to peace and stability on this island. It was agreed on 10 April 1998 and overwhelmingly approved in two referendums in both parts of Ireland in May 1998.'

with living, working and having family in Ireland, Molly states, 'contributing to the community'. Similarly, within the Drumcondra focus group discussion, community is defined in a homogenizing way within Ireland broadly and is related to ideas of assimilation into the Irish collective.

In a post-viewing response, Ryan makes several observations regarding the comments made by the first interviewee Laura and the fourth interviewee Kevin. Ryan presents outlooks additional to what had been said prior to viewing the presentation:

Ryan: The first person was talking about, you know, being, if you want to call it new Irish, or you know identity ... and, you know, about relaxing your fears, em, the challenging problems, identifying them and or ... spotting them, and the last person spoke about participating in community, engaging and contributing to the collective ... I mean they're all, they're all solid to me, reasons or ways of being part of a community is participating in that community, in that collective, I don't even think all Irish people do that so, it is interesting to hear somebody who considers themselves to be new Irish maybe, to, to say that, maybe they've, there's more of a need to do that, to be accepted ... one last thing about identity ... I think generally, there's more of a need, like you need, if you want to be accepted as part of it ... like, being Irish, like you may need to participate more or engage in the true collective, you know ... in a more obvious way, in order to be noticed ... as to say, 'oh ok, you're Irish, you're ok, we'll keep yea'

Ryan refers to the notion of the community and in particular, how certain individuals deemed as members of the collective, may not sufficiently contribute through participation, to the normative wellbeing of society. The concept of 'new Irish' is introduced and described as having a greater onus to perform to the expectations of social organization and order. Ryan goes on to discuss the expectation to participate in what is deemed as 'the true collective' and the act of 'being Irish' (Ryan). This *assimilationist* view is reliant on the notion of the existence of a homogeneous society, as well as a comprehensive understanding of what actually 'being Irish' should or would entail.

Community is also used to manufacture and describe groups as distinct from one another. In contrast, despite the recognition that, '*Irishness* doesn't actually have a colour or a language ...' and as Tony makes an additional comment following the viewing of the presentation by stating '... assimilation, as opposed to integration ... almost depends on the extent to which you have to give things up',[4] he continues to discuss and compare by using community as a means to distinguish between groups:

---

[4] To some degree in this instance, community is interpreted as acting as a locality and social configuration which promotes a *subsumption pathway* (Latham, 2010, p. 191) towards eventual assimilation of individuals or their progeny into its dominant normative values, attitudes and behaviours.

Tony: [...] I mean, I grew up in London and em, the Black community, the West Indian community particularly, it was easy for them to integrate 'cos of all, the white community, because they were Christian, so to a degree, there was less for them to give up, and then they were still black and still suffered desperate racism but when em, the Muslim community started to arrive, in numbers in my area, typical Bangladesh, it was more difficult for them to integrate because [they] weren't Christian, they were black and they were Muslim, do you know what I mean, there's levels of kinds of integration

An informed understanding of racism, disparate groups and their religious affiliations within the society of London is revealed in this extract. In this instance, the use of community is of interest along with how it demonstrates understanding of a community divided which replicates descriptions of the Northern Irish context. Overall, this seems to emphasize perceived differences between groups within society and how conflicting images of what is called community are fabricated by participants.

As Tony later surmizes, 'well yeah, one has responsibilities when they are active members of, em, in a state, to participate in the state I suppose, representation and active in the community'. Tony later recognizes the 'multiplicity of Irish identities' and acknowledges that this may not be as recent a phenomenon as commonly thought.

Tony: Well I mean, the Jewish community was always here of course, you know what I mean? em, but they, we've done them in as well
Molly: The Chinese and Indian communities
Tony: By the war you know
Molly: They've been here fifty, sixty or seventy years, they're not perceived as Irish or their kids aren't perceived as Irish
YB: So you mean –?
Tony: The Asian community in the North has been quite – Indians particularly – it's been depressing

Although evidently within both extracts above, Tony seems to express good intentions and the desire to challenge and overcome racism, Tony continues to describe people in disparate groups according to specific communities. This use of distinction within community is pronounced when considered along sectarian lines also. Community as a distinguisher enters the conversation during a description of divergence whereby it is explained that with the Northern Irish conflict, certain groups supposedly believed they could no longer identify with being 'Irish'.

Molly: [...] protestants, unionists, loyalists community no longer felt they could be Irish because of the Irish Republican Army or the ... so I think the conflict has damaged ... over that period of forty years –

Tony: Irish Unionists from the nineteen-twenties was, and that tradition survived up until the start of the troubles, they don't exist anymore, they're British Unionists now ... their Irish identity has nearly been expunged ... from large bits of the loyalist, unionist community do not consider themselves to have any Irishness at all

Evidenced in this extract of conversation is the description of a disassociation with 'Irish' identity by loyalists and unionists but importantly perhaps also the emergence of a description of people with such affiliations fitting into discrete communities that, as previously described, are separate from the notion of one collective and homogeneous community. This, along with the notion of discrete and segregated communities in relation to what may be deemed as minority groups, suggests that particular identity formations can place an individual within or external to what is perceived as 'the community' which is majority and dominant rather than 'a community'. 'The community' represents one overarching community of contesting groups, similar to the interpretation of culture prescribed by Finlay (2007, p. 342), whilst 'a community' either represents a community of communities, complementing the essence of multiculturalism, or a singular community within the broader social environment. Consequently, the notion of 'the community' seems to act as an identifying term or apparatus of segregation rather than 'a community' which appears to operate more as a harmonizing mechanism within discourse to alleviate somewhat falsely constructed notions of difference.

Nonetheless, community and segregation also manifest themselves beyond such discursive practice mentioned above. In the Drumcondra focus group discussion, Carroll describes the greater need of membership of community when living abroad in answer to what it means to be 'Irish'. This instance supports the apparent notion of association with community and inclusion/exclusion, as is described by Carroll:

Carroll: I only ever felt really Irish when I went away, when I lived and worked away in America or England because I never thought about it before that, never, ever, I remember when I was a teenager – in my nineteen, twenties but, more of an issue for me was, when I was with different people, cos if I was in Ireland then everybody was the same, it didn't matter what you were, but when I was in America or England, it was different, it felt different to be Irish cos it gave some kind of community, and some kind of basis, and some kind of people to be a part of you were like, I never thought about it before I went away, ever

Membership of the Irish community seems to insert one inside a closed and somewhat exclusive collective grouping. But what is also noteworthy is that the necessity for community association seems more definite when abroad, as a reaction to *minoritization*, whereas in Ireland, the assumed default dominant majority positioning is within the Irish community; thus, there is less impetus to self-associate with it. This aspect of being abroad, having a more pronounced sense of *Irishness*, pride and yearning to be associated with the Irish community whilst abroad, as well as the sense of returning 'home' having travelled, is evidenced in most of the focus group discussions and some interviews.[5]

Within the Limerick focus group discussion, community is juxtaposed with parochial sentiment and is perceived as a means of unifying members of society at a local level. Community is presented more positively than *parochialism*, which seems bound to the institution of the church. When society is described as 'parochial' (as evidenced above), a counterargument is given to suggest that a more community-based understanding of local society is a preferred perspective than thinking and referring to local Irish society as parish based. Keeping in mind that the Limerick focus group discussion was hosted at a local family resource centre should provide further clarity to the conversation below.

Maebh: I do think we've good community spirit as well, and someone that lives –

Charlie: Well I think the parish thing came from… what do you call them, did they start fights? …

Adrian: But sure look it

Charlie: […] then the church honed in on the parish, and actually you know what we do every year? it's community based … families, it's very hard to take the parish out of people's mind …

Maebh: Mind-set

Charlie: They have this thing, well it's not really the parish itself … and I mean we cover work in nine or ten parishes … but it's very hard to instil in people that its community based …

Juliana: What we're talking about, and we all understand that … this is called [town name] family resource centre and it's based here … but our catchment area is huge … so what Charlie is saying is that maybe people living in the outlying parishes don't actually recognise this as being their service

The implication from this conversation is that because of a more parochial mind-set that has been instilled in members of the local society, they are less likely to avail of the services being offered to a wider community at the family resource centre. This might be understood more generally to resemble how it can be challenging for the individual psyche to adjust at the same pace to societal changes in organization. Perhaps, a lack of ability in adjustment is not only an unconscious process due to past memory and habitual practice but also due to active resistance on the part of the individuals to concede to such societal alterations, due to allegiances, in this case most likely loyalty to Irish Catholicism. As Inglis (2007) concludes in a study on Catholic identity in contemporary Ireland although religious transformation is taking place through a process of de-institutionalization, 'the majority of Irish Catholics still see and understand themselves as Catholics,

---

[5]For example, Focus Group Discussions Limerick (Q4); Drumcondra (Q3); Naas (Q2); Drogheda (QA); Coolock (QG).

have a strong sense of belonging and loyalty to a Catholic heritage, and accept most of the Church's key teachings and beliefs' (p. 217).

The differentiation and separation between the church and community are also intentionally remarked upon later in the Limerick focus group discussion when it slightly diverges away from a description of the difference between being 'Irish' and being an Irish citizen.

Charlie: [...] being charitable to me has nothing got to do with religion, you can be totally against a (religion) but still (be) very good –
Maebh: [...] you're still a good Christian
Charlie: Ah, in your community and to your fellow human being ... you don't need to be religious

It is plausible that the reason the conversation deviates is because it is an issue of concern for some of the participants which they feel particularly strongly about and would like to vocalize and reiterate their opinion on the matter. Although there is the rejection of the church and most likely the institutions of *Catholicism*, Christian values are still portrayed in a positive light in relation to community life.[6]

An analysis of conversations with the eight focus groups of this study would seem to indicate the perception that traits, which are deemed to characterize *Irishness*, are attained via one's immediate family, which provides the foundational basis for the cultural diffusion of values, attitudes and behaviours and which are reproduced inter-generationally. In addition, the constructed descriptions of participants would appear to portray immediate family and Irish family life in an idealized, romanticized and enduring fashion. These views, reliant on nostalgia, seem to conflict with significant societal changes that have occurred, specifically a growing independence of the marital unit with probably fewer kinship ties to distant relatives. On the one hand, motherhood and the reproduction of parental distinctiveness are perceived as based on desires to provide for the next generation, often at the cost of self-sacrifice, yet conversely, such perceived notions may, in fact, contribute towards replicating traditional patriarchal norms. This is because the commonly perceived roles of mother seem to persist as apprehended quite conservatively, with regard to the organization and maintenance of family life.

Ancestral lineage and the prominence of one's hereditary and wider family connections would seem to provide the underlying reasoning for claims of being 'Irish'. Participant responses appear to convey a conception of both immediate and wider family as being the means by which an individual's self-association with an Irish locality and being 'Irish' can be validated. From the analysis of conversations with participants the implication is that it is 'race', not space or locality, which primarily determines the basis of being 'Irish'.

---

[6]Other interrelated topics that were discussed within the focus group discussions include waning religion, spirituality, paganism and anti-puritan themes. Nonetheless, due to constraints on limits and the primary focus of the study being on racial and ethnic considerations, these themes are not further expanded upon.

The notion of clan is associated with conceptions of family, wider family and atomic genealogical ancestry. Being of a clan is seen as a more genuine form of authenticating *Irishness* and is construed as an unbroken lineage, first and foremost through *jus sanguinis* imaginaries that extend historically to the pre-medieval era. Some participants seem to interpret clan in biogenetic terms and, thus, the strength of the clan as being determined by reproduction, as well as the expansion of essentialized kinship though propagation of the progeny which enlarges the clan. Associated with clan are the relatable notions of grudge, *begrudgery* and belittlement which are perceived traits of *Irishness* that have persisted since feudalistic times.

Community also appears to be a foundational characteristic of *Irishness*, in particular, how community is apperceived with traditional and rural living. Participants drew synonymous comparisons between cultural production and evolution or 'progress' which would seem relatable to the creation and reproduction of tradition, and its associated values, whereby tradition is constantly reinvented. For some participants, community is conceived of dualistically as either, an all-inclusive singular collective – *the* Irish community, or, to describe a distinct group within the collective – *a* community. Both interpret society as a prearranged naturally homogeneous collectivity within which there are unnatural variances that either require *assimilation* or can never truly be conceived of as part of the collective. The perceived views of some participants within the discussions would seem to challenge the theory that late modernity is resulting in the decline of family, as a fragment of community, but rather views expressed still would seem to support notion that direct kinship networks are dominant within societal organization irrespective of a decline in broader community ties.

As a means of introducing empirical results and findings pertaining to *Irishness*, this chapter commenced at the social unit of immediate family. As above and consistent with the development of the findings chapters overall, this chapter progresses by expanding outwardly from the more micro-social circumstances to more macro-level themes. Having introduced more micro-level perceived notions of 'Irish' identity in relation to day-to-day relationships on being 'Irish', at the distance of home, clan, parochial and community life the next chapter widens the focus of the lens on perceived thoughts on historical *Irishness* and becoming Irish, as expressed by the participants of the study.

118 *Redefining* Irishness *in a Globalized World*

Chapter 6

Historical *Irishness* and Becoming 'Irish'

Keywords: Irish history; social change; liquid modernity; 'The other'; self-subscription; 'Native'; idealize; sovereignty; pride; cultural awareness

This chapter commences by presenting narratives on the historical, specific to notions of *Irishness*. Subsequent to this, Irish history as perceived by participants provides the basis for expressions of social change. Societal change is inferred directly to biological evolution. The chapter continues by uncovering how participants perceive 'the other' as lacking historical connection with the nation, across a spectrum of criteria. The following section points out an inconsistency and bias within several of the focus group discussions whereby participants dismissed, in this case American, claims to 'Irish' identity based on ancient hereditary links. Progressing from conversation about ancient Irish history, the subsequent section introduces modern Irish history from the perspective of participants. Separately, the subject and discipline of history are shown to have emerged in several focus group discussions.

The following section introduces aspects pertaining to being 'Irish', such as recognizing the Irish, claiming or calling oneself Irish and feeling Irish. Inter-related to this are 'insider' self-subscription and ascription onto a person who might be perceived as more of an 'outsider' or 'newcomer'. The prevalence of conversation in relation to the mere possession of an Irish passport across all of the focus group discussions and beyond is highlighted. From here, linking to the conversations presented in the previous section on perceived *Irishness* and history, participants' perceptions of being or becoming an Irish citizen are compared with being 'Irish' and nationalistic sentiment. Leading on from this, findings show how the agency to self-define as Irish is linked to the less palpable sense of feeling Irish. In several of the focus group discussions, cultural exposure over time is shown to gain prominence. The concluding section presents a conversation whereby some participants recognize the dilemma between conforming to societal cultural norms and expectations while having the privileged ability and right to be self-expressive, unconventional and even to contest such prevailing customs.

Redefining *Irishness* in a Globalized World:
National Identity and European Integration, 119–132
Copyright © 2024 by Yaqoub BouAynaya
Published under exclusive licence by Emerald Publishing Limited
doi:10.1108/978-1-83797-941-720241007

Historical Orientations of *Irishness*

Although narratives on the historical were consistent across most of the focus group discussions, some discussions revealed alternative interpretations of the past. Discussions would often take the form of emphasizing positive attributes of being 'Irish' and also supporting claims relating to becoming Irish. Within the Naas group discussion, numerous references to the historical presented not only the conventional but also, in some respect, a more *revisionist* view of Irish history specifically. Overall, this fed into a more questioning and better informed approach by the participants of Naas focus group discussion, whereas in the other focus group discussions, references to the historical were quite sporadic and often had the tendency to reaffirm notions relating to identity as fixed, based on one-dimensional notions of history.

The historicity of Ireland as a small island, with repeated flows of 'newcomers' and migrants, complicates an accurate understanding of what might be deemed as 'native'. Thus, it exactly claims to historical pasts which likely contribute towards defining contemporary conceptions of *Irishness*. In describing characteristics of *Irishness*, within the Drogheda focus group discussion, one response seems to refer to tourism but also alludes to the ancestral roots Ireland represents to the wider world.

Machie: […] the way Ireland is perceived outside of, eh, Ireland is more of a touristy kind of perception and that's why most of the people from Germany and Spain and places like that visit Ireland, to see the more ancestral places, so I'd say touristy as well would be, it's a very nice place of Irish, ancient kind of stuff like castles and things like that

In the Belfast focus group discussion, Tony considers '… history is very important …' when describing a distinctive Irish ethnicity. What is interesting is that when other dimensions, such as culture, language and religion, are omitted, according to Tony, history appears to be reduced down to providing,

the sense that we've been here longer than anyone else, anyone else who comes in, does so on our terms, on the terms of, you know, native Irish people, you know, that phrase you see on every history book, you know, 'who are the native Irish?'

Such a critical stance on the notion of 'nativeness' is also documented by O'Brien (1971), who relates nativist claims to regressive nationalistic sentiment.

However, when this dimension of longevity of time is examined further, no specific point is established that gives closure on the 'true' authenticity of an individual's claim to *Irishness*. There is the suggestion of a greater genuineness by connecting to an ancient heritage but what is questionable is less related to the historical reality of an ancient past and more the supposed actuality of a current person's genealogical link to such a past in order to deem oneself a true 'native'.

This ambiguity could be seen alternatively in what is described as an aspiration of Douglas Hyde,

> to restore the broken continuity of the Irish nation with an ancient past by arguing that the essential reality of *Irishness* is based on Gaelic history, and by proclaiming a knowledge of Gaelic culture and traditions the birthright of all Irish people. (Tovey et al., 1989, p. 18)

In contrast, within the Naas focus group discussion, in describing the difference between being 'Irish' and being an Irish citizen, participants apparently make the argument for a more inclusive understanding of *Irishness* and challenge the constitutional changes made in the 2004 ICR.

Liam: Nowadays there's no, like there, I doubt there is any Irish person here who has just been completely Irish through the years, there has been ... mixing, there has been different cultures coming together ... so I, I don't think you can actually reject someone from becoming a citizen of their country it's, it's unfair to be honest

Colin: It's funny to say nowadays but I mean it's not just nowadays, it's been happening for a long time, what with all ... the Vikings and there was the people who came ... from Spain originally, and then there was the Celts and then the Vikings and the English, so there

Liam: There is no one that ... is pure Irish

Colin: Yeah, well ... there just is none, there's no ethnicity that is purely Irish, it just doesn't exist (pause)

The participants seem to question the idealized and notional concept of a pure 'Irish' identity. Primarily, this is achieved by stressing more accurately the historicity of Ireland and connecting such an understanding to conceptions of identity. To a degree, the views imply a level of 'frailty of concepts such as identity, nationality and history in the light of the problematic and flexible notion of perspective' as described by Monahan (2009, p. 216). Though in this case, evidence demonstrates how the participants 'produce a critique of the essentialist and mythopoeic [myth making] aspects of Irish identity' (Monahan, 2009) rather than rely on established 'protreptic (classical rhetoric) discourse' (p. 217). The conversation above highlights the ambivalence and tenuousness of claims of a fixed nature that genealogically link an Irish individual with the more ancient bygone eras. What is surprising is that such a dislocating viewpoint is only voiced in this context in the Naas focus group discussion.

In contrast, genealogical links to the historical are discussed by Kelsey in relation to modern history in a more idealized way in a separate discussion. In relation to the conversation on family names (as detailed in Chapter 5), though in the post-viewing stage of the same discussion, participant Dana suggests that having Irish descent is an essential criterion for being 'Irish' but that, 'it doesn't have to go back like thousands of years' but rather, 'one or two generations will do'. Kelsey appears to make the connection between genealogy and history and interjects by focussing on the connection to a more recent history and provides a justification for claiming *Irishness* based on ancestral links that extend only several generations or back as far as the new formation of the Irish nation state.

Kelsey:	[...] I think it's great like, having that national ... sense of like history, I mean like, 'cos Ireland is such a small country ... I think all of us can go back and do our ancestry and we can all find someone who died in nineteen sixteen rising related to us or one of us, all of us have some sort of uncle that like wrote the proclamation, I mean like I'm related to like John Redmond and Michael Collins, like all of us are gonna be related to one of them ... and it is, it is that kind of sense to say, 'well my ancestors fought for this', and it is such a small country, our ancestors generally did, and it is –
Brady:	but if you're looking back thousands of years ago you'll find that a lot of people aren't Irish ... because we were invaded by so many different cultures, it's just like ... half of us are, would be, north Europe, northern European Normans, the Scandinavians
Christine:	the Spanish armada
Brady:	the Spanish armada, the British ...
Dana:	I think it only has to go back like ... a couple of generations ...

The conversation evolves by drawing on a broad understanding of Irish migration, settlement and invasion historically to emphasize the melange of cultures and traditions that have mixed to produce what are within present day considered to be 'Irish'. The participants continue by implying that processes of integration and assimilation have occurred but that, 'there is still old Gaelic (slight pause) culture there' (Brady). Overall, observable in both conversations are references to the historical that undermine justifications for claiming *Irishness*, or a purity of 'Irish' identity, based on genealogy or familial lineage. This extract, along with the extracts immediately above and below, concurs with the historical description of Irish migration and settlement as offered by White (2008). They would seem to challenge the notion of a pure Irish homogeneity on the historical grounds that since ancient times 'waves of immigrants from various geographical locations settled and contributed to the genetic variability of the Irish' (White, 2008, p. 83).

Referencing History in Relation to Societal Change

Within the Drumcondra focus group discussion, the conception of *Irishness* being obtained through a level of inherentness is intertwined with a general emphasis on understanding social progress as being an almost intrinsic evolutionary process. Participants' perceptions seem to complement notions of *social evolutionism* which view history as a having directionality and 'reflecting certain unifying principles of organisation and transformation' (Giddens, 1990, p. 5f.).[1] Recognition of the historical melange of Irish society is described to frame how identity in the 21st century might be redefined or re-imagined. The conversation below follows on from participants expressing the view that diversity is generally positive and enriching for the host society (as detailed later in this chapter).

Eddie:	We're not the same, we're not the same people that the Fir Bolg's and Tuatha de Danann's were
Ryan:	Anyway, you know, you're not going to ...
Eddie:	Every time, every time a new group arrived, everything changed ... whether it was the Vikings or the Normans ... or the British –
Ryan:	This is a new Irish
Eddie:	Of the Scottish plantation, you know, of Ulster or whatever ... all, I mean we're constantly changing all the time and these people all brought different influences ... they changed our language ... they changed our culture, they changed our habits, they changed our dress, they changed what we ate and what we drank
Ryan:	The crucial difference is, you know, the suddenness, you know in Ireland ... you know within the, fifteen, twenty year period ... so, I think, there's a huge influx of –
Carroll:	Yeah, the numbers and –
Ryan:	Different cultures and, yeah ... I mean if it happened over a fifty year period maybe it's, it's a different thing, but it's happening a sudden way ...
Eddie:	And you know everybody is terrified of change, we don't like change
Ryan:	No, nobody does ...
Eddie:	You know what we have to realise is that ... what we are afraid is going to change, was in fact change itself, you know different to what went before it ... so it's constantly, it just, we just need to get, get a grip on ourselves really and realise that it's going to change anyway
Alana:	That change is good ultimately
Eddie:	Of course it is yeah (pause)
Carroll:	I keep telling myself that

As detailed above, there appears to be recognition of the innateness of societal change through the process of looking back to the past. The interposing supposition by Ryan that the change that Ireland has experienced is somehow extraordinary, thus alarming, seems exaggerated. The participant does, however, imply recognition of the inevitable condition of *liquid modernity* and the ambivalence of identity together with a sense of anxiety and fear, which is comparable to depictions by Bauman (2001, 2006).

---

[1] Giddens (1990) would contest such an assumption of progress as inherent to the history of humankind.

124 Redefining Irishness *in a Globalized World*

Nevertheless, the dimension of fear that accompanies change seems to be portrayed quite uniformly at a collective level but operates at the level of the individual. By claiming a fear of change among all, there is the sense that the participant/s perspective is confirming the desire to maintain the *status quo* and that with change, the position of the prevailing culture might be vulnerable to change. This aspect of fear is confronted by Eddie with the suggestion that one must know it as an inevitability, but an inescapable effect likely to produce positive societal outcomes. However, in contract to this, the exaggerated portrayal as well as claims of fear by Ryan appears to provide for an elusive sense of greater concern to conserve the *status quo* by resisting or being pessimistic about change.

This aspect of recognition of historical change and fear relates to the understanding of the inevitability of change within a contemporary Irish setting expressed in several focus group discussions (as detailed below).

Lack of lineage closely ties in with what has been previously discussed in relation to perceived 'native' and seemingly less native claims to *Irishness*, as well as the topics of family, clan and *feudalism* covered in Chapter 5. This lack of lineage understood as a lack of historical connection impedes the capacity to become Irish. In the Drumcondra focus group discussion, these issues seem to have been compounded when answering the post-viewing question, which asks about the difference between being 'Irish' and being an Irish citizen:

Ryan: I think being Irish maybe suggests you have maybe a lineage way, there could be time ... so you'd have lines of say family, family before that in various different, it can be different parts of Ireland ... but in Ireland and links probably to the land itself, there's a real link I think to the land and the landscape and nature and sport and the politics, so you have that lineage going back maybe some generations ... a new citizen wouldn't just by definition, probably just arrived in the country over a couple of years, five years, or maybe quite recently born here

Alana: She wouldn't have the history ...

This excerpt draws a connection between genealogy or family lineage, association with the physical terrain, culture and politics, longevity of stay and place of birth as mechanisms that validate claiming to be 'Irish', which is surmised by Alana as possessing 'the history', whereas a person wishing to become Irish, or an Irish citizen, may not necessarily encapsulate all of these features into their history as an Irish person. In connection to this, as Liu and Hilton (2005) describe, 'history provides us with narratives that tell us who we are, where we came from and where we should be going. It defines a trajectory which helps construct the essence of a group's, how it relates to other groups' (p. 537). The implication from above is that without knowing the representations of Irish history and having a conclusive connection to them, one cannot really be Irish.

When it is later suggested that these seemingly subtle differences between being 'Irish' and being an Irish citizen might create social stratifications, the conversation continues as follows:

Alana:	I don't think so but I think it's a reality ... it's a reality that eh, we have a history being, we'll say the old Irish, whereas the new Irish have other cultures (pause) and –
Ciara:	I don't think it's divisive, it's necessarily a divisive thing
Alana:	No, I don't see it ... but they would have their traditions ... and culture

This response, although somewhat rejecting that social stratification might occur, also implies a process of differentiation because of diverse historical pasts, traditions and cultures. The suggestion here is that the 'old Irish' are represented by a somewhat homogenized sameness historically, whereas the 'new Irish' have a melange of alternative histories. Such a benign understanding neglects to comprehend that for the reconstitution of identities, ethnic or otherwise, power relations are of immense significance (Tovey et al., 1989, p. 7)

Contradictions Within 'Nativist' Claims to *Irishness*

At this juncture, a revealing attitude is exposed relating to sentiments towards American Irish, in particular, how American Irish lay claims to *Irishness*. It would be expected that arguments espousing nativist claims to *Irishness* that are based on ancient historical links to Ireland would then support claims made by Americans or other members of a supposed Irish diaspora to be or become Irish. However, this would seem not to be the case. In truth, the responses within several of the focus group discussions appear to expose quite negative sentiments to those making such claims.

Juliana:	But, you know, so this, this view, looking at Ireland through rose tinted glasses is something that is common, if you talk to Americans especially, I just thought of history, recent history, talking to people from America and engage with them on Facebook, people through family relations, and ... they own more than an Irish man ... they just want to be Irish, they're not Irish, now if you go back in their history you might find that ... generation, or even some, don't have any Irish in their blood whatsoever, yet they want this whole Irish thing going on for them ... so there's, there's this vision of the Emerald Isle, the old country
Charlie:	It will always ...
Juliana:	And that's the land ... yes, it's rose tinted glasses

In this instance what becomes apparent is not only a rejection of Americans claiming *Irishness* but also a critique of an overly optimistic and idealized view of Ireland. There is the conflicting issue of American individuals attempting to lay claim to *Irishness* due to their genealogy while also the suggestion that with this are claims to the land or territory. Further to this, Americans are criticized for attempting to make even greater claims to *Irishness* than the Irish themselves.

Similarly, within the Drumcondra focus group discussion below, this issue is discussed in relation to whether, or not, having Irish parentage is an essential criterion for being 'Irish'.

126 *Redefining* Irishness *in a Globalized World*

Alana: Well, when you look at America and there, its three generations back that were Irish and they still consider themselves Irish, today like you know
YB: Umhmm, and are they?
Alana: Eh, well they think they are, like your man from, born in Cairo (referring to the interviewee, Kevin), in America he was Irish but in Ireland he was – (laughter) ...
Eddie: I think that ... the American situation is different because America is a very young country and they don't have a kind of history ... unless you go back to the native Americans, so it's relatively young, you know, they have a building that is a hundred years old, they're saying, 'woe, look at this, fantastic', 'ah yeah, but we have buildings five thousand years old', you know, I think they're very conscious of the fact that they are very young, they don't have a history ... and they don't have the roots and the culture, so, I think they kind of frantically look for something to hang on to ... and something to identify with and give them ... I think that is why it is important to them

This extract led by contributions from Eddie, places emphasis on the historical, or perceived lack of an historical past, in relation to a sense of the de-centred self that requires and yearns for 'something to identify with'. The impression is that, without possessing an adequate past the self, in this context the American, is seen as incomplete.

What may also be implied from the snippet from the Drumcondra discussion above is how identifying with *Irishness* and claiming to be 'Irish' may be based on a conscious recognition of a connection to not only a recent past but to an ancient history. In this instance, what becomes apparent, independent of considerations of historicity, are the assumptions that a person might make to believe they have a genealogical lineage that would trace back into ancient Irish history. Such a concept of lineage is based on essentialist notions of culture as being based on 'primordial inheritance of a people or group' (Finlay, 2007, p. 337). In effect, the individual appropriates the cultural–historical to justify and elevate their sense of being 'Irish' and conversely seems to challenge another's claim by either a lack of connection to such an historical expanse, or by undermining another's desire to become Irish in the absence of such a claim. Relating back to the extract which suggested a degree of conservatism (see above), such appropriation, albeit baseless for the majority, may relieve insecurities and may be conducted less to stabilize the sense of self by connecting to an ancient historical past, but more as a mechanism to maintain and preserve a conservative social arrangement that benefits the self. An outcome of mitigating such insecurities is the rejection of 'others' who lack their own claim to an ancient past or cannot lay claim specifically to such Irish historicity. An alternative position would complement the views (as described earlier) which suggest an Irish person's genealogical link to an ancient Irish past is quite tenuous.

The emphasis on attachment to an ancient Irish historical past over a perceived lack of connection to the historical past seems also present within the

Coolock focus group discussion, when a link is made between knowing the self, 'where you are, where are you from?' (Conlaoch), and understanding the traces of one's shared history.

Peadar: I mean is that the reason why we tend, Irish people tend to hark back to the past in many occasions, if you go to a new country, like the United States, I mean their history is what? Three or four hundred years you can say, you know, and we're talking about thousands

Conlaoch: Well their history is thousands as well, it's just they've been forgot –

Tierney: Is just they wipe away –

Peadar: No, no, no I'm talking about the white civilization

Conlaoch: Yes the white civilization ...

Peadar: No, no, no but I'm talking about ... the Westernization

Of significance in this excerpt is the recognition of an erasure of history, let alone a false or skewed understanding of the past. This presents an alternative mechanism by which the self rejects a more ancient past, as a form of collectivized amnesia.[2] Within the context of the Irish, nevertheless, claiming *Irishness* through the connection to a more ancient past could be seen as not only a means of benefiting the self over 'others' who wish to enter within, but may be a means of elevating the perceived status of the 'insider' individual in comparison with 'others' beyond the Irish collective who may not even desire to become part of a shared *Irishness*.

The Post-colonial Yet Juvenile Nation State

In the Limerick focus group, discussion about Ireland seems to distinguish between its pre-nation state condition, as a colonized land and its post-nation state reality, as a young and developing republic, to provide a justification for its shortcomings at a collective level. Apparently, what is also seen as a new characteristic of the Irish is the desire for materialistic wealth. As Maebh claims, 'I suppose em, we got more materialistic really.' When this aspect was probed into further, the historical justification was provided.

Dale: You see we're a very young country and I think we forget that, this country is really, not even a hundred years old ... so we don't have necessarily great traditions of our own making, they were always influenced by, and our history is influenced by other nations, so this, Ireland as we know today only became a country really in the forties, if you

---

[2] It may be in the American context the supremacy of grounding one's self-identification in a more recent historical epoch relates to notions of the hegemony of 'white civilization' and 'Westernization', vis-á-vis, American exceptionalism.

want to get down to it, when it became a republic, and eh, it only actually completely happened when Ireland had total independence from any other nation, so I think really, we are just like the child in the sweet shop, going out to explore, you know we give out to teenagers these days, taking things further than their own generations, those of us who are older, I think the Irish nation is like that, we're all exploring, exploring, exploring, pushing boundaries and breaking a few of them, I think at this stage everyone would agree with that

The analogy provided in this instance suggests quite a naïve understanding of the collective activities of the Irish. Drawing parallels with 'the child in the sweet shop' implies the emergence of a more *consumerist* mind-set among the Irish (discussed further in Chapter 9), similar to the description by Inglis (2008) of contemporary Ireland where 'globalization has dramatically increased the consumer and lifestyle choices through which Irish people develop new identities and realize themselves as individuals' (p. 38).

Moreover, a denial of responsibility and accountability seems to occur both pre- and post-colonial rule, as perceived by Dale. The impression is that the colonial past of Ireland is generally portrayed in a negative light due to external forces associated with British *colonialism*, whereas the more recent historical referencing negates responsibility by ascribing blame to the juvenility of the nation state collective.

Likewise, from the outset within the Drumcondra focus group discussion, Ryan appears to provide a somewhat similar perspective when describing characteristics of *Irishness*.

Ryan: [...] I think we are a complicated race, because of history, you know, because of colonization and then, well the freedom, you know, we're joined with the EU in training, training again different, it's getting more internationalized, people travel more and so on, that has changed people's perception of what the country is, (slight pause) eat different foods, so I think it's been sort of, big changes in the past forty fifty years ... we're still somewhat a complicated people, probably because we got full confidence in ourselves, although this recent economic crash there's been maybe, (pause) given some pointers as to that insecurity again, worry, you need a Troika of economies coming together to bail us out of the problem, now we're, kind of, cowing to another group, it's not the colonizer it's someone else ... it's an IMF,[3] it's a European sort of grouping that we have to sort of bow down to, like we've been bold ... you know as a nation ... maybe immature in some ways, I think, there's a lot of confidence has grown in the country, but there's still a large degree, I think at some level, or levels, there are still some

---

[3]International Monetary Fund (IMF) is an abbreviation of the International Monetary Fund.

insecurities that seep in, overall, I think very gregarious to a point but, not wild as is popularly known, quite timid and conservative, we put up with a lot, without protest ...

The conversation again suggests indirectly a deferring of responsibility away from the collective Irish towards either the past colonizer, or newer institutions of power such as the European Union or IMF. The recent historical timespan, when Ireland is seen as possessing greatest sovereignty and independence, is similarly seen as a time of immaturity and naïvety for the nation state. What is also revealed and noteworthy from this excerpt in the closing comment is how it may also provide insight into the psyche of the Irish generally in its response to 'others' who may wish to become part of the Irish collective. It would seem to suggest a sense of underlying insecurity that feeds into conservatism among the Irish.

Learning History to Gain Cultural Awareness

All the informed references to the historical, provided by participants, come across as being related to their learnt understanding of the past. Within the Drogheda focus group when discussing what it means to be 'Irish', the participants initially refer to the pragmatics, then the less tangible, such as feeling Irish but also having roots with society. In contrast to Toben's anecdotal account of a person who lives in Ireland but maintains a greater affiliation with his country of Nigeria, Irena attempts to disregard or at least downplay the obstacles facing the racialized 'Other' by detailing the process of becoming Irish irrespective of ethnic or racial associations.

Irena: [...] you have an Irish passport now ... that you think that you would like to stay here, you would like to connect with this eh, society, eh, for you, you think about, 'I should know Irish history ... because I will be, learn my children or others ... this history, because I live here ... I would like to stay here' ... for me I must be proud from this country because, I eh, I must also think I am responsible, eh, responsible ... responsible for this country, for this eh, connect, integration you know ... because I am here, now I am Irish, I decide to have Irish ... citizen, yes ...

What is evident in this extract is a clear link between satisfying the legal criteria and the granting of access to citizenship, along with a heightened sense of obligation of responsibility towards the Irish collective and the ability to self-subscribe as Irish, or at least an Irish citizen. An understanding of history specific to Ireland and the transference of historical knowledge would seem to be compulsory. Knowledge of history is acquired within notions of nationalistic pride and cultural transference. However, there is the sense that compounding these two may restrict a more critical appraisal of such knowledge re/production and overly focus on positivist accounts of history.

In the case of what was revealed from the Naas focus group discussion, evidently, the participants view their learnt history as both a mechanism of inciting pride in their past but also as a means of critical engagement. For instance, during a conversation where participants were describing their sense of pride and love in being 'Irish', Colin refers to their 'big interest in Irish history'. Subsequently, in reference to the rebellion and beyond Colin states, 'I don't know, I think again going back to history, they never gave up, for the most part, there was always somebody trying … [whereas] there are lots of countries that have and do give up freedom'. However, in keeping with the overall tone of the conversation, the same participant in a separate account later claims quite reflexively, 'everybody likes to lie about their history …' Their knowledge and critical engagement with History as a discipline would seem to indicate that their learning goes beyond what Gilroy (1990, p. 114f.) describes as a dated role of history pedagogy whereby it is understood as the transmission, reproduction and celebration of an 'authentic' national identity and culture that supposedly unifies a population through *homogenization* but excludes through 'a kind of disqualification from membership of the national community …' (Gilroy, 1990, p. 115).

This chapter commences by highlighting how the historical is afforded importance by people who customarily self-subscribe as Irish, whereby association is related to genealogical links or ancestral roots to an Irish past. However, this is challenged primarily by younger participants with respect to the perceived basis and accuracy of Irish historicity. Nonetheless, comprehending societal change seems to be dependent on references to a perceived historical past. Consequently, social transformation is expressed and conceived of as a form of progress that appears to be conceptualized akin to natural evolutionary processes. In relation to the assumption of societal change as an innate progression comparable to evolution, some reservation is expressed concerning the perceived rapidity of change in the fabric of Irish society due to migration. Compared to past migration, it is seen as either a supposedly negative phenomenon, or, as an inexorable evolutionary process with the potential to create positive social progress. Inferred from this, views would seem to assume that diachronic connections or temporal progress is integrally linked to civilizing processes.

Participants create an important distinction by claiming how 'the other' lacks historical connection with the Irish nation across a continuum of indicators. Such a deficit would seem to be perceived as lessening a person's claims of *Irishness*. Therefore, representations of history are not only used as a means to create, maintain and shape an individual's self-identity but are combined to influence their social status in relation to others. Across several of the focus group discussions, a particular bias is identified where participants divulge negative attitudes towards American claims to *Irishness* based on ancient hereditary links to Ireland. When compared with findings presented in the previous chapter, this would seem inconsistent with the justified rationale utilized to lay claim to *Irishness* for one-self, namely that connection to an ancient past is an integral part of perceived 'Irish' identity.

The perceived views by participants, of more modern Irish history, in addition to views of pre- and post-colonial Ireland would appear to act as a mechanism to disclaim accountability for what are acknowledged as past and persistent collective issues shared within Irish society. Furthermore, denying responsibility is also achieved through the portrayal of Ireland as a juvenile nation that has yet to become equipped with the means to unburden itself from the persistent societal problems it still endures. Interrelated with this, one participant reveals the sense of underlying insecurity, particularly with regard to Ireland's perceived lack of response to increased migration and integration, which is recognized as feeding into *conservatism* among the Irish.

Somewhat disparate from the previous themes mentioned above, within several focus group discussions, the importance of history as a topic of knowledge attained pedagogically is highlighted as a means of better understanding oneself individually and within a collective. Participants' views seem to emphasize the value and importance of acquiring comprehensive knowledge of Irish history so as to become completely assimilated into the Irish collective and self-subscribe as Irish.

Having broadened the scope of analysis from more localized day-to-day conceptions of *Irishness* in Chapter 5, the above results and findings in this chapter interlink and detail perceived views of the context of Irish history specific to *Irishness*. Views on history are interrelated with conceptions of family, clan and so forth vis-á-vis notions of descent, genealogical lineage and 'nativist' or *essentialist* claims to *Irishness*. Although alternative contestations in relation to Irish *historicity* are presented, in addition to more diffuse themes such as the perceived juvenility of the Irish nation state and learning history as a means to gaining cultural awareness, Chapter 6 maintains a broad focus on the perceived foundational arguments for being 'Irish'. Leading on from these more bedrock layers, Chapter 7 details the more existent and habitual means by which being Irish is ascribed.

132   Redefining Irishness *in a Globalized World*

Chapter 7

Recognizing Being 'Irish'

Keywords: 'insider'; an Irish citizen; classificatory distinctions; individuation; discursive practices; exclusions; perceived Irish; racial distinction; 'Otherness'; affinity

This chapter details the process of recognizing the Irish as discussed by participants. It differentiates between the ability to call oneself Irish or self-subscribe as Irish in comparison to ascribing *Irishness* onto a subject as an 'insider'. Both are seen as affording the 'insider' or 'native' a position of privilege that conversely disempowers by externalizing an alternative subject as 'outsider' or 'part-outsider' and as the 'newcomer'.

One mechanism that is alluded to in achieving this emerges in the conversation: there is evidence of a nuanced contrast between being 'Irish' and being or becoming an Irish citizen. Moreover, a subtle classificatory distinction is evidenced whereby a person is either recognized as 'being Irish', or in contrast, 'being an Irish citizen'. The lingual distinction made implies an imbalanced power dynamic between both within social interaction. Yet, for all intents and purposes, legally they are both analogous, with both sharing equal claim to the benefits of the state such as the provision of an Irish passport.

Although not referenced by participants there is an arbitrariness to being 'Irish' which for many affords them security as members of the nation and the freedom to travel, there is less arbitrariness to being an Irish citizen of the state. This leads to the requirement of the state to recognize morality. As Appiah (1997) deconstructs,

> since human beings live in political orders narrower than the species, and since it is within those orders that questions of public right and wrong are largely argued out and decided, the fact of being a fellow citizen – someone who is a member of the same order – is not morally arbitrary at all. (p. 623)

The Segregation of Being 'Irish' and Being an Irish Citizen

As evidenced across all of the interviews and focus group discussions, the pragmatic aspect of simply possessing a passport is stressed as tangible evidence in support of claims to being or becoming an Irish citizen. In the Drumcondra focus group discussion, upon viewing the multimedia presentation, the initial comments that were made focused on the importance of possessing an Irish passport. As Eddie observes from the responses of the interviewees, 'well I suppose, they all appreciate, eh, their Irish passport would you say? ... yeah, they showed an appreciation for it, that maybe Irish people themselves don't realize'. Within the Belfast focus group discussion, in answer to a question posed by the facilitator, '... how would you define what it means to be Irish, for you currently?' Molly simply responds, 'an Irish passport (laughter)'. Although speculative, what may be inferred here is a somewhat satirical recognition of what *Irishness* has lost and that its meaning has been reduced down to the very simple and pragmatic aspect of possessing an Irish passport. On the one hand, such an object has become so valued because of the historical context of Ireland's international relations, yet, also valued somewhat cynically for the ease and privilege it affords an Irish person to travel relatively freely.

Although the possession of a passport and other such legally afforded rights are recognized, a subtle distinction between being an Irish citizen and being 'Irish' seems to surface in most conversations. Within the Coolock focus group discussion, during a conversation in response to what it means to be 'Irish' Peadar seeks clarification as to whether both being 'Irish' and being an Irish citizen are analogous by posing the question to the other participants.

Peadar: Can I just come back and qualify ... somebody who is an Irish citizen (slight pause) ... they're Irish, correct?
Tierney: No, no
Keela: I think so, I think so
Peadar: ... well, so if you stood in the concert hall ... last week ... full of six hundred people, who are not white ... but they're Irish
Aileen: Exactly
Tierney: Yeah, yeah but ... yeah but they're not Irish, they weren't born here
Peadar: My argument is, that's my point, now are we qualifying it? ... no, no, no, I've, no, no, I'm saying ... we're talking about ourselves, I'm talking about an Irish citizen ... are they Irish?
Tierney: About ourselves
Peadar: I think they are
Aileen: Yeah I think definitely

The response as evidenced in this excerpt is varied, with both Peadar and Aileen being quite adamant that being 'Irish' and being an Irish citizen are synonymous, whereas Tierney rejects such. Tierney's rejection is based on the rationale that if 'we're talking about ourselves' and ascribing it to ourselves then both being 'Irish' and being an Irish citizen would be identical. Nevertheless, in the circumstance where one might gain citizenship and go through a formal award ceremony, such as those hosted by state representatives (referenced above), it might be inferred from the above extract that Tierney would not equate being 'Irish' as synonymous with being an Irish citizen.

Also in the Drumcondra focus group discussion, the recognition of classificatory distinction between being 'Irish' and being an Irish citizen also seems to be emphasized.

Carroll: I think there's a subtle kind of classification there in the choice of words, I think if someone said to you, 'I'm Irish' ...

Eddie: There would be a certain understanding as Ryan has said ... if someone says' 'I'm an Irish citizen' it suggests there's only a short timeline here and I may have a passport or a piece of paper but you know, I need that to establish me as being Irish ... that there are reasons perhaps, why I wouldn't be, necessarily be Irish, it kind of suggests that you have ... have kind of earned it or been given it ... as it were, rather than automatically entitled or classified as Irish, doesn't it? I think ... and certainly, I don't think we would, I don't think we would call ourselves an Irish citizen, I think we would say we're Irish

In this extract, there appears to be a clear understanding of the differences between either referring to or being referred to as an Irish citizen or as simply being 'Irish'. Eddie implies also an imbalanced power dynamic between both contexts by suggesting that being 'Irish' is a privilege afforded unconditionally to those within, whereas to become an Irish citizen, there is the conditionality of earning that entitlement.

Furthermore, in deconstructing the two terms, 'I'm Irish' and 'I'm an Irish citizen', it could be posited that within the first singular statement, there is the subtle understanding of being part of the Irish in its plural form. Thus, it suggests being a member of the collective Irish. Whereas the latter personal claim of fact individualizes the subject within their own statement. It, thus, renders the subject, albeit making a claim that may be factually true, detached from the many. Such a process of classification may be seen not only as binding specific dissimilar associations but also by segregating the discrete subject it disempowers them at a subliminal level by reducing their capacity to be conceived as part of the collective. This reflects the views of Foucault (1977) and Said (1978, 1994) who place emphasize on discursive practices through which exclusions are subtly and not so subtly created.

Diarmuid recognizes that what it means to be 'Irish' has likely changed since the 1950s. As Diarmuid states in relation to the demographic makeup of contemporary Irish society, 'about ten percent are other nationalities, and "others" who have come in, migrants ... so we are changing as a society ... very eh, significantly'. Continuing to elaborate on this, Diarmuid claims to be nationalistic, a republican and proud to speak Irish and within this context claims, 'I'm proud to be Irish (pause), but now I, I welcome other people who are now Irish citizens and we are now a more diverse society, and we have to allow for that'. This clearly stresses a perceived predicament Diarmuid faced and somewhat still is trying to reconcile, within the self-realization of the inevitability of societal change. There is the sense that expressing an affiliation with Irish national republicanism ordinarily should be understood as though it is at odds with notions of an inclusive and diverse society. Yet there seems to be the realization on the part of Diarmuid that it may in actuality not be the case. Such a position, as expressed by Diarmuid, would seem to correspond with Fossum's (2012) view that democratic constitutional states can be explicitly committed to inclusive community.[1] The extent to which Diarmuid is willing to change and afford the ascription of *Irishness* to 'the other' is limited however, with the labelling of 'Irish citizens' and the subtle inclusion of it being articulated as an obligation of choice and subsequent permission on behalf of the 'we' of Irish society. Leading from this, Busayo, perhaps acknowledging the pragmatic importance of citizenship attempts to reinforce the importance in becoming an Irish citizen:

Busayo: First off, if you're born here and, even have the Irish citizenship, (slight pause) being from a different country (pause) ... you need ... to become a citizen of the nation ... you need to gain Irish citizenship, you become ... if I'm not born here ... because it's your debt of a nation ... because of your citizenship (long pause)

This sense of indebtedness or onus of responsibility to the nation connects well with nationalistic sentiment, and viewpoints expressed by the fourth interviewee, Kevin, regarding civic duty. Inadvertently or not, it does also seem to add an additional burden not only perceived by but also projected by the broader public onto an individual who may become a citizen of the nation. It is suggestive of a heightened and unequal onus of responsibility on the new Irish citizen and a privilege afforded to the Irish, who are automatically granted citizenship and can, thus, adopt a more laissez-faire attitude to civic duties and responsibilities.

Perceiving Oneself as Irish

Molly responds to the question of whether or not being born in Ireland is an essential criterion for being 'Irish' by stating, 'no I don't think it's essential, I think it's how you perceive yourself or how you feel about your own em ... identity'. Apparently evidenced here is a confidence in the ability to self-subscribe as Irish where perhaps the aspect of external recognition has been omitted. However, specific to identity claims, and in this case being 'Irish', would seem to be the consideration

---

[1]An exemplar nation state being Canada is described by Fossum (2012) as fostering general principles of 'cultural and linguistic tolerance, inclusive community, federalism, interregional sharing, democracy, rule of law, and equality of opportunity, as well as respect for and accommodation of difference' (p. 357*f.*).

of claiming to be 'Irish' or electively belonging to Ireland and being accepted as Irish. Within the Limerick focus group discussion, Juliana informs the group that, in the context of an Irish person travelling abroad, what makes someone Irish is '... the right to be known as Irish ...' Although this feature of self-understanding and 'outsider' perspective while travelling abroad and being immersed in a 'foreign' culture is mentioned in several focus group discussions, such an externalization of recognition from the self would be applicable within Ireland also.

Although 'race' and ethnicity are discussed in more detail in the subsequent chapter, within the Naas focus group, when the question of a distinctive Irish ethnicity was discussed, it became compounded with perceived notions of racial distinction. In addition, the concluding remarks seemingly challenge such concepts of Irish ethnicity. These can be seen in relation to the idea of self-subscription and are, indeed, quite insightful.

Colin: [...] I don't think there is in any country, 'cos if you identify as Irish
YB: [...] how do you mean, if you identify as Irish?
Colin: Like if, this is your home, this is the place you love, you like being here and you like the people then, you don't want to be anywhere else
YB: So it's a kind of, an, an affection or an affinity ... an affinity to Ireland? ... is there, would it be a characteristic of an Irish ethnicity?
Colin: Would it be, be a characteristic of ... ethnicity of any country?
YB: [...] ok, that was pretty profound

Emergent in this extract, it appears that bound to self-identifying as Irish is an emotional association with Ireland that is often expressed as an affection for or an affinity with Ireland. Any understanding of a distinctive ethnicity would be based on emotional attachments that can be shared collectively. Thus, perhaps it is at this point distinctions should be made between feelings or emotions towards Ireland, and 'otherness' based on alternative ways of living or 'otherness' based on phenotypes and physiological traits. The main constituents of 'Irish' identity, in this instance, are less based on fantasy and idealization of interconnected oneness with a mythological past, as Hall (1996, p. 3*ff.*) has described. In this circumstance, by disregarding the notion of discrete nation state ethnicities, the participant instead refers to authentic *Irishness* as being an ongoing process of affinity and desire for association. From this perspective, the implication may be that through the social construction of identity, the root processes of identification are, or should be, based on desires. Although not based on innateness, this is quite similar to the Freudian perspective whereby 'identification means first of all trying to realize inadmissible desires, especially during childhood or adolescence' (Benoist, 2004, p. 19).

There is a strong emphasis within the Naas group discussion, on feelings such as affinity rather than on more concrete criteria in relation to either being or becoming Irish. When a discussion was raised on the difference between being 'Irish' and being an Irish citizen, the response was categorical and consistent with previous comments made.

138 Redefining Irishness in a Globalized World

Liam: Well any person born ... in Ireland can be can be an Irish citizen ... but to be Irish you need to love the culture, you need to ... want to be part of the ah (slight pause) –
Colin: It's not enough to have the passport
Liam: No (long pause)

Although there is an initial emphasis on *jus soli*/birthright citizenship,[2] Liam seems to place importance on the requirement of having an affinity with Irish culture and participation. This connects to discussion on the deconstruction of nationalism whereby for O'Brien (1971) love of one's country and one's people can enter the equation, but that 'it is not easy because, for the nationalist, anyone who fails to love his country in an exclusive and collectively self-righteous way, does not love his country at all' (p. 8f.).

Of course, the ability to claim *Irishness* or self-subscribe as Irish from the perspective of an 'insider' contrasts with how one might or might not be recognized as Irish from the perspective of an 'outsider'. Central to this are notions that rely on racialization and certain perceptions of physiognomies that are deemed as Irish. The section on racial and ethnic distinction highlights viewpoints raised specifically in relation to this (see below).

Jus Soli, Jus Sanguinis or Temporal Exposure to Irish Culture

Within the Clondalkin focus group discussion, there appears to be an emphasis on the importance of cultural exposure rather than birthright or bloodline association. Such views conflict with the legislative changes following the 2004 Irish Citizenship Referendum, which are described by Moriarty (2006) as 'the changing of rules of belonging in Ireland' (p. 132) (as referred to in Chapter 3). Kelsey provides an additional outlook from what they had said prior to viewing the presentation, by challenging the claim that the interviewee Kevin could be Irish exclusively through their bloodline descent and quite insightfully referring to exposure to the cultural norms of Irish society. However, there is slight disjuncture among the participants on this issue.

Kelsey: If you weren't born in Ireland and didn't grow up in Ireland, what makes you Irish? ... like I mean, just 'cos your mam and dad are Irish doesn't mean you are Irish ... you need to like be brought up in Ireland like, even if you're not born in Ireland as long as you're raised through the norms ... or in our culture like, he was brought up in Boston like
Brady: He does kind a have a right to consider himself Irish
Christine: Yeah he does yeah

---

[2]This perception is now further divergent from law following the 2004 Irish Citizenship Referendum.

Brady:	Because his mother and father are Irish but (slight pause) ... I don't know... there's two different –
Dana:	But he's been Americanized so –
Brady:	I think there's two kinds of, every nationality there's two kinds (slight pause) there's the people that their mother and fathers are born in that country but ... you were born in another country, so you can kind of call yourself half and half but –
Kelsey:	But he didn't call himself Egyptian
Brady:	At the end of the day –
Kelsey:	He was born there ...
YB:	[...] would you consider him less Irish than the second guy?
Brady:	The half and half ...
Kelsey:	I think he was actually less Irish than the one from Iraq ... cos your man from Iraq, he had a real culchie accent ... you can tell that he like, he's real Irish
Brady:	Yeah but he ... wasn't born in Ireland though
Dana:	Yeah but he went to primary school and all in Ireland, like
Brady:	I still wouldn't consider him Irish
Kelsey:	But your fella who is born in Egypt, you'd consider him Irish?
Brady:	No, I said I wouldn't ... (laughter)
Kelsey:	Oh, right, right, right ... (laughter)
Christine:	So you have to be born in Ireland? ... (laughter)
Kelsey:	No ... but I think I would consider him more Irish than the American fella ... 'cos the American fella had an American accent ... so he grew up in America ... whereas this fella had an Irish accent so he obviously grew up in ... Ireland
Dana:	It showed him like in primary school in Ireland, that he liked Irish music and stuff like that, where your man was just like, 'ah yeah, I got slagged and all, and I took offence and all'
Christine:	That's probably because we're just anti-American, what do yea reckon?
Kelsey:	Yeah, we really are ... (slight laughter)

This conversation contains quite a few key considerations in relation to perceived *Irishness*. As previously mentioned, there is an apparent emphasis on temporal exposure to cultural norms that are seen to be a primary determinant; however, there is also the suggestion of a possibility of possessing a hybridity of identities. This seems to be portrayed as a somewhat irreconcilable clash of interests, particularly in relation to the ascription of identity onto interviewee, Kevin. Being both Americanized and Irish is viewed as conflicting, through the automatic assumption that somehow possessing both cultural norms would be discordant. The justification to deem interviewee, Dijwar, as being or having become more Irish than interviewee, Kevin is primarily based on the accent he possesses which, in turn, is rationalized as being indicative of a greater longevity of exposure to Irish norms and values. The simple recognition of having grown up in Ireland, gone through the Irish educational system and having an affiliation with Irish culture, vis-á-vis, an expression towards an appreciation of 'traditional' Irish music by interviewee Dijwar would appear to be judged by the participants from the Clondalkin focus group discussion, to offer sound validation of their decision to consider interviewee Dijwar 'more Irish' than interviewee, Kevin. This would suggest a level of social stratification according to the *ethno-linguistics* of accent and language. Nonetheless, it is suggestive of a more complex internalized stratification system which now subordinates perceived non-native speakers and speakers from the United States of America. Whereas before Tovey et al. (1989, p. 22) documented a language and accent stratification system that approximated more closely the old core elite, the additional 'Other' is now present at the lowermost end of social strata.

Another focal point is the somewhat reflexive evaluation of the participants themselves, with the suggestion and confirmation that they exhibit anti-American sentiment. In the context of the analysis of all the focus group discussions, feeling anti-American does seem to surface (as highlighted above) however, it seems reasonably inconsistent with the converse self-recognition of greater adoption of perceived American traits, either by individuals within Irish society or a more general Americanization of lifestyle across multiple spheres of Irish life.

Quite unpredictably within this excerpt of conversation, the participants do not overtly discuss the observations regarding the differing physiological traits among the interviewees. There is the sense that care is being taken to be politically correct and that is why aspects that might be associated with 'race' are intentionally omitted from the dialogue. Taking this into account, the previous excerpt may be quite relevant and relatable to the conversation below from the Clondalkin focus group discussion, where the topic of growing up in Ireland is raised again (refer to Chapter 8 on 'ethnic and racial distinction').

Feelings of Affinity Towards an Irish Way of Being

At this juncture what becomes apparent among several focus group discussions is that for a person present and living in Ireland there exists an ambivalence between having an affinity with Irish culture and actively participating in Irish culture. For the most part, throughout the discussions even after deliberation and deconstruction, participants seem to create a bind by maintaining a conceptualization of Irish culture as fixed and clearly defined, while conversely acknowledging the heterogeneity of cultural practices within Irish society (as discussed in Chapter 8 in relation to the reification fallacy).

Within the Naas focus group discussion, the participants apparently attempt to reconcile this dilemma whereby Colin initially claims that, '... if you're ever going to identify as a nationality, you should love the nationality, not, you shouldn't say well ... my parents are Irish so I must be Irish ... I was born here, I must bear it'. However, as the conversation progresses, the participants seem to recognize the predicament between conforming to societal expectations and cultural norms, while having the privileged ability and right to be self-expressive, nonconformist and even challenge such perceived dominant norms.[3] When this is posed, the response incorporates discussion on the anecdotal account provided by the interviewee Niamh in the multi-media presentation, relating to the individual wearing their customary 'African' attire. The conversation is quite revealing and continues by discussing how societal or cultural expectations of the individual result in conformity.

Colin: [...] you should challenge them, if they do restrict you, then you should wonder why (slight pause)

Liam: I don't see why you should conform for anyone else, as in if you are proud of your culture, if you let's say, the third girl was it, the third girl said something about ... the lady and the African dress, like, she, that woman was obviously proud of where she was from, she likes her tradition and she likes the ... clothes, she shouldn't conform just because like, they want, the guy's boyfriend said, 'oh shouldn't she blend in?' ... because ... if people blend in it's not unique ...

Colin: It's obvious that she identifies more as being, she probably doesn't identify, or I don't know ... she probably doesn't identify as Irish and that is ok ... that's fine

YB: But she could have an affinity for, for Ireland couldn't she?

Liam: Exactly yeah, but she prefers –

Colin: I think so yeah, she prefers yeah –

Liam: Her dresses ...

Colin: At the end of the day it's what you think ... what you feel closest to you, if you feel closer to Africa than to Ireland then you're probably African (pause)

Liam: But just 'cos you are in our country, you're just in the country, it doesn't mean you have to

Colin: You can still love it and not be, but if you're ... if you're going to identify as Irish that is one of the things you should, you should love the country, I don't see why else you would, you identify as Irish

YB: [...] it's interesting isn't it? ... it leaves us in a kind of quandary, in a paradox I think

The excerpt of conversation has several discrete and subtle inconsistencies, such as the initial reference to 'our country' which is immediately corrected to a less possessive description as 'the country' by Liam. In ways the questioning of dress and outward behaviour is both a discursive practice of *subjectification* (Hall, 1996, p. 2) and also resembles how conformity is bound to the presentation of the self (Goffman, 1959) and certain expectations of performance; a performance of conforming to the conventions of Irish social norms. It is as Butler (1993) defines

---

[3]The interrelated themes of privilege, entitlement and ownership were flagged within the data analysis; however, due to constraints on the volume of content, they are not documented discretely in the results findings chapters.

a form of *performativity* identified as 'the reiterated practice of *racializing* interpellations' (p. 18). However, the outcome from the collective interaction is the recognition that having affinity to a locality or nation need not require a person's active participation in the reproduction of the perceived cultural norms which dominate that locality, region or state. In fact, taking into account what seems to be a valuing of uniqueness by Liam, adhering to the ethno-cultural expectations of society may be overly conformist. Feelings of affinity and love towards the collective nation of Ireland hold utmost value. The anecdotal account of the lady wearing what is deemed to be 'African' attire implies a zero-sum understanding of both self-identification and externally imposed identification. There does not seem to be space for the subject to express a more polygamous relationship with multiple cultures or nations, resulting in an acceptance of hybrid identities.

The ascription of being an Irish citizen in comparison to being 'Irish' seems to be indicative of a type of labelling as a process of distinction and 'otherness'. In the context of the focus group discussions, this would appear suggestive of a predisposition among some participants towards in-group exclusionary practices. In contrast, the sense is that self-identification as Irish is recognized as an emotional attachment with Ireland, as expressed through feelings of affection towards the country, as well as affinity with a perceived dominant Irish culture.

Specifically in relation to the legal requirement to being 'Irish', what emerges within several focus group discussions is that cultural exposure over a temporal period is afforded significance over either *jus soli* (birthright) or *jus sanguinis* (bloodline) forms of citizenship acquisition. This becomes slightly perplexed when participants contrariwise seem to compound notions of ethnicity as being reliant on both territorial and bloodline association with Ireland and Irish descent. The seemingly recognized importance of birthright or territorial connexion is exemplified when some participants appear to somewhat reject the legitimacy of being American and claiming *Irishness*. Thus, the idealized view of being 'Irish' would seem to exclude concepts of hybrid identities. Some participants emphasize temporal exposure to the dominant cultural norms of Irish society as a solution to the hybridity dilemma. This occurs whereby contestation is made towards supposed claims of being American-Irish, but where a person is viewed to have minimal or no direct exposure to Irish society.

Among several focus group discussions, it appears that for a person residing in Ireland inconsistencies exist between having an attraction to Irish culture and active participation in Irish culture. A further predicament is constructed by some participants whereby Irish culture is continuously conceptualized as fixed and clearly defined, while participants also inversely recognize Irish cultural practices as heterogeneous. In relation to this, conversation evolves by discussing how socio-cultural expectations of the individual may impose conformity. Both *subjectification* through discursive practice and expectations of performances are shown as ways by which Irish social norms and conventional behaviours are imposed through the prism of conformity.

> This chapter sharpens the lens of analysis to document how participants recognize being 'Irish', the power contained in the

capacity to call oneself as Irish, affiliation with being 'Irish' and further ascription to being 'Irish' linking in with the previous findings chapters. Though inseparably intertwined, broadly Chapters 5 and 6 analysed being 'Irish' in relation to *Jus sanguinis* association, while this chapter draws into the debate the more lived temporality of identity formation and being 'Irish'. In combination with *Jus sanguinis* attachments, this chapter also details participants' perceived views on being 'Irish' in connection with *Jus soli* and temporal exposure to Irish culture. Subsequently, Chapter 8 focuses in, as the principal basis of critique, to look at the social construction of 'race', ethnicity and the nation in the context of perceived *Irishness* and 'Irish' identity formation.

144   Redefining Irishness *in a Globalized World*

Chapter 8

Constructing Ethnicity, 'Race' and the Irish Nation

Keywords: Stereotypes; conformity; assimilation; integration; reification fallacy; social Darwinism; hybridity; ascription; Romanticization; civic patriotism

This chapter explores 'race', ethnicity and the nation. The initial section interconnects perceptions of the historical with notions of 'race' and ethnicity as homogeneous. Participants express the requirement to conform to perceived norms so as to be accepted within the dominant norm of Irish society. Linking back to Chapter 6, within one focus group, discussion emphasis is placed on temporal exposure and the acquisition of a sense of collective commonality. There was a slight aside, which is given further elaboration in the conclusion, Chapter 10, in relation to the use of third person plural pronouns. The subsequent section contrasts the notion of 'race' as an imaginary against 'race' as a reality of representation. Across several conversations, a form of reification fallacy is exposed in relation to the blurring of both ethnic and racial distinctions. The Irish are distinguishable, not only because they are perceived as 'white' or 'Caucasian', but further differentiated and defined as a 'race apart' that is 'spotted' or 'freckled'.

Divergent from above is the opinion that ethno-cultural transformation, as well as the erosion of the traditional in the Irish context, is seen as produced by alternative processes of *globalization* and not caused by the arrival of 'newcomers' together with the perceived ethno-racial diversification of the Irish collective. Subtle comments are shown as expressions of the transposition of Darwinian evolutionary theory onto the socio-cultural. Combined with this, 'race' and diversity are interrelated to participants' perceived sense of fear or anxiety with respect to societal change.

The concluding section of this chapter provides findings on participants' notions of the reinvention of 'Irish' identity within an era of *liquid/late-modernity*. Two highly illuminating, yet polar oppositional views are presented whereby

146   Redefining Irishness *in a Globalized World*

one participant perceives being a 'citizen is an illusion'; thus, we should renege control of entry and exit to the island of Ireland, while contradictorily another participant identifies the role and advantage of the state in more stringent migration control.

Genealogical Assumptions and Notions of 'Race'

The generalized perception, across most of the focus group discussions, of physiological traits that would characterize being 'Irish' depicts *Irishness* as of pale, 'white' or Caucasian complexion. Although there seemed to be caution in making such blatant representations within some focus group discussions, which may be due to certain participants' desire to be inclusive, it would seem that such political correctness may have resulted in over sensitivity which, in fact, may mask racialized bias among participants.

Assertions are made within the Drogheda focus group discussion, in partial response to providing a description of a distinctive Irish ethnicity, interconnecting the historical with physiological traits which persist today, in which participants recount how stereotypical notions of physiological homogeneity persistent in contemporary Irish society interdepend on notions of previous historical events, such as settlements and invasions.

Luis: [...] the original populations ... I feel, they look a lot like Northern people, like the Vikings, or, in Ireland, especially in this, it could be my idea from, I am from Spain, I don't know a lot eh, of Nordic country, but I look and feel a lot of Nordic Viking influence ... especially in this area, Dublin, Drogheda, and this eh, people walking the street, I've met my ... idea of Viking ...

Hubert: Yeah, if you're talking about the specific, the specificity of the face, even for a friend downstairs ... he's an Irish man, he's not as blond and as tall as a Nordic man, as a German or as a Scandinavian, but his hair are red ... how do you say it in English?

Dillon: Ginger

Hubert: Yeah, gin, ginger ... and his face ... is very white with a little ginger in him ... but it's maybe by the film of the cartoons, I don't know, white skin, very white skin ...

Toben: What is it? the skin looks like uh, Celtic skin ... because when you see someone for example, in France or Holland or Russia or, you know the difference between the skin of an Irish man ...

Rachel: It's because of the weather though ... the weather affects, (slight pause) for our skin and Ireland is very low ...

Toben: Physically they are not, they are not too big, they are not slim, you know they are not big guys ... it's like average (pause)

Within this excerpt, the participants initially refer to genealogical links that originate from past settlements and invasions to illustrate a perception of physiological Irish traits as being pale and of 'white skin' to the extent that it is evidently different to other countries that might also be associated with a certain Caucasian complexion. What is noteworthy, but given little prominence by how the conversation evolves, is the interjection made by Hubert, who suggests such stereotypical notions of external traits of *Irishness* may be artificially construed through media manipulation such as films or cartoons. Such a scrutinizing eye might also question the role of manipulative elites who contend for power by influencing social divisions through propaganda (Oberschall, 2010, p. 181). Nonetheless, such dimensions of identity politics are not followed up and generally remain absent from discussions.

Instead, the conversation shifts from discussing the participants understanding of Irish history in relation to the homogeneity of Irish physiological traits, to describing traits as being phenotypically determined via intergenerational exposure to Irish climatic conditions. The conversation seems to naturally progress so as to bring in other apparent physical traits of *Irishness* rather than reverting back to discussing attributes based on ethnicity, cultural qualities or questioning the foundation of their generalizations based on a more ancient past.

Becoming 'Irish' Through Conformity and Participation

Although within all of the discussions participants provided debateable views that were assimilationist, integrationist or more multicultural and intercultural in leaning, a central contested position emerged in relation to notions of becoming Irish which relates overall to expectations of conformity. When the question is posed to participants from the Leixlip focus group discussion, the response comparing the difference between being 'Irish' and being an Irish citizen initially reveals the opinion that has been stressed throughout the conversation but in different contexts. It commences by emphasizing the necessity for conformity.

Michael: Like you have to fit in, I can't ... once you stop standing out, I think you become fully Irish, if you get what I mean, (long pause)
Noel: 'cos yeah when, 'cos when you stand out you could be classified as Irish, African or there's lots of things ... you know the way like
Michael: African American
Noel: Yeah African American Irish
YB: [...] can an African American, or an African Irish person, as you say, can they ever stop standing out, because of their racial –?
Noel: No I don't think [so] ... I think they can 'cos, like, there are people in my school who would ... have been born in Africa but like ... then they moved to, at a really early age, to Ireland and like I would consider them Irish ... yeah, there's a guy on our football team who moved here from Nigeria, who was born in Nigeria and stayed there until he was ... like five and he's as much Irish as any of my other friends
Blathnaid: Yeah, I've a friend and she lived in Holland until she was nine, so that was only four years ago and she's like
Kim: [friend's name] (murmurs)
Blathnaid: Yes, [friend's name], yeah she's, like I, you, I didn't even know

Kim: Neither did I
Blathnaid: I thought that like maybe her dad, I think it was her dad was from Holland but ... like I didn't think she was like, lived there or anything
Kim: Like she just started speaking Dutch to her sister and I was like, oh my god

Although initially the emphasis on conformity is suggestive of an *assimilation/ integrationist* perspective, it seems to disregard the consideration of physiological differences that may not complement what might be considered Irish traits. However, when both of the anecdotal accounts present friends with alternative physical characteristics or past affiliations with nations other than Ireland, these seem inconsequential in the process of ascribing *Irishness* onto another person. Neither the temporal length of stay within Ireland nor the physiological traits of a person are deemed to have importance. Instead, subtly in both instances, participation in sports activities, incorporation into friendship circles and conforming to the norms of one's peers seem to permit a person generally to be perceived as Irish. Such views appear to be comparable to the Kantian notion of civic patriotism as described by Kleingeld (2003, p. 303) that refer more to a present attitude of reciprocity between citizen and state, irrespective of *jus soli* or *jus sanguinis* association.

A further consideration that ties in with feelings and emotions (discussed above) but which complements the previous views expressed relates to attaining the specific nuances of Irish culture. Within the Clondalkin focus group discussion, rather than perceiving aspects of being or becoming Irish as a process of conformity, evidently, it is explained in less oppressive terms through the notion of commonality. In describing what it means to be 'Irish', Christine explains the more subtle attitudinal distinctions that might exist such as an affiliation with people perceived as Irish, not just with the nation state itself.

Christine: I think comfortable when they meet other Irish people, that you've something in common with, not everybody but just certain times you're ... happy enough, you know you can just relax and you don't, there's no, people get the nuances, they know what you are about
Dana: There's no messing, they understand the language ...
Christine: The dialect, everything (pause) and the slagging, the behind the scenes kind of stuff, they get ... they get the cultural background, it's there in them, so it's there in you, it's just the politically or whatever you know, kind of there's, they know what's going on when you're slagging the government or when you make a little comment about something ... they knew what that was about to them, cos they were in school with yea or, (slight pause) you know ... I definitely think if kids ... were in school, if kids have come through the Irish school system, you, you don't have, if you even see skin or you just hear them, you hear that they grew up in Ireland, you know ...
Kelsey: Yeah, if they grow up in the Irish culture from a child and they have, they don't know, they don't know their actual, let's say what,

	London, they don't know the London culture, they know our culture which makes them an Irish person, 'cos they can identify with Irish culture not the English culture
Christine:	Yeah, I think your parents, (slight pause) I think schooling and parents and something, have something to do with that as well, you know… I don't know, I think they do
Kelsey:	Not necessarily being born but kind of growing up in Ireland

Although there had been no impetus placed on discussing what being 'Irish' means in relation to the perceived potential 'other', the conversation seems to shift to describe it in relation to a third person 'other'. Fascinatingly, this change seems to occur where there appears to be slight confusion in interpreting 'they' within the conversation. The third person 'they' is initially incorporated into the sentence to describe the generalized 'other' Irish person who possesses the same cultural nuances as the participant. However, the use of 'they' seems to shift in its use to become a descriptor of subjects who might have entered into Irish culture, unlike most Irish, and subsequently the pronoun, 'them' is otherwise spoken.

The use of the third person plural pronouns of 'they' and 'them' in the context of the excerpt does not seem to differentiate in an intentionally derogatory or subordinating manner. Instead, the language is used to underscore the proposition that a person's formative way of life or ethnicity is the primary determiner in one being or becoming Irish, rather than one's bloodline descent or physiological traits. The experiential, through schooling and parental upbringing within an environment of exposure to Irish culture, is given priority over both bloodline and birthright connection to the Irish collective. The mention of accent together with seeing the 'skin' of a person implies recognition of a racialized determinant in being or becoming Irish yet it attempts to commensurably maintain *Irishness* as colour or racially blind. This implies that although notions based on 'race' exist also as abstract signifiers that separate human groups socially, politically and economically (Lentin, 2008, p. 490), in the Irish context, skin colour is perceived as a defining characteristic of being, or not being, Irish.

'Race' as an Imaginary and 'Race' as a Reality

Being 'Irish' is viewed within legalistic frameworks, and through culturally normative values attitudes and behaviours, but it also seems to be weighted heavily in relation to bloodline descent or hereditary bonds. In the Drumcondra focus group discussion, the notion of the Irish 'race' is assumed factual by Ryan (as mentioned above), and similarly implied in other focus group discussions.[1] This perspective may not have been shared by all of the participants as is evidenced later when Carroll challenges notions of the existence of a stereotypical *Irishness* by stating, 'but I don't think it really is what it is (pause)' to which Ciara continues,

---

[1] Please refer to the Limerick, Drumchondra, Naas, Leixlip and Coolock focus group discussions.

referring to the heterogeneity of Irish society, by stating, 'I think there's loads of different Irish's, Irishnesses, you know...'.

Nevertheless, within the Limerick focus group discussion, when *Irishness* was referred to in racialized terms, it was nuanced and the conversational viewpoints were more indicative of a cynical understanding of the notion of an Irish 'race', and perhaps an apropos view of the racialization of peoples more generally. The perceived difference between being an Irish citizen and being 'Irish' comes to the fore in the Limerick focus group discussion when answering one of the closing questions on whether, or not, having Irish descent is an essential criterion for being 'Irish' (along with the question, can someone become Irish?). Again, the legal and pragmatic dimension of the passport is initially discussed and how the conversation evolves is quite illuminating.

Juliana: If you get citizenship, does that mean you are Irish? (pause)
Dale: Does it mean like you can get an Irish passport and have Irish citizen on it, I suppose does it?
Juliana: Yeah, but does that make you Irish?
Dale: I don't know, I've never had a problem getting an Irish passport like
Charlie: Well I think, in a few words of sense Juliana, if you haven't Irish blood in yea, (pause) yeah there's a good thing there ... if you're not, haven't Irish blood in you, [it] is only making an Irish citizen
Juliana: Yeah
Charlie: It's not making you Irish ... as in Irish blood? ...
Juliana Yeah, blood Irish
Maebh Yeah, I think you are dead right ...
Juliana You're not a member of the Irish race in other words ... but you can ...
Charlie: Or if, we'll call it species (laughter)
Adrian: Now (laughter)
Maebh: Species
Charlie: You know when you look at a monkey, well ... leaving evolution out of this, he's never going to turn into one style of giraffe (laughter)

The direction the conversation takes and the closing analogy would seem to reveal the underlying notion bound with being 'Irish'. In what appears somewhat satirical, Charlie refers to having Irish blood as being the distinguisher between being 'Irish' or being, in a lower esteem, an Irish citizen (as discussed in the previous chapter). Having Irish blood or heredity is then equated to 'the Irish race'; however, this is somewhat joked about by Charlie when he compares it to species. In fact, Charlie's analogy of the impossibility of a monkey becoming giraffe, in all its unnaturalness, is suggestive of the utter unfeasibility of a person without Irish blood ever becoming Irish. There is the sense that these comments are being made quite sarcastically, but they are also indicative of a perceived view of a dominant attitude that may prevail in Irish society more generally. As ludicrous as the sarcastic comment denotes, the questioning of the underlying logic of 'race' resonates with the position held by Balibar (1991) who claims, 'there is in fact no racism without theory (or theories) ... It is, however, quite clear that they are "rationalized" by intellectuals' (p. *18f.*).

Although this view of an Irish 'race' seems to be recognized as somewhat dubious, and referred to with some level of satirical criticism, the conversation continues to reveal that the term is also conversely used in descriptive terms making its understanding both imagined and real at one in the same time.

YB:	Does your passport mean you're an Irish citizen?
Charlie:	Citizen yeah, I don't know the wording but, put down on those documents, but ...
Maebh:	If Irish blood means that you're true Irish ...
YB:	Irish blood means you're a true, true Irish person, so you would say then you can't, so for instance your 'Chinese' friend could never be Irish?
Adrian:	But she is
Juliana:	She is possibly not part of the Irish race

That Maebh makes the conditional sentence, rather than stating as factual Irish blood equates to being truly Irish, is suggestive of a level of hesitation concerning such a claim. To add to this, Adrian's recognition of a friend they had previously discussed, who had immigrated to Ireland from China when they were young and had by now spent the majority of their life in Ireland as being 'Irish', would also seem to challenge a bloodline association with being 'true Irish'. Similarly, although Juliana claims that they may not be part of the Irish 'race', it is stated with some level of doubt. So, on the one hand, there appears to be recognition of the ambiguous nature and subjectivity of the term 'race' specifically in relation to *Irishness*, yet contrarily the notion itself remains imbedded within the psyche and conscience of the participants, thus maintaining its existence. That is to say, the participants did not get to the point of undermining the notional idea of 'the Irish race' as a core concept that had been taken-for-granted. Because 'race' is recognized as imagined, yet as a concept it is left unchallenged, fallen back on and even reproduced, it restricts different forms and comprehensions of existence that might otherwise emerge. So doing is in direct opposition to what Acampora (2007) describes as the imaginary domain activating 'the possibility for change' (p. 67).

The Reification Fallacy of Ethnic and Racial Distinction

Within the Naas focus group discussion, the initial description of a distinctive Irish ethnicity from participants focused on rural life; that 'a lot of people seem to have very strong connection with farms' (Colin), and quite mockingly on diet, in particular potatoes. Recognition is made that 'well even now, you know we're not really a farming country anymore' but that still, 'people tend to eat everything that they would've eaten if they lived on a farm' (Colin). When the perception of a distinctive Irish ethnicity is probed further, the response given relates back to an alternative interpretation of the historical (as discussed above).

152   *Redefining* Irishness *in a Globalized World*

Colin: I don't think there is one really 'cos, we all came, we came from Spain didn't we? The first people in Ireland came from Spain somewhere
Liam: Well nowadays it's a strong mixture of different countries is in Ireland ...
Colin: There is a strong mixture of different countries everywhere
Liam: There's not exactly (slight pause), yeah I know but ... there's not exactly one Irishness now because a lot of people –
Colin: Have come in
Liam: Yeah, there's a lot of different cultures in Ireland nowadays then what it would've been years ago ...
YB: [...] and are those cultures also Irish?
Colin: No, not always (pause) Irish, they're different, they may not be Irish, um (pause), sometimes they become more Irish as the longer they're here ... but they usually aren't when they first come

On this occasion, a cultural comparison seems to be made between more ancient times, when Ireland was first inhabited, with contemporary or recent historical times. The implication is that even throughout history 'newcomers' who may have possessed alternative cultural norms have since integrated into the dominant Irish culture through assimilation. Such views would seem to correspond with Latham's (2010) description of the *subsumption pathway*, as detailed in Chapter 3, whereby the supposition is that eventually integration will occur through assimilation into the larger, more dominant, collective.

As the conversation progresses however, trying to describe what people might be assimilating into or pinpointing what is an Irish ethnicity, becomes problematic. Perhaps, a generalized view is that '... years ago, do you know, we were all farmers, used to drink a lot' (Liam) and that 'it was almost exclusively Catholic' (Colin). These generalized views seemingly emphasize a commonality of perceived cultural values, attitudes and behaviours, yet there would appear to be the opinion by the participants that they paint quite an artificial representation of Irish society. In relation to this, what might be inferred from the participants' reversion to more satirical responses to the question is that the participants might have had a difficultly clearly defining ethnicity and/or they may have genuinely found it difficult to describe a distinctive Irish ethnicity beyond relying on superficial generalizations. When Eithne questioned how ethnicity was defined by asking, '... do you mean by the ethnicity, you're talking about colour as well? Or specific traits, are you specifically talking about the cultural norms?' Leaving this open for interpretation, the subsequent response is as follows.

Eithne: Well I guess the stereotype that definitely comes is the freckly face, you know ... that's what I deem of when I think of ethnicities, em, race as well, but then I think one thing that's standing out in particular, in terms of how the society is, is definitely drinking is a big part of it as well

Noticeable here is suggestion of the compounding of both cultural and what might be perceived as inherent physiological traits in an attempt to describe a distinctive Irish *ethno-racial* condition. By blending both, it provides the participant with a seemingly clearer, more concrete understanding of what they are self-describing, which, thus, prevents the questioning of the underlying notions of ethnic or racial distinctions discretely.

A previous section, elaborated in the excerpt from the Clondalkin focus group discussion, interwove ethnic notions of *Irishness* and the recognition by participants of the importance of temporal exposure to Irish culture. Continuing on what is later deliberated, the discussion relates to the effects of exhibiting physiological traits that might be interpreted as more or less Irish like. This corresponds with the problematic difficulty in distinguishing between notions of an Irish ethnicity in relation to views of 'race' or more specifically people of differing physiological traits. Kelsey overtly raises the issue in discussion on whether, or not, being born in Ireland is an essential criterion for being 'Irish'. When the conversation reverts back to justifying one's claim to *Irishness* by simply growing up in Ireland (as discussed above), racial considerations are discussed.

Dana: It's just where you grow up
Kelsey: I think even like, I know it's horrible to say but with a dark person, it's, it's very hard for (slight pause) them to integrate where ... if you actually are the skin colour it's a lot easier like ... and people won't perceive you like, I mean no one would have known I was born in Birmingham, a different country, 'cos I look Irish ... well I look Polish but am I? ... (laughter) ... but if a darker person came it's straight away, 'Are you Irish?, Are you sure?' do you know like it's ... so it's harder for a dark person to integrate as an Irish persona, whereas if you're white and from anywhere else but you look Irish you're grand ... you can get away with it

Although this aspect of not possessing the corresponding physiological traits with what is deemed as Irish is only discussed at this latter stage of the focus group discussion, the simple acknowledgement of this predicament appears significant. This is because not only is it raising an issue that seemed to be equivocated previously, it seems to indicate an outward empathic view on what might inhibit a person from truly becoming Irish. Nonetheless, it implies that the participants haven't, through participation and reflexivity, made the realization that what might be at the core of the discussion relates more to their own sense of perceived *Irishness*.

Whereas *Irishness* seems to be initially perceived within boundaries delimited by specifically recognized physiological traits, these bodily traits correspond with what is viewed as dominant normative external characteristics of a person such as paleness, 'whiteness' or Caucasian. In this way, 'race' as a signifier is more pronounced than ethnicity or gender as it is based on the corporeal state rather than acts. As Butler (1988) describes, gender identity is 'instituted through a *stylized repetition of acts*' (p. 519), so too can ethnicity, if conceived of discrete from 'race', be an enactment. Somehow because the bodily condition associated with 'race' is seemingly inescapable, so too is it implausible that a 'darker person' can be Irish. Thus, 'race' is pronounced conceptually, in the mind, and visibly, in our perceived reality.

The extract recognizes the dilemma whereby such fixed conceptions of perceived *Irishness*, thus, become disturbed by the expected initial realization that people with darker complexion may be excluded from being acknowledged within the Irish collective. Kelsey expresses a reaction towards a questioning attitude that potentially falsely perceives a person as 'other'. Her reaction also seems to illustrate the ease with which a person with supposedly similar skin who may not have any, or only tenuous links to Ireland, could be afforded privilege and be more easily incorporated into the Irish collective. Although the expectation was that this bind might be more deeply deliberated and deconstructed, evidently, the participants' attitudes in this conversation remain quite embedded in the reification fallacy of Irish physiological traits equating only to a Caucasian complexion.

Similar to several other opinions expressed in separate focus group discussions (as in the previous chapter on 'feeling Irish'), more concrete notions of being 'Irish' appear to be challenged within the Drogheda focus group discussion. Continuing on to describe what it means to be 'Irish', Toben makes an effort to go beyond conceiving *Irishness* merely through nation state affiliation and legalistically afforded criteria such as citizenship and nationality.

Toben: You know that question is a bit, it's very complicated
YB: Be frank
Toben: Yes, being Irish, is feeling Irish, you have to feel Irish yourself, to be Irish, and eh, having Irish citizenship or being born in Ireland for me that doesn't make you Irish ... and I don't know how to say this, but it's how you feel yourself, and it's hard to cut your roots, because something will bring you always there, so being Irish, for me, is feeling Irish

Leading on from this is a comment pertaining to how perceived characterizations and portrayals of *Irishness* are restrictive in racial terms. However, what is noteworthy is that such understanding of the ascription of 'Irish' identity is referenced at an earlier stage of the discussion, prior to viewing the multimedia presentation.

Toben: But also, you have to be accepted by other people as Irish, because you say you are Irish, but if people don't accept you, you are not Irish, if I say now I'm an Irish man, and people don't believe you, they will clearly say 'oh, yes he's Irish but he got Irish citizenship', but when you finish here, 'what the, why is the black man saying he is an Irish man?' (laughter) ... and he will say, 'I have a friend, no he was ... he has the passport' ... and better I calling him, 'you, you will never be Irish man, (slight pause) a black man will never be an Irish man' ... that is the truth ... and that same man, he will say, 'my country's going to play eh, next Friday', 'which country is it?' ... 'Nigeria'
Irena: Of course, yes
Toben: But he will say he is an Irish man

There appears to be an evident connection expressed within this excerpt between being deemed an Irish citizen, rather than being 'Irish', and racialized notions of what might be, or in this case, might never be perceived as Irish irrespective of the legislative reality. Initially, Toben seems to expose the actual and real implications of being a 'black man' and seems to be subtly critical of the fixed nature of generalized perceptions of *Irishness* that are exclusive and, thus, exclude. Somewhat surprisingly however, the criticism seems to be inverted to target the 'black man' who might have mixed, if not counter-allegiances. This would appear to suggest the rejection of the authenticity and compatibility of hybrid identities, yet it does not seem to discount the existence of such. As discussed (see above), not only does the participant from within the normatively dominant perspective advocate the view that exhibiting hybrid identity seems discordant with the claim of *Irishness*, Toben's view would also seem to complement such a stance.

Similarly, evidence of the reification fallacy is assumed within the Belfast focus group discussion, in the participants' description of a distinctive Irish ethnicity. Tony replies, although slightly more ambiguously, '(pause) I think we just answered that one, ethnicity, well it depends how you define ethnicity, I suppose, ethnicity for Western Europe. You rarely look at skin colour, you always accepted it as white'. Likewise in the Coolock focus group discussion, and the initial descriptions of a distinctive Irish ethnicity, from several of the participants, refer to more cultural aspects of living and traditional or past lifestyles. When the question is restated however, several participants demonstrate more evidently an incomprehension of the question, specifically the term *ethnicity*.

Without interjection and rearticulating of the question by the facilitator, Grainne proceeds by describing physiological traits.

Grainne: White
Tierney: White
Grainne: For starters yeah
Tierney: Ok
Conlaoch: What, white?
Peadar: Caucasian
Tierney: So white skinned, Celtic
Conlaoch: No –
Aileen: No?
Conlaoch: No, we're not
Tierney: White skinned
Emmet: Catholic
Conlaoch: No, we're not ... we're spotted, we are the spotted people
Tierney: ha, ok, ha
Conlaoch: We're a race apart, I mean
Aileen: Exactly
Grainne: The question was ... how do I perceive Irish
Conlaoch: Oh yeah, so you, so you assume it yourself
Tierney: Ok, so you say white, (slight pause) you say white

156 Redefining Irishness *in a Globalized World*

Grainne:	I wouldn't say Caucasian
Tierney:	Why?
Grainne:	I would actually say white
Tierney:	You say white, ok (pause)
Conlaoch:	I say spotted

The implication from this excerpt seems to go beyond Marshall's (2000, p. 16) description of the construction of the quintessential Irish stereotype as being based on physiological traits of 'whiteness', as well as other characteristics, such as heterosexual, Irish born, settled and Catholic. Physiological traits are described in even more defined and distinct terms. Conlaoch continues to seemingly justify this description by claiming that the Irish are 'freckled people'. Evidenced in this extract is not only the desire by several participants to distinguish the Irish as 'white' or 'Caucasian' but to further differentiate the Irish as a 'race apart' that is 'spotted' or 'freckled'. In the context of the overall focus group discussion, it is worth noting that Emmet, within this extract, does not make any affirmation regarding physiological traits, nor are those challenged. Instead, Emmet, on several occasions, apparently interjects in an attempt to relate *Irishness* to the religious affiliation of Catholicism. If cultural habits can be shaped by institutions of religion, this would seem a more appropriate answer to the initial question posed.

Ethno-racialized Identity Ascription

A continuation of conversation in answer to what it means to be 'Irish' within the Coolock focus group discussion leads on to discuss how the Irish have now become more heterogeneous in relation to physiological appearance. This realization seems to give rise to some awkwardness when the racialized associations made (as discussed above) are viewed in relation to what was once a supposed homogenized nation.

Aileen: I would say that the Irish people now, really, I know this is going to sound bad but, more of a mixture, like you know, yea, you can … you can be standing, I remember standing in a chemist and the, it's quite a while ago, and there weren't that many people from other nationalities living here and it was a real Dublin accent and I turned around and the girl was black and I nearly died like you know … because it wasn't something I expected …

Within this short excerpt, Aileen seems to express an acceptance of how in contemporary times the Irish can be conceived as having greater heterogeneity. By stating, 'I know this is going to sound bad but', the implication may be that such notions of homogeneity can naturally be challenged but such negation should be perceived negatively and as undesirable. It is also implied that the individual might have a nationality that doesn't correspond to their accent, which would be attained through cultural exposure over time. This is suggestive of an ascription of identity that might be termed hybridity (as elaborated above). Such speculation on the nationality of the individual in the pharmacy, as described, might also be interpreted as a means of subjugation below the status of simply being seen and perceived as Irish. Following on from expressions of conflicting views regarding *Irishness*, the conversation reverts back, somewhat reflexively, to describe what becomes as much a critique of broader society as a self-critique on the part of Aileen. Evidently, Aileen disagrees with Tierney's and Conlaoch's notional views that the Irish have inherent attributes, such as being '… wired to think a particular way and to behave in a particular way' (Conlaoch). Instead, Aileen expresses that it is a person's location of birth that determines their acceptance into the Irish collective.

Aileen: Well I disagree, I don't think that Irish people are particularly right, as I say that, that was a real turning point that day, that girl because that girl was, was black and she had the Dublin accent, so I think it's because she was born here, so you feel … she's of my people

In truth, the notion of hybridity extends beyond identification and allegiances with specific countries; it can also be interpreted in how people view hybridity in the form of external physiological traits a person might be perceived to possess. For instance, an initial post-viewing comment is made in the Drogheda focus group discussion by Machie who seems to focus attention on such external traits:

Machie: Well, out of the four interviews there … I would say the first person, would have been the most striking Irish person …yeah, even though she was from (an) African origin … she had a lot of freckles on her face … and that's an Irish person too … you know apart from that, the accent was very strong

This opening of discussion post-viewing may be revealing of how, more often than not, an individual may subliminally evaluate and read a person through the visual firstly. Within this process of constructing first impressions, bias enters in an attempt by the mind to decode, categorize and ascribe a generalized identity onto the person built on presumptions. Such processes of socio-psychological presuppositions becoming embedded in the individual's consciousness may likely occur within a collective that accentuates the immutability of singular identity distinctions rather than conceiving identities as fluid and variable. The fixity of a person's external physiological traits will likely complement such a process. Thus, the process compounds one's racialized labelling together with one's ethnicized labelling which makes it hard to challenge or transgress the association between *Irishness* and paleness, 'whiteness' or being Caucasian.

Many of the participants within each of the focus group discussions did respond to the initial post-viewing question, which was quite open and was unspecific concerning physiological traits, by referring to the interviewees' external visible traits rather than the audio content or overall disposition. Within the Belfast focus group discussion, the initial post-viewing comment as above is, 'it was very interesting to see so many walks of life, you know, and people from different parts of the world with a wee bit of family here, you know, Irishness doesn't actually have a colour or a language'.

Furthermore, in the focus group discussion, the following query is conjectured:

Eddie: [...] the first one, the girl, I wondered were you playing a game with us, did the visual in fact match the audio at all ... because the girl obviously had a, an Irish accent ... and what she was saying, I suppose, didn't give me the impression, or I didn't feel the impression that she might have had an ethnically different background ... the images clearly show that she had ... and I thought, he's playing a game with us, do-you-know ... but then when it went on then, and the images sort of fitted the audio, then I decided, no he's not playing a game that, he's not playing a game with us

Within this excerpt, Eddie appears to express, somewhat accurately, a suspicion that the visual and audio material may not match. However, Eddie's comments go beyond the manipulation that was conducted in the production by suspecting and doubting that the accent from either of the female interviewees corresponded with the visual images of the first interviewee, Laura. Similar to what is previously discussed (see above), by linking the visual stimuli with the notion that 'she might have had an ethnically different background' (Eddie), ethnicity becomes merged with physiological traits. When compounded with notions of 'race', the comprehension of ethnicity as a social identifier seems to result in the assumption that ethnicity has certain constituents that are 'assumed "givens"' (Geertz, 1973, p. 259). Furthermore, it implies that ethnic attachments are not only temporally attained through exposure but are biologically and innately acquired (Tovey et al., 1989, p. 5). By binding a perceived notion of cultural ways of life that are collectivized into distinct groups, together with racialized notions, it entraps the individual into only conceiving *Irishness* in restrictive terms that do not complement the theorization which proposes that identities are fluid and socially constructed. As such, the impression is that an ethno-racial bind based on the reification fallacy occurs in the psyche of some participants.

Societal Transformations, 'Newcomers' and Discriminating Fear

In contrast within the Leixlip focus group discussion, when a distinctive Irish ethnicity is elaborated as a distinctively Irish way of life, the participants make no reference to phenotypes or physiological traits. Instead, the participants refer to Irish sports and athletics more generally.[2] When the facilitator asks, 'can we say

---

[2]In the context of the Irish sport within other discussions reference is made to how it still exists through *parochialism*, a theme discussed in Chapter 5. Within other focus group discussions, participation in sports is also emphasized. Perceptions of sport are offered both through the act of participation and through spectatorship.

Constructing Ethnicity, 'Race' and the Irish Nation **159**

there is a distinctive Irish way of life?', the response seems relatively unequivocal among the participants.

Kim: Not really
Michael: Not really, no, umm (pause)
YB: Not really?
Blathnaid: Lots of like, people from other countries have now, like moved here so now I think it's not really, it's mixed, like cultures and stuff ... like they might do some Irish things but like, they'd still be raised like maybe how their grandparents were raised or something, some, like, a lot of people are from other countries now in Ireland
Kim: And it's mostly only the like older people who still have, like still do what they did when they were younger and all
Noel: Yeah, 'cos we watch a lot of American tv and... like Nickelodeon and stuff
Michael: Eating like processed foods, that aren't from Ireland
YB: So ... the culture that we absorb... isn't really Irish?
Kim: No
Noel: It's all imported stuff
Kim: From America and stuff like
Michael: British

Although this goes in a different tangent away from the ethno-racial considerations, the conversation does appear to reveal significant reflections concerning notions of the traditional versus cultural appropriation within the context of transnational trade and a globalizing world. Evidently, there is the subtle undertone and recognition that although there have been changes leading to a perceived greater cultural heterogeneity with migration, a more dominant effect on what seems to be perceived as a distinctively Irish way of life is media exposure and consumption patterns determined and influenced primarily from the global powers of America and Britain. These perspectives would appear to complement the description by Inglis (2008, p. 2) of the effects of *globalization*, whereby it is perceived that local everyday life in Ireland is becoming global, and to a lesser degree Americanized.

Leading on from this, the question is posed as to what the participants perceive is 'a distinctive Irish traditional way of life?' in order to elicit what might be meant by a traditionally Irish way of life and how it might be described. Although quite generalized and romanticized, the participants' views of traditional Ireland may reveal an understated component of transnationalism.

Kim: You know go out and milk or whatever
Michael: Independence I'd say
Noel: Yeah ... like on the bog and stuff ...
YB: So again, kind of generalizations though right, and how do you mean by independence?
Michael: Well I mean, when, kinda (slight laughter), I (slight pause), I like (laughter) yeah

160   Redefining Irishness *in a Globalized World*

Kim: From a young age they were like going out
Michael: Yeah like, when my granny was young and stuff like that ... she like, they wouldn't really, like in America, they would be kind of (slight pause), kind of fed by their parents, if you know what I mean, like when you think of old people in Ireland, you think of kids like, milking cows and –
YB: Ok, so you mean a kind of sustainability, like producing their own products?
Michael: Yeah, like not having to buy stuff from shops, making it themselves

Within this extract, the facilitator assumed that the 'independency' the participants refer to relates to a greater level of self-sufficiency within the lifestyles of traditional Irish living. However, what becomes apparent is that the independence may have been initially mentioned concerning the responsibility and also freedom young individuals in the past might have had, thus associating it with a higher level of independence.

Above all, implicit to the content in both excerpts above, would seem to be the perception of tradition and independence in the Irish context being challenged through exposure to hegemonic cultural production from abroad. The traditional would appear to be portrayed as having greater self-sustainability with localized food production and consumption, as well as energy resources whereas, at present, individuals' existence seems increasingly dependent on and encroached on by external forces.

Linking in with the excerpt that was documented above concerning historical change, within the Drumcondra focus group discussion, the participants respond to the idea of re-imagining identity in the 21st century by first mentioning cultural diversity. They continue by providing a more optimistic opinion of immigration and increased pluralism.

Carroll: That's a difficult ... question
Ryan: I would see it as a mix, you know a mix of new citizens ... really with whom we're bringing, you know, differences with them, you know, and I think it'll greatly enrich the country, in many different ways, so it's a –
Ciara: Different outlooks you know, they're bringing
Ryan: Different outlook, customs, you know ... there'll be ... more, you know, diverse ... and interesting country as a result ... you know, if that happens
Carroll: I think it will be very enriching
Ciara: If that happens in the right way
Carroll: You know, what, it's strong, what's strong and what's (pause), what's strong survives in any culture, and we hope it's the good parts that survive ... and if the other bits come in and they mix in with it and make it better
Ciara: An enriching of both things ... and then there's always the downside, the opposite of that as well, but one would, I personally would hope that it would all be the positive stuff ...
YB: [...] what would you see as an enrichment or 'positive'?

Ciara: Alternative solutions to situations that maybe Irish people wouldn't have viewed, whereas another culture, another group of people could come in and think, well, 'could we try this?'
Eddie: A less insular attitude ...
Ryan: Enriching the gene pool maybe ... (slight laughter) you know

The conversation progresses in a generally optimistic tone, yet it seems as though, following the previous remarks that were made throughout the focus group discussion by the same participants it is embellished and slightly contradictory (as evidenced from extracts above and detailed in Chapter 7). The participants seem to have reverted to a more politically correct and seemingly progressive stance in relation to diversity. There are subtle comments within the conversation that are nonetheless indicative of a reliance on notions of inherent naturalness and the transposition of Darwinian evolutionary thought onto the socio-cultural, such as notions of survival of the fittest and enrichment, genetic or otherwise. In fact somewhat in contrast to what was portrayed in relation to resisting change and the fear of the new, Ryan seems to refer to identity as changeable, 'it's not fixed, (pause) it would be, I think, there's an element of Darwinism in this, in this whole thing, you know, if you don't adapt or you don't change then you're going to falter ...'. Societal change in Darwinian and evolutionary terms becomes blended with a pragmatic yet quite vague view of Irish societal advancement. When combined with themes detailed within the previous excerpts, this assumption of linear progress, as critiqued by Clifford (2000, p. 105), would appear to subtly emphasize a *fatalism* of culturally assimilated oneness, being shaped by the forces of *globalization*.

What also emerges overall is a general sense that the participants' frame of reference, albeit providing apparently quite liberal stances, emphasizes the benefits quite *ethnocentrically*. Neglected in the conversation is a form of empathy (discussed in further detail in the following chapters), or the recognition and consideration of the benefits that may be gained by 'the newcomer' in becoming accepted within what is deemed as Irish.

Somewhat alternatively, the conversation on the difference between being 'Irish' and being an Irish citizen in the Coolock focus group discussion evolves away from the technical/legal aspects to seemingly point out the less tangible sense of 'feeling' or 'wanting' and 'desiring' to be 'Irish' (as discussed above).

YB: Or is there a difference?
Emmet: No ... I think what Aileen said was I think it's a feeling that Irishness, and, (slight pause) but that may not necessarily be (pause) how would I say, an all- encompassing thing because maybe as we embrace more cultures what, (slight pause) the feeling of what being Irish is, may (slight pause) become something different to us and our generation ...
Tierney: And that's a fear for us, that's a fear for us ... it's a fear that
Emmet: [...] your analogy there about you know where, where Africa is now is like where we were two hundred years ago, or whatever ... and (slight pause) yeah it's, it's on a bigger scale, it's on a huge, it's a, a much bigger scale, it's, it's much like our land was pillaged and plundered, the

whole continent and that's why they can't ... rise out of their poverty or whatever, but they are moving out into the world ... and we're actually going, 'ah hold on a minute' ...

Tierney: [...] yeah but that's a self-preservation thing right, we, like, there's we have, we will help people along the way, welcome people in here but there has to be a limit, for one, for our state of mind, I, in my opinion the state of mind, the Irishness that we have, this place that we have, cannot absorb another four million in the next say ten years, and still be the same country that we have now, that's just doesn't make sense, I, let's say twenty years, another four million ... and I, maybe I'm exaggerating the, the numbers, but I'm just saying, that it creates a fear when we say that it's open door, it's unlimited ... we will ... never ever stop anybody coming in here

Emmet: I don't think Tierney ... (multiple voices)

Peadar: Can I just come back to the question and illustrate it, I worked for a guy who –

Tierney: It doesn't make me a racist to say that

Peadar continues to describe a person from Zambia who is an engineer that came to Ireland with his family and whose son grew up and went through the Irish education system. Peadar refers to the son as Irish, by stating that the rationale for the son gaining employment was 'because he was Irish'. The conversation reverts back to discussion above.

Emmet: I mean, just to, sorry address what ... Tierney [was] going on about there ... I think that's more of a hypocritical kind of Irish thing that we have, which is, the Irish have gone out all over the world ... and we're very proud, and we actually believe ... wholeheartedly –

Tierney: We built America

Emmet: By going out we did a great thing ... but yet we can't get our heads around these people coming to us could do great things for us

Tierney: No, no, no I'm not saying, I'm saying people of course can come in here and do great stuff for us, but it's the numbers, it's the ratio ... that's unlimited

YB: In relation to the ratio that's unlimited, an unlimited number of people from Poland could come into Ireland tomorrow

Peadar: Correct

Tierney: Yes, yes that's a fear

The basis for the counter-argument presented by Emmet rests on an understanding of the historical past of Irish emigration. In contrast to the excerpt from the focus group referenced above, Emmet does seem to make some acknowledgement of the plight of 'others' within a more globalized world with widening inequality, though it is mentioned in more sympathetic, rather than empathetic terms by referring to the historical plight of the Irish during the famine. Initially, Tierney argues against a policy of unlimited migration yet this seems quite clearly directed at migration from developing economies.[3] Although there appears to be self-reflection on the sentiment of fear towards unlimited migration, it does seem to be relatively non-figurative. This anxiety based on an abstract and notional idea of an overwhelming of the Irish population via immigration seems racialized as, in fact, hypothetically at present the real and existent way such could occur would be from populations within the European Union. Although Tierney does confirm that concern would exist about migration into Ireland from the broader European Union and beyond, it would seem permissible, to an extent, once the 'newcomers' as Emmet states 'could do great things for us'. What would seem to be subtly evidenced in this extract within the Coolock focus group discussion, as well as responses to the question on having Irish descent, is a criterion for acceptance into the Irish collective being based on whether or not the respective individual will be beneficial to the country. Such a position is very unidirectional, in effect seems quite usurping, differing from the sense of an *assimilationist* view but supporting a more racial *neo-liberalist* standpoint (Goldberg, 2009; Kapoor, 2013; Lentin, 2015). It differs from *neoconservatism* in that it does not purport to conserve a traditional status-quo, instead it incorporates those that are worthy 'newcomers' if they can 'do great stuff for us' (Tierney).

In a post-viewing comment, the aspect of change evoking fear is also remarked upon by Emmanuel within the Drogheda focus group discussion and is described apparently as a reaction to a perceived threat to the stability of one's own apparent culture and self-identity.

Emmanuel: [...] our identity or identity ... it comes stronger when we feel that something might happen ... you know like, (slight pause) we become more part of our self ... when we have to fight against the losses of our culture... that's why sometimes you will, you feel you know Irish when you are, somebody asks what makes him Irish, he will tell you, eh, Catholic, you know ... and these eh (slight pause), because they, they're fighting against the change in their identity, that is the point ... so, (long pause) the fear is to loss our culture, is to lose who we are or who we believe we are, that is the fear ... and when you, change, when you leave your country, you go to another country, (slight pause) and you hear the music, that's the music, a song of your own country somewhere you feel powerful, you feel proud of being from your country ... and that ... is higher than when you are in your own country and you hear the same music

Emmanuel's concluding comments within this segment could easily be related to conversations that were prevalent within other focus group discussions on being 'Irish' abroad. It emerges in several of the discussions (as previously discussed)

---

[3]This is subtly emphasized in the final interjection stating '... that's **a** fear' rather than, 'that's **the** fear'

164   Redefining Irishness *in a Globalized World*

that one's sense of affiliation to *Irishness* and closeness would be intensified when abroad or in a setting as the minority.

This extract is revealing as it would seem to provide the perspective of the 'newcomer' having lived abroad and their sense of sentimentality. When placed within the context of the previous excerpt, it makes conspicuous a commonality between both the 'native' and the 'newcomer'. Both have constructed their self-identity based on associations with their respective nations, but with changing lives, either as the new arrival or the host, there is a heightened sense of fear and anxiety. It would not be unreasonable to conjecture that for the 'newcomer' their fear would be more accentuated and may potentially deepen regret at their extraction from the habituated lives they had led before. Also compounded within this may be that the 'newcomer' also carries the burden of a fear of rejection by the 'natives'.

Re/imagining *Irishness*

In alleviating the perception of fear or anxiety that might be related to the sense of a loss of culture or loss of self-identity within the continuum of liquid modernity, an obvious remedy would be the re-imaging of what it means to be 'Irish'. Prior to any additional questions being asked pertaining to concepts of reimagining 'Irish' identity within the Drogheda focus group discussion, conversation recurs on the importance of not only self-recognition but the recognition by 'others', or the ascription of 'Irish' identity, in legitimating one-self to fully claim *Irishness*. This seems to lead into a revealing disclosure that acknowledges an anxiety that hadn't been expressed by other participants within the other focus group discussions.

Emmanuel: […] in the modern world now eh, I think Irish, Irish man will be, (slight pause) different, will not be just black, he will not be just white, he will not be just Catholic, he will not be just Muslim but is everything together, you understand, eh, it's like a rainbow, rainbow country now we are living in (slight laughter) … yeah, we have to accept that, I believe that if we accept that way … eh, it will be a peaceful country, (slight pause) if everyone can accept that this one can be Irish … even though he looks Chinese, he can be Irish, (slight pause) really he can be Irish because, (slight pause) if someone asks me how, where I'm from, (slight pause) if I have Irish passport, I say 'I'm from Ireland' and he is Irish, you look at me again (laughter) … you understand? … I tried to do it here before you know, someone asked me, [I replied] 'well I can say I'm from Kerry' the person looked at me (laughter) … and, another just laughed (laughter) … you understand?
Ezinwa: He became satisfied
Emmanuel: Yeah (laughter) … we have to accept it that, it's not just I have to be like this to be Irish … I am Irish because I am accepted to be

	Irish, I have the citizenship ... I feel Irish, like other Irish people, and I want to give something to Ireland
YB:	So, can I, (slight pause) to me what you're suggesting is reimagining what Irishness is, or reinventing Irishness ...
Emmanuel:	I think it's already done, yeah forsaken us (laughter)
YB:	[...] ok so what's interesting, no because what you're saying, you're coming back to the law, it definitely is already done
Emmanuel:	Yes

The implication of what Emmanuel is suggesting seems to be that *Irishness* has, in recent times, been reinvented but that it has neglected to embrace people of skin colour other than 'white' and perhaps, from the perspective of Emmanuel particularly, people who may have more recent genealogical links to sub-Saharan Africa. Emmanuel appears to highlight both the differentiation that is made between being 'Irish' and having Irish citizenship, the somewhat inconsequentiality of self-subscribing as Irish without external recognition and the desire to be a 'good' citizen, who self-acknowledges both their rights and responsibilities. Yet, even after all, Emmanuel feels 'forsaken' as Ireland changes within the continuum of contemporary modernity. By referring back to law, the facilitator shows how in concrete terms, the changes in the 2004 ICR reinforce or, make exclusion tangible for certain groups and, thus, engender a sense of forsakenness. Such a sense of the forsaken subject resembles the notion of 'the abject' (Butler, 1993, p. 3*ff*.; Coates, 1997, p. 78*f*.). The person that is not recognized as being 'Irish' is instead forsaken through abjection, either literally or conceptually within the process of defining what is, and what is not Irish.

Whereas it is recognized that there always has been space to manoeuvre around the 'elusive ambiguities in Irish identity' so as 'to reimagine who "we" are' (O'Toole, 2000, p. 22), within the Belfast focus group discussion, participants more directly propose civic *Irishness* as a means of re-imaging an alternative to ethnic *Irishness* and seem to somewhat dismiss the idea of having Irish descent as an essential criterion for being 'Irish'.

Tony:	[...] there's this idea of an ethnic Irishness and whatever that means, I know it's a complex area, and civic Irishness ... you know that ... and yes if you came here at eighteen and had been here for five years and had got the Irish passport and living in, you know, no-one would have a (problem), well apart from the old, well plenty of racists, most progressive people wouldn't have a problem with you saying I'm Irish person, I can live here, I have a family here, you may know him maybe five years, but even those people wouldn't consider you to be ethnically Irish ... probably for good, for good reasons usually, because you have, you don't have those ... genetic is a horrible word, you know what I mean, ancestry links here, so that ethnic versus civic is perhaps where the debate lies, you know, what you do is, we always promote civic

166 *Redefining* Irishness *in a Globalized World*

nationalisms as a more positive way forward rather than ethnic nationalisms, cos that gets into kind a horrible, you know Ukraine, Kiev territory, you know what I mean, Nazis and fascists so, but I haven't had a problem with someone Irish, cos they've only been here for three or four years and got a passport

Reagan: That's their choice
Molly: Yeah, if they want it, who I am I to tell them

Although the general perception from contributions within this extract does seem to suggest a more inclusive understanding of *Irishness*, it does nonetheless appear to contain some latent foundational views that are left unchallenged. Individuals, irrespective of their ethnic or genealogical background, are viewed equally as Irish and a proposed solution to overcoming dominant ethnic nationalistic sentiment is civic nationalism. There is even a questioning of self-identity based along essentialized ethnic lines in comparison with civic *Irishness* which implies a level of understanding of identity as being similar to what Hall (1996, p. 3*f.*) suggests as multi-layered whereby superficially imposed 'selves' layered over the deeper buried true self. However, by alluding to the perceived views of the dominant norm that might deem the 'newcomer' as not being ethnically Irish, the participants would appear to avoid criticizing the foundational basis of ethnic *Irishness* in the first place. Again, the reference to genetics and ancestral links would seem to compound ethno-racial notions that create a bind through its reification fallacy. The justification for not extricating both may be because to do so might perturb the participant's self-recognized value and the capital put into developing and appropriating perceived Irish cultural norms into their private family lives and their own sense of 'Irish' identity.

Not all ethnic characteristics traditionally associated with a stereotypical 'Irish' identity are accommodated within the participants' views of maintaining cultural practices. Similar to above, what seems to emerge as the conversation progresses is a direction that develops on the notion of civic *Irishness*. The impetus of such appears driven by a rejection of the historical role of religion in the formation of an Irish ethnicity.

Molly: [...] what I'll work towards is a settler socialist society of Ireland ... I'm never gonna get it, you know, in my lifetime, but that's what I would like Irishness to represent, if you know what I mean, em, so you try to create your own reality as opposed to going, 'well Jesus, it's just the way that it is' ...
Tony: Which is why you opt your kids out of religion ... why you work for an anti-racist organization ... why you challenge fascism and racism when you see it, but –
Molly: And support trade unions
Tony: But on ... your own terms, not on liberal, woolly multicultural terms, but on fairly strong political terms

The consensus from the participants seems to be an orientation and emphasis on what is termed as a 'settler socialist society of Ireland' that has rejected religion, fascism and racism. Instead what is given prominence is the agency of the politically engaged individual that has the free will to fashion their own reality which concurrently supports 'others' through trade unionism. In a sense, this extract would seem to provide an understanding and definition of civic *Irishness* as a concept to supplant notions of ethnic *Irishness*. Their inclination would appear more supportive of the concept of *civic patriotism*, as described by Kleingeld (2003), but with conceivably less *cosmopolitan* qualities.

Somewhat complementing the stressed importance of the political, within the Coolock focus group discussion, participants discuss the difference between being 'Irish' and being an Irish citizen. Tierney views political participation as having greater significance and states, 'well voting ah, is very important, being 'Irish' and an Irish citizen, you must vote, I think that's, that's ... that one should transcend both'. Although this seems quite rudimentary and self-explanatory, it does appear to indicate the pragmatic and legal similarity between both. By observing *Irishness* in current political terms only and by exaggerating the democratic process, it neglects to fully contemplate an alternative that listens to the voices of minorities, nor does it directly challenge the construction of the majority–minority dynamic that may remain persistent over time.

Within the Coolock focus group discussion, a very revealing debate on who is entitled to be an Irish citizen ensues primarily between Conlaoch and Tierney. Both participants provide starkly contrasting opinions and the discussion leads towards an analogy provided by Tierney which is quite illuminating.

Tierney: Who's entitled?
Conlaoch: Anybody who wants to be as far as I'm concerned
Keela: Anyone, yeah
Tierney: No, I don't agree with that ...
Keela: No?
Conlaoch: I'd say anybody that wanted to be, I mean citizen, is ... citizen is an illusion and –
Keela: If you want to be they're obviously here, aren't they?
Tierney: No
Conlaoch: But citizen is an illusion ... does citizen mean that you belong to a state? I don't belong to the state ... I do not belong to the state
Emmet: Citizenship is a very bureaucratic thing
Conlaoch: It is yeah ... it's a Roman, it's of these Roman things that the Romans brought into England, and then, or into Europe anyway and then they inflict it on us, we don't want it
Grainne: That wasn't the question
Conlaoch: Sorry
Grainne: If they want, obviously who's entitled, if ...
YB: I think it's a valid answer
Grainne: If they're looking for entitlements ... but if they're looking for entitlements surely they want to be a citizen ... so

Conlaoch: Yeah but they mightn't –
Grainne: Anybody who wants that
Conlaoch: If they want to ... if they want to live on the island ... who wants to live, people who want to live on the island and –
Tierney: No I'm more, more protective of the island o' that to be honest with you
Conlaoch: No but the –
Tierney: I'm protective of what's here ...
Conlaoch: They're all our own people coming home, people, the people who come here are our own people, we don't get any foreigners here ...
Emmet: And again Tierney there's people all over the world claimed citizenship ... and they never came back here
Tierney: I'm just saying like a lot of ... just because someone decides that they want to be a citizen of the country ... we're not eh, I don't regard the island of Ireland open door like that, and no, I may be wrong ... but that's just my position on it, that's the way I feel about it
Conlaoch: Well I'm more egotistical than that, because I actually believe that the people who are coming here to settle here are ... they won't be returning home

Up until this point the debate has exposed counter-opinions that either challenge the very notion of citizenship itself or attempt to rely on citizenship as a mechanism of *protectionism*. The discussion would seem to highlight the difference between having acquired Irish citizenship in contrast to the consideration of actually being physically present on the island of Ireland. Participant Conlaoch seems to value 'newcomers' settling in Ireland with the intention of staying and being completely part of Irish life; however, Conlaoch appears to reject the notion of 'newcomers' being foreigners in the first place. Whereas, implied from Tierney's response, the state concept of citizenship is valued because it can be utilized to restrict access to the island.

The homogeneity of Irish physiological traits, in particular pale and 'white' skinned, is perceived as reliant on a fixed historical understanding that links back to a Celtic aeon. It seems to be phenotypically determined though intergenerational exposure to the Irish environmental setting and climatic conditions. The portrayal is that such perceptible phenotypes are deeply imbedded in historical ancestry, so they have become naturalized to become synonymous with an imagined purity of *Irishness*.

From the perspective of the participants, it would seem that conformity is an expected requirement towards being recognized as a member within the dominant norm of society and that such views seem more aligned with an *assimilationist* or *integrationist* perspective rather than an inter- or multi-culturalist perspective. Within considerations of becoming Irish, it appears that physiological traits are inconsequential within the process of reading *Irishness* onto somebody. Noteworthy is that within one focus group discussion, the notion of commonality, as opposed to conformity, stimulates greater attention. As described by one participant, commonality is acquired through temporal exposure and maturation within Irish society, which, in turn, can lead to social integration.

Emergent from the transcribed material seems to be that the concept of 'race' as an imaginary is juxtaposed against 'race' as a reality. It is assumed and implied within several focus group discussions that the Irish are a discrete 'race' sometimes as imagined through myths and historical tales, but also at times in perceived reality, through the ascribed notion of a phenotypically determined *Irishness*.

As evidenced in conversations, a process is exposed whereby the compounding of ethnic and racial distinctions creates a form of *reification fallacy*. From the analysis of participants' conversation, it would seem that ethno-racial first impressions are related to socio-psychological processes which arise with the ascription of identity. Interpretations of ethnicity seem to be perceived by some participants as reliant on primordial or even innate attachments. Thus, the occurrence of such a reification fallacy appears to be when Irish ethnicity is conceived of as innate, together with racialized notions of a purity of *Irishness*. At the psychological level, this creates an ethno-racial impasse and the effect of such presumptions results in the accentuation of recognizing distinctions based on a single identity which is absolute rather than hybrid, multiple and changeable.

Contrary to views which seem reliant on the reification of racial-ethnocentrisms, cultural change, along with the extinction of what is deemed traditional, seems superficially caused by processes of *globalization*, rather than the arrival of 'newcomers' and the apparent ethno-racial hetergenization of contemporary Irish society.

Further evidence is presented which seems to highlight that although social change is perceived by participants as inexorable, social progression is conceived of under *Social Darwinist* terms. Specifically, the transposition of the biological concept of evolutionary change onto the social creates a sense of linear advancement, which would seem to originate from fixed understandings of the historical.

Furthermore, with respect to social transformation, contemporary notions of 'race' and diversity give the impression of affecting people's perceived sense of anxiety. The notional view that immigration will overwhelm the Irish population is perceived as an anxiety that creates a sense of fear among the broader public. Characteristically, the appearance presented by participants would seem to be that such a perceived sense of fear among the wider population is discriminatory. Conversely, evidence describes how fear, as felt by the 'newcomer', is likely heightened and may also be compounded with a sense of fear of rejection from the dominant 'indigenous' population.

The perception presented within one focus group discussion is that although *Irishness* has been reinvented, it still denies the possibility that people of skin colour other than 'white' can be Irish. The feeling seems to be that Ireland, within the continuum of contemporary modernity, has forsaken some people and that this has been reinforced through the legislative changes in the 2004 ICR. Another noteworthy view expressed, pertaining to re/imagining *Irishness*, is the proposition of *civic nationalism* rather than *ethnic nationalism*. Although this occurs, participants seem to sidestep reflecting on and criticizing the foundational basis of ethnic *Irishness* overall. In relation to redefining or reinventing *Irishness*, a view that is advanced, but is challenged by another participant within the same focus group discussion, seems to express a completely alternative comprehension of citizenship whereby the notion of 'newcomers' as being foreigners is rejected outright, with the implication that no-one can lay claim to belong more or less than another to any locality universally.

Within the holistic framing of this thesis, the focal-point from the outset has been notions of 'race', ethnicity and the nation state as assumed absolutes or otherwise. Thus, the findings and results culminate in this chapter by building on previous findings from discussions to present more depth on cultural and physiological traits that are notionally Irish, under the terms of 'race' and ethnicity. The focus of this chapter has been less the use of such terminology in data analysis and more the use of such terminology, or explicit associations with such terminology, as expressed by participants. What emerges is how participants' understandings of *Irishness*, which have been presented thus far, have, in fact, been tacitly dependent and essentially underpinned by perceived views of ethno-racial in/distinction. Continuing on from this point, Chapter 9 opens the perspective more widely to picture perceived 'Irish' identity in its entirety in relation to visions of 'good' governance, migration controls and *globalization*.

Constructing Ethnicity, 'Race' and the Irish Nation   171

172   Redefining Irishness *in a Globalized World*

Chapter 9

Irishness, Governance, Migration Controls and World Views

Keywords: Conservative; welfare state; reciprocity; ownership; neoliberalism; governance; globalization; financial capitalism; racism; status quo

The initial section of this chapter addresses participants' perceptions of Irish governance specifically with regard to the welfare nation state. From here, participants' sense of the benefits of the welfare state, as well as rights and responsibilities are explored. A significant theme that emerged relates to participants' understandings of 'free' education, healthcare provisions and the welfare state. The following section details how the welfare state is perceived as flawed both because of maladministration of state policies and practices and because of abuse by citizens. Participants also allude to the oppositional condition of 'us' and 'them' in discussing who can avail of state provisions. The notion of 'us' as opposed to 'them' is described in a simplistic anecdotal account which relies on notions of familial association and is underpinned by ideology associated with private ownership.

The second section of this chapter addresses perceptions of *conservatism* more explicitly. Participants also recognize the shift from welfare-based provisions towards a more *neoliberalist* approach. Within the Belfast focus group discussion, participants go so far as to imply in a critical manner that *Irishness* is characterized by values of *conservatism*. Linking with the discussion in Chapters 7 and 8 is the significance of nation state governance in the management and conservation of border and migration controls. Opposing views are presented, one justifying more stringent controls to counter the perceived threat to security, while in contrast, intra-European migration based on labour economics is viewed as ultimately counterproductive.

174 Redefining Irishness *in a Globalized World*

The third section of this chapter focusses on the juxtaposition of rational or irrational pragmatisms within predilections towards *neoliberal* cognisance and governance. Further analysis of some participants' responses to the outcomes of the 2004 Irish Citizenship Referendum exposes compliant support of legislation as fixed and predetermined. Evidence is presented to indicate an *assimilationist* position held by some participants, who would necessarily oblige the assumed migrant 'other' to acquire English, specifically because it is the dominant language spoken in Ireland. A subsequently detailed example of *perceived rational pragmatism* relates to *consumerism*. Some participants express propensities towards buying Irish and prioritizing the Irish, but these are juxtaposed against a lack of reflection and conversation on altruism, resource acquisition and global inequalities. A further example of *perceived rational pragmatism* is evident in the management of cultural appropriation and assimilation through emigration and returnee migration. An inversion of *perceived rational pragmatism* is presented whereby one participant proposes that anyone should have true freedom of movement, residence and equal claim to Ireland. Nonetheless, it is refuted by another participant from the same focus group discussion for being unmaintainable and indefensible.

The final section of this chapter examines perceptions of governance, *regionalism* in the context of European governance and *globalization*. Quite polarized positions on Irish versus European governance are identified. Participants view European governance and authority as having political and legal power to obligate the Irish state to enact laws of equality, thus perceived positively. Conversely, the European Union (EU) is also stated to be an undemocratic entity. The final section expands on perceptions of the Irish economy within the more globalized macro-structure of *financial capitalism*.

Perceived Benefits and Flaws of the Irish Welfare State

Beyond the benefit of being a legally recognized citizen of the nation state of Ireland and the ability to then travel with an Irish passport (as discussed in the previous chapter) are benefits associated with the provisions of the Irish welfare state. Within the Naas focus group discussion what may be evidence of a realization, or at least what may have been brought to the fore of the participants' consciousness, from viewing the multimedia presentation, relates to openly distinguishing the perceived benefits from what is deemed the Irish social welfare state model. This is explicated in the response provided by participant Liam who appears to describe an additional outlook from what they had said prior to viewing the presentation. Liam directly refers to comments made in the multimedia discussion primarily in relation to education.

Liam: I suppose in ways we don't realize how lucky we are, I mean in Ireland, I mean I know we complain a lot but Irish people moan an awful lot … but overall we are extremely lucky with what we have like … I mean, we have decent, we have a good education, we like, hospitals they're good I mean, compare that to other countries like, it is no surprise that some people want to become Irish … it's a pretty nice place

Irishness, Governance, Migration Controls and World Views 175

Colin: There's a good em, you know, they take care of people who aren't well off, I mean a lot, then do a lot of other countries, like America and things, I mean it's awful to be poor in America, but there is, even though some people don't think of it like that, but when we compare, how we take care of the poor, the hungry and things in Ireland ... the poor weren't hit as bad as they were in America by the recession here because of, there's a, you know there's a big social safety net here

Liam: We have more opportunities too then a lot of people would have, like I know people say America land of ... opportunity, but I mean –

Glenn: It doesn't really work

Liam: You have to be, it depends like ... their colleges cost an awful lot of money, like I know, our colleges do cost money but not half as much as like Harvard or ... anything like that but (slight pause), you know, for being Irish there are a lot of benefits that go with it so like (slight pause), I was going to make a good point there and now I've forgot ...

YB: Well coming back to what you had said, you know, where it is not surprising that people would want to become Irish or come to Ireland, and you know in relation to opportunity and benefits, do you see that as being a good thing, or ... do you think that access to benefits should be restricted or feel that it is a good thing to share the benefits, the wealth of the country, or, if we can consider them wealth?

Liam: I wouldn't say that we should, like, let's say if any, if someone comes to the country, let's say ok, you don't get all of the benefits of being Irish, you only get some of them and the rest are kept for the Irish cos that's, that wouldn't be fair on people ... that's just, but –

YB: So like, a partial access to benefits ... wouldn't be fair?

Liam: Well because I mean (pause), it would just be kind of like shutting people off, if someone wants to come to Ireland ... wants to take part in the society and wants to become part of the culture ... then, they should

The discussion exhibited above and input primarily from Liam seem to highlight the apparent difference between Irish societal structuring when compared with the United States of America. For the participants, apparently there is the tendency to make comparative analyses based on assumed differences between the Irish nation state and the United States of America welfare model. Not only is Liam's addition to the discussion in parallel with the contribution from the first interviewee, Laura, it seems to go further progressively by explicitly declaring that state benefits and provisions should be afforded to both nationals and non-nationals living within Irish society.

Colin: If you're going to sit around and do nothing then no matter where you are from or who you are, whether you are Irish or not, you're going to sit around and do nothing, you ... it's a bit unfair to the people that are really poor and really don't have anything, if you're one I, I unfortunately know some people that waste their lives away on drugs and smoking and, you know, they half the time don't show up to school, things like that and ... the way they are right now they're destined for a life on social benefits and not doing anything or you know, living off of other people, but you know those kind of people don't, I feel they don't deserve it

Liam: There are some people, like let's say you take some people who are Irish, Irish, who you know are one hundred percent Irish ... some of them don't take part in the community, they don't really have any pride in Irishness, when my little sister does Irish dancing and she goes to the 'Worlds' to compete and it's generally in different places in Ireland and tonnes of different countries, like Americans, I think this year there was –

Colin: There was lots of English people too

Liam: Yeah, I mean and they love the culture, they love the music, they love the dancing ... and if they, they have shown interest in it, they want to be part of the culture but they aren't what you would call one hundred percent Irish ... so, saying Irish people like, back to the partial thing, you, some people who have more respect for the culture and show more interest in the culture ... then some people who are meant to be Irish, meant to be their culture

Significant aspects, detailed in the continuation of conversation above, include a shared opinion by both Colin and Liam which evidently criticizes people deemed and recognized to be full members of Irish society. The disparagement would seem based on perceiving some members as not possessing the desire to participate in community life. This social non-participation and lack of communal involvement would appear to be equated to a lack of pride in Irish society, which, in turn, gives the participants justification to claim that some members are underserving of the provisions of the welfare state. Linking such conceptions to discussion on access to state resources and welfare to the 'non-Irish' from a normative perspective of fairness may have some justification; however, it also acts to subtly feed into critique of the welfare state and an attitude of 'us' against 'them'. It would also seem to complement Anderson's (2013) central argument and description of the community of value, where

> modern states portray themselves not as arbitrary collections of people hung together by a common legal status but as a community of value, composed of people who share common ideals and (exemplary) patterns of behaviour expressed through ethnicity, religion, culture, or language – that is, its members have shared values. (p. 2*ff.*)

Implied from the discussion above is the importance of the extrinsic relationship to the country irrespective of the person's subscribed or ascribed citizenship affiliation. In contrast, the other implication from above is the viewpoint that both participants seem to impose the maintenance of a dominant cultural normative position. It would seem an expression of interest in Irish culture would suffice to deem one satisfactorily entitled to state welfare provisions, yet the participants do not acknowledge the bind this leads to when envisaging a more *ethno-pluralist* society.

In the Drogheda focus group discussion, the opening response to the notion that being born in Ireland is an essential criterion for being 'Irish', the impression is that Diarmuid rejects birthright citizenship as an essential criterion, which is warranted on the basis of reciprocity between rights and responsibilities.

Diarmuid: I don't think being born in Ireland or being of Irish descent is essential criteria for being Irish but what I believe is, (pause) to live in a free country and obey the law, and with rights comes responsibility, I'm a firm believer that we don't just get rights, (slight pause) automatically given, we have responsibilities, we have duties, I was in the defence forces for twenty years, and I, before that I was in the part time reserve forces and I swore an oath of loyalty to the constitution of Ireland, so I'm well aware of what my patriotic duty is, it's my loyalty to the constitution of Ireland, (slight pause) that's how I regard myself as an Irishman

This response encapsulates several themes of analysis together. For instance, it would seem to refer to the notion of freedom and how such autonomy is conversely bound to being lawful. As in other focus group conversations and also affirmed by the second interviewee, Dijwar, conforming to the notion of a law-abiding citizen seems paramount to living freely and assuredly within a democracy. As above, this perspective also corresponds with the ideal notion of the *community of value* (Anderson, 2013). As Anderson (2013) describes 'the community of value is populated by "good citizens", law abiding and hard-working members of stable and respectable families' (p. 3). Conversely implied is that the individual recognized as a free citizen should not challenge the law or should do so perhaps only by seeking changes to the law through democratic processes. Directly associated with this idealized lawful citizen is then the access to rights such as state welfare provisions, in direct juxtaposition with the notion of being a citizen responsible to the nation state. Again this duality of rights and responsibilities seems to replicate comments made by the forth interviewee, Kevin. Tantamount to being a dutiful citizen are the virtues of loyalty and patriotism. Thus, evidently for Diarmuid, to claim *Irishness* does not require bloodline nor birthright citizenship but instead quintessentially demands the possession of the virtues of loyalty and patriotism specific to the constitution of Ireland.

Within the Clondalkin focus group discussion, the participants respond post-viewing the presentation by discerning and accentuating the comments made by

178   Redefining Irishness *in a Globalized World*

the first interviewee, Laura, on education and medical services provided by the state through welfare.

Kelsey: I know the first girl said she got free education and free healthcare, I was like 'what Ireland are you living in?' ...
Christine: She kind a caught herself ... it's the principle of it rather, it's not free ... but it is freer than some countries
Kelsey: Well yeah ... it's considerably cheaper than America ... and access for other countries, but it's not free
Christine: No, it's not free, no
Brady: No she probably did get free healthcare (pause)
Kelsey: Medicard, yeah ... maybe, medication –
Brady: I think in some cases you can get free medication
Christine: But how free is free? ...
Cillian: But yeah, what's your definition?
Brady: Well, it depends on your situation
Christine: Yeah, that's true
Cillian: Yeah, are they financial backing?
YB: But is it not interesting that she highlights that as being ... a real benefit to being Irish? (slight pause)
Kelsey: Well I know like in college like a lot of people would come over to Ireland ... to study 'cos it's like a fraction of the price ... in Ireland
Christine: Even as an overseas (student)
Dana: Yeah it's expensive
Brady: I wouldn't say, is that more a benefit of being Irish, that's a benefit of being a refugee?
Kelsey: Yeah
Brady: 'Cos Irish people don't all get that

This extract initially exposes the opinion that some of the welfare provisions which are described as ostensibly free by the first interviewee, Laura, are contrariwise perceived by Kelsey as not free, in the financial sense of the term. The notion of 'free' is questioned more generally, both in the sense that there can be a direct cost or that it is paid for through taxation and more generalized reciprocity. Of significance is that the conversation also would seem to reveal a sense of resentment towards 'outsiders', either as 'outsiders' coming to study at a reduced cost than the burden they would have to pay in their respective countries or as 'outsiders' recognized as refugees. The portrayed perception would appear to be that refugees receive more benefits relative to Irish people with the connotation that this would seem unfair and biased. Of relevance to this, Moriarty (2005) documents how,

> key government officials, particularly the Minister for Justice, Equality and Law Reform, and media commentators have served to construct asylum seekers childbearing as being associated with

crime, welfare abuse, exploitation, cultural dilution, economic pressure and a threat to Irish citizenship. (p. 99)

Thus, the participants' views may plausibly hint at the ways in which elites and media manipulation can and do shape and influence the opinions of the public

Similarly, within the Coolock focus group discussion, there is discussion and critique of the notion of 'free' in relation to the input from the interviewee, Laura. This emerges within the discussion when participant Emmet initially responds with a post-viewing comment. However, more varied opinions are expressed in this focus group discussion, which seem to provide opposing views on the concept of 'free', particularly in relation to education.

Emmet: I was intrigued by the youth, the first one, it was the last day as well, one of the first things that jumped out at me, was, her definition of free (slight pause) as in free education and free health, we wouldn't necessarily consider it to be free ... she saw it as ... the best thing about our citizenship I think ... it gave her access to free education, free healthcare, now ... I certainly wouldn't (say) that we have a free education system –
Peadar: And sure, sure if her American cousins –
Emmet: Or free healthcare
Tierney: Well ok but –
Grainne: It's a lot more free than
Peadar: Have spent thousands and thousands of dollars
Tierney: No let's tease that one out like, well like, primary school is free ... no fees there
Peadar: [...] well it's not actually, if you think of the extra fees and monies you have to pay, you know, there's always extras, there's art and there's this and that
Tierney: Well you have to buy books and
Grainne: You can go through it free
Tierney: Yeah
Peadar: Oh no, no, no, no
Tierney: But it is free
Peadar: I mean –
Emmet: You can go through it free, but there's a small minority going through the whole schooling system from –
Peadar: If you go to third level education in the states it would probably cost you thirty grand a year ...
Emmet: Yes, absolutely
Grainne: Yeah

As the conversation progresses to debate the notion of 'free', Grainne seems to attempt to clarify the interpretation made by the first interviewee, Laura by describing, '... I think when she says "free" I think she understands that it's not

180   Redefining Irishness *in a Globalized World*

totally free, but it's free as in the access ...'. However, it is only after some debate that acknowledgement appears to be made of the generalized reciprocity associated with welfare provisions. An example of this is when Aileen evidently claims in relation to education, 'and o' course we pay for it through our taxes'. The discussion continues to contemplate how people conceptualize the welfare state model, prior to recognizing the fundamental value and significance of such a system.

Emmet: It's a perspective thing and I suppose that comes back to, (slight pause) the question of Irishness, is our perspective as Irish people different to that girl's perspective ...?
Tierney: She was born in Dublin ... she knows the story yeah
Keela: I think we're just more encouraged and we have more choice ... [that] might be a better way of putting it you know ... like there are options, if you want to do something, where a lot of countries, those people were from, you know, it's a lot more restricted and ... they're not encouraged ... particularly the women you know
Aileen: And maybe people from outside can see and value things that we might take for granted as well ... 'cos she might've been looking and saying 'well if you were there you'd have to pay that', where we sort of feel ... you know, we get it so we don't [know] –
Tierney: We can't see the wolf
Aileen: What it would be like not to have it like, you know ... we don't see what it would be like ... [to] be grownup and not be able to go to school, and when you see children abroad, especially in Africa and developing nations, how eager they are to go to school ... and then you see our kids, 'oh I have a pain in my tummy, oh I've a cold'

Within the extract above, participants would appear to compare benefits attained through the Irish welfare state model with other countries that may not have a well-developed welfare model structure. Not only is comparison seemingly made between differing modes of state governance among 'developed' nation states, Keela also appears to make reference to the economic and cultural conditions in developing world economies that impact on educational attainment. The overall implication is that, as is subsequently stated by Aileen in reference to the comments made by the first interviewee, Laura, irrespective of a person's birth, the Irish may take the provisions of the welfare state model for granted.

The empathetic recognition of the circumstance of 'others', that may be in less fortunate situations due to their social structures, and/or societal economic predicament, is a rarity among the focus group discussions. Although at times responses appear to take a less egocentric form, they do not make a further advancement by considering issues in more altruistic terms. It is surprising that there would seem to be an absence of altruistic expressions or that they do not evolve at this stage or later in the discussion when it might seem to have relevance during the discussion of 'the other'. In fact, instead of identifying the positive value 'newcomers' might contribute, not just economically but also through their perspectives of social functioning, such *socio-cultural capital* seems reasoned as best attained through the process of returnee migration. This is expressed when participant Peadar acknowledges, '... I think there's no question about it, that when you travel em, and experience other cultures and other experiences, you do have a different perspective'.

There is a sense of pride and independence in being able to claim that the social functioning of Irish welfare state orientation is superior to other nation states, such as Britain or America, as well as developing world nations. However, a major caveat would appear to be the concern that it is also a system being abused by its beneficiaries. Although there are more liberal egalitarian perspectives expressed among most of the participants in the Coolock discussion, dissatisfaction is projected towards mismanagement of state policies and practices, as well as criticism of values, attitudes and behaviours of citizens potentially misusing the system.

Peadar: [...] historically, there's an issue I feel very, very strongly, is that (slight laughter) we go, look back the biggest problem that ever caused, that ever happened in this country was in the seventy-seven election, when rates were taken, and we, we, we developed this hand out culture ... there's nothing for nothing in this world you know, but there's an attitude of many Irish people now, that they expect things for nothing ... that is a new experience, I think in Ireland because, if you, if you go to other cultures ... that doesn't exist

Tierney: I think there's a demographic attached to that expectation, to be honest with you ...certain demographics that expect everything for nothing, like for example, my wife works in a post office in [Dublin suburb name] and she's dealing with three generations of a family who've never worked ... their expectation is never to work ... they live on welfare ... that's it, work is sort of ... something for somebody else ... and it's bred into them, and I think the expectation of hand-outs, I would say ... it's definitely a demographic area, eh, geographical, call it what you want ... I don't expect, hand-outs ... I'm, I, as a human, as an Irish person, I don't ... but I know, I know other people who do

Aileen: Well I think that there's a lot of people, and there'd be a, a few demographics where people expect that they have an entitlement ... and you could say that very about people in the country who are extremely wealthy, take [wealthy family dynasty name] for example ... like the, (slight pause) [name of wealthy family dynasty patriarch] himself did a lot of work but his children just expected that they had a right ... to huge wealth, which they actually didn't have a right to wealth, that they felt that they should have a right to, and I think that, you know across the board, you can find that in a ... fair few different situations, where people have an entitlement whether they're getting it off the state, whether they're refusing to pay taxes, or whatever you know ...

To some extent, this excerpt exemplifies two opposing views concerning the misappropriation of Irish welfare state provisions. Initially, Tierney seems to describe certain cohorts within the Irish population through anecdotal evidence that suggests specific groups are exploiting benefits. As is implied, because individuals from such groups are trapped in a cycle of intergenerational unemployment, such groups would seem associated with the lowest socio-economic strata of Irish society. However, as a counterargument Aileen appears to interject by emphasizing how subjects from elite spheres in Irish society also look to defraud the state by manipulating the Irish revenue and taxation system.

Within the conversation from the Clondalkin focus group discussion, the notion of the Irish welfare state appears to be described as imperfect by Christine. This is revealed with the progression of the discussion on access to education and educational attainment.

Christine: I think it's a flawed welfare state ... I like the principles of it ... but I think it needs tightening up ... and it's being abused by (slight pause) all sectors of society and manipulated by policies and stuff, but I do think yeah ... basic, ah I don't know what the baseline is on health in welfare, in medical, in education, but I do think there are abuses to the system but I would be kind of going more towards a welfare state than privatized

Kelsey: I think we would be more welfare than privatized at the same time like we could be, it's not like, very welfare, like (slight laughter) ... I suppose, like we're not speeding (slight laughter), like we haven't got, like we still pay our GP and we've got like, it's very expensive like, a medical care centre compared to like England, our education might be cheaper ...

Christine: I think some sectors pay a price for the general welfare system, it's not equal, equitable kind a system in terms of just because you're working and stuff ... doesn't mean you've any access to anything, you're sort of supplementing an awful lot to keep that welfare state at a baseline level for other people as well

The subsequent extract would seem to somewhat recognize the complicity of both sectors within the general public and the state itself, in the utilization of state provisions. It implies that state welfare provisions are not only being misappropriated, but also, that the policies themselves are knowingly constructed so as to benefit certain sectors more than others in a prejudicial manner. This, along with a discussion on educational attainment, is analogous to the Bourdieusian notion of *cultural capital*, which favours those with familiarity of the dominant culture in society (Bourdieu, 1986; Sullivan, 2001).

While discussing if having Irish descent is an essential criterion for being 'Irish', or not, the conversation digresses by talking about a stereotypical situation of being abroad and identifying (with) fellow Irish because one can 'spot the physical similarities' (Christine). However, the conversation reverts to drawing conclusions from the perceptions of both interviewee, Laura and Niamh in a comparative manner beyond their physiological appearances. The suggestion is that the contributions from both interviewees are perceived to be quite complementary of one another.

Christine: It wasn't even so much for the physical thing, it was more the values seemed to be quite similar ... I heard family, I heard safety, safe passage, education so there's sort of to me fundamentals of again basic rights and entitlements and that's kind of what it means to be Irish as well you know, and not that, I don't think they're level across the playing field but ... I think, we kind of, sort of aspire to them, we have to manipulate for them for some people as well, 'cos they're not getting them ... but there's a certain thing there that I would see as an Irish aspiration or something

The submission being made by Christine would seem to be that people will bend rules or find ways to circumnavigate restrictions in order to access certain welfare provisions, but that such behaviour may be, to an extent, condonable as it would be a way for such members of the public to fulfil their aspirations of obtaining their 'basic rights and entitlements' (Christine). Christine's perception implies that it is the structural flaws in the provisions of welfare that excuse values, attitudes and behaviours that would typically be deemed corrupt.

From a more detached and impartial position, a similar dichotomous comparison between the deserving 'us' versus the less or potentially underserving 'them' is also presented within the Drogheda discussion. Evidently, Machie makes the reflection through anecdotal reference to the situation in Calais which reveals a perceived pragmatic relationship between the sought acquisition of national identity and the welfare state model.

Machie: You know and the ... system there, my brother in law was talking about the identity problem, if any of those people are not sitting there, are they any worse off than myself? ... but if any of those people were to enter the society and become part of the society, their children become French citizens, you know that's, that's the identity problem that ... people have a problem with like, 'oh you're coming in ... and they're gonna get the same benefits' as others ... who have been here fifteen years or hundreds of years, and at the end of the day, he's gonna, you know disappear, whenever they feel like it ... that's not the way to go forward, if you want to do it properly, you come into society ... (make) roots ... and then be part of us or part of society, not just ... take what you want ...

The implication from Machie's remarks seems that in acquiring citizenship and being able to identify as a specific nationality, in this case French nationality, it then affords the once 'outsider' the ability to avail of the rights and provisions of the welfare state. Reservation would appear to be made towards the 'outsider' who, in becoming 'insider', is, thus, equally able to gain the same benefits as previously recognized 'insiders'. As implied above, the more 'authentic insider', however, should presumably have greater entitlement to such provisions through the process of *generalized reciprocity*.

In the previous chapter, an exchange of views within the Coolock focus group discussion is documented in relation to who is entitled to be an Irish citizen. Conlaoch's views of citizenship seem unique in the context of responses from both the participants in the same focus group, as well as in the other focus group discussions. However, the rebuttal provided by Tierney and the subsequent counter response are also of importance in relation to notions of the welfare state governance. The conversation continues on, primarily from the perspective of Tierney through the analogous account that is provided in describing the neighbour down the street.

Tierney: I'm going to use an analogy, I'm living in a housing estate right ... (slight pause) and let's say there's forty-five different families in it ... right, and we're all doing different things, I'm going out to do this, I'm living my life the way I want to do it and I'm, I'm married and ... buying a house, I'm ... doing my stuff, I'm looking after my kids and I'm doing, I'm doing everything reasonable right ... and there are other houses around the way which (slight pause) most of them are doing the right things and some of them are not ... but the guy who was living down in, in that house down there decides, 'you know what it is, it's really chaotic where I live here, you know and ... I'm suffering, (slight pause) it's not working out the way I want it to, and (slight pause) my standard of living is not really ... the way I think it should be, do you know what I think I'm gonna do? I'm gonna go up to Tierney's [and surname] door, and I'm gonna say, I wanna come in and live in your house', (slight pause) ... and I say 'what?' ... I says, 'sorry, no, this is my house, I have certain situations going on here ... which I'm in control of', and this that and the other ... that's the analogy I use

Conlaoch: Yeah, no, that's fine for your house because you won that house, in theory, you are –

Keela: In your castle

Tierney: I've, I've done my, I have my little space on planet earth –

Conlaoch: No but you see –

Tierney: Forget about it being a house, it's my little space on planet earth, where everything is in control, where I am the leader of the family ... my children are being fed and watered and all of that but there's another guy down the way and (slight pause), eh, ok, you have to be charitable I suppose, maybe one of the children of that house ... is having a problem, then that's a different story, do I take them in and say, I look after them and then ... when things are sure, foster them and then, and then move it on to something else, but I don't think –

Conlaoch: But I, but eh, the notion, the notion that –

Tierney: Citizenship is there, I did go a bit

Conlaoch:	That you're espousing is that ... that you own the land and that, that collectively the citizens of, of this state
Tierney:	Forget about me owning the land
Conlaoch:	Own the land
Tierney:	I'm running the land
Conlaoch:	Yes, that's the same –
Tierney:	I'm running and I'm living on it –
Conlaoch:	But they don't –
Tierney:	And I'm living by a decent set of, (slight pause) traditions
Conlaoch:	The land, the land actually owns us, and we serve the land
Tierney:	Ok, well that's my answer anyway

This exchange primarily between Tierney and Conlaoch portrays two outspokenly opposing views that can be related to the concept of property and private ownership. Conlaoch seems to perturb the sense of control, ownership, maintenance and dominance of space as described by Tierney, by inverting the position and stating that 'the land actually owns us' (Conlaoch) humans. Such a position would seem to better supplement the critique of the social sciences for its 'inherent nation-state bias, or "methodological nationalism"' (Fossum, 2012, p. 341).[1] In contrast, Tierney's hu/man dominant position exposes how bound within *anthropocentrism* is the creation of divisions along national, racial and ethnic lines.

The analogous description provided by Tierney seems quite one-dimensional in its account and does not reflect on the complexities of migration. Tierney's position seems equivalent to what are described as 'traditional conceptualizations of the state' (Brown, 2011, p. 54), which are reliant on insular policies and statist defences to protect culture, nationality and national patriotism. In particular, it appears to be referring specifically to migration of asylum seekers and refugees. It may, however, capture a sentiment that is prevalent more broadly within Irish society. The analogy creates a clear differentiation between those that are within the family and those that are external to it. Furthermore by reducing it in such a simplistic manner, the implication is that it neglects consideration of more collectivized mechanisms which occur placing someone or a group of people in the predicament that would necessitate them to feel the requirement to leave and seek refuge elsewhere. Evidently, there is an assumption of responsibility on the individual who is a victim for the difficulty they may face. There is also a lack of recognition of the power of societal order that may impinge on a person's quality of life, security and safety. It would seem to exemplify the paradoxical condition of *neoliberalism* that, on the one hand, shifts onus of responsibility onto the individual while diminishing rights by maintaining state interest and investment in oppressive apparatuses of control, policing and security, as described by Goldberg (2009, p. 333).

---

[1] As Beck (2003) has stressed, 'To some extent, much of the social sciences is a prisoner of the nation-state' (p. 454).

The analogy itself would seem conflicted. Family would appear to be equated to one closed society and relied upon to justify group inclusion, whereas, exclusion would seem to be achieved on the basis of the individuals' circumstance without consideration that the group or family may impose, or had historically imposed, sanctions on the alternative society or its individuals. Thus, the seeming implication is that, in the same instance, there is the recognition of 'family' dominance, or collectivized organization that transcends the individual for the 'insider', while conversely the omission of family dominance of the 'outsider'.

Conservatism and *Irishness*

Within several of the focus group discussions, there is recognition of the shift from the structure of a welfare state to a more neo-liberalist state. In some participants' remarks, this seems to be seen as a beneficial transition, in others' as having a negative impact, or in others' as an unavoidable inevitability. Common across all three positions is the sense of processual change in governance and social organization and with this, subtle concern that traditional or past forms of state organization are being undermined or eroded.

An example that links this change in governmental structure, away from a more traditional *welfare state model* towards more *neo-liberal governmentality*, would appear to be expressed in the Drumcondra focus group discussion. Moreover, an underlying perceived outcome of such societal change may reveal a more reflective and thoughtful consideration of the impending consequences. This seems to materialize in a post-viewing comment when Ciara discusses the remarks made by the first interviewee Laura (similar to the discussion above), who compares fees and access to education in the United States of America with the Irish context.

Ciara: [...] I'm not sure if it was the same woman but she was talking about education and free education and how much freedom that gave, and I thought that was interesting where her cousin who was the same age as her in America ... he would have to go into a private company in order to pay back his loans, I just didn't realize the freedom that that would give a person to choose work in the voluntary sector or maybe a sector that wasn't as well paid

YB: The outcomes of that ...

Ciara: You get far more choice, exactly it was opened up to her rather than have to pay back this huge loan ... it is a huge thing, I think

Eddie: Oh, absolutely, I mean the university education ... in the States, I mean you are talking about forty five thousand dollars or that kind of money ... em, you know for starter

Carroll: [...] and as people would say, well that's the point of it, is to keep people ... like if you read some of this stuff, it's about control ... and about keeping the status quo, so you are educated in this way ... so that you will fit in with society in that way ... you know, you're gonna keep on in the corporate thing ... and if it ... Chomsky's written a lot about it, Chomsky's written a lot about it

Irishness, *Governance, Migration Controls and World Views*   *187*

This exchange and interaction in conversation between participants Carroll and Ciara seem to reveal an interpretation of a reversion towards access to education being based on economic status or the nation state being in economic debt. The impression is that such a policy is seen as having a detrimental impact on affording individuals certain freedoms. This is understood to be the case for many in the United States of America. There would seem to be an assumed link between what may be interpreted as a shift from welfare state-based provisions in education to a more neo-liberalist approach, restricting freedoms and similarly, the reinforcement of status-quo positions that are attained through such control. Implied is that the incremental retrenchment of the Irish social welfare state may be evolving into a government system based on neo-liberal ideology.

What is also illuminated from this short interchange is the absence of involvement from the other male participants present. It may be observed that the other participants generally express more conservative positions throughout the Drumcondra focus group discussion and that they are personally more accepting and sympathetic of the shift towards a more neoliberal form of governance.

Within the Belfast focus group discussion, it is apparent that there is a clear consensus opinion which views *Irishness* as being characterized by values of conservatism. The participants portray an enthusiasm and awareness of political activism which underscores their professional lives and interests, as documented in earlier conversation excerpts. In detailing characteristics of *Irishness*, two forms of conservatism would seem to be identified and defined.

Tony: Well it's one of the most conservative countries in Europe ... moral conservative
Reagan: Moral conservatism yeah, anti-abortion and anti-gay and yeah
Molly: Which all feeds into religiosity I suppose
Tony: Although that's probably changing isn't it?
Molly: Not completely ...
Tony: There is a bigger minority of, you know, people who are more open to different identities, you know, and women's rights and LGBT rights, but it's still small compared to other parts of Western Europe
Molly: And I suppose em, racism, in terms of you know Irish –
Tony: Oh yeah, very racist –
Molly: As an Irish culture, in terms of a hierarchy of culture, we think we are top of the tree, you know it's great to be Irish and –
Tony: As long as you're white
Molly: Yeah, and everybody wants to be Irish
Tony: As long as you're white, you can't really be Irish if you are not white ... I think Ireland was the most homogenous countries up until the late 90s, in terms of statistics, in terms of you know whites, Christian, you know Ireland and Lithuania or someone ... then again we did have one of the largest fascist movements up until the nineteen-thirties, that is why it's hardly surprising, (pause) what else is *Irishness*? our political conservatism, not just our moral conservatism, Ireland is politically conservative and has been since partition and not before it

Molly: Yeah

Tony: I mean, the fact that our labour party, which is, well the Irish labour party, which is what I am talking about ... it's never been Marxist, it's always been social democrat, well weak socially democrat and the rest of the country is very politically conservative, Fianna Fail, Fine Gael ... I think right wing policy, quite a lot of class prejudice, hatred of inner city Dubliners, you know from the political elites ... despised them really, and that continues today you know, yeah it's pretty shit really isn't it? when you think about *Irishness*

Within this extract, both moral conservatism and political conservativism are discussed in a critical manner by the participants. The excerpt appears to provide quite an opinionated understanding of Irish conservatism and within a relatively short frame contemplates issues (highlighted in previous chapters) pertaining to religion, racism, homogeneity, desire to be 'Irish' and understandings of the context of modern history and the emergence of the Irish nation state republic. The concluding dimension, critiquing class prejudice, is revealing as it would seem to suggest that the existent status quo functions within an ideological framework of democratic and egalitarian republican values, yet maintains contempt for the urban working class. *Irishness* would seem to be viewed as the adoption of a value system that can simultaneously accommodate conservatism, yet purports to uphold notions of equality. The participant refers to such a value system as 'neoliberalism' (Tony). However, such a generalized orientation within Irish society would also seem to be blurred with conservative and neo-conservative principles.

At a later stage within the same focus group discussion, Tony reflects on how someone can become Irish by stating, '... Ireland is not different to most other European countries, it's just completely racist, conservative and –'. In the context of how someone can become Irish, inferred is that Tony not only views the Irish as racist but that the Irish state is racist. This opinion would seem supportive of the view of Ireland fitting into the notion of the racial state (Goldberg, 2002; Lentin, 2007; Lentin & McVeigh, 2006). The remark by Tony directly contradicts the viewpoint previously stated contrasting other European countries as being generally more progressive than Ireland, so there is also a level of inconsistency when comparing Irish governance with European governance. This may be dependent on when looked at from a Eurocentric point of view or the opposite. Both stances substantiate and are analogous to what Benhabib (2004, p. 13) describes as the predicament facing the EU where it is caught in a contradiction between legislating norms of *cosmopolitan justice* within the EU and maintaining outmoded conceptions of sovereignty to restrict those outside the EU.[2]

---

[2]Another trope that emerges in discourse, under which Irish governance and the preserving of conservative values, is based on the perceived dominant role the Catholic institution in Ireland.

The Nation State Perpetuating Migration Controls and Nationalism

Within the Belfast focus group discussion, the role of the nation state as a medium for control, particularly control of the movements of people, is not seen as waning but as of greater and valued importance within a structure of *transnational capitalism*.

Tony: Well I don't think nationalism's, there's a big myth that, a big globalization, neoliberal myth that national borders are less important, that free movement of labour, a break-down of national identities, we'll all be traversing around the globe as … entrepreneurs just enjoying ourselves with our ipods and that bullshit and that's what tells people … and that will not disappear because, well international capitalism needs them to, to control laws to control local parliament so, they can go and exploit the removal of resources for their own benefit … the only people who are choosing to be national, you know, international travellers, there's a very small elite group of f*** capitalists, the rest of us are going to be down at the bottom scrambling for the scraps at the top of the table, fighting among each other for them, I mean it suits them, and they'll encourage that, as they do in Kiev, you know, and places like that

YB: But you are kind of suggesting then that, nation states will be used as –

Tony: Well they are already, I think –

YB: Are being used as tools to enforce laws or controls on the people

Tony: Yeah, on behalf of the implementation of capitalism … that's where you need nation states, you can't do without them, 'cos those territories will remain, national border will, so will all the negative associations of identity and national identity and all the rest of it you know, and when they need to they'll play one off against the other, as you're seeing in Ukraine at the moment, aren't you? what is really about economics is now ethnic Russians versus f*** ethnic Ukrainians you know, nothing to do with that but, (pause)

YB: […] could we challenge that setup by a re-imagination of identity do you think? I mean, there's a parallel … I think it's completely correct but, I'm trying to look at it less from … a movement of production, of a movement of goods and looking at it from the control or mobility of people (pause)

Tony: It depends on how it is … there is this idea that I am comfortable with, which is mobility is a free choice

Tony seems to interpret the importance of nation state governance as being one which operates in a functional capacity, such as managing the mechanisms of control over the movements of people. These mechanisms are at the behest of *capitalist* advancements rather than necessarily the good of the populace.

190 Redefining Irishness *in a Globalized World*

This relates back to previous comments which compare European governance and Irish governance within the Belfast focus group discussion, whereby the mass movements of populations, certainly within the European Union, are seen as shifts of transient migration. Although ostensibly considered 'free' movement, they are described as being governed by the demands of *capitalism* and regional economic fluctuations. This perspective would seem to challenge the idealized *patriotic cosmopolitan* view as described by Appiah (1997, p. 618) where flows of migration could be celebrated if determined by the free decisions of individuals or of groups. Instead, it quite fittingly would appear to complement Goldberg's (2009) description whereby

> now relatively undeterred and deregulated flows and mixture have been germane to promoting globalized neoliberal commerce. Within the European theater they have been helped along, if unevenly, by more or less resonant informal social intercourse across racial lines. But the promotion of a racially muted sociality within has been supplemented by a more forceful if sometimes symbolic cementing of racially circumscribed border barricades around "fortress Europe" at its geographical limits. (p. 152)

Tony describes how,

> they're not backpackers, trying to backpack around Europe, they're people who have been wrenched out of their own cultures, forced to go somewhere else, to work in shitty, low paid work, abused by racists while they're there and then, they have to go somewhere else with the next boom, 'cos that boom is over.

This section focusses primarily on views and perceptions of immigration. Discussion below highlights the concern expressed by Sassen (2005) who states,

> What is now experienced as a crisis in the state's control over its borders may well be the sign that we need to redraw the map within which we confront the difficult question of how to regulate and govern immigration flows in an increasingly interdependent world. (p. 37)

Within the Belfast focus group discussion, the discussion on immigration control seems to focus on the differentiated control systems for people within the European Union juxtaposed against people that are outside the European Union. Explicitly bound to such control regimes is the legislative condition determining who is officially deemed to be a member of the Irish or European collective and of equal important for governance controls, who is excluded. When asked specifically about the outcomes of the 2004 ICR, several participants from the Belfast discussion appear to show a definitive and expressed understanding of

Irishness, *Governance, Migration Controls and World Views*   191

the consequences in quite explicit terms. The response brings to the fore several intertwined issues.

Tony: Well I'm not sure to be perfectly honest, I know we had a racist referendum
Molly: The outcome is where, just because a child is ... born in Ireland, (it) did not automatically guarantee them Irish citizenship, so then they have to go through an application
Tony: There was a change in the constitution, wasn't it? ... yeah there was a change, a constitutional change ... Ireland only, well yeah, (pause) it was racist
Molly: It is racist
Tony: Purely racist, the whole impetus behind it was racist, it was small minded, it was national chauvinistic ... yeah it was f*** ... to do with this place ... it was embarrassing too internationally; it was one of the first times that Ireland on an international stage in Europe showed its true colours, since the blue shirts in the thirties ... it showed what it is really like, you know
Reagan: I don't really know about –
Tony: If you were born in Ireland before the referendum you're Irish ...
Molly: Listen, my mate ... [friend's name], his partner is South African so the first kid was born before two thousand and four and became an automatic citizen, the second child was born, they had to apply for citizenship for their second child because ... he's from Ireland, she's from South Africa ... and that was the change to the Irish constitution
YB: It was a fundamental shift away from, being born, your link to the land of the country rather than the link to ... descent
Tony: The impacts were very controversial, the very idea that before, when that constitution was written, no one envisaged mass, well they should've, but they didn't envisage mass movements of populations potentially ... not mass movements, but immigration, that was a response to say 'well we're part of the European Union' which implies open borders, but you know, anyone outside those open borders, particularly non-EU nationals, you've got to ask special permission, you know ... and of course the people that are asked are people that are from North Africa or Africa, or sub-Saharan Africa, or you know, the far-east, so people of colour, so they would argue it was coincidentally racist ... whereas we know it wasn't

This excerpt combines an interpretation of the changes of the 2004 ICR as racist and nationally chauvinistic with an anecdotal account grounded in personal experience of a close acquaintance of participant Molly. Tony crucially also discusses the perceived rationale for such an amendment and implies that it is falsely based on uncontrollable levels of mass immigration. By highlighting in the concluding statement that the amendment is racist because of its exclusion of people of colour primarily, Tony would seem to be affirming the 'race'-based materialization of an 'us' versus 'them' dichotomy (as discussed in the previous section) imbedded within the supreme level of Irish nation state legislation.

Within the Limerick focus group discussion, Charlie seems to express the justification for the amendments made in the 2004 Irish Citizenship referendum. However, the impression is that modern trends in mobility, migration and processes associated with *globalization* are provided as rationalizations necessitating such legislative revisions (this would seem to complement discussion below on *opportunism* and *perceived rational pragmatism*).

Charlie: [...] I would assume that the law was changed because of the movement throughout the planet of people either through ... persecution ... and whatever, that laws had to be modernized to take account of that

Juliana: Yeah, because there's a culture of people from non-European states, getting in anywhere in Europe ... having babies

Charlie: And therefore if you get in Europe, then you've free access to Ireland ...

Maebh: Yes

Juliana: Ireland, that's right

Charlie: You know, in theory, because I suppose I'm not treating this ... as something sort of, but yea-know, we have this preconceived idea that people, and I can understand it, cannot freely travel ... it's like nearly when the ... you know ... moving from grazing to say you can't cross over a border, now that's simplified but with the, remember with the, taking flights before Osama BinLaden, it was envisaged you could turn up at an airport ... and you could fly, the same as you hop on a train ... and when Osama BinLaden ... and the twin towers, stopped all of that ... of course you have to have (pause), laws on immigration, migration, but generally I think most countries, I know here, most especially in the trades, most people gave out about the Polish, (pause) I thought it was about half a million at one stage, I don't remember

Juliana: I'm not sure, exactly

Adrian: The Polish

Charlie: Yeah, and they were doomed, eh, people on the ground said that they were taking –

Juliana: I don't think it was as much as that

Charlie: A portion of Irish work ... and there was the thing that they were working for cheaper ... rates and you can understand that because I mean, people have to live ... but a lot of it was judged on eh, most of it was the Polish and other nationalities took the work because the Irish workers wouldn't do it, and they definitely wouldn't do it for the ... the pay that was involved, now subsequent to that, I mean,

Irishness, *Governance, Migration Controls and World Views*   *193*

> pay has dropped in this country, and with the luck of it, it's not a bad thing because I mean ... ordering in a solicitor or some, an electrician in, it costs a lot of money, and, (pause) prices have to be controlled, you know ...

Initially considered within this excerpt is the plight of refugees and asylum seekers as a basis for the amendments introduced from the 2004 ICR. Consequently, it is expressed that legislative changes were required in order to become more modernized, explicitly within the reorganization of Ireland as a member of the European Union and the increased mobility of persons between nation state members. There seems to be the perceived fear and threat of non-Europeans, entering Europe, reproducing (assumedly to improve chances for leave to remain) and then accessing Ireland with the legitimacy to stay. Although there appears to be a questioning of the control on free movement of people, Charlie's argument seems to move from directly discussing the non-European migrant 'other', to the perceived threat to security. It is at this stage that a perspective based on experience and anecdotal evidence is provided to discuss intra-European immigration. Exaggerated numbers of migrants, particularly from Poland, are suggested to have immigrated into Ireland, and although participant Charlie creates distance from the opinion, the perceived sense is that the Irish begrudge 'newcomers' because they are seen to have taken Irish jobs. Charlie seems to view such resentment as unwarranted by suggesting that the Irish at the time wouldn't do the required work because of pay and work conditions. No basis is provided to support the initial claims that non-European migrants had exploited the ease of mobility within Europe in order to gain access and immigrate to Ireland.

On the one hand, the opinion would seem to be that migration controls are justified to restrict non-European migrant 'others', without any substantive rationale behind it besides prejudice. In contrast, freedom of movement as a generalized philosophy would appear to be acceptable as it accommodates new workers required to conduct jobs that would otherwise be avoided by the Irish themselves. To some degree, participants' views would appear to support the notion that Ireland pursues competitive corporatist national interest as an endorsement of developmental modernity (Fanning, 2010, p. 410; O'Donovan, 2009, p. 103*f.*). However, the restriction of non-European migrant 'others' would seem to complicate the more benign notion of developmental modernity because such a condition may have only marginally, to what Fanning (2010) suggests may be the case, 'undermined ethno-nationalist rules of belonging' (p. 410). The evidence also would seem to support the *Ordo-liberal* perspective theorized in the second chapter. Furthermore, detailed above is indicative of opinion, which shifts from being supportive of exclusivity and contrarily supportive of inclusivity. Shifting opinion does not occur on the basis of perceived moral ideology, though it is framed within discourse based on ideology, instead, it is based on a supposed rational pragmatism. This aspect or process of obscuring racism through the presentation of perceived rational pragmatisms is further detailed below.

Authority and *Perceived Rational Pragmatism* in Conversation

This section further exposes and elaborates on the juxtaposition of ir/rational pragmatisms, opportunism and moral dis/regard within inclinations towards neoliberal thinking and political authority. *Perceived rational pragmatisms* are seen to substantiate a logical rationale of moral disregard and act to obscure racism. For instance, where morality and principles would reject racism because of its baseless and refuted logic, *perceived rational pragmatisms* offer the individual or collective a (falsely) construed pretext to conduct their actions or sanctions that are essentially racially biased. Such *perceived rational pragmatism* is, in fact, wholly irrational; nonetheless, it provides the groundless basis for dominant advancement and preferment. In reality, it is less pragmatic and more opportunistic in its composition. *Perceived rational pragmatisms* provide the socio-psychological basis for opportunistic behaviour with moral indifference. It, thus, complements the ideology of *neoliberalism* which drives such a self-perpetuating process of opportunism.

As exposed in the previous chapter, within the Limerick focus group discussion, the differentiation between being an Irish citizen and being '*truly* Irish' seems to be constructed by participants in a somewhat satirical way. However, the requirement of having Irish descent as an essential criterion for being 'Irish' is also discussed in quite a pragmatic sense in relation to acquiring citizenship and getting an Irish passport. When a similar question was asked previously in relation to who is entitled to be an Irish citizen, the initial response appears to be definitive and direct.

Juliana: People who ... meet the criteria of the legislation
Charlie: Yeah, I, I agree with that ...
Dale: If you're born in Ireland or if you're born in a different country to Irish parents, (pause)
Juliana: Yeah, I don't personally have a problem with the Irish legislation, I don't fully understand it either ... but I don't have issues with it, I don't ... I've no issues with the legislation, so, I'm kind of, I wouldn't be too rigid in saying 'two Irish parents' ... if you meet the criteria, like people have moved here ... lived here for ten years and said, you know ...'I wanna stay here' ...

The impression is that although Juliana expresses an element of incomprehension, Juliana's response seems to reflect an unquestioning support of legislation as fixed and predetermined, thus somewhat beyond the influence of the public realm. Within this focus group, there would seem to be a majority of opinion supportive of the legislation. Responses also suggest a weighted view towards the necessity for bloodline descent, or alternatively having spent an adequate temporal period within Ireland together with the conscious desire to reside in Ireland. Notable is the underlying determination of the responses which appear to resolutely support the legislation. Such may be a genuine opinion, but it may also reflect a more pragmatic attitude towards law, order and status quo.

Continuing on from this dimension of acceptance of legislative norms, within the Drumcondra focus group discussion, the aspect of *perceived rational pragmatism* would appear to materialize in the discussion. The participants provide a well-informed description of the outcomes of the 2004 Irish Citizenship Referendum.

Ciara:	If the child is born in Ireland it's not automatically granted Irish citizenship ... umm, ok, (pause)
Ryan:	Well?
Ciara:	That's all I know about it (slight laughter)
Carroll:	I don't know about it
Ciara:	If a child is born in Ireland they're not automatically –
Ryan:	Not only that now
Eddie:	They're not automatically
Ryan:	(cough)
Carroll:	[...] Ireland, is that the thing?
Eddie:	Yep, unless I think ... one of their parents is Irish ... there was an automatic entitlement to citizenship once you were born in Ireland ... but they removed that ... that was the essential thing
Ryan:	(There were) incidences where people were preparing for here eight months pregnant and having their child and a lot of black people are citizens
Eddie:	I thought they were, they were one week off eh, giving birth, they were arriving at the Coombe hospital, you know
Carroll:	That's dangerous
Eddie:	And, and, it was terrible
Carroll:	Sad
Ryan:	It did happen, by the way
Eddie:	It did happen, I know

This interchange and argument seems to provide the supporting rationale for the constitutional changes which are framed within the context of a perceived moral concern for the health and welfare of pregnant 'newcomers' arriving into the Irish state. Noteworthy is the apparent association made which contextualizes the 'newcomers' into a specific cohort that is racialized. Although since discredited (please refer to Chapter 3), reference is made to dominant mass media reports on migrant influxes and their health and welfare conditions. Paradoxically, Ryan seems to reaffirm knowledge and an awareness of such discrediting yet maintains the stigmatizing narrative nonetheless. When this stance is challenged by the facilitator, with both the supposed health conditions and exaggerated numbers of immigrants being refuted, the conversation evolves to position itself with an alternative justification in support of the legislative changes.

YB: [...] people have done studies of newspaper cuttings ... that were purporting ...you know, this sudden influx ... of Nigerian mothers with triplets and boarding planes ... about to give birth, but ... there's no evidence to suggest that that was actually the case (relative) to the numbers they were stating

Eddie: No, they were suggesting there was huge amounts, which there wasn't

Ryan: Well we didn't want the numbers to increase either ... you know, so if you see something happening and ... word goes around very quick as to what makes a difference through social media ... that this is an easy place ... to get EU citizenship for a child, and if numbers do increase then you do have a real problem ... so I would say if the numbers were small, now is the time to make that law ...

Carroll: It was about economics, it was about having to support those children then, thinking that they weren't going to be supporting themselves ... they weren't going to participating back or whatever ... that's what it was about

Ryan: Absolutely yeah, so they took the, I think that removal to right to [the] land

Evidently, what emerges from this excerpt is a shift away from the supposed moral concern justifying the 2004 ICR legislative changes, towards a more pragmatic position allegedly based on deterrence and unsubstantiated economic necessity.[3]

Overall pragmatism emerges juxtaposed against either a moral regard or disregard. In fact, it becomes a rational pragmatism, as it is perceived, which seems to be a key underlying feature used to vindicate opinion which shapes some participants' subjectivities in relation to and beyond questions of migration. *Perceived rational pragmatism* seems to be a fundamental feature that shields the individual from perceiving their own moral stance. As such, it is a mechanism of nullification that permits the subject to uphold beliefs, attitudes and behaviours with moral disregard, while at the same time perceiving oneself to be a moralizing subject. Such a *perceived rational pragmatist* approach would seem to be a part of the cultural repertoire of both the Irish liminal and subconscious psyche which seems reliant on amorality and opportunism. Either through self-deceit or through deceiving 'others', pragmatism remains rationally constructed even if quite blatantly inherently illogical and/or immoral.

Such *perceived rational pragmatism* is not a contemporary phenomenon and may not be a unique condition of the Irish consciousness though perhaps it may

---

[3]The economic contradiction is not referred to in relation to Direct Provision managed by private bodies and forced dependency on state provisions for certain 'newcomers' due to work permit restrictions, while 'other newcomers' are legally permitted to work as essential contributors to the Irish economy. Nor is there reflexive query that contrasts Irish-born children of 'non-Irish' parents with those of Irish parent/s who still maintain entitlement and are afforded state provisions.

Irishness, *Governance, Migration Controls and World Views* 197

be accentuated within the doctrine of *neo-liberal governmentality*. One somewhat unique condition in the Irish context is the acquisition of language and the dominance of the English language in contrast to the ostensibly more native Irish language.

Within the Drumcondra focus group, in order for someone to become Irish, a twofold dimension in relation to the pragmatics of learning the dominant language appears to surface. Initially, the conversation seems to focus on the assimilationist view of the obligation for a migrant to acquire the dominant language when Ciara makes the point that, 'speak in English ... they should learn the language'. The rationally pragmatic justification for such obligatory measures is that, 'it can lead to ghettoization if people are not made to learn the languages of the country ...' (Ciara).

Continuing on from this, a question relating to the importance of acquiring Irish language is posed to evoke further thought and deliberation on the underlying dilemmas relating to language acquisition.

Ciara: I do think the Irish culture is a bit ... diluted to a certain ... not diluted, but it is not as rich as it could be ... because people in Ireland, including myself ... don't speak the language, or a lot of people don't speak it, but I'd say really language is part of Ireland and part of the physical location and the words that describe the physical features of the country, I think, you know, eh, I think it's sad that we don't all speak Irish, cos I do think we are losing

Ryan: [...] it's very difficult to know, I mean, we, do this in a different class, we speak about it a lot ... in, what's the class, in language and cultural identity ... and, I mean, the Irish language itself has been rolled back over a hundred years or more, more ... but I mean it's, it's a different thing, colonizers, you know, forced us out of our land, you know, over many years ... Irish being indigenous ... the majority language ... the first ... people and that happened over a very long period of time, so, it became a minority language because of that, so it, now English is the, the spoken language, and when you look around at business –

Ciara: [...] I think there was a kind of snobbery about English being a better language because the dominant people at the time spoke it

Carroll: Yeah colonization

Ryan: [It] would be ... Ciara if you look at ... sorry ... we were doing this last week about ... you take on the identification of the master ... and the colonizer ... would've been the master ... so you take on their identity ... and their norms and their language and everything else, and you associate the Irish culture a little bit and the Irish language being inferior, it takes a long time to knock that out of you

Within this extract, there would seem to be a clear association made between language and cultural identity formation. Initially, it appears the loss of Irish language over a temporal period is seen as a form of cultural dilution, but it is then

198 Redefining Irishness *in a Globalized World*

seemingly argued that adopting the language used by those in a dominant position is perceived as favourable (as detailed in Chapter 2). Importantly, the historic position of Ireland in the context of British colonialism seems to be expressed as being socially advantaged through the exposure to and acquisition of the English language. The attainment of English language, with the waning of Irish language, appears to be translated as beneficial for presumably international business in current times by Ryan. Ciara seems to concur with this view and perceives the attainment of English as an enabler of social development mobility. The inference is that both positions combine to highlight a *perceived rational pragmatist* view of cultural appropriation which is rationalized according to economic development and elevated relative social status.

Ciara also seems to draw from a more nuanced position to pose the proposition of the subordinate becoming the dominant, evidently revealing both an understanding of the power/knowledge paradigm but also, though not explicitly stated, conceivably suggesting a link to demands of assimilation nowadays of 'newcomers' and the uneven power dynamic that may exist between the Irish and 'newcomers'. There is also the sense that society is always entrapped in such a power dichotomy between inferior/superior cultures. It is such a predestined condition that manifestly forces the collective status quo to dominate and excuses such a *perceived rational pragmatist* approach to demand integration through assimilation, rather than negotiate and arbitrate *interculturalism* and/or an interlingual society.

When the conversation during the Clondalkin focus group progresses to discussing how one might re-imagine the issue arises of welfare exploitation by 'outsiders' contrasted with activities of vulture capitalists, Irish or otherwise. There seems to be recognition that with mobility and assumedly globalization, 'it's not just about Irish ripping us off, it's Europe as well' (Christine), together with reference to American vulture capitalists and China being able to buy up Irish assets. Apparently, it is because external players are seen to have the financial capital and that, at a pragmatic level, as is somewhat rhetorically posed 'it's all about money and resources, isn't it?' (Christine).

Also, interwoven with mobility would seem to be access to resources. When it is implied within the Clondalkin discussion, that certain vulture capitalists may have benefited from their 'Irish' identity or connections to Ireland in acquiring Irish assets, Kelsey views this as 'not really fair'. An appeal to fairness is counterposed with consumer choices that place emphasis on 'insider' allegiance towards supporting people within the 'home country' (Christine). When asked what the appeal in 'Guaranteed Irish' is for the consumer, the conversation continues as follows.

Brady:	Buying Irish
Christine:	Where it grows
Dana:	Yeah, cos you're saying –
Kelsey:	Spending in Ireland
Dana:	Yeah, you're gonna give ... put money back into the country

YB:	But yeah, but why?
Dana:	Because like, we need to like think of ourselves before others, in all fairness, like you have to take care of yourself and then when you're well off and stuff then you can, have the ability to help others

Evidently, there is the estimated opinion that supporting Irish produce through particular consumption habits means, as Kelsey later substantiates, 'you're keeping the money in the country so we can get it back'. There seems to be a rational pragmatism towards improved quality of life for those deemed to be members of the Irish collective through such a financially cyclical production/consumption process. Nonetheless, while this would assume generalized continual improvement of the quality of life within Ireland, this dimension of development and increased wealth of the Irish nation does not appear to be reflected upon in an altruistic manner, that is, welcoming of asylum seekers or 'others' less wealthy. That is to say, neither the more outward looking view of immigration being the result of poverty, which Sassen (2005, p. 36) claims is overly simplistic, nor the consideration that inequitable trade relations between wealthy nations/regions and developing nations may be a cause of immigration (Mancini & Finlay, 2008, p. 11) would seem to be reflected upon by participants.

Furthermore, this individualistically based *perceived rational pragmatism* of consumption patterns contrasts with perceived views of collective action in relation to what is deemed 'the national interest' (Christine). When prompted, Christine expands on the ambiguity of the concept of national interest.

Christine:	[...] it's very hard to define what the national good is, or who defines what it is ... and I think people will assert their, even out of spite, they'll nearly say, 'ah I don't know up in Dublin, not them', you know like ... Dublin only represents one county in the whole country and there's a little bit of, we don't pull together in that national sense, I don't think ... we're divided on it ... all the legions of county and stuff, so I think that somehow goes into the bigger political picture where we are divisive, we're not kind of altruistic for the national good, we might be at a small level but –
Kelsey:	I think a lot of Irish food is like now getting more bought because Aldi and Lidl use Irish goods so I mean like they use Irish
Christine:	Produce yeah
Kelsey:	Meat and ... fruit and veg, so it's a bit, a lot of it, and it is cheaper, it is, it would be a lot cheaper so it is getting more, a lot more ... but
Christine:	But not everybody would go with the melon thing, even though knowing it might be, others will say 'to hell with the Irish jobs, I'll take the cheaper melon' ... even knowing the consequences, or to spite they might say, 'ah feck, let them go down the swannee like, we'll still buy the dearer one, the cheaper one ... because, that's our choice, freedom of choice and' ... they won't see the bigger picture, you know ... 'cos they only [live] for themselves

Within this retort what is described is a sense of disproportionate political influence from Dublin in contrast to the rest of Ireland more generally, and perhaps rural Ireland. The divisiveness within Irish society is seen to produce a limited level of altruistic attitudes and behaviour, and this may be linked back to the discussion on parochialism and historicity (please refer to Chapters 5 and 6). The conversation progresses to describe the pragmatic juxtaposition between purchasing Irish and buying the cheapest produce irrespective of source. Evidenced here is a perceived pragmatist rationale that jostles between emphasizing taking care of your own in the first instance and the perceived pragmatic consumer choices individuals make, rationalized on economic circumstances. It may be the fact that the historical insecurity of an 'Irish' identity within the ambiguity of racial theory, as described by O'Toole (2000, p. 27), lends itself towards such contemporary ambiguities within the collective consciousness of people self-subscribed as Irish.

Overall, it would seem the supporting basis for perceptions that are rational pragmatic can shift between economic, cultural and social dimensions, thus facilitating conscious choices that negate genuinely considering moral implications of the subject's actions. It could be conjectured that such juxtaposition of *perceived rational pragmatisms* not only provides individuals within the Irish collective, with the privilege of making politically persuaded voting decisions and being influenced by dominant media positions that construct the pragmatics for an individual's perceived rationale. Quintessentially, it also facilitates an individual's ability to maintain certain justifications or perspectives that might ordinarily conflict with their own self-ascribed ideological positions. In effect, a process such as *perceived rational pragmatism* disavows ideology or the self-sense of morality, without necessitating perception of oneself as amoral.

Migration and the Management of Cultural Appropriation

As discussed previously, the blurring of conservative and *neoliberal* values can also be exposed in relation to emigration and immigration. This section focusses on several discussions on emigration which primarily frame it within the context of returnee migration and the partial benefits such migration affords the island nation state.

Within the Drumcondra focus group discussion, more contemporary forms of outward mobility and emigration are discussed as alternatively occurring processes counter-posed with immigration. Unlike previous generations of Irish emigration, the view seems to be that contemporary flows are more transient and that returnee migration is a more likely phenomenon.

Alana: I suppose one thing about Ireland is, because the country is so small ... lots of young people have travelled abroad ... so they would have had experience, well I happen to have an awful lot of, my parents wouldn't have travelled ... but I know my siblings children they have gone all over the globe and brought back that difference, so although there was a huge influx of people, people would have been aware in Ireland of different cultures and stuff like that, and

Carroll: I think that came from the country being as small as it is ... and if you wanted to go anywhere you had to leave Ireland ... you know, I mean even if you went on holidays and things like that but for people that were travelling sure they went to the other side of the world I think that brings up something else though because you have an expectation if your child or children ... go to another country that they're treated decently ... so you should have the same expectations

Within this excerpt, Alana would seem to make a generational comparison between the generations prior to their own, with that of young people, as well as the change in mobility over such a time period. Apparently, increased mobility beyond the nation state is seen to facilitate exposure to and experience of new cultures with the transference of such acquired knowledge through returnee migration. Such emigration flows of young Irish people are seen as enablers of cross-cultural appropriation of alternative ethnic attributes and customs. In this way, what seems to be perceived as beneficial is the adoption of certain forms of cultural knowledge by young Irish people, rather than the incorporation of the 'newcomer' who might possess a diverse range of cultural repertoires. Underlying this is a subtle dynamic whereby the judgement which places value and deems what is worthy of cultural appropriation would appear to be internalized within the Irish collective. The implication is that, it is the choices of journeys and discoveries of young Irish people which determine the adoptions of what is appropriated, as well as the status quo of Irish society at a given time, which governs what is deemed of value from such cultural appropriation through rewards.[4]

In a sense, returnee emigration would seem to be a process by which intercultural learning occurs, but it is externalized from the nation state. Furthermore, emigration in this manner may then be a way of creating and managing cultural appropriation. Conceivably, this is because it demands a level of assimilation by creating mechanisms that favour the returnee migrant's newly acquired skills, which are deemed beneficial for the status quo. Overall, albeit within a period of liquid modernity, what may be occurring is a system that maintains *conservatism* through the selective management (acceptance or rejection) of flows of cultural appropriation.

Although from the extract above, the impression gained contains the implication that such emigration and returnee migration is a recent phenomenon, within the Coolock focus group discussion, Tierney suggests otherwise when Conlaoch challenges the concept of citizenship.

---

[4]This would also supplement the opinion that the state looks to control, though active confinement of refugees and asylum seekers, so as to manage inter-cultural interaction (Fanning, 2002, p. 87*ff.*). As described by O'Donovan (2009, p. 103) by creating such isolation, it reduces cultural impact on the assumed homogeneous and dominant society.

Conlaoch: People who are attracted ... to this island are coming here for the purpose, they're either our own returning or they're people that are coming here that they need to learn before they go back out again, and so they should have, they should have the right to live here, [as] I would claim the right to live anywhere on this planet

Tierney: Would yea?

Conlaoch: I belong to the planet ... I don't actually go anywhere 'cos I'm not allowed off the island anyway but

Keela: 'Cos you've no passport

Conlaoch: I don't have, well no I can get off the island without a passport but ... I've gone off the island but ... I could physically go if I wanted to but ... I'm spiritual, I'm tied to this land ... and I, I am for the rest of my life, I mean I knew that when I came here ... I knew that I wasn't going to go anywhere (slight laughter) but em –

Tierney: So you are an Irish citizen?

Conlaoch: No

Tierney: Oh are you not?

Conlaoch: I don't vote, I don't participate ... in the fictions that are here at all, I am, I will be, I consider myself as part of Éire –

Tierney: Um, ok

Conlaoch: Which is the spiritual entity of, of the island, I would consider myself as part island, and I have a right to live here the same as all other people who don't vote here and they, they don't consider themselves as citizens of this republic, this em, republic of Ireland which was eh, which was created in nineteen-forty-eight, as a, as a company, as –

Tierney: So, if half a billion people arrive tomorrow that there's, want to be citizens of this island –

Conlaoch: They're not going to arrive

Tierney: You've no problem with that?

Conlaoch: Half a billion people are not going to arrive here

Tierney: Well if they all arrive together and say, 'look I wanna be part of this thing that you're bangin' –

Emmet: Well again Tierney

Tierney: What are you going to say?

Conlaoch: I'd say welcome and come in but they're not going to happen ...

Tierney: Ok ...

Conlaoch: The reality is everyone looks after themselves ... the island will decide how many people are, are welcome to come here ... she will herself decide that ... and, you're never going to get this ... huge influx of people, that people always talk about, and dodge they're going to

Tierney: No, I, I, that's just

Grainne: I'd like to ... I think it's really hard, I don't think it's that simple ...

Conlaoch: I think that Irish citizenship is a construct and it's not real, and so I couldn't possibly consider ... in all honesty I could not consider

Irishness, Governance, Migration Controls and World Views

YB:
Conlaoch:

myself a citizen of Ireland ... because ... the government of Ireland, the state, the state of Ireland ... have a notion that they can inflict suffering on the people, on the living people of I, of this land ... in order to keep their economic books balanced, (slight pause) anybody who considers that they can cause harm to living beings ... I couldn't possibly be a part of that ... grouping

I think yeah, you've kind of highlighted a really important point which is this aspect of it being a social construct

I mean because I was born on this island, they, the state of the Republic of Ireland, well the free state, where I was born in the free state, but ... the state of the republic of Ireland consider that I am a citizen, and try to inflict all their restrictions on me as they would on any other citizen, but, I'm not a citizen, I never will be a citizen ... because I cannot support any system that is willing to cause suffering to living beings

This extract presents the adamant position held by Conlaoch who appears to challenge the notion of citizen and citizenship and, concordantly, the notion of organized society and (inter)dependency. The argument Conlaoch gives seems to be an inversion of a *perceived rational pragmatist* perspective. Conlaoch justifies the mobility and inward migration of people from anywhere based on the view that if Conlaoch can and should claim the right to go and live anywhere, then anyone should be able to claim the same right to live in Ireland. Conlaoch's position would seem to endorse complete free mobility for anyone on the planet. When this is challenged with the prospect of overpopulating the island, participant Conlaoch presents an illuminating refutation by implying a more natural process would occur whereby the land of the island would determine the population size of inhabitants. This position inverts the argument and would seem to have a more *posthumanist* leaning.

Conlaoch appears to expand on the justification for such a position through disassociation with the nation state's notional construction of citizen and citizenship. Irish citizenship is suggested to be, not only merely a construct, but a concept that is based on an imaginary. Conlaoch then leads on to describe how it is a concept invented by the state and utilized by government so that state authority can inflict suffering on people. In support of this, Conlaoch seems to make reference to the recent economic predicament Ireland faced and claims that Irish governance is commensurate to a system that inflicts suffering on a populace. In a generalized yet very real sense, the appearance is that Conlaoch desires no association or allegiance to the nation state, in particular, non-participation in an assemblage that restricts and inflicts suffering.

Governance, Regionalism and Globalization

As discussed above, when conversation relating specifically to Irish governance arises, it can be portrayed as quite a flawed or corrupt nation state. Other than this, in most of the focus group discussions, minimal referencing appears to be made to Irish governance prior to the additional question comparing European governance with Irish governance. Irish state governance seems to be perceived as either in need of top down EU governance within the natural progression of regionalism, or conversely, Irish governance lacks the representative determination to develop self-autonomous 'good' governance as a successful functioning democratic nation state. In either instance, Irish state governance would appear to be infantilized by its depiction as weak and underdeveloped.

European governance seems to be portrayed as being either one of benefit or in juxtaposition as a burden for the nation state of Ireland. In each instance, quite polarized views seem represented yet the commonality between both positions would seem to be that European governance is seen as an overarching and dominant force impacting on Irish society. Thus, evidently, it is a governing force that should either be confronted and vetoed by the state, or, one that should be fully embraced and capitulated to by the Irish state.

Within the Limerick focus group discussion, in answer to the latter additional question comparing European governance in relation to Irish governance, Charlie seems to respond by concentrating on the perceived constructive powers European governance brings to Ireland.

Charlie: [...] I actually think that most of equality laws that were introduced in here came from our European basis, where we had to comply, which was to me, now it could've been bad laws, and it may be bad laws in the future, but all these equality laws that came in were a plus I think for the Irish people, because our own government, still are – and they can't even comply with some of the laws even on the environment – ... dragging their heels, obviously they don't have the money to comply as quickly as you'd want to, but ... I think being part of Europe has given the Irish people, (pause) ... a balanced standing in the eyes of the world, as if we were, rather than if we didn't join it, I think it's a good vessel to economically grow and be a part of, if you like a powerful ... and I mean as far as I know, we always have the option to get out
Juliana: Do we? (murmurs)
Charlie: And, you know, without Europe our motorways wouldn't've been built
Juliana: Ah no
Charlie: They would've some of them but not to the extent

This extract seems to concisely capture a certain sentiment towards European governance as well as Irish governance. The suggestion is that European supremacy is one that has power to oblige the Irish state to enact laws of equality, yet somewhat paradoxically; such imposition would imply the erosion of self-determination and, thus, could be interpreted as autocratic. What also emerges, yet what seems explicitly unobserved by the participants, is the juxtaposition between the top down obligation towards environmental protection in contrast to European-level financial support for the expansion of transportation infrastructure.

Thus, the expressed perceptions of Ireland would seem to be of a peripheral sub-state, within a more imperial super-state. Ireland would seem to be perceived as dependent on and subordinated by European affairs rather than as an equal member of a decentralized political Europe with self-directing regions in which cultural plurality is maintained (Tovey et al., 1989, p. 2).

Similarly, the responses from the participants in the Belfast focus group, looking at European governance in comparison with Irish governance, seem to portray an aversion towards European governance. Molly claims, 'Irish governance is gombeen politics, it's corrupt, it's misogynistic, it's capitalist', to which Tony additionally affirms, 'it's nepotistic' and later asserts, 'Ireland is corrupt, Europe's anti-democratic'. The implication from these statements is a double-bind between corruption and autocracy. Such perceptions could be seen as a facilitation of what Chandler (2010) refers to as a 'façade democracy' (p. 150) (as detailed in Chapter 3).

Within the Drumcondra focus group, when European governance is considered in relation to Irish governance, a similar recognition of the supremacy of European law appears to be made, as well as the apparent relatively minor position Ireland possesses in affecting outcomes at a transnational level. There are, however, apparently divergent opinions within the focus group discussion that were either outright dismissive of EU governance or saw EU governance as the panacea to Ireland's economic woes. The initial response to the question of European governance from Alana seems quite striking.

Alana: They're dictators
Ryan: Well about control, we've ceded a lot of our control to the European Union
Carroll: Sovereignty yeah
Ryan: Governance anyway, and in particular we don't control our own eh, interest rates, you know, so that's a huge thing ... and a lot of laws, I mean the European laws, you know, they're above the supreme court laws in theory, if you take back action in Europe above supreme courts in Ireland's judicial system at its upper levels ... it's actually ruled by –
Carroll: Budgets and fiscal and things like that –
Ryan: Is run by a different grouping in the European Union ...
Carroll: And we're a very small part of that, we're a very small influence on that
Eddie: [...] we have ceded some of our, our control ... the question I would ask is 'have we ceded enough control?' ... if we had conceded our, if there was more control from Europe, would we have gotten into the mess that we're in? if we had more control, if perhaps the French and the Germans have more of a say in the way we run the country, would we be in the mess we're in? ... you know, I don't think we would have but I think the fact that we've had them control things for a while helped us get back on track ... Ryan talks about, 'we weren't able to control our own interest rates', we had the most

206 *Redefining* Irishness *in a Globalized World*

	historically low interest rates in the world, had we been able to control our interest rates, would we have started to, you know, put up our interest rates, eh, so that we couldn't compete, you know, in the world? I'm not sure that, that argument stands up
Ciara:	I don't know, I kind of think, you, kind of local government and everything like that is important ... for even, kind of looking for Europe, em, to Europe ... for your economic structures and, I just feel that that's very, handing over power, it's kind of like saying, 'we're not mature enough to handle this ourselves because we've made a balls of the last time'
Eddie:	We've just proved it
Ciara:	They've even offered this .... they're kind of infantilising us you know, (pause) we're children so therefore we need Brussels to look after us
Alana:	Eddie's after presuming that even they know what they're doing

Eddie makes a significant admission in relation to control over interest rates which implies that it is better to concede control of fiscal policy etcetera to the European level of governance. Eddie concurrently seems to provide justification which emphasizes the lack of leverage Ireland has when operating within the global financial system as an independent nation state. This would imply an inescapable bind whereby globalized financial systems drive and determine regionalization. These views would seem on a par with Sassen's (2005) observations, who writes more generally,

> the state itself has been transformed by the growth of a global economic system and other transnational processes. These have brought on conditions that bear on the state's regulatory role and its autonomy ... [They have also] affected the power of different agencies within it, and furthered the internationalization of the inter-state system through proliferation of bi- and multilateral agreements. (p. 38)

Also present within this extract would appear to be the notion of Ireland as an immature and, thus, irresponsible nation. Whereas this is the perceived view from those in power external to Ireland, it is also comparable with earlier comments whereby participants seem to give excuses for Ireland's shortcomings because of its relatively recent independence and attained sovereignty.

The reality of the effects of an ever globalizing world is discussed in several of the conversations and is related to the question of governance. Within such conversations, the aspect of *perceived rational pragmatism* would seem to become prominent again, whereby economic necessity would seem to become the dominant context in which it is framed. Towards the closing of the Drogheda discussion, Diarmuid appears to refer to what is perceived to be the existential reality of the situation for the Irish economy in the context of *transnationalism* and broader regionalization.

Diarmuid: We tend to think as ourselves as insular, we're an island obviously … we're, we're cut off from everywhere, we're not, we're part of the EU, and we have laws and responsibilities as part of the EU, Brussels, links between the United Nations … and we're, as you know, financial situations and economic situations in this country has been dire for the last few years, and who provides us with most of the employment now? multinational companies … we are dependent very much on the outside world … we couldn't exist without it, you know

Diarmuid's remarks would seem very pragmatic and grounded in the reality of contemporary times. They appear to provide recognition of the circumstance of the nation state economy operating within a macro more globalized financial capitalist structure but also refer to the absolute requirement to maintain our presence within such as a matter of economic survival. The suggestion is that this dependency creates a sense of powerlessness and futility in conceptualizing any alternative. Participants' perceptions challenge the less threatening notion of *glocalization* (Inglis, 2008; O'Donovan, 2009; Ritzer, 2011; Robertson, 2001) which seems to imply a relatively balanced crossover between micro/bottom up and macro/top down processes of cultural and economic interexchange. Instead, there would seem to be recognition of regional actors in globalization dominating from a supranational level of governance. Participants' accounts do not seem to support the idea that identities have become adapted to globalization in a complementary manner, as Inglis and Donnelly (2011, p. 129) imply. Instead, and plausibly in part as a reaction to the macro processes of globalization, which are perceived as subordinating, evidence does suggest *Irishness* is understood in more mythological *ethno-racial* and what O'Donovan (2009, p. 100) point towards, *regressive nationalist* terms.

Nonetheless, the acceptance of transnational corporate contribution to the Irish social fabric would seem incongruent with the denial of other processes of globalization that might plausibly warrant envisaging conceptions of identities as hybrid or more fluid (Faas, 2010, p. 11). This may also lead to the occurrence of a form of ambivalence whereby there is a reluctance to conceive of 'Irish' identity in more inclusive terms, as evidenced in the general acceptance by participants of the 2004 Irish Citizenship Referendum legislative amendments (as discussed previously), and an acceptance of autocracy and/or corporate authority.

This chapter begins by presenting a discussion by participants on how the known benefits of the welfare state model in Ireland are deemed to surpass those of the US welfare model. Discussions seem to make apparent that, by expressing interest in what is believed to be 'Irish' culture, it should be a satisfactory means to determine an individual's claim to state welfare provisions. Besides, the 'perfect' citizen appears to be perceived as law abiding, dutiful and responsible to the nation state, and this is reciprocated through access to rights and welfare. Progressing from this, the notion of 'free' state assistance is contested and counterarguments refer to the Irish taxation system and either direct or *generalized reciprocity*. Such cost–benefit reasoning seems to provide an excuse for feelings of resentment towards 'newcomers' who are believed to unevenly benefit from welfare provisions. Instead of appreciating the potential gain of tangible economic, immaterial profit and *socio-cultural capital* from 'newcomers' and diversification, the impression is that returnee migration is the preferred substitute in acquiring new forms of *capital*, knowledge and prosperity.

Generally, the current welfare state model is perceived as deficient. This seems to manifest in disapproval aimed at the maladministration of state policies and practices, as well as towards citizens who abuse the welfare state model across the social-class strata of Irish society. What emerges is a politics of a deserving 'us' versus an undeserving 'them' which creates a perceived binary division based on classist and racist assumptions. In relation to such a dichotomy, a basic anecdotal account, of property ownership and the allocation of land, is overtly contested as being *anthropocentric*. Instead, the apparent counter-position exposed by one participant is an inversion whereby the deemed reality is that the land and nature own humans; thus, no one should claim governing access over the Irish territorial expanse.

What materializes from the transcribed material is that *conservatism* is an ascribed inclination among the Irish, at an individual and political level. Thus, the impression is that *Irishness* is viewed as being characterized by values of *conservatism*. The erosion of the traditional would seem to be comprehended as undermining conservative leanings, along with sustaining unfair rights of access to state provisions. The shift towards *denationalization* and *economization* seems to be recognized as a development within national governance towards the acceptance and implementation of *neoliberal* policies. Within the Belfast focus group discussion, comprehension of *conservatism* seems slightly more nuanced. The impression seems to be that the Irish value system is based on moral and *political conservatism*, while purporting to uphold notions of equality might more aptly intimate *neo-conservative* predilections. Intermeshed with this appears to be an historical understanding of Catholicism, and its institutions, as having acted as proxies for what should have been provided for by the state. More importantly, in the context of this book, conservatism within contemporary times is explicitly discussed with regard to the management of migration controls. *Transnational capitalism* and regional economic uncertainties seem to be perceived as governing immigration.

Although it would initially seem to contrast general views presented thus far, discussion on the outcomes of the 2004 ICR gives the impression that various participants perceive its motion, constitutional approval and enactment as being founded on racism and national chauvinism. Nonetheless, by some this is resolved whereby justifications for its ratification are made on the grounds of a perceived sense of threat to security from the non-European, non-developed world, 'other'. Intra-European migration which is perceived as driven by principles of economic supply and demand is also perceived as in quite negative light. Some participants' perspectives appear to hint at a degree of regressive nationalistic sentiment caused by both racism and protectionism; however, this seems to remain present even during the rebound in economic prosperity in the Irish national context.

Interrelated to the topic immediately above, although concealed within discourse, the discussion progresses towards a description of the central findings. The main findings culminate by highlighting the juxtaposition of rational or irrational pragmatisms within tendencies towards *neoliberal* thinking. In support of this thesis, further evidence is unfolded to elucidate the notion of *perceived rational pragmatism* in conversation. As mentioned above, some participants challenge the outcomes of the 2004 ICR and, as detailed in previous chapters, there seems to be the view that citizenship can and should be attained through bloodline descent, birthright and/or temporal exposure to Irish society. Nevertheless, several participants would appear to be decisively in favour of the 2004 ICR legislative changes. Fascinatingly, such support is not contained within a vacuum of unawareness. There is a consciousness of how dominant media representations and political discourse falsely presented arguments during the 2004 ICR campaign. Even with the benefit of such hindsight, as explicitly accepted, some participants maintain and espouse support for its passing into legislation by relying on the newly found basis of perceived security threat and economic necessity. A further example of *perceived rational pragmatism* emergent within the thematic analysis relates to the dominant usage of English language over Irish language. Some participants actively differentiate *Irishness* from 'otherness' and endorse the *assimilationist* view that demands the migrant 'other' to acquire English. Conflicting with ideological views on the importance of acquiring Irish language (as detailed in relation to *linguistic capital* in Chapter 5), integration is gratified through *acculturation* rather than mediated through *interculturalism* or the conception of an inter-lingual society. Participants' notions on *consumerism* provide further evidence in support of the theory being espoused. The perception is that it is logically pragmatic to express a predilection towards consuming Irish produce, as well as prioritizing the Irish over 'others', because it is internally cyclical, thus perceived as beneficial for the Irish economy and Irish collectivity. This seemingly rationally pragmatic view neglects reflection upon altruism. Furthermore, in the context of consumption, *perceived rational pragmatism* negates adequately considering the means of attainment of commodities that are acquired and imported via broader world systems relating to *globalization*.

The closing section of this chapter focusses attention on governance, *regionalism* and *globalization*. Irish state governance is portrayed as what would seem to be immature within the circumstance of contemporary *regionalism*. Governance in Ireland is also deemed to be frail whereby the nation state is depicted as having a deficiency in political experience. Thus, it lacks capability towards sovereignty, independent management and autonomous determination. For this reason, some participants seem to perceive European dominance as a positive development as it obliges the Irish state to enact progressive laws of equality. Conversely, such an undemocratic arrangement would seem to imply that Ireland is in a bind between state ineptitude and European-level autocracy. To add to this, some participants refer to the global financial system and *transnationalism* as further binds on the ability of the Irish state to adequately manage its independency, yet, paradoxically

Ireland seems perceived as inextricably dependant on *globalization, as well as* foreign direct investment from transnational corporations.

This concluding chapter, of the results and findings, presents a selection of the more expansive motifs concerning both inter- and intra-state governance and globalization. In keeping with the overall directionality of the study and orientation of analysis in the previous chapters, this closing results and findings chapter focusses attention on contemporary perceptions of governance as a means of inclusion/exclusion. For this reason, it primarily observes perceived views on the welfare state model, in conjunction with immigration and migration control regimes. This chapter culminates by introducing and substantiating the socio-psychological concept of *perceived rational pragmatism*. The concept is elaborated on, both theoretically and descriptively, in the subsequent chapter which also documents the overall conclusions. Thus, interlinking with this and previous chapters, the following chapter commences by presenting an overview of the findings and results interwoven with theory and more inferred interpretations of the data as documented and analyzed heretofore.

Irishness, *Governance, Migration Controls and World Views* 211

Chapter 10

Epilogue

Keywords: Social evolutionism; traditionalism; Hobbesian theory; egocentrism; ethnocentric; Kantian theory; *perceived rational pragmatism*; pseudo-rational; language; empathy

Although the general theme of this project is immensely expansive, the focus and motivation from the outset relate both to how 'Irish' identity is perceived, primarily by members within the dominant norm of Irish society and how such perceptions reflect onto the lives of 'others', as included, excluded or marginal. Thus, by being intentionally less assumptive, this research endeavours to raise thought, deliberation and reflection on the impact of more subtle nuances associated with identity formation which have an effect on the most marginalized 'other' within the society of Ireland, for example, people barely living within the Direct Provision system and people physically excluded from the comforts of a developed world economy, such as Ireland. It is for this reason that the focal point of the concluding section will be on addressing emergent thoughts, discussions and sociological critique pertinent to the contemporary spatio-temporal condition of individual people that are 'othered'. The justification is that, upon reflection of how we define ourselves, we might expose the gratuitous hardships we inflict on other people through antonymic exclusion.

This concluding chapter details the emergent leitmotifs relating to how *Irishness* is perceived within the current era of *liquid modernity*. Within the remit of this qualitative study, this chapter describes and reflects upon some of the substantial ways in which 'Irish' identity is redefined and socially (re)constructed in contemporary Ireland.

The initial section details an overview of the book's contributions to the body of knowledge on identity, being and the self within the ever mutable social fabric. The second section reviews the findings of the dissertation by discursively deliberating on perceived *Irishness* and the processes by which identity is redefined in Ireland within the continuum of an ever-changing society. This progresses into the third section which further deconstructs and theorizes the process of *perceived rational pragmatism* in the context of *liquid/late-modernity* and *ordo-liberalism*. The final section provides an overall closing to redefining *Irishness* in a globalized world.

In summary, there are five main findings that emerge and are identified in redefining 'Irish' identity within this globalized world and the continuum of contemporary modernity. These findings are considered to be an empirical addition to the body of knowledge on 'Irish' identity. Most noteworthy is the unambiguous centrality of essentialist notions of 'race' in the social construction of *Irishness*. Although numerous mechanisms affecting identity formation are established, the redefining of an 'Irish' identity occurs through these fundamental processes.

Firstly, at a micro-level, justifications for claims of being 'Irish' are linked to genealogical lineage and the importance of one's heredity, wider family ties, clan and community. Secondly, claiming *Irishness* through the connection to an ancient past is practised as a means to elevate and project status of 'native' above all other people. Thirdly, a new construction that differentiates between being 'Irish' and being an Irish citizen is reliant on the superficial visual, which is racialized and hierarchical. Fourthly, compounded ethno-racial distinctions are reified and conceived of in essentialist terms; the singular ideal of an 'Irish' identity is extrapolated and superimposed onto the collective. These processes combine to constrain conceptions of identity as dynamic and fluid. Finally, a crucial process exposed is that identity in Ireland is formed within the social condition of *conservatism*, and propensity towards *ordo-liberalism*, which create an environment that lends itself to the socio-psychological process of *perceived rational pragmatism*.

Perceived rational pragmatism is presented as thesis synthesis herein and as a contribution, albeit incremental, to the body of knowledge on socio-psychological theory. The third section of this chapter explores and develops further theorization on this process of *perceived rational pragmatism*. By scrutinizing and deconstructing specific discourse, the theory emerges organically and becomes evident in the research overall. The agential dimension of the socio-psychological process posed is that it exposes and challenges the illogical bias which occurs within the production of a classificatory schema reliant on the very notion of 'race' in defining who the Irish are in contemporary Ireland. In addition, the qualitative methodological approach detailed in Chapter 4 which incorporates the viewing of a multimedia presentation, made from one-to-one interviews, midway through the focus group discussions, is an evidently productive addition to the body of knowledge on qualitative methodological approaches to researching contemporary issues of identity formation, definitions and (re)constructions.

Review: *Irishness* as Perceived in an Era of *Liquid Modernity*

Many forms of identity and their constructions become apparent throughout the research. Participants build a sense of *Irishness* based on family and genealogical linkage, physiological traits, political identification, national cultural identity affiliation (such as language and music) and often through differentiation from 'others'.

Similar to research by Inglis and Donnelly (2011) what is found 'is a *mélange* of identities and senses of belonging. Deep-rooted belonging is mixed with elective belonging and both come together with a general sense of belonging to Ireland' (p. 139).

Across all of the stages of the research, it becomes apparent that one's immediate family is perceived as a foundational prerequisite for the cultural transmission of values, attitudes and behaviours which are re/produced trans-generationally. The particularities of such traits would seem to be deemed as explicitly Irish, and often even more specifically localized. The subject-constructed narratives of participants portray an emphasis on the importance of immediate family in an idealized, romanticized and static way, similar to what Byrne and O'Mahony (2012, p. 58) detail in relation to classical studies of dominant narratives in the monolithic and enduring portrayal of Irish family life.[1] Evidently, the impression is that little consideration is given to a growing independence of the conjugal unit with potentially fewer kinship ties to distant relatives and where families, both nationally and internationally over the past century, may have become more democratic, smaller, less stable and more diverse in form (Fine-Davis, 2011, p. 5*ff*.; Goode, 1963, p. 1; Seward et al., 2005, p. 411). Within the discussions, the participants do not seem to take into account the significant societal changes that have occurred, as reported by Fine-Davis (2011),

> since the 1960s there have been vast social changes which have led to changing gender roles, changes in the nature of the family and a falling birth rate in Ireland and in Europe. In Ireland, we have witnessed major shifts in gender role attitudes and behaviour, including notably a major increase in women's labour force participation, and these shifts have been accompanied by changing patterns of family formation. (p. 4)

What also becomes evident, directly in relation to immediate family, and which is conversed about within several of the focus groups, is the perceived view of the role of the mother not only in family life but also in creating and continuing a distinctive sense of *Irishness*. The reproduction of parental distinctiveness based on desires to provide for the next generation at the cost of self-sacrifice is suggested as stemming from a historical viewpoint of the Irish as underdogs, having suffered under colonial oppression and a sense of yearning to succeed and progress.

---

[1] Arensberg et al. (1940) published *Family and Community in Ireland* following an in-depth anthropological study of Irish families in County Care in the early 1930s as part of the Harvard Irish Study. Although of classical status, according to Seward et al. (2005), 'Studies completed since the 1970s have overwhelmingly documented that the reign of stem-extended families (children reared beyond immediate parents) was primarily ideological and that they were not typical even in the area that Arensberg and Kimball had studied. Yet their descriptions of Irish families became the standard and the primary basis for claims that Ireland's families were an exception to the convergence pattern' (p. 422).

Although, on the one hand, this may be understood positively in a maternal and protective sense, on the other hand, such perceived notions associating motherhood and *Irishness* may have the effect of contributing towards reproducing traditional hegemonic patriarchal norms.

Genealogical lineage and the importance of one's hereditary and wider family ties would seem to provide justification for claims of being 'Irish'. The wider family comes across also as portrayed as integral to producing a sense of 'home' that is not merely the physical locality of one's living space, but a place, real or imagined, that encapsulates closeness among members of the wider family both spatially and emotionally. Members of the wider family, who may be based in Ireland, provide a sense of emotional attachment not only to the physical locality of Ireland but also for claiming *Irishness*. As Inglis and Donnelly (2011) contest,

> [...] place is more than a space for performing identities. It is [an] integral part of how individuals see and understand themselves, another identity block in the ongoing construction of a sense of self. It is about feeling at home with 'others' who are seen as similar, as having shared understandings, dispositions and ways of being in the world. This sense of belonging, of being at home, is obviously strongly associated with family and community. (p. 130)

Although generally family or marital status are considered the principal forms of social identity for people who deem themselves to be 'Irish', Inglis and Donnelly (2011) maintain emphasis on 'place'.[2] However, participant responses appear to impart an understanding of both immediate and wider family as being catalytic in an individual's self-association with an Irish locality and being 'Irish'. Essential to this is that such definitions of identity and sense of belonging are heavily rooted in perceived genealogical linkages irrespective of affiliations with the actual land of Ireland or even ethno-cultural exposure. That is to say, from the responses from participants, the impression is that it is 'race', not space,[3] which principally determines underlying associations of being 'Irish'. In the context of globalization and migration, it may be that as real or imagined sense of place becomes unsettled, individuals resort more to reliance on family and 'race' as a social indicator of distinction and, conversely, it leverages so that when an individual's homogeneity becomes perturbed their contingent reaction is the reliance on place and locality to provide a sense of a foundational belonging.

---

[2] This does not reduce from the consideration that 'place is seen as a major social indicator, of culture, class, nationality, urbanity and so forth'. And where place 'establishes similarities and differences and the strength of the bonds and boundaries that could unite or divide strangers' (Inglis and Donnelly, 2011, p. 131).

[3] In reference to Hagedorn's (2006) work entitled, 'Race not Space: A Revisionist History of Gangs in Chicago'.

Layered into this is what Gilroy (1990) describes,

> The term culture has expanded to displace any overt references to 'race' in the older, biological sense of the term. Culture is reductively conceived and is always primarily and 'naturally' reproduced in families. The nation is, in turn, conceived as a neat, symmetrical accumulation of family units and the supposedly homogenous culture – secured in part by sustained exposure to national history in the classroom – culminates in the experience of unified and continuous national identity. (p. 114)

Linked to conceptions of family, wider family and irreducible genealogical lineage is the notion of clan. This notion of clan would seem parallel to some definitions of the nature of kinship, emphasizing biological over social relationships, whereby 'irreducible genealogical connections, the given relations of actual connectedness … are utilized in building up kinship relations and categories' (Fortes, 1969, p. 52; Strathern, 1973, p. 21).[4] Being a part of a clan is seen as a more authentic way of validating claims of *Irishness* and is interpreted as a lineage primarily through bloodline descent-constructs that extend back to the pre-medieval period. This comes across as corresponding with Strathern's (1973) description of clan where

> it refers both to the world of processes in which local groups actually interact with one another and to the world of constructs in which (wo/)men posit common descent from ancestors, common substance in the form of semen or blood and so on. (p. 26)

Several participants also seem to interpret clan in biogenetic substance or bloodline terms, whereby the strength of the clan is dependent on reproduction but also on the expansion of essentialized kinship through the propagation of the progeny which increases or widens the clan.

An interpretation given for the historical construction of social life in a feudalistic manner relates to the notion of grudge and is also linked to feudal conflict. Its perpetuation even into contemporary times within Ireland links into notions of *begrudgery* or belittlement more generally, which is touched upon in several of the focus group discussions.

Parochialism appears to be particularly associated with rural Irish life.[5] With parochialism, 'people were seen and saw themselves as belonging to extended

---

[4] Kinship may be polysemic whereby its meaning is derived from genealogy and it may imply a metaphorical extension of such descent (Strathern, 1973, p. 31).
[5] As revealed in the findings, rural life is idealized across many of the focus group discussions. Such expressions complement O'Toole's (1985) description in 'Going West: The Country versus the City in Irish Writing', but are based on a real sense of tradition that persists. To a degree, traditional culture has dissolved, but perhaps, it persists in new forms; thus, there isn't the sense of demoralization or break-down because of that but from elsewhere (economics, dominance of state and beyond).

families from particular parishes ...' (Inglis, 2009, p. 2; Inglis & Donnelly, 2011, p. 131). Nonetheless, parochialism can also be seen to differ from clan as it transcends clan loyalty and centres the community around the parish. People may be included in the parochial life but excluded through the construction of boundaries from membership in the clan category and vice versa (Strathern, 1973, p. 26). What is fascinating from the discussions is the lack of dialogue of religion, specifically Christianity, in relation to *parachialism*.

The subsequent theme is community. It comes across as a foundational characteristic of *Irishness*, in particular, in its association with traditional and Irish rural life. This would correspond with the view that 'tradition is a mode of integrating the reflexive monitoring of action with the time-space organisation of the community' and as Giddens (1990) continues, 'tradition is not wholly static, because it has to be reinvented each new generation as it takes over its cultural inheritance from those preceding it' (p. 37). Giddens' notion of the reproduction and development of tradition would seem relatable to participants drawing synonymous comparisons between cultural production and evolution or 'progress' (as further detailed below).

Furthermore, for some participants, community is understood and discussed in a dualistic manner. It generally seems to be either used with polarity to describe an all-encompassing singular collective – the Irish community – or to describe groups within this as distinct from one another. It is used as a means of distinction and with this as a means to create linkages and bonds. In both cases, the sense is that it homogenizes either, by placing individuals into discrete groups that are internally uniform, or, by interpreting society as a prearranged naturally homogeneous collectivity. Although conceptions of community may manifest themselves in slightly different forms, it can be identified within this dichotomy, which is expanded further below. The feeling is that community is also intentionally described as disparate from notions of *parochialism*, as the latter is seen to relate directly to religious institutions, which are viewed as having negative connotations.

For community what becomes evident appears to be recognition of the continued importance of family (as above) yet, contradictorily, participants' views also complement Halberstam's (2003, p. 315) notion that community is becoming an archaic thing of the past. Inglis and Donnelly (2011) suggest that 'the trend seems inexorable: the more the local becomes penetrated by global flows, the more people move around the world, the more family and community become "disembedded"' (p. 127).[6] Although Inglis and Donnelly's (2011, p. 127) interpretation implies that both family and community are inseparable, it is plausible that one maintains strong family bonds irrespective of the erosion of community in its outmoded sense, imagined or otherwise. In fact, as Giddens (1990) states, 'kinship relations, for the majority of the population, remain important, especially within the nuclear family, but they are no longer the carriers of intensively organised social ties across time-space' (p. 108).

---

[6]In reference to the work by Giddens (1991) entitled, *Modernity and Self-identity: Self and Society in the Late Modern Age*.

The implication from the perceived views of participants in the discussions is that they seem to challenge the notion that late-modernity results in the decline of the family but rather perhaps still support that 'some local milieux continue to be the hub of substantial kinship networks of rights and obligations' (Giddens, 1990, p. 108). Similarly, Corcoran et al. (2010, p. 138) looking at *Suburban Affiliations: Social Relations in the Greater Dublin Area* refer to work that implies an intensification in the trend for suburban families to spend more social time with immediate family members and less with friends and neighbours. Perhaps evidenced from the findings are the perpetuation and maintenance of familial and clannish associations in the construction of identities, as well as a reversion away from more collectivized views of community in the Irish context, communal existence being associated with religion and *parochialism*. Nonetheless, the fact that community is used to describe and create a foundational basis for an all-inclusive singular Irish collective would also support the central theorization presented from the findings on *perceived rational pragmatism* (as detailed below).

Claims made by individuals who would ordinarily self-subscribe as Irish in relation to the historical seem portrayed as associated with genealogical links or ancestral roots to an Irish past. The abstract idea of claiming a purity of 'Irish' identity based on the protracted longevity of familial lineage is brought into question in relation to the perceived accuracy of Irish historicity by some participants. This occurs within a focus group discussion with primarily younger participants, who highlight a noteworthy dimension in cross-analysis. An assumption might be made whereby *conservatism* appears as allied with older age and creativity with youth. Loaded with this supposition would be the view that, with age, greater knowledge has been attained, thus providing a greater excuse for conservative values. Evidenced from the focus group discussions, however, seems to be the inference that some of the younger participants were, in fact, not only more open to alternative understandings of *Irishness* but were also contemplative and evaluative, in a deconstructive manner, of aspects pertaining to *Irishness* which were conversed about by older participants, such as supposed unambiguous histories. Conceivably, it may be also indicative of a shift in pedagogy in recent years that takes, for example, a more revisionist approach to historical education and challenges what Doherty (1996) several decades ago describes as,

> the inculcation of the belief in the inherent spirituality of the Irish people, which constituted the dominant motif in school instruction, supplemented by a more sophisticated popular historical consciousness than has usually been allowed ... the point to be emphasised here is that the purposefulness of Irish popular thought, as instanced by the teaching of History, defies the categories prescribed for it by intellectuals, and has produced a variegated cultural milieu in which the political substratum nestles comfortably. (p. 325*f.*)

It is worth mentioning that gaeilgóir students, who likely value highly Irish language and nationhood, appear to display a level of cynicism towards *Irishness* that is based on identifying with fixed historical understandings associated with *revivalism*. Inferred also is that the younger participants may recognize how the acquirement of the Irish language is not so as to strengthen mythical racial distinctiveness but rather more simply an appreciation of cultural distinctiveness which can be valued inclusively. The younger participants seem to have transcended the *postcolonial* backlash that viewed the restoration of the Irish language as a means to counter 'the extinction of the Irish race' as described in Seanad Debates on 18 March 1943 (Doherty, 1996, p. 336). Their views give the appearance of having removed an assumed *intrinsicism* of the Irish language and other traits and characteristics. Such views seem to correspond more closely with *subjectivist* views. Such self-reflective and critical evaluation of past and present also lean towards *cosmopolitanism* or, conceivably even, 'a cosmopolitan patriotism' as described by Appiah (1997, p. 618). These young participants show signs of appreciating locality and community while transcending local attachments at the same time. This aspect of *patriotism* and *cosmopolitanism* is afforded more in-depth attention in the section below.

Conversation on history provides the means to express an understanding of societal change. The comprehension of social change is expressed and conceived of based on a form of progress that seems conceptualized similarly to natural evolutionary processes. Instead of what Giddens (1990) describes as a 'loss of a belief in "progress"' (p. 10) which is underlain by 'the dissolution of "narratives" of history' some participants' responses seem to rely on historical narratives for the restoration of the belief in social evolutionary 'advancement'. Such views appear to correspond with *social evolutionism* which supposes that '"history" can be told in terms of a "story line" which imposes an orderly picture upon the jumble of human happenings' (Giddens, 1990, p. 5). To a degree, such cognitive positioning may then limit participants' perceptions on discontinuities that may have occurred and occur in both modernity and post/late-modernity. There is some reservation whereby viewing societal change as an innate process comparable to evolution, rapid change in the fabric of society due to migration is seen either as a potentially detrimental abnormality, or as an inevitable process with the prospect of creating positive societal advancements. The impression is that the former detracts from serious, existential concerns (discussed below), while the latter indicates a sense of blind acceptance or *fatalism*, which adds to the depreciation of self-agency and sense of autonomy. The *Social Darwinian* evolutionary narrative, that expresses perpetual progression, may hint as to why participants generally did not allude to more dysfunctional social phenomena relating to environmental degradation, political totalitarianism/empire and military power with the industrialization of military intervention and war (Giddens, 1990, p. 9; McNeill, 1982, 1983). Such views seem to assume diachronic links or temporal progress to be integrally linked to civilizing processes or the advancement of civility.

Participants distinguish 'the other' by claiming how 'the other' lacks historical connection with the Irish nation across a continuum of measures. Such a deficit is perceived to lessen one's claims of *Irishness*. In the practice of creating such differentiations, although it is not perceived as being necessarily divisive, the suggested inference is that it may unwittingly exacerbate social stratification.[7] Here what is identified is that representations of history not only help to define the social identities of peoples but how groups relate to other peoples both in the context of international politics and with regard to internal diversity (Liu & Hilton, 2005, p. 537). Important too, is the observed relationship between representations of history in creating, maintaining and shaping an individual's identity, combined with their social standing.

A certain bias emerged across several of the focus group discussions whereby negative sentiments are expressed towards American claims to *Irishness* based on ancient genealogical links to Ireland. This would seem inconsistent with previous justifications that allow one-self to claim *Irishness*. Such a contradiction appears to be less as the need to construct one's own identity within a fixed historical past and more as a confirmation of a strategic manoeuvre; as means to fulfil the desire to preserve a social arrangement that benefits the self. Furthermore, claiming *Irishness* through the connection to an ancient past comes across as a means to elevate and project the status of 'native' above all other people. Such elevation of nativeness seems constructed even by participants who may not ordinarily associate themselves with supposed progressive or conservative inclinations although typically it would more aptly complement leanings towards the latter. Accordingly, Gilroy (1990, p. 166) refers to the doggedly *ethnocentric* character of the desire and aspiration of leftist nationalists 'to produce a popular culture which the left can somehow orchestrate or even command ...' and also raises issue with 'left nationalism and the statist conceptions of political change that bolster it' (p. 166). Gilroy (1990) continues by referring to the compounding of 'race', nation, culture and ethnicity and how such historiography creates a nativist impulse which 'represents a great intellectual weakness' particularly as far as 'the politics of racism are concerned' (p. 166).

Participants' perceptions of more modern Irish history and views of pre- and post-colonial Ireland appear to negate responsibility and accountability for recognized past and persistent social problems. Ireland is portrayed as a juvenile nation that was and is inadequately equipped to deal with its own collective societal dilemmas.

In the context of modern Irish history and *postcolonial* Ireland, and although unspoken, such negation could also be how Ireland distances itself from European colonialism. Conversely, such distancing may also neglect or even, through a process of historical amnesia, eradicate reflection and deliberation

---

[7]The relationship between ethnic identity and social-economic status is not a wholly new phenomenon. In modern Ireland, the predominantly bipolar religious denominational axis distinguished between Protestantism and Catholicism and was seen to have social significance for status inequality. During the 19th and 20th centuries, religion was a key characteristic or ethnic determinant of an individual's identity, and labelling on religious grounds was starkly related to social position. Although inequalities have diminished, certainly in the Northern Irish context, differences remain (Coakley, 2002).

on intersecting ethno-religious and social divisions that culminated in the Rising and ensuing civil war. Furthermore, although a neutral state at the time of the Shoah Holocaust, a certain level of complicity was present. Although not a colonizing country like other European nations, nonetheless for Ireland also there would seem to be a

> silence about race today, its censoriousness, its denial. Race is an embarrassment. A family past that has passed, or must be made pass. Better that it not be mentioned, that it not have to be thought or thought about. Only it doesn't comply, it won't cooperate, it refuses to remain silent. (Goldberg, 2009, p. 155)

Perhaps such discomfiture which creates an abstinence from discussing 'race', and the fear of an alternative 'other', is leading to the regressive phenomenon of perverse views of 'race' as expressed in explicit racist sentiments. The impression is that, as a juvenile state, we are excused for knowing no better, or for lacking the socialization of civility and respect.

Alternatively, or in combination, silence about 'race' would seem not be a localized phenomenon. Lentin (2008) conveys the view in *Europe and the Silence about Race* that, '… contemporary, western, postcolonial societies are imbricated in an idea of their constitutive nature as tolerant and democratic and, by association, non-racist or indeed anti-racist' (p. 488). In accordance with this, the overall argument presented is that,

> the silence about race in Europe allows European states to declare themselves non-racist, or even anti-racist, while at the same time continuing to imply an inherent European superiority, which determines both international relationships and relationships with those seen as 'in but not of Europe' within its domestic spheres. (Lentin, 2008, p. 487)

History, as a subject and discipline, is shown to have been discussed in several focus groups. The impression from the participants' discussions is that a sound and comprehensive knowledge of Irish history is considered indispensable in order to become fully integrated into Irish society and self-subscribe as Irish.

The discrepancy between being an Irish citizen and being 'Irish', when brought to the fore, apparently emphasizes a form of labelling as a process of differentiation. The resultant effect may be the projection of an unequal onus or responsibility on the new Irish citizen rather than the 'native' Irish. Nonetheless, with regard to the notion of being 'native Irish' as Inglis (2008) writes,

> there has never been a unique, essential way of being Irish. But this has not stopped people – and the groups and organizations to which they belong – from trying to make out that there are core characteristics to being Irish. These range from being born in Ireland, to having Irish ancestors, speaking the Irish language,

listening to Irish music, playing gaelic sports, supporting the nationalist struggle in the North and so forth. (p. 41)

Overall, what may be observed, with shifting dynamics because of increased variation among the Irish population due to migratory flows and globalization, is the occurrence of a more contemporary form of distinction. The possibility is that the process of labelling and differentiating has moved from less explicit culturally assumed habits to the superficial visual, which is racialized. Within the continuum of *liquid modernity* instead of a more enlightened approach whereby the very conceptual notion of belonging is challenged and changed, simply the rules of belonging may have partially shifted. Such an adjustment to the rules maintains inequitable power dynamics which are an undercurrent of Irish society. In this context, a seemingly invariable outcome in the dynamics of populations and power is the socio-psychological disposition towards making superior/inferior distinctions. In this Irish context, some perceptions of participants studied suggest a propensity towards in-group exclusionary practices.

When comparing the agency to call oneself "Irish" with the less tangible sense of feeling Irish, what becomes evident is the contrast between self-subscribing as Irish and being externally recognized and accepted as 'Irish' by other people. Bound to self-identification as 'Irish' is an emotional association with Ireland that is often expressed as an affection or affinity with the country, and a perceived Irish way of life.

The importance of cultural exposure over a temporal period in several of the focus group discussions appears to shift the focus away from either *jus soli* (birthright) or *jus sanguinis* (bloodline) kinship-based arguments. What may seem incongruent from this is that although participants did seem orientated towards temporal duration and residency rather than birthright or bloodline descent affiliation and Irish citizenship acquisition, as further elaborated below, participants' understandings of ethnicity imply that 'mere residence within a locality is not in itself enough to generate local solidarity' (Tovey et al., 1989, p. 9). An ostensibly plausible antidote to this dilemma is in the classificatory distinction that is made between 'being Irish' and 'being an Irish citizen'.

Being both Americanized and Irish through exposure to Irish cultural norms would seem discordant with an idealized view of being 'Irish' which somewhat rejects the possibility of expressing identity hybridity. In this instance, there is the preclusion of the notion of *cultural hybridization* associated with *cosmopolitan patriotism* as detailed by Appiah (1997, p. 619). Furthermore, the expression of anti-American sentiment does not seem to complement the self-recognition of the adoption of perceived American traits, attitudes, values and behaviours by assumed members of Irish society.

The contestable issue between performing alternative cultural practices and expressing feelings of affinity for Ireland would seem to show an imbalance towards privileging individuals deemed as members of the Irish collective. Linking in with this is the rejection of notions of hybrid identities, whereby a paradox is highlighted between expressing an affinity with a given locality or country while also maintaining an appreciation of self-expression that may have stemmed from cultural exposure elsewhere. Again, in reference to above, this seems to challenge Appiah's (1997) desire for *cultural hybridization* within *cosmopolitan patriotism* and the sentiment expressed by Appiah (1997) who suggests that, 'there is no reason to suppose that everybody in this complex, ever-mutating world will find their affinities and their passions focused on a single place' (p. 622).

This might lead to the inclination to ask the question, 'why might society discourage understanding self-identification in such a manner?' An assumption might be because there is the association between historical events, such as the 1916 Rising and the Irish civil war, and *nationalism* fuelled by over-romanticization and sentimentality. Past conflict is conflated with the perception of excess emotion yet, as detailed above, affection for and affinity with a perceived ethnic tradition seem based on the arousal of feelings. Emotive feelings based on a sense of connectedness to the past can also be seen as woven into the present and also future projections, as described by Tovey et al. (1989):

> Whatever cultural elements emerge to symbolize identity, over time these develop an accretion of additional meanings which amplify the group's representation of itself to itself and others. They become the bearers of an interpretation of historical continuity – myths of origin or a shared historical past; they come to stand for a much broader, explicit or implicit ethos and set of aspirations for the future of the people. Thus, they both define the epitome of peoplehood and express in a multidimensional way a common consciousness of kind. (p. 6)

As described above, the immense importance of history is evidenced. Power is exerted to maintain control into the future by those who can outwardly claim linkage to Irish history, define it and self-subscribe as associated with it, both physically and emotionally. It is the means by which descendent rises over those without claim to ancestry.

Progressing on from this is the examination of the construction of ethnicity, 'race' and 'Irish' national identity. The homogeneity of Irish physiological traits, in particular pale and 'white' skinned, is seen to be dependent on a specific understanding of a Celtic historical epoch, as well as phenotypically determined via intergenerational exposure to Irish climatic conditions. Thus, as the word phenology implies, the external environmental habitat and climate are seen to be functional in affecting an Irish person's physical disposition. Such recognized phenotypes would seem to be so imbedded in historical ancestry, they have become naturalized to equate to an imagined purity of *Irishness*.

The requirement to conform so as to be recognized as a member within the dominant norm of society, as perceived by participants, is related to an *assimilationist/integrationist* perspective in contrast to *multiculturalism* or *interculturalism*. Yet, directly in contradiction to above, where imagined purity is based on inherited and an evolved bodily condition, physiological traits are not deemed to be of importance within the process of inscribing *Irishness* onto a person. Of equal importance, though with a slightly dissimilar nuance, commonality rather than conformity is focussed upon in a separate focus group discussion. As referred to above, according to one participant, one gains an appreciation of commonality within the collective through temporal exposure and 'growing up in Ireland' (Adrian), which can be assumed as progression towards social cohesion.

Nonetheless, additional evidence does emerge which reaffirms a more fixed view on the homogeneity of *Irishness* based on a supposed essential nature of a person. With the further disentanglement of the notion of 'race', revealed somewhat conflicts with the stance above which seems to value extrinsic factors. Thus fittingly, the notion of 'race' as an imaginary is juxtaposed against 'race' as a reality. The notion of the Irish as a discrete 'race' is assumed and implied in several focus group discussions, yet may not be shared by all of the participants within each of the groups. Either way, in the social and public sense observed is how perceived reality and the perceived imaginary domain become mechanisms of limited representation rather than an exercise of minds that provides individuals with 'freedom of personality' and self-determination (Acampora, 2007, p. 67; Cornell, 1998, p. 33). Instead of the imaginary domain activating what Acampora (2007) describes as 'the possibility for change – insofar as different forms of existence emerge as options to pursue or reject, and hence the imaginary domain facilitates a more rigorous exercise of our agency' (p. 67) – the collectivized racialized imaginary domain of *Irishness* produces the opposite, by restraining agency both of ourselves and 'others'. If phenotypical *Irishness*, as described above, is imagined but constructed externally at a social level to then become absorbed and internalized at the individual level, then there may well be a moral obligation for a democratic society, purporting to uphold the values of freedom, to undermine and destabilize such notions of 'race' built on false consciousness.

Two noteworthy aspects of discourse become evident from analysis of the focus group discussions. Firstly, as discussed in Chapter 8, attention is given to the use of third person plural pronouns which might be perceived as a language mechanism to intentionally differentiate in a derogatory or subordinating manner. Instead what is inferred is that it is a mechanism to stress the importance of cultural exposure through the experiential in being or becoming 'Irish'. Secondly, in certain instances although comments are made which seem to ironically portray *Irishness* as being solely bound to intrinsic bloodline descent, they could be indicative of a perceived view of a dominant attitude that may prevail within broader Irish society below the surface.

A form of *reification fallacy* pertaining to the compounding of both ethnic and racial distinctions is identified and exposed in conversations. Participants refer to generalized descriptions of a stereotypical understanding of a unique Irish way of life, yet almost simultaneously recognize the difficulty in describing a distinctively authentic Irish ethnicity. Suggested from the analysis is the implication that participants have not, in a reflexive manner, made the realization that what might be at the core of the question relates to their own sense of perceived *Irishness*. As compounded by participants, ethno-racial first impressions seem to be related to socio-psychological processes that occur with the ascription of identity. More traditional understandings of the concept of ethnicity appear unveiled, particularly as perceived by older participants. Their interpretations of ethnicity complement

Geertz's (1973) description whereby ethnicity as a social identifier can be perceived based on attachments and sentiments that are primordial; 'assumed "givens" – of social existence' (Geertz, 1973, p. 259). Comprehending ethnicity in such a manner implies 'that ethnic attachments are temporal (rudimentary, unresponsive to change) and even biological (innate, almost genetic)' (Tovey et al., 1989, p. 5). Such presuppositions are seen to become embedded in an individual's consciousness with greater effect when the collective group accentuates the absoluteness of singular identity distinctions rather than conceiving identities as fluid and adaptable. Through conceiving *Irishness* in restrictive terms and an inability to imagine more varied ethno-racial arrangements, an ethno-racial bind occurs within the consciousness of participants that is based on the *reification fallacy*.

Overall, comprehension of the Irish social fabric is achieved through a compounding of intrinsic notions of evolutionary change within the context of history (as is further expounded below), together with the reification of ethno-racial distinctions, *ethnocentrisms*, as well as the belief that society can be and is shaped by environmental externalities. Such an interpretation of social order and potential societal progress conveys a level of illogicality. It suggests that through social interaction, between members of the dominant normative group within Irish society, a blending occurs to facilitate transmission of racial/ethnocentric and conversely *anti-essentialist* values which merge within the psyche of individuals. On the one hand, through a process of social construction, the socio-psychological condition perpetuates ethnocentric biases; while on the other hand, there is a cognisant understanding that such ideas of the inherent are actually quite fragile, baseless and abstract. Nonetheless, acceptance, reconciliation and the condoning of such conditioning are reached because there is the fear (as introduced in the previous findings chapters) and belief that any undermining would entail the destabilization of the status quo, or an alteration of the social fabric which ultimately would be personally counter-beneficial for the increasingly egocentric individualized Irish person.

In contrast to above, cultural change, as well as the loss of what is deemed traditional (also discussed below), seems to be perceived as caused by processes associated with *globalization*, rather than the arrival of 'newcomers' and the perceived *ethno-racial heterogenization* of the Irish collective. Cultural appropriation and absorption through media exposure and consumption patterns are described as determined and influenced primarily by the global powers of Anglophone America and Britain. Notions of traditional Ireland are portrayed as having greater self-sustainability, whereas current existence appears to be more susceptible to and reliant on external forces operating transnationally.

There seems to be acceptance of the inevitability of social change, yet the biological concept of evolution is transposed onto notions of social progression. Evolutionary ideas provide elucidation and create a sense of linear social advancement with underlying racist/ethnocentric rationalizations. Additionally, 'race' and diversity are related to people's perceived sense of anxiety with respect to societal transformation. Fear is shown to stem from anxiety that is based on an abstract or notional idea that immigration will overwhelm the Irish population. However, quintessentially the fear is discriminatory. Conversely, it is conjectured that for the 'newcomer' their fear would be more accentuated and that this may be compounded with the burden of the fear of rejection from the 'natives'. This dimension of fear can be seen in relation to *egocentrism* and *social Darwinism*, which are referenced in Chapter 8 and further developed in the subsequent section.

With changing times and the perceived re-imagination of *Irishness* within broader contemporary society, a critical neglect has been the recognition and inclusion of people of varying physiological dispositions, in particular people of skin colour other than 'white'. This would seem tenuous because, as evidenced, it is recognized that notions of a pureness in *Irishness* are quite unfounded, yet participants maintain reliance on antiquated stereotypical notions of 'Irish' identity when discussing *Irishness* in ethno-racial terms. It is understood that such a clash in conceptualizing *Irishness*, instead of finding a greater resolution, has been reinforced by legislative changes in the 2004 Irish Citizenship Referendum with the erosion of *jus soli*-based citizenship acquisition, even while, the existential reality is that Irish society continues to diversify.

Discussions within the groups draw attention to and focus on the recognized benefits the welfare state model affords the population. The Irish welfare state model is contrasted with perceptions of the US model and is discerned to be superior. Apparent from the conversation is that simply the expression of interest in supposed Irish culture would be sufficient to deem an individual satisfactorily entitled to state welfare provisions. Participants' sense of the benefits of the welfare state, with particular regard to perceived rights and responsibilities, highlight that notions of freedom associated with membership of the nation state are conversely intertwined with law-abiding acts. The idealized person seems to be perceived as a law-abiding citizen, dutiful and responsible to the nation state and in return is afforded rights.

The notion of 'free' provisions, as an emergent theme within several conversations, is contested by participants and counterarguments are presented, suggestive of either direct or generalized reciprocity through taxation. This cost–benefit rationale seems to provide justification for a sense of resentment towards 'others' who are 'newcomers' that appear to chiefly profit from the benefits of the welfare state. New and alternative forms of socio-cultural and potential economic capital are reasoned as most aptly acquired through processes of returnee migration rather than through integration of diverse 'newcomers'.

The welfare state is perceived as relatively flawed, with apparent disapproval being directed by participants both towards the mismanagement of state policies and practices, as well as towards citizens potentially abusing the features of the welfare state model across the strata of Irish society. Institutional structural flaws in the provision of welfare are seen to excuse corrupt values, attitudes and behaviours exhibited by members of the public, who are deemed as simply acquiring their basic rights and entitlements. Where there is cultural recognition of misuse of provisions, 'insider' social capital may be beneficial for individuals in acquiring welfare provisions, whereas for 'outsiders' navigating such an imperfect system becomes a more arduous task. In a similar vein, the dichotomous comparison appears to be made by participants between the deserving 'us' versus the potentially undeserving 'them'. What results from the politics of 'us' and 'them' is the (fabricated) creation of a perceived binary division which eradicates the opportunity for adequate anti-racist and anti-classist intervention.

The impression is that, having contributed through the process of *generalized reciprocity*, the 'insider' who originates within is deemed as more eligible for state provisions. The quintessential view, as detailed in the rudimentary anecdotal account of man's ownership of property and the carving up of nature/land, which could be read as natural resources, is outwardly challenged as anthropocentric (as discussed further below). Instead of divisions along national, racial and ethnic lines, it is apparently counter-posed by one participant that in actuality it is the land or nature that owns 'us' humans, the implication being that anthropocentric world views inexorably make subhuman racism a given (as further contended in the following section).

The informative anecdote detailed in Chapter 9 supports the view that the perceived issues associated with immigration and the perception of the welfare model are flawed, which all feed into justifications towards the reconfiguration of the socio-democratic welfare state model. What was neglected or under discussed, however, was a shift in governance towards neo-liberal policies. In fact, some views may, inadvertently or not, endorse *neo-liberalist governmentality*. Although the participants generally express an appreciation of the welfare model, certain reservations expressed may well fit into a shift towards neo-liberal authority. Perhaps unbeknownst to most participants such an agenda seeks the transformation towards a new politics and new social order by delinking social problems from socio-structural factors and alternatively links problems to individual-subjective categories. According to Lemke (2001, p. 13), from a Foucauldian perspective, *neo-liberal governmentality* is based on a logic that attempts to render the social domain economic and justifies a reduction in welfare state services and security systems to the increasing emphasis on individual responsibility and personal care.

Conservatism is seen both at the level of the individual, as a characteristic of *Irishness*, and also within political organization. The erosion of the traditional (as mentioned above), either in the form of state organization or societally, seems to be perceived more complexly as a condition challenging *conservatism*, while also reinforcing existent inequitable access to provisions. There also appears to be the ostensible recognition of a shift from welfare-based provisions towards a more *neo-liberalist* approach. As noted predominantly by female participants, the more economizing approach of state policy would seem to create financial binds which stifle altruism at an individual level, yet absurdly within *ordo-liberal* rationale, the impression is that care is often outsourced to charitable bodies and organizations that depend on the charity of individual people and personages.

The example provided of the choice to partake in voluntary work would seem also to be associated with altruistic acts. The implication is that the erosion of the welfare state and the shift towards *neo-liberal governance* apparently produces financial binds that negatively affect the opportunity and ability of individuals to be as altruistic as they might ordinarily wish to be. Inferred from this, it would seem acts of altruism have become less a choice and more a matter of personal circumstance.

From the perspective of the participants within the Belfast focus group discussion, it seems that both moral and political *conservatism* are distinguished and discussed in a critical manner. Although *Irishness* is perceived as having adopted a value system that simultaneously accommodates *conservatism* and aspires to uphold notions of equality, such incompatibility may more aptly reflect *neo-conservative principles*.

The institutions of Catholicism seem to be comprehended historically to have been substitutes for provisions which the state had otherwise left neglected. From this, it would appear that contemporary privatization simply shifts responsibility from religious orders to corporations, thus the (more secular) intermediary state maintains its negation of social obligations leaving status quo structures unchallenged.

Conservatism is explicitly discussed, specific to the importance of nation state governance and the management of mechanisms of migration controls (as discussed above). Within one focus group in particular, notions of ostensibly 'free' movement are described as being governed by the demands of transnational capitalism and regional economic instabilities, rather than uncompelled migration.

The outcomes of the 2004 ICR are deliberated on and perceived as a more regressive and conservative step based on racism and national chauvinism. Further to this, because the amendment exerts inordinate exclusion of people from developing regions, it is perceived as the manifestation of an 'us' versus 'them' dichotomy (as detailed above) imbedded in the supreme level of Irish nation state legislation. One justification for more stringent controls on the migration of the non-European, or non-developed world, 'other' seems based on the perceived threat to security. In contrast, negative opinion of intra-European migration that is based on economic supply and demand would seem perceived as irrational antipathy. What emerges is that perceptions and positions of opinion may shift but maintain balance through their presentation in discourse as rational pragmatisms.

In the late 1980s, Kirby (1988) wrote of '... the evidence of a conservative backlash' (p. 8) triggered by economic and social problems of a decade of economic recession and emigration. Whereas it has not been an uncommon phenomenon throughout the history of modernity for nation states and peoples to slip into a more regressive stance politically when the nation state suffers shock from economic failures, the inference must not be made that economic stagnation is the principal cause of increased conservatism. As supported by the viewpoints expressed by some of the participants, regressive nationalistic sentiment can occur due to racism and protectionism even during a period of relative economic prosperity.

The culmination of the findings is the juxtaposition of rational or irrational pragmatisms within predilections towards *neo-liberal* cognisance and governance. Such leanings are comprehended as the means to justify a supposed logical rationale of moral disregard. Perceptions of rational pragmatism are, in fact, quite irrational; nonetheless, they justify the unjustifiable basis for dominant advancement and elevation. Described in the subsequent section is a more thorough and in-depth explanation of the concept being advanced in this thesis, namely *perceived rational pragmatism*.

Although some participants express an acceptance of citizenship acquisition through both bloodline descent and through temporal exposure to Irish society, there is an underlying absoluteness held by some, which resolutely supports legislative norms associated with the passing of the 2004 Irish Citizenship Referendum. Awareness of dominant media representations, now discredited, during the 2004 ICR campaign is evidenced; nonetheless, maintenance of a view complementing such a position still seems to be espoused by several participants; instead, the perceived rational pragmatist position surfaces, based on deterrence and economic necessity.

The historical imposition of English language, as well as its dominant usage over the Irish language in the contemporary context, is, to an extent, indicative of juxtaposed ir/rational pragmatism. This is particularly evident when framed in parallel with analysis of discourse that definitively looks to differentiate *Irishness* from 'otherness' or presents the assimilationist position which obliges the migrant 'other' to acquire the dominant language in Ireland, namely English. Historically, in the context of British colonialism, exposure to and acquisition of the English language appears to be expressed as being a social benefit for Ireland. What may also be interpreted is a predestined condition between inferior/superior cultures, which unavoidably demands that the status quo remain dominant, thus excusing the demand for integration through assimilation rather than mediated through *interculturalism* or an inter-lingual society.

The consecutive example of *perceived rational pragmatism* detailed relates to consumerism. Propensities towards buying Irish produce and prioritizing the Irish over 'others' is perceived as rationally pragmatic as it is cyclical and, thus, benefits development within the nation state. A financially cyclical production/consumption process is assumed logically favourable for the improved quality of life of recognized members of the Irish collective. However, the impression is that such *perceived rational pragmatism* based on consumption patterns that are individualistic and neglect to reflect upon altruism which would share development and resources with 'others' less affluent, the welcoming of asylum seekers or external development aid. Furthermore, such perceptions based on assumed consumption patterns fail to truly consider resource acquirement beyond the nation state and paint an abstracted picture blind from the existent processes of globalization.

When the alternative concept of non-governance is proposed with the promotion of true freedom of movement, it appears to be rebuked and challenged as irrational and entirely impractical. The contrary argument implying a more natural process of population equilibrium would seem to complement *posthumanist* inclinations (as discussed earlier in relation to anthropocentrism and conserving migration controls). The rational pragmatist perspective is one that argues for emigration, cultural appropriation and returnee migration instead of affording more lenient access to the 'newcomer' and incorporating the 'newcomer' whose alternative cultural repertoires will bring potential enrichment. In this way, stricter status quo management of subjective value and selective cultural appropriation are kept internalized within the Irish collective. Also notable is that Irish state governance seems to be depicted as weak or undeveloped due to either the natural progression of regionalism or the lack of political competency towards self-management and self-determination (linking in with perceptions of flawed governance discussed above).

The apparent view of participants is that European dominance has manifested political and legal power to obligate the Irish state to enact laws of equality. However, such imposition would imply the disavowal of autonomy and thus could paradoxically be interpreted as undemocratic. It is implied that Ireland is caught in a double bind between state inefficiency and pan-European autocracy. It would seem that along with such autocratic governance is the risk that '... ethnocentrism may be enhanced amidst the cultural order of a new Europe in which chauvinistic concern with ethnic particularity has been rehabilitated even as the political and economic integration of nation states proceeds' (Gilroy, 1990, p. 116).

Some participants allude to the lack of political leverage at the Irish nation state level when operating within the global financial system, thus implying an inescapable bind that is determining Ireland's diminished control through *transnationalism*. Discussion on the Irish economy in the context of *global financial capitalism* suggested that participants seem to perceive Ireland in a state of dependency on processes of globalization and transnational corporate contribution. This creates a sense of powerlessness and futility in making any alternative societal level abstractions: there seems to be an inability to conceive of a balanced approach to sovereignty and interdependency, where the former is overly *isolationist* and is perceived as running the risk of stalling prosperity and enhanced quality of life. A sentiment that seems persistent – although the social, political and economic landscapes have changed since then – complements what De Paor (1979) wrote in the late 1970s where it is claimed that 'it is not possible to build a wall, paper or otherwise, around Ireland and to maintain here a kind of frugal republican virtue, while the outside world indulges in an orgy of greedy affluence' (p. 23).

Perceived Rational Pragmatism

This subsequent section, which postulates the idea of *perceived rational pragmatism*, is considered an addition to the body of knowledge on socio-psychological theory.[8] Consistent with the Grounded Theoretical approach employed the concept of *perceived rational pragmatism* emerges from analysis of the empirical data that has been detailed heretofore. Within the limitations of this thesis, the endeavour at this point is to deconstruct the concept focussing on examples in discourse that emerge within the focus group discussions presented, with respect to Kantian concepts of the self. By detailing such, the ambition is to clarify and justify the argument, with the intention that it might evoke thought and consideration on the implications of such a theorization, in the context of contemporary Irish society and beyond.

---

[8] As presented in the methodology section, the methodological approach is also deemed to be an addition to the body of knowledge, but in this case, it is a supplementary to knowledge on contemporary principles of methodology.

For Kant, the concept of personhood, as rational agency reliant on the formation of the self, is a form of understanding the rational dispositions of the self. Thus, personhood in Kantian terms is based on the 'conception of the self as rationally unified consciousness' (Piper, 1991, p. 2). From this point, empirical evidence or *a posteriori* knowledge is presented to substantiate how consciously perceived rationality manifests itself and how it may become defective when relegated under pragmatisms that are perceived in/accurately to be a priori based. Ordinarily, the assumption is that a priori constructions of knowledge produce logical truths and also transcendental verity. However, the rationale of pragmatism need not always initiate such directionality. Under an exacting doctrine of pragmatism, the inverse could just as easily be substantiated such that the course of supposed knowledge production becomes destructive.

What has, thus, emerged is the cognitive construction of rational pragmatism as perceived by individuals both at the liminal level and subconsciously. Nonetheless, the self justifies their pragmatic stance through the edifice of a supposed rationality that is not subjectively perceived by discrete individuals; rather it is specifically experienced through social exposure. This materializes when the self finds reaffirmation that collectivizes and makes real the rationality of pragmatism. In this way, the expressions that are formed within a *perceived rational pragmatic* frame of consciousness are tested between individuals and are confirmed or rejected along two vectors that interact along a rational/irrational vector and a pragmatic/impractical vector and are, within the cognisance of persons, inseparable. A sense of rationality can, thus, be deferred below, or elevated above, its perceived practicality or impracticality.

Evidence detailed below presents the argument that within this current spatial and temporal frame, as indicated among some participants in 21st-century Ireland, perceptions and views are determined predominantly by a process of pragmatism that then augments itself through cognitive constructions of rationality. This supposition is demonstrated by detailing participants' specific discussions on *Irishness*. Certain responses are revealed in relation to research on political and public discourse in the framing of the undeserving 'other' and legislative amendments made following the 2004 ICR, as documented in the introductory chapters. These very social processes, and their resulting outcomes, provide the basis for evidencing that the causation of *perceived rational pragmatism* may be societally determined rather than the inverse, outward from the individual, at the psychological level.

Within *liquid modernity*, an external effect of manipulation and exposure to mythological notions reinforces notions along supposed pragmatic positions. The sense-perception within current spacetime would seem to position perceived rationality as the exclusive constitutive measure by which knowledge is deemed rational. With simultaneity, these are validated through social interaction and discourse, which act to shape an individual's consciousness and impose pragmatism as a dominant thought process that looks to justify a specific rationale. As such perceived notions may lack autonomous contemplation, they may occur without necessarily having a comprehensive rational foundational basis. Instead of avowing principle, morality and/or ethics *perceived rational pragmatism* becomes a mechanism that circumvents such considerations by playing rationality off pragmatism, or the inverse. In effect, the reinforcement and affirmation of specifically pragmatically driven perceived rationalities render an ostensibly moral position cogent for the individual. This is likely to occur because, as Piper (1991) elucidates 'internal rational coherence is necessary for preserving a unified and rationally integrated self' (p. 2).

It is the paradox of living within the social environment while striving for *individualism* which breeds the conditions for *perceived rational pragmatism*. Perceived rationality allows the individual to identify themselves as being able to self-constitute with a level of autonomy and freewill while also being subsumed under culture and society. When the self is positioned in relation to 'others', it would seem to necessitate a loss of control. To maintain rational coherence within the self and between 'others', such forfeiture is justified with supposedly pragmatic arguments.

In this sense, morality, as realized through a level of *autonomous self-constitutionality*, becomes relegated below, neither moral nor immoral but 'non-moral' actions. 'Non-moral' practices occur in order to preserve the interests of the self in a heteronomous world that primarily drives self-interest. Such 'non-moral' practices are achieved because reasoned thought is apprehended on superficial pragmatic grounds. The external imposition of a societal structure dominated by the singular economic rationale together with apparent pragmatisms, thus, inhibits the range of perceptions attained by the intertwining of conceptualization and intuition. Instead of allowing for a multiplicity of data to inform the organization and synthesis of a perceived rational position, the process of pragmatism within an aesthetic frame negates the burden of more fully-rounded and complete cognition. What was 'out of sight, out of mind' becomes 'out of mind, out of sight', both in the hypothetical and literal sense.

Pragmatisms disavow morality from thought, or conscience from cognisance, by generating a pseudo-rational condition through which the self falsely perceives themselves as entirely sensible and reasoned actors within the context of their surroundings and situation.

Piper (1991) argues that xenophobia may be 'a self-protective reaction to violation of one's empirical conception of people, and involves a cognitive failure to apply the transcendent concept of personhood consistently across all relevant cases' (p. 3). The fear of something foreign, strange or different from the self is dependent on how one self-identifies. By socially constructing identifications of the self, through processes discussed above, a pseudo-rationality then becomes created. This is because *perceived rational pragmatisms* are heteronomous yet appear to the self as autonomous. What occurs is a form of mind trickery to defraud oneself of morality, while seemingly having the conscious knowhow to think with morality.

Thus what becomes evident at the core of this condition is a skewed function of classification and/or categorization under such a state. Essentially the Kantian thesis of rationalism proposes that in order to have a conscious experience, the prerequisite is that one must be able to make sense of the experience by identifying properties of it '... in terms of a set of coherent concepts that structure our experience' (Piper, 1991, p. 5). As mentioned above, the cognitive organization that is deemed a requisite of existing as a rationally unified subject relies on both fundamental categories (a priori transcendental concepts of the self) and categories based on experience (a posteriori gained knowledge). As Hicks (2004) explains, 'the knowing subject is something: its processes are causal and definite, and they shape the subject's awareness' (p. 34).

Within the context of identity formation and identity ascription, of primary interest is how the relational aspect of categorization effects the shaping of perceived identities. To register a conscious experience means that the construction of identifiable properties is relational to previous experiences that obey processes of categorization, grouping and classification. It would seem a logical necessity for knowledge, in all its subjectivities, to still be reliant on learnt perceptions and perceived truths of identity. It is, thus, through subjectivity that one makes their own sense of empirical knowledge. Kant (1781/1922) first elucidated in the 18th century the doctrine of *Transcendental Idealism* as,

> everything in space and time, and therefore all objects of experience possible to us, are nothing but appearances, that is, mere representations; and that these, as presented to us – as extended bodies, or as a series of changes – have no self-subsistent existence apart from human thought. (p. 400)

In the context of *perceived rational pragmatism*, logics exist both externally and internally to the self, such that the distinction between a priori and a posteriori overlap but in a chaotic manner to both fix and unfix simultaneously a reason of logic attained through a supposed pragmatic rationale. While pragmatism spurs the freeing of the conception, rationality looks to bind it to senses of morality. *Perceived rational pragmatism* as pragmatic rationalism might seem reiterative less the value of perception, but it is this renunciation of subjective positioning that allows the subject to perceive their positioning as universally logical but fundamentally wanting of morality. Thoughts and will towards the universality of the individual's situation are evaded through purposeful, though perhaps not so explicitly conscious, whitewashing by pragmatism. The pragmatic component allows the coherent ordering of experience and rational conception, while neglecting already attained knowledge which might be conflicted or indicate an inherent illogicality underlying such reasoned pragmatism.

In the context of the exclusion of 'the other', *transcendental* concepts, which are abstractions from experience, inform the judgement of the subject, yet such a process of cognizance is merely perceived and has been radically influenced by external empiricism that is imposed on the subject through dominant forms of social interaction (e.g. media representation and public discourse). These *pseudo-transcendental* concepts inform the individual and trouble transcendent ideas or more abstract and learnt ideals of personhood and human behaviour. If such transcendent ideas produce unified morality, universal reason and ideal humanity, then *pseudo-transcendental* concepts intrude on such unified morality or humanity. Thus, perceived comprehensive judgement is (re)constructed by false abstractions from self-experience and imposed empiricism. Pseudo-transcendentally constructed consciousness imposes on a person's self-consciousness, whose requisite is unified thinking selfhood, to inflict debilitation of further transcendent cognisance. In addition, the assigning of personhood through transcendent processes is neglected through the process of self-conceived pragmatism.

In substantiation of this theorization, evidence is presented below that interrelates three dimensions, firstly, the analysis of conversations presented in the previous results and findings chapters; secondly, the historicity in relation to *Irishness* discussed in Chapter 2; and finally, the legislative predicament following the passing of the two thousand and four Citizenship referendum and subsequent acts.

In Chapter 9, findings that emerge centring on the concept of *Perceived Rational Pragmatism* are presented. Being 'Irish' and becoming 'Irish', or an Irish citizen, are framed within the prism of bloodline descent (*jus sanguinis* citizenship), birthright affiliation (*jus soli* citizenship), or thirdly, spatiotemporal association with Ireland. Although contradictory to the general view presented whereby participants stressed the importance of physical attachment with Ireland over a specific longevity of time, participants expressed responses which were resolutely supportive of the amendments made with the ratification of the 2004 Irish Citizenship Referendum. Not only is this symptomatic of a more conservative view towards the formalized aspect of being and becoming 'Irish', it may also reflect a pragmatic attitude towards law and order of the conventional *status quo*.

Though not limited to the examples below, rational pragmatism as it is perceived by participants in the focus group discussions becomes conspicuous within several noteworthy themes. What becomes apparent in the operation of *perceived rational pragmatism* is less a zero-sum positioning and more an orientation that accepts multiple conditions and is context dependent. For instance, Irish language and English language, Assimilation and Multiculturalism, Open access and closed entry. The overarching prerequisite circumstance that determines whichever stance is taken would seem almost invariably determined within the basis of *perceived rational pragmatism*.

The Language of Irish and English

Over two decades ago, Tovey et al. (1989, p. 3) described the juxtaposition between perceptions of and belief in the value of the Irish language among the majority of Irish people, as well as the erosion and progressive marginalization of the actual use and maintenance of what is deemed by Tovey et al. (1989) as an affirmative quality of Irish collective identity. Evidence is presented in relation to language acquisition and the *perceived rational pragmatist* view that the attainment of English, and assumed maintenance as the dominant language, is perhaps paramount to economic prosperity and advancement. Within contemporary times, examples of the recognized relegation of the Irish language in the pursuit of *ordo-liberal* economic advancement within post-colonial Ireland are provided in several focus group discussions. From the discussion on the role of immediate family in the transmission of core values across generations, it can be inferred from one snippet of conversation that adopting the Irish language becomes a means of differentiation or 'self-othering'. Thus particularly evident in the Belfast focus group discussion, there is also evidence of the re-appropriation of the Irish language from what was deemed a degenerative characteristic for centuries of colonial rule, which goes beyond mere language parallelism. So although Tovey et al. (1989) proposed the desire to reverse such a trend, that is, to promote and revitalize Irish language use, what would seem to have materialized since the 1980s would be a more nuanced *perceived rational pragmatist* approach to acquisition and use of the Irish language. This is whereby its adoption and learning are encouraged as a form of *cultural capital* in order to distinguish or to make distinguished. In both instances, there is a *perceived rational pragmatic* approach taken but also in both are purposeful processes of exclusion rather than inclusion. As such actions based on what is perceived as rationally pragmatic perform as a mechanism to justify, or ostensibly nullify one's own self exclusionary practices.

Assimilation and Multiculturalism

Nonetheless, *perceived rational pragmatism* may not always manifest itself in terms of exclusion. It may also promote inclusion, but such inclusionary forms seem ultimately to be justified on *egocentric* or *self-preservationist* grounds, through the inexorable course of societal change. To provide further substantiation for such a proposition and to bolster the argument that this is socially reproduced, an example comparing the emphasis on *assimilationist* rationale rather than *interculturalist* leanings will be specified. What transpires from several discussions on *assimilation, integration, interculturalism* and *multiculturalism* is ultimately a reversion towards conformity within what is apparently, singularly stated, 'the community'. As much as there is the expectation to be 'Irish' by contributing through community participation, there is the elevated expectation on the 'new Irish' to assimilate more into this notional culturally homogeneous society. The justification for such an *assimilationist* approach is given along the lines of *perceived rational pragmatism* in relation to language acquisition, as discussed above, but also in order 'to fit in' (Michael). This in itself may project itself as simply reasonable speak, yet when this notion of assimilation or 'fitting in' is understood within the dimension of a cognisant understanding of social hierarchy and contemporary *neo-liberal order*,[9] within the conception of *perceived rational pragmatism*, 'to fit in' is less about the benefits it may bestow on the 'other' and more about knowing that fitting in for the 'new Irish' is about subordination and ethnocentric preferment. *Perceived rational pragmatism* in this sense is a means by which one convinces oneself and 'others', both collectively and individually, of expressions of compassion while simultaneously being realist. Though superficially dissimilar, when *assimilationist* leanings are sometimes challenged within some discussions, when seemingly more progressive stances are taken in relation

---

[9]Please refer to Carroll's remarks in relation to education in Chapter 9. It could be plausible to infer that a similar understanding of conformity is also viewed in relation to the maintenance of status quo more generally.

to the promotion of diversity and *multiculturalism*, in certain instances, these are justified under a social Darwinist rationale, which is not at all too distant from contrived thinking on eugenics. What becomes apparent is less a benign desire to share and perhaps empathize through a diversification of society and more a way of thinking that comprehends diversity in *egocentric* or *pseudo-ethnocentric* terms for either self-benefit or collective 'insider' benefit. The combining of both *assimilationist/integrationist* stances, in certain instances, with more *multiculturalist/interculturalist* propensities would seem to aptly fit the notion of manoeuvring under the pretences of *perceived rational pragmatism*.

Egocentrism, Altruism – Empathy and Sympathy

As introduced above, *egocentrism* is a pronounced dimension that emerges from various focus group discussions and among several participants. At times it subtly projects itself as both a form of self-centring, but vitally for this thesis, it occurs in combination with sympathy that is explicitly Irish-centric. In contrast, there is a noticeable absence of empathy from some participants. Evidence of this is observable in the process of minoritization within discussions on either anecdotal accounts that are personal or specific to kin relatives, presented as Irish, whereby sympathy is sought in the context of the self or of 'the other' as Irish. Correspondingly, participants refer to and discuss the historical context of Irish emigration and assumed general hardship that is perceived to have been imposed on the Irish populace. Yet in both of these instances, neither sympathy, in relation to the experienced processes of minoritization having been abroad, nor empathy, even in reference to historical circumstance, is developed as a means to justify altruistic tendencies towards the excluded 'other'. If anything, altruism as it seems to emerge is exclusively self-centred, familial-centric or Irish-ethnocentric. What is troubling about this is that it is doubly flawed. Firstly, such a position is oxymoronic when at the roots of altruistic sentiments or selflessness is basically a self-centred core. Secondly, such expressions of altruism are ethnocentrically determined by what is considered to be 'Irish'. Thus as discussed throughout, if narrow definitions of *Irishness* are maintained through notions that are fundamentally *essentialist*, and altruism forms predominantly in the fashion described above, then humanistic favouritisms become subhuman. Again the latter would seem to be either in-humane or quintessentially racist.

Open Access and Closed Entry

This progresses to another characteristic of *perceived rational pragmatism*, racism under the guise of participants' opinions on conceptual access to what is deemed Irish, as well as actual physical access to Ireland via legislative ruling on migration and existent migratory control regimes.

Within the findings, the younger participants, in particular, challenge the notion of a pure Irish ethnicity, 'race' and so forth. Similarly, although some participants place value on genealogical connections with Ireland, there is general acknowledgement of the continuous yet mutable nature of the Irish fabric that comes with societal change. Also evidenced are expressions of orientation away from the *jus sanguinis*, and even *jus soli*-based citizenship and instead the accentuation of the importance of having a spatio-temporal association with Irish society. The combination of these positions implicitly undermines the constitutional changes made in the 2004 Irish Citizenship Referendum.

Nonetheless, in direct conflict with this is evidence relating to, among other aspects, the purposeful differentiation between being 'Irish' and being an Irish citizen.

Following participants' responses to defining *Irishness*, which are more supportive of a comprehension of identity as fluid, mutable and less labile, the expectation would have been that through reflection on participants' own responses to *Irishness* the participants would provide expressions supportive of greater fluidity in both access to the nation state itself and the conceptualization of being 'Irish'. However, participants revert back to a rejection of fluidity both in permission to enter and remain within the nation state itself and also in being deemed as Irish. Multiple justifications are discussed, such as the modernization of the state as a member of the European Union, fear based on the perceived mass influx of 'newcomers', or the threat to security, or, an ostensible moral concern for the health and welfare of pregnant 'newcomers'. This becomes evident when analysing responses of participants when confronted with the outcomes of the referendum or when participants express a relatively comprehensive understanding of the irregularities associated with the 2004 Irish Citizenship Referendum. The fact that the legislative changes from the 2004 ICR are left uncontested would seem purposeful; even when justified along seemingly pragmatic grounds such positioning would seem to complement the *perceived rational pragmatist* perspective. Opinions and viewpoints of participants provide pragmatic arguments that are rationalized based on their perceptions as they are presented in conversation, which seem highly subjective and unsubstantiated. Moreover, despite participants being cognisant that their perceptions may be in actuality baseless, or lacking well-considered moral foundations, they choose to manoeuver to uphold certain perspectives nonetheless.

An inversion of a sense of morality dictating economic choices occurs in relation to consumption. On the one hand, consuming Irish produce and goods is justified in the national interest, while recognition of everyday lifestyle choices of many is individualistic and seems to disregard 'the bigger picture' (Christine). This would seem to imply the valuing of economic rewards over more moralistic orientations. Economic necessity is argued on multiple grounds, not just consumption but also those discussed hereto now. Reverting to the subject of access and migration, ultimately economics is argued by a participant to justify more restrictive access to Ireland or becoming 'Irish'. Compulsions towards economic necessity are used as means to leverage moral stances and thus create justification of opinions under *perceived rational pragmatism*. Similarly, one participant's anecdotal account provides opinion based on *perceived rational pragmatism* that argues for restrictive access because of the desire to preserve their rightful ownership of their home or society. When unveiled, while arguments based on *perceived rational pragmatisms* attempt to portray well-reasoned moral vis-à-vis economic justifications, they are, in fact, utilized as a means of reinforcing egotistic and self-preservationist positions. Furthermore, there is the projection of viewpoints that complement what Goldberg (2009) refers to as 'continental nativism', whereby there is the Irish and European preference of 'native' Europeans. Thus, importantly, the discrepancy in differentiating once 'outsiders' somewhat welcome to become part of the Irish fabric (i.e. European nationals), and 'outsiders' deemed as less or undeserving would seem to have racist undertones. One can surmise that participants within several of the focus group discussions express a shared psychic mechanism that employs *perceived rational pragmatism* as an attempt to conceal racist undertones, therefore acting to reinforce egotistic and self-preservationist positions.

Divergent from what has been discussed hitherto is evidence which is overtly empathetic though sometimes negated or seeming to be relatively minimal either in the context within each of the discussions or among the discussions overall. Examples of the emergence of empathic considerations are presented with specific regard to the racialized 'other', and in relation to the perceived lack of welfare provisions in developing countries. Also, though slightly more nuanced, empathetic reflections come to the fore pertaining to a counterargument which refers to the hypocrisy of the Irish historically relying on and benefiting from emigration, 'but yet we can't get our heads around these people coming to us could do great things for us' (Emmet). Evidenced is a clear contradiction of the notion that the constitutional amendments have a reasonable justification when a participant claims that the 2004 ICR was 'a racist referendum' (Tony). Also in contestation of the idea of ownership and preservation from 'outsiders', Conlaoch, insightfully, contends that 'the land actually owns us, and we serve the land' (Conlaoch). This presents a shift in consciousness and conscience, which is less egocentric or human-centric leaning towards a more posthumanist collective and self-understanding. Combined with this, Conlaoch presents the argument, in relation to *neoliberalism* and the management of migration, that the nation state should have no authority to 'cause harm to living beings' (Conlaoch). Conlaoch rejects the association with the nation state that constructs a system which privileges certain peoples over 'others', through limitations, boundaries and frontiers as it not only permits human suffering but becomes agential in inflicting suffering.

The overall picture is of the wilful relationship between the Irish subject and the Irish nation state, whereby the Irish subject seeks to protect their collectivized egocentric position by mandating the authority of the Irish nation state to make certain exclusions; one most blatant mandate being the passing of the 2004 Irish Citizenship Referendum and fixing into constitutional law greater onus on *jus sanguinis* descent. Such *protectionism* is at the cost of a rejection of not only the perceived 'other' but their humanity and ultimately a denial of a more *posthumanist* understanding of one's own existence both spatially and temporally. It seems to be a means of clinging onto, somewhat blindly, a sense of immortality if not through familial bloodline, then through the imagined Irish collective. If being eternal becomes increasingly elusive, at least the illusory notion of racial superiority and desire for perpetuation is accomplished through the exclusionary policies and practices of both the Irish nation state and the European Union, manifested, in part, through their concerted border migration regime.

The association between racism and immortality is no recent phenomenon. As Crew (1998, p. 16) affirms, Peukert's argument is that the 19th-century old dilemma of understanding death and im/mortality was resolved through the logic of science and reason based on racism rather than theology. Crew (1998, p. 16) writes how, under such scientifically rational logic, attaining the eternal is shifted from the body of the self, to the eugenic 'body' of the 'Volk', or societal collective. 'Although each individual must eventually die, the healthy race could survive. But while racism promised immortality for each individual's "healthy" genes, it also advocated the "elimination" of the "unfit" carriers of "deficient genes"' (Crew, 1992, p. 322f.; 1998, p. 16). The historical significance is that what emerged out of the Weimar Republic in the early 20th century was a Germany underpinned by such social racism with 'hopes of national reawakening and fears of national extinction' (Peukert, 1993, p. 277).

As Rodby (2009) writes,

> The system of immortality found in the totalitarian ideology creates a national or supranational organic collective which is defined and defended biologically. The continuation of the whole depends on the reliable and continual reproduction of the individuals within the collective, hence the extraordinary level of concern in matters that would ordinarily be considered personal and private. Anything that constitutes a threat to the collective reproductive system of the totalitarian movement constitutes a threat to collective immortality. (p. 35)

Although such notions are considered a constituent of authoritarian belief, as the evidence suggests, such concepts are not unique to such oppressive dogma but can be found simmering within the logic and conscience of modern man existing collectively within a supposedly egalitarian-based democratic nation state. For both Peukert and Crew, 'social racism' is considered to have been produced by the 'human sciences' themselves, existing as a constituent of 'the pathologies of modernity' (Crew, 1992).

What has changed, however, is the basic difference that individuals within *ordo-liberal* society perceive of themselves as rational liberated beings whereas, according to Randel (1975),

> supporters of totalitarian ideas believe that man does not, in most cases, act on rational grounds. They maintain that, in general, due to factors of emotion or personality, he is not master of his own actions thus he cannot control them. Therefore, he must be led or, in some way, have his course of action illuminated by what is conceived to be a better group of men. (p. 19)

In an individuated, self-concerned society, the attempt at immortalization within *ordo-liberalism* complements the perception of oneself as rationally pragmatic, for 'Death is the scandal, the ultimate humiliation of reason' (Beilharz,

2000, p. 148). Though we are powerless to 'know' death, thinking from a *perceived rational pragmatic* position permits the construction of racisms in order to immortalize and, thus, provides a sense of resolution for the *ordo-liberalist* modern human condition. It falsely elevates human status as masters of our universe, fully knowing subjects, operating within reason.

What has been charted up until this point is the exposure of a subtle socio-psychological mechanism, theorized as *perceived rational pragmatism* that materializes within a conversation on the collective self, in this case, the Irish and *Irishness* and the assumed 'other'. It is revealed to be complementary to Arendt's (1964) views on *the banality of evil* and is contained within a logic associated with modernity. As Lentin (2008) claims,

> racism in Europe following the Nazi *Shoah* has predominantly been interpreted as a particularity of the Hitlerian regime, an aberration from European politics rather than, as several scholars such as Hannah Arendt (1966) and Zygmunt Bauman (1989) have argued, a possibility contained within the idea of modernity itself. (p. 489)

The trajectory of arguments above has led to the consideration of immortality and racism which is seen as embedded within classical modernity itself, and now is even more accentuated with the rise of *ordo-liberalism* within a globalizing, yet regressive nationalistic sentiment.

Concluding on Perceived *Irishness*

The centrality of socially constructed ethno-racial distinctions and creations of 'otherness', in relation to perceived *Irishness*, should not be underestimated. Conceptions of 'Irish' identity that are dependent on such distinctions may be a cause of, if not throw fuel on the fire of a propensity towards a dominant culture of values, attitudes and behaviours reliant on the socio-psychologically fabricated process of *perceived rational pragmatism*. Thus, in order to break such a tautological bind so as to advance normatively, not only a more truly knowledgeable society but a more compassionate society, both processes ought to be unequivocally confronted and counteracted.

Prior to the commencement of this study, it might have been assumed that with *liquid modernity*; mobility, migration, globalization, transnationalism and communications new, more labile and fluid perceptions and conceptions of self-identification might be occurring in Ireland. These might debase more racialized constructions of 'Irish' identity, or even support more circumspect understandings of *Irishness* itself. Nonetheless, the findings imply that participants tend to rely on redefining 'Irish' identity in a bind with the predicament of reproducing essentialized and racial notions of *Irishness*. The theorization above even suggests that participants resort to expressing a mechanism of *perceived rational pragmatism* so as to justify and convince themselves of a foundational basis for the criteria for 'Irish' identity that may be the antithesis of their very own self-knowledge.

An expectation might be that the effects of globalization on demographics, communications and information exchange have meant that time and space, both physically and cognitively, are less bound by locality or place (Appadurai, 1996; Hannerz, 1996; Inglis, 2009) such that people's sense of national identification and belonging may have become troubled. A prospect might be that, instead of a regressive shift towards nationalistic tendencies of exclusion, there would be its converse: the diminishment of national identity and the emergence of a new form of identification. Such a decline might have the effect of convergence across humanity with a heightened or empathic concern for the unknown 'other' and desires for greater inclusion. However, participants expressed more nuanced, complex and often conflicting views on identity formation which through conversation sophisticatedly manoeuvred between these three scenarios. Overall, the resultant effect is that of an underlying *conservative* and *traditionalist* nature which seeks status quo preservation, particularly in the context of access to citizenship and the very real and figurative aspect of citizenship legislation.

Moreover, the supposed basic rational justification is repeatedly reinforced through processes of constructing ethno-racial distinctions. In this 21st century, within our globalized world, is it not high time to finally discard such *Hobbesian* theoretical foundations of 'human nature' being competitive and so deterministic whereby, as Arendt (1958) warns, 'humanity could carry the endless process of capital and power accumulation through to its logical end in self-destruction' (p. 157)? Surely, it is about time to reject,

> naturalist ideologies which hold nations to be tribes, separated from each other by nature, without any connection whatever, unconscious of the solidarity of mankind and having in common only the instinct for self-preservation which man shares with the animal world. If the idea of humanity, of which the most conclusive symbol is the common origin of the human species, is no longer valid, then nothing is more plausible than a theory according to which brown, yellow, or black races are descended from other species of apes than the white race, and that all together are predestined by nature to war against each other until they have disappeared from the face of the earth ....

> Racism may indeed carry out the doom of the Western world and, for that matter, of the whole of human civilization. When Russians have become Slavs, when Frenchmen have assumed the role of commanders of a *force noire*, when Englishmen have turned into 'white men', as already for a disastrous spell all Germans became Aryans, then this change will itself signify the end of Western man. For no matter what learned scientists may say, race is, politically speaking, not the beginning of humanity but its end, not the origin of peoples but their decay, not the natural birth of man but his unnatural death. (Arendt, 1958, p. 157)

Our humanity, along with the transformative capacity of new knowledges, obliges us to finally transcend the unnatural condition of thinking in essentialized terms. Our conscience endows us with the hypothetical capacity to replace *sub-humanist falsities*, by means of *posthumanist* thinking, and to avail of knowledge production ethically and holistically. Only by doing so will it help overcome the impending challenges of our time, such as the conflict of war, ecological degradation, resource depletion, population growth and changing climatic conditions.

Postscript

To give a schematic review of the depth and latitude of 'Irish' identity, notwithstanding its complexity and perplexity, would be to exceed the limitations of this book. For this reason, this study confines discussion of perceived *Irishness* to that displayed by participants through an in-depth and comprehensive analysis. Some features of 'Irish' identity are dealt with only cursorily, or have even been omitted. Furthermore, this study engages only concisely with certain themes of perceived *Irishness* which are central to unravelling an understanding of 'Irish' identity but which can either be easily studied elsewhere or would diverge from the empiricism built into the methodological process.

Irrespective of the debate about the Celticness of Irish origins, which Nash (2006) refers to as 'an internal postcolonial process of rethinking history, belonging and identity' (p. 27), it would seem paramount that the reassessment of historical notions of 'Irish' identity, from a post/late-modernist standpoint, would complement the justification of a more inclusive approach to Irish immigration policies. Particularly in an ever more interdependent and globalizing world which creates dramatic social change, it would seem that more flexibility in defining and modifying existing conceptions of the collective self is a prerequisite of any contemporary society (Wight, 2006, p. 84). Thus, one clear avenue of future research would be historical studies that expand on historical revisionist narratives, with particular focus on dynamics of migration and cultural adaptation.

It would seem pertinent from the findings and inferences discussed hereto that the theoretical proposition on *perceived rational pragmatism* be explored and scrutinized further, both in the Irish context and elsewhere. Exploration within alternative jurisdictions, such as Europe, or further afield, would lend to the view that such theorization is not a unique phenomenon of the Irish collective, but rather it may be a collective socio-psychological condition inherent to *ordo-liberalist* thinking irrespective of locality. In this regard, it would be beneficial to attempt to construct and visualize the more substantial conditions that either encourage or alleviate tendencies towards *perceived rational pragmatism* within our globalized reality. How the framing of positions may differ based on *perceived rational pragmatic* grounds, or not, within and between diasporas' networks, migrant groups, commuters, hybrid persons, etcetera, would also prove fruitful. Although worthy of focussed research in itself, such studies could be incorporated into broader research on the socially (re)constructed nature of identity and how identities are redefined during contemporary times more generally.

References

Acampora, C. (2007). Authorising desire. In C. Acampora & A. Cotten (Eds.), *Unmaking race, remaking soul: Transformative aesthetics and the practice of freedom* (pp. 59–80). State University of New York Press.
Agamben, G. (1998). *Homo sacer: Sovereign power and bare life*. Stanford University Press.
Agamben, G. (2005). *State of exception*. University of Chicago Press.
Agassi, J. (1990). *Change research or action research: A promising methodological tool that combines applied sociology with empirical research in organisations*. http://www.tau.ac.il/~agass/judith-papers/change.pdf
Ahmad, A. (1992). *Theory: Classes, nations, literatures*. Verso.
Anderson, B. (1983). *Imagined communities: Reflections on the origin and spread of nationalism* (Rev. extended ed., 2006). Verso.
Anderson, B. (2013). *Us and them?: The dangerous politics of immigration control*. Oxford University Press.
Anthias, F., & Yuval-Davis, N. (1992). *Racialized boundaries: Race, nation, gender, colour and class and the antiracist struggle*. Routledge.
Appadurai, A. (1996). *Modernity at large: Cultural dimensions of globalization*. University of Minnesota Press.
Appiah, K. (1997). Cosmopolitan patriots. *Critical Inquiry (Front Lines/Border Posts), 23*(3), 617–639. https://doi.org/10.1086/448846
Appiah, K. (1998). Cosmopolitan patriots. In P. Cheah & B. Robbins (Eds.), *Cosmopolitics: Thinking and feeling beyond the nation* (pp. 91–114). University of Minnesota Press.
Arendt, H. (1958). *The origins of totalitarianism* (2nd enlarged ed.). The World Publishing Company.
Arendt, H. (1964). *Eichmann in Jerusalem: A report on the banality of evil* (2nd rev. and enlarged ed.). Viking Press.
Arensberg, C. M., & Kimball, S. T. (1940). *Family and community in Ireland*. Cambridge Harvard University Press.
Arendt, H. (1966). *The origins of totalitarianism*. Harcourt Publishers, Inc.
Armstrong, A. (2008). Beyond resistance: A response to Žižek's critique of Foucault's subject of freedom. *Parrhesia Journal, 5*, 19–31.
Bakhtin, M. (1981). *The dialogic imagination: Four essays*. University of Texas Press.
Balibar, E. (1991). Is there a "neo-racism"? (C. Turner, Trans.). In E. Balibar & I. Wallerstein (Eds.), *Race, nation, class: Ambiguous identities* (pp. 17–28). Verso.
Barth, F. (1969). Introduction. In F. Barth (Ed.), *Ethnic groups and boundaries: The social organization of culture difference* (pp. 9–38). Universitetsforlaget.
Bauböck, R., Ersboll, E., Groenendijk, K., & Waldrauch, H. (2006). Introduction. In R. Bauböck, E. Ersbøll, K. Groenendijk, & H. Waldrauch (Eds.), *Acquisition and loss of nationality: Policies and trends in 15 European states* (Vol. 1). *Comparative analyses* (pp. 15–34). Amsterdam University Press.
Bauman, Z. (1989). *Modernity and the holocaust*. Polity Press and Blackwell Publishing Ltd.

Bauman, Z. (1990). Modernity and ambivalence. In M. Featherstone (Ed.), *Global culture: Nationalism, globalization and modernity* (pp. 143–170). Sage Publications.
Bauman, Z. (2000). *Liquid modernity*. Polity Press (in Association with Blackwell Publishing Ltd.).
Bauman, Z. (2001). Identity in the globalising world. *Social Anthropology*, 9(2), 121–129. https://doi.org/10.1017/S096402820100009X
Bauman, Z. (2006). *Liquid fear*. Polity Press.
Bauman, Z. (2012). *Liquid modernity* (2012 ed.). Polity Press.
Beck, U. (2003). Toward a new critical theory with a cosmopolitan intent. *Constellations*, 10(4), 453–468. https://doi.org/10.1046/j.1351-0487.2003.00347.x
Beilharz, P. (2000). *Zygmunt Bauman: Dialectic of modernity*. SAGE Publications Ltd.
Benhabib, S. (2004). *The rights of others, aliens, residents and citizens*. http://www.crassh.cam.ac.uk/oldwww/events/2003-4/BenhabibPaper.pdf
Benoist, A. (2004). On identity. *Telos*, 128, 9–64.
Bhabha, H. (1990a). The third space: Interview with Homi Bhabha. In J. Rutherford (Ed.), *Identity: Community, culture, difference* (pp. 207–221). Lawrence & Wishart.
Bhabha, H. (1990b). *Nation and narration*. Routledge.
Bhabha, H. (1994). *The location of culture*. Routledge.
Billig, M. (1995). *Banal nationalism*. SAGE Publications Ltd.
Billig, M. (2009). Reflecting on a critical engagement with banal nationalism – Reply to Skey. *Sociological Review*, 57(2), 347–352. https://doi.org/10.1111/j.1467-954X.2009.01837.x
BouAynaya, Y. (2011). *Perceived Irishness: An exploration of the superficiality of identity using a reflexive social experimental approach*. Department of Sociology, Trinity College Dublin.
Bourdieu, P. (1977a). *Outline of a theory of practice*. Cambridge University Press.
Bourdieu, P. (1977b). The economics of linguistic exchanges. *Social Science Information*, 16(6), 645–668. https://doi.org/10.1177/053901847701600601
Bourdieu, P. (1986). The forms of Capital. In J. Richardson (Ed.), *Handbook of theory and research for the sociology of education* (pp. 241–258). Greenwood Publishing Group Press.
Brah, A. (1996). *Cartographies of diaspora: Contesting identities*. Routledge.
Brandi, S. (2007). Unveiling the ideological construction of the 2004 Irish citizenship referendum: A critical discourse analytical approach. *Translocations*, 2(1), 26–47.
Brown, G., & Held, D. (2010). *The cosmopolitan reader*. Polity Press.
Brown, G. W. (2011). Bringing the state back into cosmopolitanism: The idea of responsible cosmopolitan states. *Political Studies Review*, 9(1), 53–66. https://doi.org/10.1111/j.1478-9302.2010.00226.x
Brubaker, R. (2001). The return of assimilation? Changing perspectives on immigration and its sequels in France, Germany, and the United States. *Ethnic and Racial Studies*, 24(4), 531–548. https://doi.org/10.1080/01419870120049770
Burawoy, M. (2005). Presidential address: For public sociology. *American Sociological Review*, 70(1), 4–28.
Butler, D., & Ruane, J. (2009). Identity, difference and community in Southern Irish Protestantism: The Protestants of West Cork. *National Identities*, 11(1), 73–86. https://doi.org/10.1080/14608940802680920
Butler, J. (1988). Performative acts and gender constitution: An essay in phenomenology and feminist theory. *Theatre Journal*, 40(4), 499–531. https://doi.org/10.2307/3207893
Butler, J. (1990). *Gender Trouble: Feminism and the subversion of identity*. Taylor & Francis.
Butler, J. (1993). *Bodies that matter: On the discursive limits of 'sex'*. Routledge.
Byrne, A., & O'Mahony, D. (2012). Family and community: (Re)telling our own story. *Journal of Family Issues*, 33(1), 52–75. https://doi.org/10.1177/0192513X11421121
Campbell, D. (1998). *National deconstruction: Violence, identity, and justice in Bosnia*. University of Minnesota Press.

Chandler, D. (2010). The uncritical critique of "liberal peace". *Review of International Studies, 36*(S1), 137–155. https://doi.org/10.1017/S0260210510000823
Chaney, D. (2002). *Cultural change and everyday life*. Palgrave.
Charmaz, K. (1995). Between positivism and postmodernism: Implications for methods. *Studies in Symbolic Interaction, 17*, 43–72.
Charmaz, K. (2001). Qualitative interviewing and grounded theory analysis. In J. Gubrium & J. Holstein (Eds.), *Handbook of interview research: Context and method* (pp. 347–365). SAGE Publications, Inc.
Charmaz, K. (2011). Grounded theory methods in social justice research. In N. Denzin & Y. Linkon (Eds.), *The SAGE Handbood of qualitative research* (pp. 359–380). SAGE Publications, Inc.
Clark, J., Hall, S., Jefferson, T., & Roberts, B. (1976). Subcultures, cultures and class: A theoretical overview. In S. Hall & T. Jefferson (Eds.), *Resistance through rituals: Youth cultures in post-war Britain* (pp. 8–79). Hutchinson.
Clifford, J. (2000). Taking identity politics seriously: "The Contradictory, Stony Ground…" In P. Gilroy, L. Grossberg, & A. McRobbie (Eds.), *Without guarantees: Essays in honour of Stuart Hall* (pp. 94–102). Verso Press.
Coakley, J. (2002). Religion, national identity and political change in modern Ireland. *Irish Political Studies, 17*(1), 4–28. https://doi.org/10.1080/714003140
Coates, N. (1997). Can't we just talk about music? Rock and gender on the Internet. In T. Swiss, J. Sloop, & A. Herman (Eds.), *Mapping the beat: Popular music and contemporary theory*. Blackwell Publishing.
Cole, P. (2000). Philosophies of exclusion: Liberal political theory and immigration. *Edinburough*. Edinburgh University Press. 1990. *Foundations of Social Theory*. Belknap Press of Harvard University Press.
Coleman, J. S. (1990). *Foundations of social theory*. The Belknap Press of Harvard University Press.
Colosi, R. (2010). A return to the Chicago school? From the "subculture" of taxi dancers to the contemporary lap dancer. *Journal of Youth Studies, 13*(1), 1–16. https://doi.org/10.1080/13676260903214183
Constitution of Ireland ([1937] 2004). *Twenty-seventh Amendment of the Constitution Act of 2004*. https://www.irishstatutebook.ie/eli/2004/ca/27/enacted/en/html
Corcoran, M., Gray, J., & Peillon, M. (2010). *Suburban affiliations: Social relations in the greater Dublin area*. Syracuse University Press.
Cornell, D. (1998). *At the heart of freedom: Feminism, sex, and equality*. Princeton University Press.
Crevoisier, O. (2015). The economic value of knowledge: Embodied in goods or embedded in cultures? *Regional Studies, 50*(2), 189–201. https://doi.org/10.1080/00343404.2015.1070234
Crew, D. (1998). *Germans on welfare: From Weimar to Hitler*. Oxford University Press, Inc.
Crew, D. F. (1992). The pathologies of modernity: Detlev Peukert on Germany's twentieth century. *Social History, 17*(2), 319–328. https://doi.org/10.1080/03071029208567840
Crowley, T. (2005). *Wars of words the politics of language in Ireland 1537–2004*. Oxford University Press, Inc.
Crowley, U., Gilmartin, M., & Kitchin, R. (2006). *Vote Yes for Common Sense Citizenship': Immigration and the paradoxes at the heart of Ireland's "Céad míle Fáilte"* [NIRSA Working Paper, No. 30, NUI Maynooth]. Retrieved September 8, 2011, from http://eprints.nuim.ie/1541/1/WPS30.pdf
De Frëine, S. (1978). *The great silence* (2nd ed.). Mercier Press.
De Lauretis, T. (1987). *Technologies of gender: Essay on theory [Film], and Fiction*. Indiana University Press.
De Paor, L. (1979). Ireland's identities. *Crane Bag [The Question of Tradition], 3*(1), 22–29.

Derrida, J. (1967). *Of grammatology*. The Johns Hopkins University Press.
DFA. (2016). [Department of Foreign Affairs and Trade]. *The Good Friday Agreement and today*. Retrieved May 25, 2016, from https://www.dfa.ie/our-role-policies/northern-ireland/the-good-friday-agreement-and-today/
Dobbernack, J., & Modood, T. (2011). *Tolerance and cultural diversity in Europe: Theoretical perspectives and contemporary developments (ACCEPT Pluralism)*. European University Institute.
Doherty, G. (1996). National identity and the study of Irish history. *English Historical Review, CXI*(441), 324–349. https://doi.org/10.1093/ehr/CXI.441.324
Durkheim, É., & Mauss, M. (1963). *Primitive classification*. Cohen and West Limited.
Faas, D. (2010). *Negotiating political identities: Multiethnic schools and youth in Europe*. Ashgate Publishing Limited.
Fanning, B. (2002). *Racism and social change in the Republic of Ireland*. Manchester University Press.
Fanning, B. (2010). From developmental Ireland to migration nation: Immigration and shifting rules of belonging in the Republic of Ireland. *Economic and Social Review, 41*(3), 395–412.
Fanning, B., & Mutwarasibo, F. (2007). Nationals/non-nationals: Immigration, citizenship and politics in the Republic of Ireland. *Ethnic and Racial Studies, 30*(3), 439–460. https://doi.org/10.1080/01419870701217506
Fatsis, L. (2014). *Making sociology public: A critical analysis of an old idea and a recent debate*. Retrieved February 28, 2015, from http://sro.sussex.ac.uk/51588/
Fine-Davis, M. (2011). *Attitudes to family formation in Ireland: Findings from the nationwide study*. Family Support Agency, Trinity College Dublin.
Finlay, A. (2004). Me too: Victimhood and the proliferation of cultural claims in Ireland. In A. Finlay (Ed.), *Nationalism and multiculturalism: Irish identity, citizenship and the peace process* (pp. 131–156). LIT.
Finlay, A. (2007). Irish studies, cultural pluralism and the peace process. *Irish Studies Review, 15*(3), 333–345. https://doi.org/10.1080/09670880701461860
Fortes, M. (1969). *Kinship and the social order: The legacy of Lewis Henry Morgan*. Aldine.
Fossum, E. (2012). Cosmopolitanisation in Europe and beyond. In E. Eriksen & J. Fossum (Eds.), *Rethinking democracy in the European Union* (pp. 179–200). Routledge.
Foucault, M. (1970). *The order of things*. Tavistock Publications.
Foucault, M. (1977). *Discipline and punish: The birth of the prison*. Vintage Books.
Foucault, M. (1982). The subject and power. *Critical Inquiry, 8*(4), 777–795. https://doi.org/10.1086/448181
Foucault, M. (1993). About the beginning of the hermeneutics of the self: Two lectures at Dartmouth. *Political Theory, 21*(2), 198–227. http://www.jstor.org/stable/191814
Fraser, N. (1990). Rethinking the public sphere: A contribution to the critique of actually existing democracy. *Social Text*, (25/26), 56–80. https://doi.org/10.2307/466240
Gaine, C. (2008). Race, ethnicity and difference versus imagined homogeneity within the European Union. *European Educational Research Journal, 7*(1), 23–38. https://doi.org/10.2304/eerj.2008.7.1.23
Gallie, W. (1955). Essentially contested concepts. *Proceedings of the Aristotelian Society, 56*, 167–198.
Garner, S. (2007). Babies, bodies and entitlement: Gendered aspects of access to citizenship in the Republic of Ireland. *Parliamentary Affairs, 60*(3), 437–451. https://doi.org/10.1093/pa/gsm017
Gaventa, J. (1980). *Power and powerlessness: Quiescence and rebellion in an Appalachian valley*. Clarendon Press and Oxford University Press.
Geertz, C. (1973). *The interpretation of cultures: Selected essays*. Basic Books, Inc.
Gellner, E. (1983). *Nations and nationalism*. Blackwell Publishing.

Gerth, H. H., & Mills, C. W. (1946). Chapter 3: Intellectual orientations. In *From Max Weber: Essays in sociology* (pp. 45–74). Oxford University Press.
Giddens, A. (1990). *The consequences of modernity.* Cambridge Polity Press.
Giddens, A. (1991). *Modernity and self-identity: Self and society in the late modern age.* Stanford University Press.
Gilroy, P. (1990). Nationalism, history and ethnic absolutism. *History Workshop Journal, 30*(1), 114–120. https://doi.org/10.1093/hwj/30.1.114
Gilroy, P. (1998). Race ends here. *Ethnic and Racial Studies, 21*(5), 838–847. https://doi.org/10.1080/014198798329676
Gilroy, P. (2000). *Between camps: Nations, cultures and the allure of Race.* Routledge.
Gilroy, P., & Ouseley, H. (2005). *Race and faith post 7/7.* Retrieved April 19, 2011, from http://www.guardian.co.uk/uk/2005/jul/30/july7.race
Giroux, S. (2006). On the state of race theory: A conversation with David Theo Goldberg. *JAC, 26,* 11–66.
Goffman, E. (1959). *Presentation of self in everyday life.* Doubleday Anchor Books.
Goldberg, D. T. (2002). *The racial state.* Blackwell Publishing.
Goldberg, D. T. (2009). *The threat of race: Reflections on racial neoliberalism.* Blackwell Publishing.
Goode, W. (1963). *World revolution and family patterns.* Free Press.
Gramsci, A. (1971). *Selections from the prison notebooks of Antonio Gramsci.* International Publishers.
Gray, B. (2002). The Irish diaspora: Globalised belonging(s). *Irish Journal of Sociology, 11*(2), 123–144. https://doi.org/10.1177/079160350201100207
Grewal, D. S., & Purdy, J. (2014). Introduction: Law and neoliberalism. *Law and Contemporary Problems, 77*(4), 1–23.
Grillo, R. D. (2003). Cultural essentialism and cultural anxiety. *Anthropological Theory, 3*(2), 157–173. https://doi.org/10.1177/1463499603003002002
Guba, E., & Lincoln, Y. (1989). *Fourth generation evaluation.* SAGE, Inc.
Gunaratnam, Y. (2003). *Researching race and ethnicity: Methods, knowledge, and power.* Sage Publications.
Habermas, J. (2018). *Between facts and norms. Contributions to a discourse theory of law and democracy.* John Wiley & Sons.
Habermas, J., & Ben-Habib, S. (1981). Modernity versus postmodernity. *New German Critique, 22,* 3–14. https://doi.org/10.2307/487859
Hagedorn, J. M. (2006). Race not space: A revisionist history of gangs in Chicago. *Journal of African American History, 91*(2), 194–208. https://doi.org/10.1086/JAAHv91n2p194
Halberstam, J. (2003). What's that smell?: Queer temporalities and subcultural lives. *International Journal of Cultural Studies, 6*(3), 313–333. https://doi.org/10.1177/13678779030063005
Hall, S. (1996). Who needs "identity"? In S. Hall & P. Du Gay (Eds.), *Questions of cultural identity* (pp. 1–17). SAGE Ltd.
Hall, S. (1997). *The floating signifier [transcript].* Retrieved June 8, 2016, from http://www.mediaed.org/transcripts/Stuart-Hall-Race-the-Floating-Signifier-Transcript.pdf
Hall, S. (2000a). Old and new identities, old and new ethnicities. In L. Back & J. Solomos (Eds.), *Theories of race and racism* (pp. 144–153). Routledge.
Hall, S. (2000b). Conclusion: The multi-cultural question. In B. Hesse (Ed.), *Unsettled multiculturalisms: Diasporas, entanglements, transruptions* (pp. 209–241). Zed Books. https://doi.org/10.5949/liverpool/9780853235866.003.0006
Hannerz, U. (1996). *Transnational connections: Cultures, people, places.* Routledge.
Hansen, J. T. (2006). Counseling theories within a postmodernist epistemology: New roles for theories in counseling practice. *Journal of Counseling and Development, 84*(3), 291–297. https://doi.org/10.1002/j.1556-6678.2006.tb00408.x

References

Hardt, M., & Negri, A. (2000). *Empire*. Harvard University Press.
Hayes, R., & Oppenheim, R. (1997). Constructivism: Reality is what you make it. In T. Sexton & B. Griffin (Eds.), *Constructivist thinking in counseling practice, research and training* (pp. 157–173). Teacher's College Press.
Heald, S. (1989). *Controlling anger: The sociology of Gisu violence*. Manchester University Press.
Heaney, T. (2000). Politics of explanation: Ethical questions in the production of knowledge. In R. Bahruth, M. Krank, P. McLaren, & S. Steiner (Eds.), *Freireian pedagogy, praxis and possibilities: Projects for the new millennium* (pp. 117–134). Falmer Press (the Taylor & Francis Group).
Hicks, S. (2004). *Explaining postmodernism: Skepticism and socialism from rousseau to Foucault*. Scholargy Publishing.
Holton, R. (2005). *Making globalization*. Palgrave Macmillan.
Honohan, I. (2010). *The theory and politics of jus soli*. Retrieved March 3, 2011, from http://eudo-citizenship.eu/docs/Iseult_Honohan.pdf
Huntington, S. (1996). *The Clash of civilizations and the remaking of world order*. Simon & Schuster Paperbacks, Inc.
Inglis, T. (2006). From self-denial to self-indulgence: The class of cultures in contemporary Ireland. *Irish Review, 34*(34), 34–43. https://doi.org/10.2307/29736295
Inglis, T. (2007). Catholic identity in contemporary Ireland: Belief and belonging to tradition. *Journal of Contemporary Religion, 22*(2), 205–220. https://doi.org/10.1080/13537900701331064
Inglis, T. (2008). *Global Ireland: Same difference*. Routledge.
Inglis, T. (2009). *Local belonging, identities and sense of place in contemporary Ireland*. Retrieved February 4, 2016, from http://www.ucd.ie/ibis/publications/discussion-papers/localbelongingidentitiesandsenseofplaceincontemporaryireland/P&D_Disscussion_Paper_4.pdf
Inglis, T., & Donnelly, S. (2011). Local and national belonging in a globalised world. *Irish Journal of Sociology, 19*(2), 127–143. https://doi.org/10.7227/IJS.19.2.9
James, P. (2006). *Globalism, nationalism, tribalism: Bringing theory back in*. SAGE Publications Ltd.
Joppke, C. (2003). Citizenship between de- and re-Ethnicization. *European Journal of Sociology, 44*(3), 429–458. https://doi.org/10.1017/S0003975603001346
Joppke, C. (2007). Transformation of citizenship: Status, rights, identity. *Citizenship Studies, 11*(1), 37–48. https://doi.org/10.1080/13621020601099831
Kant, I. (1781). *Critique of pure reason* (2nd rev. ed., M. Muller, Trans.). Macmillan and Co. Ltd. (Original work published 1922)
Kant, I. (1795). *Towards perpetual peace: A philosophical project* (M. Gregor Ed. & Trans.). Cambridge University Press. (Original work published 1996)
Kapoor, N. (2013). The advancement of racial neoliberalism in Britain. *Ethnic and Racial Studies, 36*(6), 1028–1046. https://doi.org/10.1080/01419870.2011.629002
Kiberd, D. (1995). *Inventing Ireland: The literature of the modern nation*. Vintage Books.
Kiberd, D. (2000). *Irish classics*. Granta Book Company.
Kirby, P. (1988). *Has Ireland a future?* Mercier Press Ltd.
Kleingeld, P. (2003). Kant's cosmopolitan patriotism. *Kant-Studien, 94*(3), 299–316.
Koopmans, R., Statham, P., Giugni, M., & Passy, F. (2005). *Contested citizenship*. University of Minnesota Press.
Laclau, E. (1990). *The impossibility of society in new reflections on the revolutions of our time*. Verso.
Larson, M. (2001). *The ethical imperative of knowledge*. Retrieved February 10, 2013, from http://www.academia.edu/454485/The_Ethical_Imperative_of_Knowledge
Latham, R. (2010). Border formations: Security and subjectivity at the border. *Citizenship Studies, 14*(2), 185–201. https://doi.org/10.1080/13621021003594858

Lears, T. J. J. (1985). The concept of cultural hegemony: Problems and possibilities. *American Historical Review*, *90*(3), 567–593. https://doi.org/10.2307/1860957

Lee, J. (1989). *Ireland 1912–1985: Politics and society*. Cambridge University Press.

Lemke, T. (2001). 'The birth of bio-politics': Michel Foucault's lecture at the College de France on neo-liberal governmentality. *Economy and Society*, *30*(2), 190–207. https://doi.org/10.1080/03085140120042271

Lentin, A. (2008). Europe and the silence about race. *European Journal of Social Theory*, *11*(4), 487–503. https://doi.org/10.1177/1368431008097008

Lentin, A. (2015). What does race do? *Ethnic and Racial Studies*, *38*(8), 1401–1406. https://doi.org/10.1080/01419870.2015.1016064

Lentin, R. (2007). Illegal in Ireland, Irish illegals: Diaspora nation as racial state. *Irish Political Studies*, *22*(4), 433–453. https://doi.org/10.1080/07907180701699182

Lentin, R. (2009). Migrant women's networking: New articulations of transnational ethnicity. In G. Bhattacharyya (Ed.), *Ethnicities and values in a changing world* (pp. 71–88). Ashgate Publishing Ltd.

Lentin, R., & McVeigh, R. (2006). *After optimism?: Ireland, racism and globalization*. Metro Éireann Publications.

Lévi-Strauss, C. (1978). *Myth and meaning*. Routledge and Kegan Paul.

Levy, J. (2004). National minorities without nationalism. In A. Dieckhoff (Ed.), *The politics of belonging: Nationalism, liberalism, and pluralism* (pp. 155–174). Lexington Books.

Liu, J. H., & Hilton, D. J. (2005). How the past weighs on the present: Social representations of history and their role in identity politics. *British Journal of Social Psychology*, *44*(4), 537–556. https://doi.org/10.1348/014466605X27162

Lu, C. (2000). The one and many faces of cosmopolitanism. *Journal of Political Philosophy*, *8*(2), 244–267. https://doi.org/10.1111/1467-9760.00101

MacCormack, C., & Strathern, M. (1980). *Nature, culture and gender*. Cambridge University Press.

MacIntyre, A. (1994). Is patriotism a virtue? In M. Daly (Ed.), *Communitarianism: A new public ethics* (pp. 307–318). Wadsworth Publishing.

MacPherson, J., & Hickman, M. (2014). *Women and Irish diaspora identities: Theories, concepts and new perspectives*. Manchester University Press.

Mancini, J., & Finlay, G. (2008). "Citizenship Matters": Lessons from the Irish referendum. *American Quarterly*, *60*(3), 575–599. https://doi.org/10.1353/aq.0.0034

Marshall, T. (2000). *Racism and immigration in Ireland: A comparative analysis*. Retrieved June 22, 2011, from http://www.tcd.ie/sociology/ethnicracialstudies/assets/documents/Marshall_01.pdf

Marx, K. (1973). The fragment on machines. In *Grundrisse* (N. Martin, Trans., pp. 690–712). (Original work published 1857).

McCann, T. V., & Clark, E. (2003). Grounded theory in nursing research: Part 3 – Application. *Nurse Researcher*, *11*(2), 29–39. https://doi.org/10.7748/nr2004.01.11.2.29.c5920

McNeill, W. (1983). *The pursuit of power: Technology, armed force and society since A.D. 1000*. University of Chicago Press.

McNeill, W. H. (1982). The industrialisation of war. *Review of International Studies*, *8*(3), 203–213. https://doi.org/10.1017/S0260210500115608

McRobbie, A. (1977). *Feminism and youth culture*. Macmillan.

McVeigh, R. (2007). 'Ethnicity denial' and racism: The case of the government of Ireland against Irish travellers. *Translocations*, *2*(1), 90–133.

Mills, J., Bonner, A., & Francis, K. (2006). The development of constructivist grounded theory. *International Journal of Qualitative Methods*, *5*(1), 25–35. https://doi.org/10.1177/160940690600500103

Monahan, B. (2009). *Ireland's theatre on film – Style, stories and the national stage on screen*. Irish Academic Press.

Moriarty, E. (2005). *Telling identity stories: The routinisation of racialisation of Irishness.* Sociological Research Online, *10*(3), 90–106. https://doi.org/10.5153/sro.1111. Retrieved December 7, 2013, from http://www.socresonline.org.uk/10/3/moriarty.html

Moriarty, E. (2006). *Ireland and race: Ideas, intellectuals and identities* [PhD Department of Sociology. Trinity College Dublin].

Munhall, P. (2001). Ethical considerations in qualitative research. In P. Munhall (Ed.), *Nursing research: A qualitative perspective* (3rd ed., pp. 537–550). Jones and Bartlett Publishers.

Nash, C. (2006). Irish origins, celtic origins: Population genetics, cultural politics. *Irish Studies Review, 14*(1), 11–37. https://doi.org/10.1080/09670880500439760

Nass, C., Fogg, B. J., & Moon, Y. (1995). How powerful is social identity? *Affiliation effects in human–computer interaction.* Retrieved April 14, 2011, from http://www.stanford.edu/group/commdept/oldstuff/srct_pages/Affiliation_conformity.html

Nichols, R. (2010). State of the disciplines: Postcolonial studies and the discourse of Foucault: Survey of a field of problematization. *Foucault Studies, 9,* 111–144.

Ní Chonaill, B. (2009). *Perceptions of migrants and their impact on the blanchardstown area: Local views.* Retrieved August 15, 2011, from http://www.itb.ie/researchatitb/documents/Perceptionsofmigrants-FinalReport.pdf

Nussbaum, M., & Cohen, J. (1996). *For love of country: Debating the limits of patriotism.* Beacon Press Books.

Nussbaum, M. C. (2008). Toward a globally sensitive patriotism. *Daedalus, 137*(3), 78–93. https://doi.org/10.1162/daed.2008.137.3.78

Oakley, A. (1981). Chapter 2 – Interviewing women: A contradiction in terms. In H. Roberts (Ed.), *Doing feminist research* (pp. 30–61). Routledge and Kegan Paul.

Oakley, A. (2016). Interviewing women again: Power, time and the gift. *Sociology, 50*(1), 195–213. https://doi.org/10.1177/0038038515580253

Oberschall, A. (2010). Chapter 10 – Conflict theory. In K. Leicht & C. Jenkin (Eds.), *Handbook of politics: State and society in global perspective* (pp. 177–194). Springer Science+Business Media.

O'Brien, C. (1971). Nationalism and the reconquest of Ireland. *Crane Bag, 1*(2), 8–13.

O'Connor, B. (1997). Chapter 3 – Gender, class and television viewing: Audience responses to the "Ballroom of romance". In M. Kelly & B. O'Connor (Eds.), *Media audiences in Ireland: Power and cultural identity* (pp. 63–87). University College Dublin Press.

O'Donovan, F. (2009). Irish identity is far from "ideal". *Socheolas, 2*(1), 95–115.

OECD (Organization for Economic Co-operation & Development). (2010). *International Migration Outlook – Sopemi 2010.* Retrieved March 21, 2011, from http://www.oecd.org

Ong, A. (1993). On the edge of empires: Flexible citizenship among Chinese in diaspora. *Positions: Asia Critique, 1*(3), 745–778. https://doi.org/10.1215/10679847-1-3-745

Ong, A. (1998). Flexible citizenship among Chinese cosmopolitans. In P. Cheah & B. Robbins (Eds.), *Cosmopolitics: Thinking and feeling beyond the nation* (pp. 134–162). University of Minnesota Press.

O'Reilly, E. (2013). Asylum seekers in our republic: Why have we gone wrong? *Studies: An Irish Quarterly Review, 102*(406), 131–149.

O'Toole, F. (1985). Going West: The country versus the City in Irish writing. *Crane Bag (Irish Ideologies), 9*(2), 111–116.

O'Toole, F. (2000). Green, white and black: Race and Irish identity. In R. Lentin (Ed.) *Emerging Irish identities* (pp. 17–24). Retrieved July 7, 2011, from http://www.tcd.ie/sociology/ethnicracialstudies/assets/documents/emerging_irish_id.pdf

Parekh, B. (2000). *Rethinking multiculturalism: Cultural diversity and political theory.* Macmillan.

Peillon, M., & Corcoran, M. (2004). *Place and non-place: The reconfiguration of Ireland.* Institute of Public Administration.

Peukert, D. (1993). *The Weimar Republic: The crisis of classical modernity*. The Penguin Press.
Pidgeon, N., & Henwood, K. (1997). Using grounded theory in psychological research. In N. Hayes (Ed.), *Doing qualitative analysis in psychology* (pp. 245–274). Psychology Press.
Piper, A. (1991). *Xenophobia and Kantian rationalism*. APRA Foundation. Retrieved March 3, 2010, from http://www.adrianpiper.com/docs/WebsiteXen&KantRat(1991).pdf
Quinn, E. (2010). *Satisfying labour demand through migration: Ireland* Economic and Social Research Institute.
Randel, L. (1975). *Roots of totalitarianism: The ideological sources of fascism, National Socialism, and communism*. Crane Russak, & Co.
RIA (Reception and Integration Agency). (2011). *Direct provision*. Retrieved August 4, 2016, from http://www.ria.gov.ie/en/RIA/Pages/Direct_Provision_FAQs
Ritzer, G. (2011). *The McDonaldization of society* (1st ed., 1993). Pine Forge Press, an imprint of SAGE Publications, Inc.
Robertson, R. (2001). Globalization theory 2000+: Major Problematics. In G. Ritzer, Smart & B. Smart (Eds.), *Handbook of social theory* (Chapter 34, pp. 458–471). SAGE Publications Ltd.
Rodby, K. (2009). *The dark heart of Utopia: Sexuality, ideology, and the totalitarian movement*. iUniverse, Inc.
Rosenau, J. N. (1992). The relocation of authority in a shrinking world. *Comparative Politics, 24*(3), 253–272. https://doi.org/10.2307/422132
Said, E. (1978). *Orientalism*. Vintage Books.
Said, E. (1994). *Culture and imperialism*. Vintage Books.
Sassen, S. (2005). Regulating immigration in a global age: A new policy landscape. *Parallax, 11*(1), 35–45. https://doi.org/10.1080/1353464052000321083
Sawicki, J. (1991). *Disciplining Foucault: Feminism, power and the body*. Routledge.
Scheffler, S. (2002). *Boundaries and allegiances: Problems of justice and responsibility in liberal thought*. Oxford University Press.
Schwartz, S. (2001). The evolution of Eriksonian and, Neo-Eriksonian identity theory and research: A review and integration. *Identity: An International Journal of Theory and Research, 1*(1), 7–58.
Seward, R. R., Stivers, R. A., Igoe, D. G., Amin, I., & Cosimo, D. (2005). Irish families in the twentieth century: Exceptional or converging? *Journal of Family History, 30*(4), 410–430. https://doi.org/10.1177/0363199005278638
Shachar, A., & Hirschl, R. (2007). Citizenship as property. *Political Theory, 35*(3), 253–287. https://doi.org/10.1177/0090591707299808
Skey, M. (2011). *National belonging and everyday life: The significance of nationhood in an uncertain world*. Palgrave Macmillan.
Spivak, G. (1988). Can the subaltern speak? In C. Nelson & L. Grossberg (Eds.), *Marxism and the interpretation of culture* (pp. 271–316). Macmillan.
Spivak, G. (1997). *Jaques Derrida of grammatology*. Johns Hopkins University Press.
Strathern, A. (1973). Kinship, descent and locality: Some new guinea examples. In J. Goody (Ed.), *The character of kinship* (pp. 21–34). Cambridge University Press.
Strauss, A. (1987). *Qualitative analysis for social scientists*. Cambridge University Press.
Strauss, A., & Corbin, J. (1990). *Basics of qualitative research: Grounded theory procedures and techniques*. SAGE.
Strauss, A., & Corbin, J. (1994). Grounded theory methodology: An overview. In N. Denzin & Y. Lincoln (Eds.), *Handbook of qualitative research*. SAGE.
Strauss, A., & Corbin, J. (1998). *Basics of qualitative research: Techniques and procedures for developing grounded theory* (2nd ed.). SAGE.

References

Sullivan, A. (2001). Cultural capital and educational attainment. *Sociology, 35*(4), 893–912. https://doi.org/10.1177/0038038501035004006

Sullivan, T. (2016). 'Hip to be Irish': Ethnicity and Bourdieu's "forms of capital". *Ethnic and Racial Studies, 39*(10), 1773–1790. https://doi.org/10.1080/01419870.2016.1142103. Retrieved February 9, 2016, from http://www.tandfonline.com/action/showCitFormats?

Tajfel, H. (1981). *Human groups and social categories: Studies in social psychology*. Cambridge University Press.

Tamir, Y. (1993). *Liberal nationalism*. Princeton University Press.

Thomas, G., & James, D. (2006). Reinventing grounded theory: Some questions about theory, ground and discovery. *British Educational Research Journal, 32*(6), 767–795. https://doi.org/10.1080/01411920600989412

Thoreau, H. (1849). On the duty of civil disobedience. In L. Hyde (Ed.), *The essays of Henry D. Thoreau (2002)* (pp. 123–146). North Point Press.

Thornberg, R. (2012). Informed grounded theory. *Scandinavian Journal of Educational Research, 56*(3), 243–259. https://doi.org/10.1080/00313831.2011.581686

Thornton, S. (1997). General introduction. In K. Gelder & S. Thornton (Eds.), *The subcultures reader* (pp. 1–10). Routledge.

Tovey, H., Hannan, D., & Abramson, H. (1989). *Why Irish? Irish identity and Irish language*. Bordna Gaeilge.

UNESCO. (2005). *Towards knowledge societies: UNESCO world report*. UNESCO Publ., Cop.

Weber, M. (1948). Chapter: VIII Bureaucracy. In H. H. Gerth & C. W. Mills (Eds.), *From Max Weber: Essays in sociology* (pp. 196–244). Oxford University Press.

White, T. (2004). Myth-making and the creation of Irish nationalism in the 19th century. *Studi Celtica, 3*, 325–339.

White, T. (2008). Redefining ethnically derived conceptions of nationalism: Ireland's Celtic identity and the future *Studia celtica fennica N. V.* 81–95.

Widdicome, S., & Wooffit, R. (1994). *The Language of Youth Subcultures: Social identity in action*. Prentice Hall.

Wight, C. (2006). *Agents, structures and international relations: Politics as ontology*. Cambridge University Press.

Willis, P. (1977). *Learning to labour: How working-class kids get working-class jobs*. Cambridge University Press.

Wodak, R., de Cillia, R., Reisigl, M., & Liebhart, K. (1999). *The discursive construction of national identity*. Edinburgh University Press.

Young, I. (1990). *Justice and the politics of difference*. Princeton University Press.

Index

A posteriori, 228, 230
A priori, 70, 228, 230
Acculturation, 4
Affinity towards Irish way of being, feelings of, 136–140
Altruism, 233
27th Amendment of the Constitution Act (2004), 52
Ancestral lineage, 112
Anthropocentric, 204
Anthropocentrism, 181
Assertions, 142
Assimilation, 60, 232–233
Assimilationist, 37
Authority in conversation, 190–196
Autonomous self-constitution, 62–64
Autonomous self-constitutionality, 229

Banal Nationalism, 32
Banal nationalism, 35
Begrudgery, 93, 105–107, 113
Belfast focus group discussion, 107, 116, 183, 185–186, 201
Belonging, sense of, 112
Biopolitics, 34–35
Biopower, 34, 49
Body politic, 23
Borders, 31
Bureaucracy, 33

Capitalism, 26, 186
Categorization, ethical imperative of, 5–10
Celtic historical epoch, 220
Celtic revivalism, 38
Citizenship
  acquisition, 54
  criteria, 52
Civic nationalism, 165

Civic patriotism, 46, 163
Civic-republican, 60
Civic-state, 49
Civil disobedience, 63
Clan, 105–107
  genealogical lineage and, 103–105
Classificatory distinction, 129, 131
Clondalkin focus group discussion, 96, 134, 144, 149, 173, 178, 194
Colonial rule, 232
Colonial subordination/'otherness', relic of, 56–61
Colonialism, 12, 58, 61
Colonization of self, 61–62, 64
Community, 27, 47, 110, 113, 214
  unifies or community of distinction, 107–114
Community of value, 20, 173
Consanguineous relation, 104
Conservatism, 169, 182–184, 204, 210, 215, 224–225
Conservative positions, 183
Constitutional vote, 53
Constructivist approach, 71
Constructivist grounded theory, 71
  approach, 71
  framework, 73
  iterative approach to, 70–71
Consumerism, 205
Contemporary identities, 18
Contemporary *Irishness*, 37
Contemporary theory, 19
Continental nativism, 235
Conversation analysis, 72
Coolock focus group discussion, 105, 123, 130, 151, 163, 175, 180
Cosmopolitan justice, 184
Cosmopolitan law, 46
Cosmopolitan nationalist, 48

Cosmopolitan patriotism, 47, 219–220
Cosmopolitanism, 7, 20, 47, 49, 216
    as panacea, 44–50
Cosmopolitans, 45–46
Cultural appropriation, migration and management of, 196–199
Cultural assimilation, 4
Cultural awareness, learning history to gain, 125–128
Cultural capital, 178
Cultural exposure, 219
Cultural hegemony, 74
Cultural hybridity, 37
Cultural hybridization, 219–220
Cultural relativism, 47, 61
Cultural transmission, 94–98
Culture, 213

Data analysis techniques, 76
Data collection tools, 82
De-institutionalization, 111
Democratic process, 163
Denationalization, 204
Deracination, 8
Design innovation, 75–77
Developmentalism, 38
Dilemmas of post-national nation state, 42–44
Direct Provision system, 209
Discourse analysis, 69, 72
Discursive practices, 131, 137–138
    seeking knowledge of, 64–65
Distinction, community of, 107–114
Dominant group, 71–73
Dominant universality, 28
Drogheda focus group discussion, 159, 173
Drumcondra focus group discussion, 106, 108, 118, 130–131, 145, 156, 193, 196, 201
Dublin City Council, 88

Economization, 204
Egalitarianism, 11, 46, 67
Egocentrism, 223
Empathy, 233
Empire, 58

English, language of, 231–232
Englishness, 37
Essential *Irishness*, 38–42
Essentialism, 14, 17, 43
    within social constructivism, 20–24
Ethical imperative of knowledge, categorization and classification, 5–10
Ethnic absolutism, 9
Ethnic distinction, reification fallacy of, 147–152
Ethnic nationalisms, 162
Ethnicity, 133
Ethno-national identifications, 30
Ethno-nationalist protectionist approach, 41
Ethno-racial heterogenization, 222
Ethno-racialized identity ascription, 152–154
Ethnocentric character, 217
Ethnocentrisms, 222
Eurocentric neoliberalism, 60
European dominance, 227
European governance, 200–201
European Migration Network, 53
European Union (EU), 57, 59, 125, 170, 186, 189
Exclusion, 19, 131
Existential reality, 31

Façade democracy, 60, 201
Family, 94–98, 102
    lineage, 120
Fatalism, 4
Feudalism, 105–107, 120
Financial capitalism, 170
Flawed democracy, 42
Flexible citizenship, 43
Floating signifier, 8
Fluid modernity concept, 19
Focus group discussions, 138, 154, 182
    additional post-viewing questions, 91
    and analysis, 78–86
    key emergent themes from main stage discussions, 83–85
    pre-and post-viewing questions, 90

Free provisions, 223
French nationality, 179
Friendliness, 102

Genealogical assumptions and notions of 'race', 142–143
Genealogical lineage, 212
 and clan, 103–105
Genealogical links, 117
Genealogy, 118, 120
Generalized reciprocity, 180, 203, 224
Global financial capitalism, 227
Globalism, 7
Globalization, 5, 41, 43, 59, 141, 155, 165, 188, 199–207, 222
Glocalization, 39, 41, 203
Governance, 199–207
Governmentality, 9, 11, 16, 23, 27, 33, 35, 42, 62–63
 of self, 61–62
Grounded theory model, 71, 87
Grudges, 105–107

Habitus, 4
Heterogeneity, 17
Historical amnesia, 217
Historical *irishness* and Irish
 contradictions within 'nativist' claims to *irishness*, 121–123
 historical orientations of *irishness*, 116–118
 learning history to gain cultural awareness, 125–128
 post-colonial yet Juvenile nation state, 123–125
 referencing history in relation to societal change, 118–121
Historicity, 127
History, 218
Hobbesian theory (on human nature), 238
Home, 93, 96
 wider family as lineage to *irishness* and notions of, 98–103
Homogeneity, 17, 36
 of Irish physiological traits, 164
Homogeneous nation, 28, 36

Homogenization, 126
Hybrid identities, 18
Hybridity, 23, 153

Identification, 19
Identity, 30–35
 formation, 72
 problematizing, 17–20
 social construction of identities and knowledge-based society, 2–5
Ideological naturalization, 55
IMF, 125
Immortality, 236
Imperialism, 61
Incorporation, 37
Individual interviewees, 78
Individualism, 229
Insider, 129
Insiderism, 9
Institutional policy, 51
Institutional racism, 59
Institutional structural flaws, 223
Institutionalization, 61
Integration, 60, 232
Interculturalism, 47, 62, 205, 220, 232
Internationalism, 7
Intolerant autonomous liberalism, 62
Intra-European migration, 204
Intrinsicism, 216
Ireland, 27
Irish, language of, 231–232
Irish, recognising
 feelings of affinity towards Irish way of being, 136–140
 Jus Soli, Jus Sanguinis or temporal exposure to Irish culture, 134–136
 perceiving oneself as Irish, 132–134
 segregation of 'Irish' and being Irish Citizen, 130–132
Irish citizen, 129, 131, 138
 segregation of 'Irish' and being, 130–132
Irish Citizenship of Children of Non-national Parents, 52
Irish Citizenship Referendum (2004), 11, 51–55, 61–62, 134, 170

258 Index

Irish clan, 104
Irish community, 110, 113, 214
Irish conservatism, 184
Irish Constitution, 53
Irish context, 23
Irish cultural norms, 219
Irish culture, 136
Irish descent, 178
Irish governance, 200
Irish Granny rule, 56
Irish historicity, 127
Irish history, 115, 120, 127
Irish maternity system, 55
Irish physiological traits, 164
Irish social fabric, 222
Irish society, 25, 75, 209
Irish stereotype, 152
Irish through conformity and participation, 143–145
Irish welfare state
   authority and perceived rational pragmatism in conversation, 190–196
   conservatism and *irishness*, 182–184
   governance, regionalism and globalization, 199–207
   migration and management of cultural appropriation, 196–199
   model, 176
   Nation state perpetuating migration controls and nationalism, 185–189
'Irish' identity, 2, 10–13, 21, 40, 89, 93, 160, 196, 239
'Irish' national Identity, historical construction of, 35–38
Irishness, 15, 17, 19, 24–29, 35, 49–50, 61, 64, 72, 88–89, 102, 112, 113, 115, 120, 145–146, 149–150, 162, 165, 169, 182–184, 204, 209–210, 214, 224, 234, 237
   contradictions within 'nativist' claims to, 121–123
   criteria of, 36
   ethical imperative of knowledge, categorization and classification, 5–10
   historical orientations of, 116–118
   Irish' identity, 10–13
   misconceptions of, 10
   mythological representations of, 55–56
   overview, 13–16
   as perceived in era of liquid modernity, 210–227
   racialization of, 36
   re/imagining, 160–167
   regionalization, 1–2
   social construction of identities and knowledge-based society, 2–5
   wider family as lineage to, 98–103
Iterative analytic process, 71
Iterative approach to constructivist grounded theory, 70–71

Jus sanguinis, 12
   association, 139
   citizenship, 56
   criteria, 54
   jus sanguinis/jus soli-based citizenship legislation, 55
   legislation, 52–55
   or temporal exposure to Irish culture, 134–136
Jus soli
   criteria, 54
   or temporal exposure to Irish culture, 134–136
Juvenile Nation State, 123–125

Kinship paternalism, 105
Knowledge, ethical imperative of, 5–10
Knowledge construction, 6
Knowledge society, 3, 5–6, 61
Knowledge-based society, social construction of, 2–5

Language, 69, 72
  of Irish and English, 231–232
Legal-technical mechanisms, 61
Leixlip focus group discussion, 154
Liberal democracy, 43, 60
Liberal individualism, 63
Liberal multiculturalism, 42, 51, 62
Liberal nationalist, 48
Liberalism, 62
Limerick focus group discussion, 111, 123, 188, 190, 200
Linguistic capital, 101
Linguistic production relations, 69
Liquid modernity, 2, 11, 40, 119, 209, 219, 228, 237
  irishness as perceived in era of, 210–227
Localism, 7
Lockean humanist perspective, 59

Manifest authority, 6
Manipulative elites, 21
Marginalization, 23
Methodological approach, 12, 14, 67, 71
Methodological justification, 71–73
Methodological nationalism, 181
Methodological theory, 70
Migration
  and management of cultural appropriation, 196–199
  migration-related diversity, 18
Minoritization, 110
Modern 'Irish' identity, 37
Modernity, 10, 29, 40
Monarchical system, 52
Moral conservatism, 184
Morality of patriotism, 46
Multiculturalism, 28, 220, 232–233
Multimedia presentation, production of, 77–78
Multipolarity, 58
Multistage approach, 79

Naas focus group discussion, 117, 126, 136, 147, 170
Nation building, 38–42
Nation State, 25–35
Nation state perpetuating migration controls and nationalism, 185–189
National identity, 22, 26
National parallelism, 38, 100
Nationalism, 7, 9, 22, 24, 27, 32, 38, 45, 220
  nation state perpetuating migration controls and, 185–189
Nationality, 26
Native, 116, 120
Nativism, 38
Naturalization, 55
Neo-colonial capitalism, 59
Neo-colonialism, 56, 59
Neo-colonialism/neo-imperialism, 61
Neo-liberal governmentality, 24, 32–33, 182, 193, 224
Neo-liberalist governmentality, 224
Neoliberal governance, 62
Neoliberalism, 9, 32–33, 39, 56–57, 62, 181, 190
Neopragmatic perspective, 70
Neopragmatic utilitarian approach, 70
Nihilistic determinism, 4
Non-governance, 226
Notions of home, wider family as lineage to, 98–103
Novel research model, 70

Open access and closed entry, 233–237
Opportunism, 188
Ordo-liberal liquid modernity, 15
Ordo-liberal perspective, 189
Ordo-liberal society, 236
Ordo-liberalism, 39, 56, 236
Otherness, 133, 138
  relic of, 56–61
Ownership, 46, 181

Index

Parochialism, 93, 105, 111, 213–214
Participants, 86, 221
   Clan, feudalism and Grudges, 105–107
   community unifies or community of distinction, 107–114
   genealogical lineage and Clan, 103–105
   immediate family, cultural transmission and sacrifice, 94–98
   wider family as lineage to *irishness* and notions of home, 98–103
Participatory development, 67
Participatory process, 75
Patriotic cosmopolitan, 186
Patriotism, 45–46, 216
Perceived *Irishness*, 237–239
Perceived rational pragmatism, 15, 170, 202, 205–206, 209–210, 225–233, 239
   in conversation, 190–196
Perceived rational pragmatist, 194
Performativity, 24, 68, 138
Personhood concept, 228
Phenotypical *Irishness*, 221
Physiological traits, 152
Political conservatism, 204
Political conservativism, 184
Political racelessness, 9
Politics of immigration, 20
Polity-public, 7
Positive collective action, 107
Post-modernists, 22
Post-national nation state, 49
Post-nationalism, 7
Post/late-modernist relativism, 70
Postcolonial/post-colonialism, 23
Posteriori knowledge, 228
Postscript, 239–243
Power, 29
Pragmatism, 192
"Pre-modern" societies, 4
Pride, 126
Primordialism, 20

Print media, 26
Progressive self-constitution, 62–64
Protectionism, 164, 235
Pseudo-objectivity, 47
Pseudo-rational condition, 229
Pseudonyms, 86
Pseudotranscendental concepts, 230

Qualitative approach, 15
Qualitative participatory, 69

'Race', 8–9, 27, 39, 44, 61, 97, 112, 133, 136, 141, 146, 149, 154, 165–166, 188, 212–213, 217–218, 220–222, 233
   genealogical assumptions and notions of, 142–143
   as imaginary and 'race' as reality, 145–147
   Irish, 147, 216
   social construction, 139, 210
Racial distinction, 131, 134, 141
   reification fallacy of, 147–152
Racial neoliberalism, 9
Racialization, 14, 36
   of *Irishness*, 27
   of state, 51
Racialized and ethnicized globalization, 1
Racio-ethnic, 8–9
   constructions, 8
   injustices, 9
Raciology, 8
Racism, 27, 184, 204, 236, 238
Rational justification, 238
Reciprocity, 73–75, 173
Reconciliation, 47
Reflexive conscience, 52
Reflexive self-constitutionality, 74
Regionalism, 12, 170, 199–207
Regionalization, 1–2, 12
Regressive nationalism, 39, 41, 62
Reification fallacy, 20, 30, 165, 221
   of ethnic and racial distinction, 147–152
Republicanism, 46

Research methodology, 88
  building reciprocity between individual and collective, 73–75
  design innovation, 75–77
  ethical considerations, 86–87
  iterative approach to constructivist grounded theory, 70–71
  limitations and reflections, 88–89
  main stage, 78–86
  methodological justification, 71–73
  preliminary stage, 77–78
Revivalism, 31

Sacrifice, 94–98
Segregation, 110
  of 'Irish' and being Irish Citizen, 130–132
Self-constitutionality, 52
Self-subscription, 102, 115, 133
Singular collective community, 107
Social change, 115, 222
Social construction, 24
  of identities and knowledge-based society, 2–5
Social constructivism, 17, 23, 31, 63
  essentialism within, 20–24
Social constructivist approach, 21, 48
Social Darwinian evolutionary narrative, 216
Social Darwinism, 223
Social evolutionism, 118, 216
Social racism, 236
Social transformation, 165
Socialization, 4
Societal change, 115
  referencing history in relation to, 118–121
Societal transformations, 154–160
Socio-cultural capital, 204

Sovereignty, 125
Space-time, 7
State administration, 58
State of exception, 34
Status quo, 4
  of Irish society, 197
  positions, 183
Subhumanist falsities, 239
Subject constitution, 27
Subjectification, 18, 34, 51, 137–138
Subjectifiction, 24
Subjectivity, 6
Substantive identity, 43
Substantive knowledge, 6
Subsumption pathway, 60, 148
Supranational governance, 12, 60
Sympathy, 233

Technologies of self, 33
'The other', 115, 126, 230
Thematic approach, 82
Tolerant universalist post-nationalism, 62
Trans-Europeanization, 73
Transcendental concepts, 230
Transcendental idealism, 230
Transnational capitalism, 185, 204
Transnationalism, 202, 205, 227

UNESCO, 3, 5
Universalism, 28, 47
Universalist post-nationalism, 62
Utilitarian approach, 41
Utilitarian liberalist, 38

Welfare state model, 182, 204, 223
Westernization, 4

Younger participants, 233

Printed and bound by CPI Group (UK) Ltd, Croydon, CR0 4YY

21/11/2024

14596801-0003